A CONCORDANCE

TO

THE ENGLISH POEMS

OF

THOMAS GRAY

EDITED BY

ALBERT S. COOK

PRESIDENT OF THE CONCORDANCE SOCIETY

36510

GLOUCESTER, MASS.

PETER SMITH

1967

TO

GEORGE HERBERT PALMER

AT WHOSE SUGGESTION

THE CONCORDANCE SOCIETY WAS BEGUN

PREFACE

THIS Concordance is the first to appear under the auspices of The Concordance Society, which was organized at Yale University in the Christmas vacation of 1906. The choice of an author was dictated by these considerations: his historical importance; the public interest in him; and the moderate compass of his works, so that the compilation might be effected by few hands in a brief time, and the subvention required by the publishers might not unduly tax the slender resources of the Society. The making of the excerpts was begun, and virtually concluded, in the Christmas vacation of 1907; the quotations, most of which had been alphabetized within the smaller groups by the compilers, were then fully alphabetized by the editor, and the head-words normalized, where it appeared necessary. The next step was to secure a publisher, and to arrange for the details of publication. The copy was forwarded to the publishers in April of the present year.

The readers who excerpted the material were as follows: —

Dr. CHARLES G. OSGOOD, Preceptor in English, Princeton University, Secretary of The Concordance Society.

Dr. ELBERT N. S. THOMPSON, Instructor in Rhetoric, Yale University.

Mr. FREDERIC T. BLANCHARD, Assistant in Rhetoric, Yale University.

Mr. ALFRED A. MAY, University Fellow in English, Yale University.

Miss ERNESTINE L. MILLER, Wellsboro, Pennsylvania.

THE EDITOR.

As none of the readers had had any experience in concordance work, the speed and accuracy displayed were most gratifying.

Those who have participated in the reading of the galley-proofs are the following: —

Professor CURTIS H. PAGE, Columbia University, Treasurer of The Concordance Society.

Professor CHARLES W. HODELL, Woman's College, Baltimore, Member of the Executive Committee of The Concordance Society.

Professor LANE COOPER, Cornell University.

Professor CHAUNCEY B. TINKER, Yale University.

Professor ARTHUR ADAMS, Trinity College, Hartford.

Dr. ELBERT N. S. THOMPSON, as above.

Mr. ALFRED A. MAY, as above.

Miss MARY W. SMYTH, Graduate Student in English, Yale University.

THE EDITOR.

None of the galley-proofs were given out to the readers before June 15, and with one exception all were returned before July 1; what this means in the closing days of a busy academic year, in our climate, no American teacher, at least, will need to be told.

The basis of the Concordance is Gosse's edition of Gray (4 vols., London and New York, 1884): the poetry is contained in Vol. I, but a few variants have been culled from the letters in Vols. II and III. Quotations from the poems which Gosse characterizes as doubtful have been distinguished from the rest by a prefixed dagger. Gosse's order of poems has been followed, except that variants have been placed under the poems to which they belong; this applies also to the List of Poems on pp. ix, x.

The question of normalization was a somewhat difficult one. The orthography of Gray's editions and manuscripts is so capricious and inconsistent that it seemed impracticable to conform the head-words to it in all cases. Should one make the head-word *Riseing*, for example, as Gray twice spells it? or *Redning* (*Sonnet on the Death of Richard West*, line 2)? Should one write *Chearful* (*Elegy* 87), or *Cheerful* (*Alliance of Education and Government* 66)? *Horror* (*Fatal Sisters* 49), or *Horrour* (*Progress of Poesy* 93)? *Rhymes* (*Stanzas to Mr. Richard Bentley* 9), or *Rhimes* (*Elegy* 79)? In such doubtful cases as these, some choice must be made, and consistency required that similar words should be similarly treated. Thus, one could hardly normalize to *Horror*, and write *Warriour* as the head-word (of course the spelling of the *quotations* is kept). Often such a choice will be, or seem, arbitrary; I have given the preference to full forms (*Roused*, not *Rous'd*), and to forms generally preferred by scholars, for etymological or other reasons, in America: thus *Rime* (not *Rhime* or *Rhyme*), and endings in -*or*, not -*our*, like Gray's *Rumor* (thus *Ardor, Armor, Colors, Flavor, Honor, Horror, Labor, Manor, Parlor, Rigor, Tenor, Vigor, Warrior; Honorable, Neighboring*, etc.). Words hyphenated by Gray are so kept, and the second element of such words is entered in its alphabetical place, with a cross-reference to the complete word. In general, cross-references have been freely employed — too freely, some will think — but it seemed desirable to enable every inquirer to find with ease what he sought.

The following words, forty-seven in number, have been omitted, following the precedent of Strong's Concordance to the Bible: *a, an, and, are, as, be, but, by, for, from, he, her, him, his, I, in, is, it, me, my, not, O, of, our, out, shall, shalt, she, that, the, thee, their, them, they, thou, thy, to, unto, up, upon, us, was, we, were, with, ye, you;* but contracted or quasi-contracted forms of these words, such as are found in *don't* and *'em*, are given. These omissions, again, may seem rather arbitrary, and so indeed they are; but so perhaps would any omissions be, in the light of some needs or expectations.

As to punctuation, quotation-marks have been omitted when only the quotation has been given; otherwise they have been retained. The same principle has been observed with respect to parentheses. Gray's punctuation, like his capitalization, is frequently erratic, but both have been retained.

In the excerpts, it has been difficult in many cases to decide whether to give the immediate context of a word, without particular regard to the construction and sense, or to seek a subject or verb, perchance, in another line. We have inclined toward the latter, but our practice has not been strictly uniform, and perhaps could not be. Suggestions to collaborators will be interpreted with more latitude by one than by another, and when the material has once been collected, an attempt on the part of the editor to secure greater uniformity would involve considerable labor in looking up references, and passing judgment upon each doubtful case. Such are the disadvantages of collaboration in the making of a concordance, but perhaps an ideal uniformity in this respect would hardly be worth the effort it would cost.

Occasionally homonyms, when different parts of speech, have been separated: see, for example, under *Art*. This has been done only in cases which the editor thought extreme for one reason or another; perhaps it would have been better to distinguish all homonyms, but little practical inconvenience is likely to result where the quotations are so few under each word as here.

The courtesy and consideration shown by Houghton Mifflin Company in the negotiations looking to the publication of this volume have been most gratifying, and augur well for the success of The Concordance Society in a very important respect.

This preface may fitly end with a quotation from an anonymous writer in a recent number of *Book News:* "No poet can be fully mastered without either dictionary or concordance. You have no grasp on a poet's use of words without one aid or the other."

ALBERT S. COOK.

GREENSBORO, VERMONT, Aug. 10, 1908.

LIST OF POEMS

IN THE ORDER OF GOSSE'S EDITION
(save for titles in square brackets)

[II and III refer to Vols. II and III]

ABBREVIATIONS

[The references in parenthesis are to the prefixed numbers in the List of Poems preceding. The references to pages are to Vol. I of Gosse's edition, except as otherwise designated.]

The following abbreviations designate variants under the poems in question: —

Dods. Dodsley's edition.
MS. Any MS. variants where only one manuscript is quoted under the text.
Nich. Nicholls.
Pem. Pembroke MS.
Wal. Walpole MS.
Whar. Wharton MS.

A CONCORDANCE

TO THE

ENGLISH POEMS OF THOMAS GRAY

A, *omitted.*

Abandoned.
Old, and abandon'd by each venal friend, *View* 1.

Abode.
To chear the shiv'ring Natives dull abode. *P. P.* 57.
That leads to HELA's drear abode. *Odin* 4.
draw his frailties from their dread abode, *El.* 126.
The rough abode of want and liberty, *E. G.* 97.
road That to the grotto leads, my dark abode.
Tasso 38.

About.
What a pother is here about wenching and roaring!
C. C. 23.
— for he talks about God — *C. C.* 30.
I grop'd About among their cold Remains
Dante 78.

Above.
but far above the Great. *P. P.* 123.
Above, below, the rose of snow, . . . we spread:
Bard 91.
While spirits blest above . . . Join *Inst.* 87.

Abyss.
The secrets of th' Abyss to spy. *P. P.* 97.

Acarnania.
A third arose, of Acarnania he, *Stat.*[1] 11.

Accent.
†K, as a man, with hoarser accent speaks,
Ch. Cr. 47.

Accents.
Methinks I hear in accents low *Spring* 41.
in accents [murmurs, MS.] dread, *Odin* 23.
In still small Accents whisp'ring *El. Mas.* 83.

Accept.
In lieu of penitence, . . . Accept my vengeance.
Agr. 180.

Accepts.
She half accepts, and half rejects, my Fires,
Prop.[3] 22.

Acclamations.
By acclamations roused, came tow'ring on.
Stat.[1] 14.

Accord.
And thus they speak in soft accord *Inst.* 55.

Accursed.
bending o'er th' accursed loom *Bard* 95.

Achaians.
two youths advance, Achaians born, *Stat.*[1] 10.

Aches.
My thought aches at him; *Agr.* 160.

Achievements.
Each pannel in achievements cloathing, *L. S.* 6.

Aching.
Visions of glory, spare my aching sight, *Bard* 107.
The Widow feels thee in her aching hip;
Com. Lines 5.

Aconite.
they love not aconite. *Agr.* 21.

Acres.
Scarce to nine acres Tityus' bulk confined,
Prop.[2] 43.

Across.
Her artful hand across the sounding Strings.
Prop.[3] 16.

Act.
†throw . . . half an act into the Fire: *Ode* 34.

Adamantine.
Bound in thy adamantine chain, *Adv.* 5.

Add.
What if you add, how she turn'd pale *Agr.* 9.

Admire.
let the Muse admire, *Bent.* 2.
The band around admire the mighty mass,
Stat.[1] 7.

Admired.
his native land Admired that arm, *Stat.*[1] 36.

Admitted.
That grim and antique Tower admitted *Dante* 23.

Adoration.
A stranger To adoration, *Agr.* 34.

Adore.
Prostrate with filial reverence I adore. *Ign.* 10.

Adores.
Where grateful science still adores *Eton* 3.

Adorn.
The verse adorn again Fierce War, *Bard* 125.

Adorned.
each Grace adorn'd his frame, *Williams* 3.

Adown.
Swift shoots the Village-maid . . . adown the
shining way, *Tasso* 20.

Adrastus.
Then thus the King: — *Adrastus.* *Stat.*[1] 1.

Advance.

the bull, . . . On surrounding foes advance?
Caradoc 3.

The love of honour bade two youths advance,
Stat.[1] 9.

Advanced.

the sun is high advanc'd, *Agr.* 158.

Adventurers.

Some bold adventurers disdain *Eton* 35.

Adventurous.

If with adventrous oar and ready sail *E. G.* 104.

Adverse.

For adverse fate the captive chief has hurl'd
Tasso 33.

Advise.

it rekes not That I advise thee. *Dante* 18.

Ædileship. *See* **Edileship.**

Ægis.

Thy leaden ægis 'gainst our ancient foes? *Ign.* 14.

Æmonian.

Th' Æmonian hag enjoys her dreadful hour,
Stat.[1] 58.

Æolian.

Awake, Æolian lyre, awake, *P. P.* 1.

Aëron.

But none . . . return, Save Aëron brave,
Hoel 21.

Ætna's.

from Ætna's smoking summit broke, *Stat.*[2] 18.

Afar.

Till down the eastern cliffs afar *P. P.* 52.
Till fierce Hyperion from afar *P. P. MS.* 52.
the Norman sails afar Catch the winds, *Owen* 15.
Oft o'er the trembling Nations from afar *E. G.* 46.

Affability.

Commend me to her affability! *L. S.* 139.

Affection.

Affection warm, and faith sincere, *Clerke* 5.

Affinity.

The Master of Trinity To him bears affinity;
Satire 12.

Afflict.

The Bad affright, afflict the Best! *Adv.* 4.

Afflicts.

Who thus afflicts my troubled sprite, *Odin* 29.

Afford.

no eye, afford A tear *Bard* 65.

Affright.

The Bad affright, afflict the Best! *Adv.* 4.
Severn shall re-eccho with affright *Bard* 54.
With headlong rage and wild affright *Hoel* 2.

Affrighted.

far aloof th' affrighted ravens sail; *Bard* 37.

Affrights.

With such a gleam affrights Pangæa's field,
Stat.[1] 29.

Afield.

How jocund did they drive their team afield! *El.* 27.

After.

†Queen Esther next — how fair e'en after death,
Ch. Cr. 9.

Again.

with looks intent Again . . . she stretch'd, *Cat* 26.
again she bent, *Cat* 26.
they vow their truth, and are again believed.
Adv. 24.
The verse adorn again Fierce War, *Bard* 125.
Ne'er again his likeness see; *F. S.* 46.
Let me, let me sleep again. *Odin* 34.
Once again my call obey, *Odin* 51; MS. 59.
Once again arise, and say, *Odin* 60.
Enquirer come To break my iron-sleep again;
Odin 89.
Again the buried Genius of old Rome. *Agr.* 141.
Oh take me to thy peaceful shade again. *Ign.* 6.
And breathe and walk again: *Vic.* 48.
A fairer flower will never bloom again: *Child* 4.
and send again to War; *Prop.*[3] 82.
†Till again the rolling Sun Bursts *Ode* 43.
†Late to find it: — and, again,
Rond. 3, 11, 19, 27, 35.
†but soon pops in again; *Ch. Cr.* 30.

Against. *See also* **'Gainst.**

Right against the eastern gate, *Odin* 17.
Squadrons three against him came; *Owen* 10.
And all that *Groom* could urge against him.
L. S. 116.
Against thee, liberty and Agrippina: *Agr.* 152.
With double light it beam'd against the day:
Stat.[1] 27.
Against the stream the waves secure he trod,
Tasso 15.

Aganippe.

Where Aganippe warbles as it flows; *Prop.*[2] 4.

Age.

Chill'd by age, their . . . dance They leave,
Spring 39.
And slow-consuming Age. *Eton* 90.
to shine Thro' every unborn age, *Inst.* 17.
The slacken'd sinews of time-wearied age.
Agr. 139.
Oh! sacred age! Oh! times for ever lost! *Ign.* 31.
But not to one in this benighted age *Bent.* 17.
Age step 'twixt love and me, *Prop.*[2] 12.
Be love my youth's pursuit, and science crown my
Age. *Prop.*[2] 52.

Aged.

Grav'd on the stone beneath yon aged thorn.
El. 116.

Ages.

unborn Ages, crowd not on my soul! *Bard* 108.
And bring the buried ages back to view. *Ign.* 35.
Thro' Ages by what Fate confin'd *E. G.* 38.

Aghast.

Stout Glo'ster stood aghast in speechless trance:
Bard 13.

Agonizing.

Shrieks of an agonizing King! *Bard* 56.

Agony.

There . . . Agony, that pants for breath,
Owen 39.

In agony, in death resign'd,   *Clerke* 7.
Her latest agony of mind   *Clerke MS.* 10.

Agrippina.
Against thee, liberty and Agrippina: *Agr.* 152.

Agrippina's.
the blood Of Agrippina's race,   *Agr.* 38.

Ague.
A sudden fit of ague shook him,   *L. S.* 119.

Ah.
Ah, happy hills, ah, pleasing shade,   *Eton* 11.
Ah, fields belov'd in vain,   *Eton* 12.
Ah, shew them where in ambush stand   *Eton* 58.
Ah, tell them, they are men!   *Eton* 60.
ah! why should they know their fate?   *Eton* 95.
But ah! 't is heard no more —   *P. P.* 111.
Ah, ignorance!   *Ign.* 9.
Ah! could they catch his strength,   *Bent.* 13.
Ah, gallant youth! this marble tells the rest,
                                      Williams 11.
"Ah!" said the sighing peer,   *View* 17.
Ah! say, Fellow-swains,   *Am. Lines* 7.
Ah! what means yon violet flower!   *Song* 3.
Ah! let her ever my Desires control,   *Prop.*³ 76.

Aid.
Some speedy aid to send.   *Cat* 33.
Join the wayward work to aid: *F. S.* 19.
And beg'd his aid that dreadful day.   *L. S.* 92.
That Slumber brings to aid my Poetry. *Prop.*³ 20.

Aim.
Taught his . . . hand To aim the forked bolt;
                                       Agr. 31.

Aimed.
'T was there he aim'd the meditated harm,
                                      *Stat.*² 22.

Air.
hark, how thro' the peopled air   *Spring* 23.
arms sublime, that float upon the air, *P. P.* 38.
Thro' the azure deep of air: *P. P.* 117.
They mock the air with idle state.   *Bard* 4.
Stream'd, like a meteor, to the troubled air
                                       Bard 20.
What strings symphonious tremble in the air,
                                      Bard 119.
Iron-sleet . . . Hurtles in the darken'd air.
                                       F. S. 4.
snowy veils, that float in air.   *Odin* 78.
And all the air a solemn stillness holds, *El.* 6.
And waste its sweetness on the desert air. *El.* 56.
To celebrate her eyes, her air —   *L. S.* 33.
Her air and all her manners shew it.   *L. S.* 138.
these walls alone And the mute air   *Agr.* 23.
Melts into air and liquid light.   *Vic.* 16.
Mute was the musick of the air,   *Vic.* 23.
The common Sun, the air, the skies,   *Vic.* 51.
such a pick-pocket air!   *C. C.* 6.
song-thrush . . . Scatters his loose notes in the
   waste of air.   *Birds* 2.
Nor changing Skies can hurt, nor sultry Air.
                                      *Prop.*³ 94.

Airs.
Parent of sweet and solemn-breathing airs,
                                       P. P. 14.
So draw Mankind in vain the vital Airs, *E. G.* 9.

Airy.
their airy dance They leave,   *Spring* 39.
in fancy's airy colouring wrought   *Bent.* 7.

Aisle. *See* **Ile, Isle.**

Aix.
At Aix, his voluntary sword he drew,   *Williams* 5.

Ajar.
But that they left the door a-jarr,   *L. S.* 74.

Alas.
Alas, regardless of their doom   *Eton* 51.
Alas, who would not wish to please her! *L. S.* 36.
These Ears, alas! for other Notes repine, *West* 5.
alas, my fears! Can powers immortal   *Ign.* 25.
Or if, alas! it be my Fate   *Prop.*³ 69.

Albion.
They sought, oh Albion! next thy sea-encircled
   coast.   *P. P.* 82.

Alecto's.
the hissing terrors round Alecto's head, *Prop.*² 42.

Alexandria's.
And scepter'd Alexandria's captive Shore,
                                      *Prop.*³ 45.

Alike.
Alike the Busy and the Gay   *Spring* 35.
Condemn'd alike to groan,   *Eton* 92.
Alike they scorn the pomp of tyrant-Power,
                                       P. P. 79.
Awaits alike th' inevitable hour.   *El.* 35.
There they alike in trembling hope repose,
                                       El. 127.
Alike to all the Kind impartial Heav'n *E. G.* 28.

All.
Not all that tempts your wand'ring eyes *Cat* 40.
Nor all, that glisters, gold.   *Cat* 42.
Yet see how all around 'em wait   *Eton* 55.
To each his suff'rings: all are men,   *Eton* 91.
give to rapture all thy trembling strings. *P. P.* 2.
Night, and all her sickly dews,   *P. P.* 49.
All hail, ye genuine Kings,   *Bard* 110.
Horror covers all the heath,   *F. S.* 9.
Nor on all profusely pours;   *Owen* 6.
And all the air a solemn stillness holds, *El.* 6.
all that beauty, all that wealth e'er gave, *El.* 34.
all he had, a tear,   *El.* 123.
He gain'd . . . ('t was all he wish'd) a friend.
                                       El. 124.
By this time all the Parish know it   *L. S.* 42.
She curtsies, . . . To all the People of condition.
                                       L. S. 112.
And all that *Groom* could urge against him.
                                       L. S. 116.
Her air and all her manners shew it.   *L. S.* 138.
All that on Granta's fruitful plain . . . bounty
   pour'd,   *Inst.* 51.
All shall be confess'd,   *Agr.* 166.
The Fields to all their wonted Tribute bear;
                                       West 11.
And all was ignorance, and all was night. *Ign.* 30.
Alike to all the Kind impartial Heav'n *E. G.* 28.
could not save His all   *Clerke MS.* 12.
And I, the meanest of them all,   *Hoel* 23.

And all the town rings of his swearing and roaring!
        C. C. 16.

But what awaits me now is worst of all. *Shak.* 8.

and all his [he, Lett.[4]] scribbles, tear.   *Shak.* 16.

The Master of King's Copies them in all things;
        Satire 18.

The Master of Catherine Takes them all for his
  pattern;   *Satire* 20.

The Master of Clare Hits them all to a hair;
        Satire 22.

The Master of Peter's Has all the same features;
        Satire 32.

As to Trinity Hall We say nothing at all. *Satire* 36.

And mimic desolation covers all.   *View* 16.

All but two youths th' enormous orb decline,
        Stat.[1] 24.

Phlegyas . . . call'd forth all the man. *Stat.*[1] 33.

All eyes were bent on his experienced hand,
        Stat.[1] 34.

Collecting all his force, the circle sped; *Stat.*[1] 48.

Brac'd all his nerves, and every sinew strung;
        Stat.[2] 7.

the orb . . . Far overleaps all bound, *Stat.*[2] 12.

Dismiss'd at length, they break through all delay
        Tasso 1.

a River . . . all further course withstood;
        Tasso 8.

All stones of lustre shoot their vivid ray, *Tasso* 65.

And all its jetty honours turn to snow; *Prop.*[2] 14.

When Pindus' self . . . Shakes all his Pines,
        Prop.[2] 32.

All angry heaven inflicts, or hell can feel,
        Prop.[2] 45.

And all the scenes, that hurt the grave's repose,
        Prop.[2] 49.

From Cynthia all that in my numbers shines;
        Prop.[3] 3.

To Cynthia all my Wishes I confine;   *Prop.*[3] 68.

A little Verse my All that shall remain;
        Prop.[3] 101.

Of all our Youth the Ambition and the Praise!
        Prop.[3] 104.

To thee and all unknown   *Dante* 19.

nor wept, for all Within was Stone: *Dante* 53.

All that whole Day, or the succeeding Night
        Dante 58.

straight Ariseing all they cried,   *Dante* 65.

†Or Poppy-thoughts blast all the shoots. *Ode* 12.

†Buzzing with all their parent Faults;   *Ode* 46.

†Elizabeths all dwindled into Betties; *Ch. Cr.* 12.

†They 're all diverted into H and B. *Ch. Cr.* 14.

†All with fantastic clews, fantastic clothes,
        Ch. Cr. 17.

†all, all, but Grannam Osborne's Gazetteer.
        Ch. Cr. 20.

†See Israel, and all Judah thronging there.
        Ch. Cr. 28.

†Proteus-like all tricks, all shapes can shew,
        Ch. Cr. 43.

†Slow follow all the quality of State, *Ch. Cr.* 51.

†And brings all Womankind before your view;
        Ch. Cr. 59.

Allay.

May the long Thirst of Tantalus allay, *Prop.*[3] 89.

Allotted.

Few were the days allotted to his breath; *Child* 5.

Aloft.

Now the golden Morn aloft Waves   *Vic.* 1.

Alone.

purple Tyrants, . . . unpitied and alone. *Adv.* 8.

Nor circumscrib'd alone Their growing virtues,
        El. 65.

Alone, unguarded and without a lictor,   *Agr.* 5.

much I hope these walls alone   *Agr.* 22.

Let me not fall alone;   *Agr.* 186.

'T is man alone that Joy descries   *Vic.* 27.

Alone in nature's wealth array'd,   *Hoel* 9.

Along.

Wanders the hoary Thames along   *Eton* 9.

the rich stream of music winds along *P. P.* 7.

Shafts . . . Shoot the trembling cords along.
        F. S. 14.

Black and huge along they sweep,   *Owen* 17.

Along the cool sequester'd vale of life   *El.* 75.

Along the heath,   *El.* 110.

The Greenwood Side along,   *El. Mas.* 117.

along some winding entry   *L. S.* 102.

while Bentley leads her sister-art along,
        Bent. 3.

while yet he strays Along the . . . vale *Clerke* 12.

Whose walls along the neighbouring Sea extend,
        Tasso 4.

†Q draws her train along the Drawing-room,
        Ch. Cr. 50.

Aloof.

far aloof th' affrighted ravens sail;   *Bard* 37.

And scornful flung th' unheeded weight Aloof;
        Stat.[1] 22.

Aloud.

Triumphant tell aloud,   *Bard* MS. 110.

she cries aloud   *Inst.* 67.

Alpheus'.

oft on Alpheus' shore   *Stat.*[1] 36.

Already.

the ghostly Prudes . . . Already had condemn'd
  the sinner.   *L. S.* 130.

already 'gan the Dawn To send: *Dante* 25.

Altars.

round heav'n's altars shed The fragrance *Inst.* 73.

Altered.

hard Unkindness' alter'd eye,   *Eton* 76.

The times are alter'd quite and clean! *L. S.* 136.

Always.

and skies serene Speak not always winter past.
        Song 10.

Am. *See* **I 'm.**

Amain.

Now rowling down the steep amain,   *P. P.* 10.

And Sigismundo, and Gualandi rode Amain,
        Dante 34.

Amazement.

Amazement in his van,   *Bard* 61.

Amazon.

The other Amazon kind Heaven Had arm'd
        L. S. 29.

Amber.
Or where Mæander's amber waves   *P. P.* 69.

Ambient.
That rise and glitter o'er the ambient tide *E. G.* 107.

Ambition.
Ambition this shall tempt to rise,   *Eton* 71.
Let not Ambition mock their useful toil,   *El.* 29.
If bright ambition from her craggy seat   *Agr.* 51.
Of all our Youth the Ambition and the Praise!
                                            *Prop.*³ 104.

Ambition's.
ye manes of ambition's victims,   *Agr.* 174.

Ambitious.
ambitious of the power To judge   *Agr.* 40.

Ambush.
shew them where in ambush stand   *Eton* 58.

Amid.
laughing . . . Amid severest woe.   *Eton* 80.
Famine at feasts, and thirst amid the stream;
                                            *Prop.*² 47.

Amidst.
Ye died amidst your dying country's cries —
                                            Bard 42.

Among.
whose flowers among Wanders the hoary Thames
                                            Eton 8.
He rests among the Dead.   *Bard* 68.
fame Has spread among the crowd;   *Agr.* 168.
In silent gaze the tuneful choir among,   *Bent.* 1.
Rise the rapturous choir among;   *Vic.* 18.
among their cold remains   *Dante* 78.

Amorous.
the rosy queen Of amorous thefts: *Agr.* 189.
The Birds in vain their amorous Descant joyn;
                                            West 3.
the long Iliad of the amorous Fight.   *Prop.*³ 26.

Ample.
Nor the pride, nor ample pinion,   *P. P.* 114.
Give ample room, and verge enough   *Bard* 51.
Soon their ample sway shall stretch   *F S.* 39.
Knowledge . . . her ample page . . . did ne'er
  unroll;   *El.* 49.
'T is ample Matter for a Lover's Book;   *Prop.*² 28.

An, *omitted.*

Ancient.
Has reassum'd her ancient right;   *Odin* 92.
Molest her ancient solitary reign.   *El.* 12.
An ancient pile of buildings stands: *L. S.* 2.
Thy leaden ægis 'gainst our ancient foes?   *Ign.* 14.
Its ancient lord secure of victory.   *Stat.*² 13.
The torrent-stream his ancient bounds disdains,
                                            Tasso 9.

Anciently.
as somewhat rare That anciently appear'd,
                                            Agr. 136.

And, *omitted.*

Androgeon.
And Phœbus' Son recall'd Androgeon *Prop.*³ 84.

Anew.
†Then have left, to love anew: *Rond.* 7.
anew revived, with silver light   *Prop.*² 21.

Angel.
Two angel [beauteous, Wal., Dods.] forms were
  seen to glide,   *Cat* 14.

Angels.
Where Angels tremble, while they gaze, *P. P.* 100.

Anger.
Disdainful Anger, pallid Fear,   *Eton* 63.

Angry.
Burthens of the angry deep.   *Owen* 18.
All angry heaven inflicts,   *Prop.*² 45.

Anguish.
but to the voice of Anguish?   *P. P.* 72.
My lonely Anguish melts no Heart but mine;
                                            West 7.
To weep without knowing the cause of my anguish: *Am. Lines* 2.
Anguish, that . . . wrings My inmost Heart?
                                            Dante 5.
either Hand I gnaw'd For Anguish,   *Dante* 64.

Animate.
They breathe a soul to animate thy clay. *Bard* 122.

Animated.
Can storied urn or animated bust   *El.* 41.
This spacious animated Scene survey   *E. G.* 22.
In swifter measures animated run,   *Bent.* 11.

Animates.
O'erpower the fire that animates our frame;
                                            E. G. 65.

Anjou's.
And Anjou's heroine,   *Inst.* 43.

Annals.
The short and simple annals of the poor.   *El.* 32.

Anne.
A moment's patience, gentle Mistress Anne:
                                            Shak. 1.

Annual.
Thrice hath Hyperion roll'd his annual race,
                                            Ign. 11.

Anon.
Anon, with slacken'd rage comes quiv'ring down,
                                            *Stat.*¹ 51.

Another.
another *Arthur* reigns.   *Bard MS.* 110.
Another came; nor yet beside the rill,   *El.* 111.
Another touch, another temper take,   *E. G.* 79.
Another orb upheaved his strong right hand,
                                            *Stat.*¹ 15.
it be my Fate to try Another Love,   *Prop.*³ 70.
That Day, and yet another, mute we sate,
                                            Dante 70.

Another's.
The tender for another's pain,   *Eton* 93.

Anselmo.
first my little dear Anselmo Cried,   *Dante* 55.

Answer.
Their answer was, If the son reign,   *Agr.* 66.
bids the pencil answer to the lyre.   *Bent.* 4.

Answered.
yet wept I not, or answer'd   *Dante* 57.

Anthem.

The pealing anthem swells the note of praise.

El. 40.

Antic.

With antic Sports, and blue-eyed Pleasures,

P. P. 30.

Antiquated.

Ye gothic fanes, and antiquated towers, *Ign.* 2.

Antique.

Ye distant spires, ye antique towers, *Eton* 1.

Minds of the antique cast, *Agr.* 126.

That grim and antique Tower admitted *Dante* 23.

Antium.

Say, she retir'd to Antium; *Agr.* 7.

I will be gone, But not to Antium — *Agr.* 166.

Anxious.

This pleasing anxious being e'er resign'd, *El.* 86.

Give anxious Cares and endless Wishes room;

El. Mas. 86.

Any.

If any spark of wit's delusive ray *Ign.* 19.

Ape.

meaner Beauties . . . vainly ape her art *L. S.* 28.

Apparatus.

So cunning was the Apparatus, *L. S.* 85.

Appear.

Fair Venus' train appear, *Spring* 2.

gorgeous Dames, and Statesmen old . . . appear.

Bard 114.

Before His high tribunal thou and I appear.

Agr. 144.

Here should Augustus great in Arms appear,

*Prop.*³ 41.

†Part in a Chrysalis appear. *Ode* 42.

†See Folly, Fashion, Foppery, straight appear,

Ch. Cr. 16.

†The walls of old Jerusalem appear, *Ch. Cr.* 27.

Appeared.

as somewhat rare That anciently appear'd,

Agr. 136.

Appears.

when lo! appears The wondrous Sage: *Tasso* 11.

And in the midst a spacious arch appears.

Tasso 42.

†E enters next, and with her Eve appears, *Ch. Cr.* 5.

Applause.

She saw; and purr'd applause. *Cat* 12.

Th' applause of list'ning senates to command,

El. 61.

the senate's joint applause, *Agr.* 77.

Appleby.

At Broom, Pendragon, Appleby and Brough.

Par. on Ep. 3.

Approach.

That fly th' approach of morn. *Eton* 50.

Slow melting strains their Queen's approach declare: *P. P.* 36.

Approach and read . . . the lay, *El.* 115.

Approached.

now the Hour Of timely Food approach'd;

Dante 50.

Approaching.

Approaching Comfort view: *Vic.* 40.

When Pindus' self approaching ruin dreads,

*Prop.*² 31.

April.

Till April starts, and calls around *Vic.* 5.

Aprons.

With . . . aprons long they hid their armour,

L. S. 38.

Apt.

For folks in fear are apt to pray *L. S.* 90.

Arbitrary.

pleasures That wait on . . . arbitrary sway:

Agr. 79.

Arch.

And in the midst a spacious arch appears.

Tasso 42.

the vivid arch of Jove; *Prop.*² 29.

Arched.

Things, that . . . Have arch'd the hearer's brow,

Agr. 169.

Arches.

Turrets and arches nodding to their fall, *View* 14.

Arching. *See* O'er-arching. *Inst.* 27.

Ardent.

With many an ardent wish, *Cat* 21.

Ardor.

How vain the ardour of the Crowd, *Spring* 18.

First the genuine ardour stole. *Inst.* 22.

†But, tho' Flowers his ardour raise, *Ode* 15.

Ardour. *See* Ardor.

Are, *omitted.*

Argive.

Ye Argive flower, ye warlike band, *Stat.*¹ 16.

Arguments.

Disprov'd the arguments of *Squib*, *L. S.* 115.

Arise.

The portals nine of hell arise. *Odin* 16.

Prophetess, arise, and say, *Odin* 52; *MS.* 74.

Once again arise, and say, *Odin* 60.

Goddess! awake, arise! *Ign.* 25.

Here mouldering fanes and battlements arise,

View 13.

†If a plenteous Crop arise, *Ode* 7.

Arising.

straight Ariseing all they cried, *Dante* 65.

Arm.

Who . . . delight to cleave With pliant arm

Eton 26.

To arm the hand of childhood, *Agr.* 138.

Let him stand forth his brawny arm to boast.

*Stat.*¹ 3.

his native land Admired that arm, *Stat.*¹ 36.

Now fitting to his gripe and nervous arm,

*Stat.*¹ 43.

His vigorous arm he tried before he flung,

*Stat.*² 6.

True to the mighty arm that gave it force,

*Stat.*² 11.

And scarce Ulysses 'scaped his giant arm.

*Stat.*² 23.

Armed.

kind Heaven Had arm'd with spirit,	*L. S.* 30.
her that arm'd This painted Jove,	*Agr.* 29.

Armenia.

That in Armenia quell the Parthian force *Agr.* 111.	

Armor.

With . . . aprons long they hid their armour,	
	L. S. 38.

Armor's.

Their scaly armour's Tyrian hue	*Cat* 16.

Armour. *See* **Armor.**

Armour's. *See* **Armor's.**

Arms.

arms sublime, that float upon the air,	*P. P.* 38.
Stretch'd forth his little arms,	*P. P.* 88.
"To arms!" cried Mortimer,	*Bard* 14.
their hundred arms they wave,	*Bard* 25.
In glitt'ring arms and glory drest,	*Owen* 21.
Their Arms, their Kings	*E. G.* 49.
Who trust your arms	*Stat.*[1] 17.
Augustus great in Arms	*Prop.*[3] 41.
†Battles, Sieges, Men, and Arms,	*Ode* 25.

Arose.

A third arose,	*Stat.*[1] 11.
Till a new Sun arose with weakly Gleam, *Dante* 59.	

Around.

Yet see how all around 'em wait	*Eton* 55.
Hyperion hurls around his . . . shafts	
	P. P. MS. 53.
Inspiration breath'd around:	*P. P.* 74.
heap'd his master's feet around,	*Owen* 29.
the sacred Calm, that broods around, *El.* Mas. 81.	
many a holy text around she strews,	*El.* 83.
Around them call The gilded swarm	*Agr.* 146.
where the face of nature laughs around, *E. G.* 70.	
calls around The sleeping fragrance	*Vic.* 5.
The band around admire	*Stat.*[1] 7.
to send the laughing bowl around,	*Prop.*[2] 7.
If the loose Curls around her Forehead play,	
	Prop.[3] 7.

Aroused.

too soon they had aroused 'em	*Dante* 48.

Array.

He wound with toilsome march his long array.	
	Bard 12.
with dirges due in sad array	*El.* 113.

Arrayed.

Wisdom in sable garb array'd	*Adv.* 25.
Alone in nature's wealth array'd,	*Hoel* 9.

Arrows.

Cobham had . . . tip'd her arrows	*L. S.* 32.

Arrowy.

Iron-sleet of arrowy shower Hurtles	*F. S.* 3.

Art. *See also* **Sister-art.**

Where China's gayest art had dy'd	*Cat* 2.
Dear lost companions of my tuneful art, *Bard* 39.	
Lord of every regal art,	*Owen* 7.
ape her art of killing.	*L. S.* 28.
To hide her cares her only art,	*Clerke* MS. 7.

Art he invokes new horrors still to bring. *View* 12.

Art it requires, and more than winged speed.	
	Tasso 30.
Each in her proper Art	*Prop.*[3] 62.

Art, *vb.*

no Traveller art thou, King of Men,	*Odin* 81.
No boding Maid of skill divine Art thou,	*Odin* 85.
I know not, who thou art;	*Dante* 10.
Oh! thou art cruel,	*Dante* 45.

Artful.

with many an artful fib,	*L. S.* 113.
And blended form, with artful strife,	*Vic.* 43.
Artful and strong	*Stat.*[2] 3.
With native spots and artful labour gay, *Stat.*[2] 25.	
Her artful hand across the sounding Strings.	
	Prop.[3] 16.

Arthur.

No more our long-lost Arthur we bewail. *Bard* 109.	
another *Arthur* reigns.	*Bard* MS. 110.

Arthur's.

born of Arthur's line	*Bard* Lett.[2] 116.

Artless.

their artless tale relate;	*El.* 94 ; *Mas.* 78.

Arts.

Fix and improve the polish'd Arts of Peace:	
	E. G. 41.
Here Arts are vain,	*Prop.*[3] 85.

Arvon's.

On dreary Arvon's shore they lie,	*Bard* 35.

As, *omitted.*

Ascalon.

And first to Ascalon their steps they bend,	
	Tasso 3.

Ashes.

E'en in our Ashes live their wonted Fires. *El.* 92.	
buried ashes glow with social fires. *El.* Mas. 108.	

Asia.

Why yet does Asia dread	*E. G.* 59.

Ask.

Rap'd at the door, nor stay'd to ask,	*L. S.* 55.
You ask, why thus my Loves I still rehearse,	
	Prop.[3] 1.

Askance.

Whom meaner Beauties eye askance,	*L. S.* 27.
Askaunce he turn'd him,	*Dante* 83.

Asked.

He ask'd no heaps of hoarded gold;	*Hoel* 8.
He ask'd and had the lovely maid.	*Hoel* 10.

Aspect.

And hoary Nile with pensive Aspect	*Prop.*[3] 49.

Aspire.

With damp, cold touch forbid it to aspire, *Ign.* 21.	

Assassinations.

Sorceries, Assassinations, poisonings — *Agr.* 172.	

Assign.

The different doom our Fates assign.	*Bard* 140.

Assigned.

To different Climes seem different Souls assign'd?	
	E. G. 39.

Astonished.

So from th' astonish'd stars,   *Stat.*[1] 53.

At.

At ease reclin'd in rustic state   *Spring* 17.
Scar'd at thy frown terrific,   *Adv.* 17.
drop'd his thirsty lance at thy command. *P. P.* 19.
Hurls at their flying rear,   *P. P.* MS. 52.
and Pleasure at the helm;   *Bard* 74.
boast at home,   *Odin* 87.
at the shrine   *El.* Mas. 71.
at the peep of dawn   *El.* 98.
at the foot of yonder nodding beech,   *El.* 101.
at noontide would he stretch,   *El.* 103.
nor at the wood was he: *El.* 112.
Rap'd at the door, nor stay'd to ask,   *L. S.* 55.
at the chappel-door stand sentry;   *L. S.* 104.
at the blush of dawn   *Inst.* 30.
At least there are who know   *Agr.* 15.
Scar'd at the sound,   *Agr.* 32.
eyed at distance Some edileship,   *Agr.* 39.
wonder'd at its daring: *Agr.* 55.
tremble at the phantom   *Agr.* 86.
shake 'em at the name of liberty,   *Agr.* 132.
My thought askew at him;   *Agr.* 160.
shed at Ev'n a cheerful ray   *E. G.* 66.
At length repair his vigour lost,   *Vic.* 47.
At Aix, his voluntary sword he drew, *Williams* 5.
No — at our time of life 't would be silly, *C. C.* 10.
She swept, . . . At Broom,   *Par. on Ep.* 3.
the champions, trembling at the sight, Prevent
    disgrace,   *Stat.*[1] 22.
Dismiss'd at length, they break through all delay
    Tasso 1.
Famine at feasts, and thirst amid the stream;
    Prop.[2] 47.
At once give loose to Utterance,   *Dante* 9.
when at the Gate Below I heard   *Dante* 50.
When Gaddo, at my Feet out-stretch'd, *Dante* 73.

Athwart.

And furthest send its weight athwart the field,
    Stat.[1] 2.
As when athwart the dusky woods by night
    Tasso 47.

Atoms.

shake . . . To its original atoms —   *Agr.* 92.

Attempered.

Attemper'd sweet to virgin-grace.   *Bard* 118.
All stones . . . mix attemper'd in a various day;
    Tasso 66.

Attend.

Still on thy solemn steps attend: *Adv.* 29.
O Cambridge, attend To the Satire I 've pen'd
    Satire 1.
A train of mourning Friends attend his Pall,
    Prop.[3] 97.
Attend, and say if he have injured me. *Dante* 21.

Attends.

Weddell attends your call,   *Com. Lines* 1.

Attic.

The Attic warbler pours her throat,   *Spring* 5.

Attire.

Fields resume their green Attire: *West* 4.

Attracts.

The diamond there attracts the wondrous sight,
    Tasso 69.

Audience.

The Audience stare,   *L. S.* 109.

Augments.

Augments the native darkness of the sky; *Ign.* 8.

Augustus.

Here should Augustus great in Arms appear,
    Prop.[3] 41.

Aunt.

Rummage his Mother, pinch his Aunt, *L. S.* 59.

Auspicious.

from that auspicious Night   *Prop.*[3] 25.

Author.

Who the Author of his fate.   *Odin* 54.

Autumnal.

pour the autumnal rain;   *Prop.*[2] 26.

Avail.

Nor even thy virtues, Tyrant, shall avail *Bard* 6.

Avails.

The Bed avails not,   *Prop.*[3] 93.

Avaunt.

Hence, avaunt, ('t is holy ground)   *Inst.* 1.

Avenger.

say, Who th' Avenger of his guilt,   *Odin* 61.

Avengers.

Avengers of their native land: *Bard* 46.

Averse.

What Cat 's averse [a foe, Wal., Dods.] to fish ?
    Cat 24.
When, less averse, and yielding to Desires,
    Prop.[3] 21.

Averted.   *See* **Half-averted.**

Avoid.

That to avoid, and this to emulate.   *Stat.*[2] 5.

Avon.

where lucid Avon stray'd,   *P. P.* 85.

Await.

Man's feeble race what Ills await,   *P. P.* 42.
What dangers *Odin's* Child await,   *Odin* 53.

Awaits.

Awaits alike th' inevitable hour.
    El., Dods., Pem., Eg. 35.
Whom what awaits,   *Clerke* 11.
But what awaits me now is worst of all. *Shak.* 8.

Awake.

Awake, Æolian lyre, awake,   *P. P.* 1.
Prophetess, awake [arise, MS.], and say, *Odin* 74.
Can honour's voice awake the silent dust,
    El. Mas. 43.
Awake, and faithful to her wonted Fires.
    El. Dods. 92.
Goddess! awake, arise!   *Ign.* 25.
She bids each slumb'ring energy awake, *E. G.* 78.
To local symmetry and life awake!   *Bent.* 8.
Or if to Musick she the Lyre awake, *Prop.*[3] 13.

Aware.

They are aware Of th' unpledg'd bowl, *Agr.* 20.

Away.

Brushing with hasty steps the dews away   *El.* 99.
Hence, away, 't is holy ground!   *Inst.* 12.
their Kings, their Gods were roll'd away.   *E. G.* 49.
A tiger's pride the victor bore away,   *Stat.*[2] 24.
†Some spin away their little lives   *Ode* 39.
†'Till they loved their love away;   *Rond.* 6.

Awe.

Rever'd With custom'd awe, the daughter,
Agr. 118.

Awe-commanding.

Her [A, MS.] lyon-port, her [an, MS.] awe-
commanding face,   *Bard* 117.

Aweful, Awful.

did unveil Her aweful face: *P. P.* 87.
Sighs to the torrent's aweful voice beneath!
Bard 24.
And bad these awful fanes and turrets rise,
Inst. 53.
Let majesty sit on thy awful brow,   *Agr.* 145.
Tell them, tho' 't is an awful thing to die,
Stanza 1.
vigorous he seem'd in years, Awful his mien,
Tasso 13.

Awhile.

Yet awhile my call obey;   *Odin* 73.
Then to my quiet Urn awhile draw near,
Prop.[3] 105.

Awoke.

The Morn had scarce commenc'd, when I awoke:
Dante 41.

Azure.

China's . . . art had dy'd The azure flowers,
Cat 3.
Thro' the azure deep of air: *P. P.* 117.
While proudly riding o'er the azure realm
Bard 72.
A brighter Day, and Skies of azure Hue ; *E. G.* 55.

B.

†They 're all diverted into H and B.   *Ch. Cr.* 14.

Babbles.

pore upon the brook that babbles by.   *El.* 104.

Bacchus .

My soul in Bacchus' pleasing fetters bound;
Prop.[2] 8.

Back.

Back to its mansion call the fleeting breath ?
El. 42.
bring the buried ages back to view.   *Ign.* 35.
Back to it's Source divine the Julian Race.
Prop.[3] 58.
Take back, what once was yours.   *Dante* 68.

Backed.

The Godhead would have back'd his quarrel,
L. S. 93.

Backward.

Backward Meinai rolls his flood;   *Owen* 28.

Bacon.

Yet hop'd, that he might save his bacon: *L. S.* 126.

Bad.   *See also* Bade.

The Bad affright, afflict the Best!   *Adv.* 4.
She had a bad face   *Mrs. Keene* 2.

Bade.

he . . . bad to form her infant mind.   *Adv.* 12.
And bad these awful fanes and turrets rise,
Inst. 53.
bade him strike The noble quarry.   *Agr.* 46.
You bade the magi call   *Agr.* 64.
who oft has bade, Ev'n when its will   *Agr.* 69.
The love of honour bade two youths advance,
Stat.[1] 9.
Who measured out the year, and bad the seasons
roll;   *Prop.*[2] 38.

Badest.

What sorrow was, thou bad'st her know,   *Adv.* 15.

Baffled.

A baleful smile upon their baffled Guest. *Bard* 82.

Baiæ.

ere mid-day, Nero will come to Baiæ. *Agr.* 159.

Balder.

'T is the drink of *Balder* bold: *Odin* 46.

Balder's.

Balder's head to death is giv'n.   *Odin* 47.

Baleful.

black Misfortune's baleful train!   *Eton* 57.
A baleful smile upon their baffled Guest. *Bard* 82.

Ball.

Or urge the flying ball ?   *Eton* 30.
yon puny ball Let youngsters toss: *Stat.*[1] 19.
And now in dust the polish'd ball he roll'd,
Stat.[1] 41.

Balls.   *See* Eye-balls.

Baltic.

blue-eyed Myriads from the Baltic coast. *E. G.* 51.

Band.

To seize their prey the murth'rous band! *Eton* 59.
Poverty, to fill the band,   *Eton* 88.
Not circled with the vengeful Band   *Adv.* 36.
a griesly band, I see them sit,   *Bard* 44.
Lo! Granta waits to lead her blooming band,
Inst. 77.
and strok'd down her band —   *C. C.* 22.
The band around admire the mighty mass,
Stat.[1] 7.
Ye Argive flower, ye warlike band,   *Stat.*[1] 16.

Bands.

Joy to the victorious bands;   *F. S.* 55.

Bane.

Orkney's woe, and *Randver's* bane.   *F. S.* 8.

Banners.

Confusion on thy banners wait,   *Bard* 2.
Thousand Banners round him burn: *Owen* 32.

Barbaric.

Like old Sesostris with barbaric pride; *Ign.* 37.

Barbarous.

sacrifice perform'd with barb'rous rites   *Agr.* 62.

Bard.

The bard, . . . Had in imagination fenc'd him, *L. S.* 113.

There sit the sainted sage, the bard divine, *Inst.* 15.

Sacred tribute of the bard, *Conan* 3.

Still may his Bard in softer fights engage; *Prop.*[1] 3.

Bark.

to his gilded bark With fond reluctance, *Agr.* 196.

Baron.

Girt with many a Baron bold *Bard* 111.

Baronets.

From fumbling baronets and poets small, *Shak.* 6.

Barons.

Youthful knights and barons bold *Bard* MS. 111.

Barristers.

Pert barristers, and parsons nothing bright, *Shak.* 7.

Bars.

I heard the dreadful Clash of Bars, *Dante* 51.

Base.

Nor Envy base, *Inst.* 9.

On this base My . . . revenge shall rise; *Agr.* 120.

Basilisk.

not the basilisk More deadly to the sight, *Agr.* 161.

Batter.

And batter Cadmus' walls *Stat.*[1] 18.

Battle.

Heard ye the din of battle bray, *Bard* 83.

outcry of the battle? *Agr.* 96.

Battlements.

mouldering fanes and battlements *View* 13.

Battle's.

Echoing to the battle's roar. *Owen* 26.

Battles.

†Battles, Sieges, Men, and Arms, *Ode* 25.

Bays.

Hoarse he bays with hideous din, *Odin* 9.

B—d's.

nor B—d's promises been vain, *View* Nich. 18.

Be, *omitted.*

Beach. *See* **Desert-beach.**

Beak.

The terror of his beak, *P. P.* 24.

Beam.

that in thy noon-tide beam were born? *Bard* 69.

Nor see the sun's departing beam, *Odin* 68.

with glitt'ring beam, *Tasso* 63.

Beamed.

With double light it beam'd against the day: *Stat.*[1] 27.

Beaming.

†Bright beaming, as the Evening-star, her face; *Ch. Cr.* 8.

Beams.

†Youth, his torrid Beams thay [that?] plays, *Ode* 13.

Beans.

So the Master of Queen's Is as like as two beans; *Satire* 16.

Bear.

Wide o'er the fields of Glory bear *P. P.* 104.

That the Theban Eagle bear *P. P.* 115.

A Voice, . . . Gales from blooming Eden bear; *Bard* 132.

A wond'rous Boy shall *Rinda* bear, *Odin* 65.

The dark unfathom'd caves of ocean bear: *El.* 54.

to bear the blaze of greatness; *Agr.* 45.

The Fields to all their wonted Tribute bear; *West* 11.

Beard.

Loose his beard, and hoary hair Stream'd, *Bard* 19.

His bushy beard, and shoe-strings green, *L. S.* 13.

Bearded.

In [Of, Lett.[2]] bearded majesty, *Bard* 114.

Bears.

by Juno, It bears a noble semblance. *Agr.* 120.

The Master of Trinity To him bears affinity; *Satire* 12.

Beat.

on these mould'ring bones have beat The winter's snow, *Odin* 31.

Beating.

To brisk notes in cadence beating, *P. P.* 34.

Beaufort's.

we trace . . . a Beaufort's grace. *Inst.* 70.

Beauteous.

Two beauteous forms were seen to glide, *Cat* Wal., Dods. 14.

Shall sink this beauteous fabric *Prop.*[2] 28.

Beauties.

From hence, ye Beauties, *Cat* 37.

Whom meaner Beauties eye askance, *L. S.* 27.

And realis'd the beauties which [ruins that, MS.; horrors which, Nich.] we feign: *View* 20.

and thousand beauties see *Prop.*[3] 19.

Beautified.

beautified by fire, *View* MS. 21.

Beauty.

all that beauty, all that wealth e'er gave, *El.* 34.

With beauty, with pleasure surrounded, to languish, *Am. Lines* 1.

Because.

I . . . weep the more because I weep in vain. *West* 14.

Become.

†as might a King become, *Ch. Cr.* 49.

Bed. *See also* **Summer-bed.**

Brave Urien sleeps upon his craggy bed: *Bard* 31.

That calls me from the bed of rest? *Odin* 36.

Drest for whom yon golden bed. *Odin* 42.

shall rouse them from their lowly bed. *El.* 20.

And o'er the bed and tester clamber, *L. S.* 64.

tost On the thorny bed of Pain, *Vic.* 46.

the obedient river's inmost bed ; *Tasso* 44.

The Po was there to see, Danubius' bed, *Tasso* 55.

stretch'd on their iron bed, *Prop.*[2] 41.

To die is glorious in the Bed of Love. *Prop.*[3] 64.

The Bed avails not, *Prop.*[3] 93.

Bee.

The pure bev'rage of the bee,   *Odin* 44.

Beech.

the rude and moss-grown beech   *Spring* 13.
the foot of yonder nodding beech,   *El.* 101.

Been.

"Ah!" said the sighing peer, "had Bute been
   true,   *View* 17.
nor B—d's promises been vain,   *View* Nich. 18.

Bee's.

The bee's collected treasures sweet,   *Inst.* 62.

Bees.

drink Nectar that the bees produce,   *Hoel* 17.

Beetle.

Save where the beetle wheels his droning flight,
   El. 7.

Befall.

fair befall the victors.   *Agr.* 153.

Befell.

Ah! say, . . . how these symptoms befell me?
   Am. Lines 7.

Before.

With pangs unfelt before,   *Adv.* 8.
Yet oft before his infant eyes   *P. P.* 118.
Till full before his fearless eyes   *Odin* 15.
The Seal, and Maces, danc'd before him. *L. S.* 12.
there before His high tribunal   *Agr.* 143.
Let him feel Before he sees me.   *Agr.* 164.
The dusky people drive before the gale; *E. G.* 105.
When you rise from your Dinner as light as before,
   Couplet 1.
His vigorous arm he tried before he flung,
   *Stat.*² 6.
before the warriors' eyes . . . the waves disparted
   rise;   *Tasso* 39.
Before the Goddess' shrine we . . . bend, *Prop.*¹ 2.
my other three before my Eyes Died *Dante* 75.
†And brings all Womankind before your view;
   Ch. Cr. 59.
†With Woe behind, and Wantonness before.
   Ch. Cr. 61.

Began. *See also* '**gan.**

they that fly, Shall end where they began.
   Spring 34.
Phlegyas the long-expected play began, *Stat.*¹ 32.
thus Began. Would'st thou revive *Dante* 4.

Beget.

the telling may Beget the Traitour's Infamy,
   Dante 7.

Begged.

And beg'd his aid that dreadful day. *L. S.* 92.

Begin.

There the thund'ring strokes begin, *Owen* 23.
†Or, soon as they begin to blow   *Ode* 5.

Beginning.

What, in the very first beginning! *L. S.* 17.

Begins.

Now the storm begins to lower   *F. S.* 1.

Begone.

'T is well, begone!   *Agr.* 1.

Begs.

'T is Willy begs,   *Shak.* 3.

Beguiled.

The slipp'ry verge her feet beguil'd, *Cat* 29.
have beguil'd . . . the dazzled sight' *Agr.* 190.

Beheld.

Has he beheld the glittering front of war? *Agr.* 94.
his helpless offspring soon O'erta'en beheld,
   Dante 39.
when I beheld My Sons,   *Dante* 61.

Behind.

Still as they run they look behind, *Eton* 38.
And Shame that sculks behind;   *Eton* 64.
Amazement in his van, . . . and solitude be-
   hind.   *Bard* 62.
cast one longing ling'ring look behind? *El.* 88.
Behind the steps that Misery treads, *Vic.* 39.
She felt the wound she left behind, *Clerke* 8.
†With Woe behind, and Wantonness before.
   Ch. Cr. 61.

Behold.

Behold, where Dryden's less presumptuous car,
   P. P. 103.
High on her car, behold the grandam ride *Ign.* 36.
And bids the pure in heart behold their God.
   Stanza 4.
†Behold K struts,   *Ch. Cr.* 49.

Being.

This pleasing anxious being   *El.* 86.
To her that gave it being,   *Agr.* 29.

Beldams.

Wrinkled beldams teach it   *Agr.* 134.

Believe.

Who will, believe.   *L. S.* 73.

Believed.

they vow their truth, and are again believed.
   Adv. 24.
he believed in a God: *Char.* 4.

Belike.

might serve belike to wake pretensions *Agr.* 103.

Bellisle's.

Victor he stood on Bellisle's rocky steeps —
   Williams 10.

Bellow.

created but to . . . bellow in the Circus *Agr.* 131.

Belly.

She strok'd up her belly,   *C. C.* 22.
And Balguy with a bishop in his belly.
   Com. Lines 7.

Beloved.

Ah, fields belov'd in vain,   *Eton* 12.

Below.

Selima . . . Gazed on the lake below. *Cat* 6.
th' expanse below . . . survey   *Eton* 6.
Above, below, the rose of snow, . . . we spread:
   Bard 91.
And the weights, that play below, *F. S.* 11.
Tell me what is done below,   *Odin* 40.
And men below Join with glad voice *Inst.* 87.
Insult the plenty of the vales below? *E. G.* 99.

Far below,   the crowd.   *Vic.* 57.
Her infant image here below, Sits smiling *Clerke* 9.
when at the Gate Below I heard   *Dante* 51.

Bend.
Virgins . . . That bend to earth their solemn
    brow,   *Odin* 76.
a team of harness'd monarchs bend   *Ign.* 38.
And first to Ascalon their steps they bend,
              Tasso 3.
Before the Goddess' shrine we too, love's vot'ries,
    bend,   *Prop.*[1] 2.
In golden Chains should loaded Monarchs bend,
           Prop.[3] 48.

Bending.
bending o'er th' accursed loom   *Bard* 95.

Bends.
Meek Newton's self bends from his state sublime,
             Inst. 25.
Where melancholy friendship bends, and weeps.
           Williams 12.

Beneath.
in the vale of tears beneath   *Eton* 81.
beneath the od'rous shade   *P. P.* 58.
Beneath the Good how far —   *P. P.* 123.
Sighs to the torrent's aweful voice beneath!
           Bard 24.
Boar . . . Wallows beneath the thorny shade.
           Bard 94.
The groaning earth beneath him shakes, *Odin* 14.
Beneath those rugged elms, that yew-tree's shade,
           El. 13.
bow'd the woods beneath their sturdy stroke.
           El. 28.
the stone beneath yon aged thorn.   *El.* 116.
in the park beneath an old-tree,   *L. S.* 122.
Fade and expire beneath the eye of day? *E. G.* 67.
Where Ocean frets beneath the dashing oar,
           Stat.[2] 20.
The river boil'd beneath,   *Tasso* 24.
he led Beneath the obedient river's inmost bed;
           Tasso 44.
If realms beneath those fabled torments know,
           Prop.[2] 39.
†reclined beneath the Tree-zes;   *Ode* 22.

Benefits.
benefits too great To be repaid,   *Agr.* 74.

Benet.
The Master of Benet Is of the like tenet; *Satire* 27.

Benighted.
steep in slumbers each benighted sense? *Ign.* 18.
not to one in this benighted age   *Bent.* 17.

Benign.
Thy form benign, oh Goddess, wear,   *Adv.* 41.

Bent.
Again she bent,   *Cat* 26.
While some on earnest business bent   *Eton* 31.
All eyes were bent on his experienced hand,
           Stat.[1] 34.

Bentley.
While Bentley leads her sister-art along, *Bent.* 3.

Bereft.
the panting Sire Of Strength bereft,   *Dante* 38.

Berkley's.
The shrieks of death, thro' Berkley's roofs that
    ring,   *Bard* 55.

Beside.
nor yet beside the rill,   *El.* 111.
His young ones ran beside him.   *Dante* 32.

Besides.
Besides, he repents —   *C. C.* 30.

Bespangled. *See* **Dew-bespangled.**

Best.
The Bad affright, afflict the Best!   *Adv.* 4.
Her household cares, a woman's best employment.
           Agr. 8.
Grease his best pen,   *Shak.* 16.

Bestow.
A momentary bliss bestow,   *Eton* 16.

Bestowed.
you bestow'd The very power he has   *Agr.* 80.

Bestride.
Each bestride her sable steed.   *F. S.* 63.
Now your sable steed bestride,   *F. S.* MS. 63.

Bethel.
The prophet of Bethel, we read, told a lie: *C. C.* 27.

Betray.
sickly Plants betray a niggard Earth,   *E. G.* 1.

Betrayed.
Betray'd a golden gleam,   *Cat* 18.
that I was betray'd By trusting,   *Dante* 16.

Better.
Better to bottom tarts   *Shak.* 17.
Better the roast meat from the fire to save,
           Shak. 18.
Better be twisted into caps for spice,   *Shak.* 19.
Far better [other, MS.] scenes than these *View* 19.

Betties.
†Elizabeths all dwindled into Betties; *Ch. Cr.* 12.

Between.
Nor knew the gulf between.   *Cat* 27.
DIVINITY heard, between waking and dozing,
           C. C. 19.
†And seems small difference the sounds between;
           Ch. Cr. 46.

Betwixt.
Age step 'twixt love and me,   *Prop.*[2] 12.

Beverage.
The pure bev'rage of the bee,   *Odin* 44.

Bewail.
No more our long-lost Arthur we bewail.
           Bard 109.

Bewitched.
Bewitch'd the children of the peasants, *L. S.* 46.

Beyond.
Nor care beyond to-day: *Eton* 54.
In climes beyond the solar road,   *P. P.* 54.
Beyond the limits of a vulgar fate,   *P. P.* 122.
Charity, that glows beyond the tomb. *Inst.* 50.
extends Beyond their chronicle —   *Agr.* 138.
Beyond the confines of our narrow world:
           Tasso 34.

Bid.
She smiled, and bid him come to dinner. *L. S.* 132.
bid it . . . shed The fragrance of its blushing
    head: *Inst.* 73.
raise, and bid it fire A thousand . . . hearts,
            Agr. 16.
†Whose influence first bid it live.   *Ode* 54.

Bids.
sacred Calm, . . . Bids ev'ry . . . Passion cease;
            El. Mas. 82.
She bids each slumb'ring energy awake, *E. G.* 78.
bids the pencil answer to the lyre.   *Bent.* 4.
And bids the pure in heart behold their God.
            Stanza 4.
†Bids the poetick Spirit flourish;   *Ode* 14.

Big.
Big with hosts . . . Squadrons . . . came;
            Owen 9.
Big with the important Nothing's History.
            Prop.³ 30.
†So big with Weddings, waddles W, *Ch. Cr.* 58.

Billows.
The flood on either hand its billows rears,
            Tasso 41.

Binds.
And winter binds the floods in icy chains, *Tasso* 18.

Bird. *See also* **Newgate-bird.**
No tree is heard to whisper, bird to sing; *View* 10.

Birdlime.
Transparent birdlime form'd the middle, *L. S.* 83.

Birds.
and Birds of boding cry,   *P. P.* 50.
The Birds in vain their amorous Descant joyn;
            West 3.
To warm their little Loves the Birds complain:
            West 12.
The Birds his presence greet: *Vic.* 12.

Birth.
To thee he gave the heav'nly Birth,   *Adv.* 11.
Science frown'd not on his humble birth, *El.* 119.
High potentates, and dames of royal birth,
            Inst. 37.
flinty Bosom starves her generous Birth, *E. G.* 2.
the human fabric from the birth Imbibes *E. G.* 84.
The birth of rivers riseing to their course, *Tasso* 52.

Bishop.
And Balguy with a bishop in his belly.
            Com. Lines 7.
The Bishop of Chester,   *Ext. Keene* 1.
Lord Bishop of Chester,   *Ep. Keene* 1.
Here lies Mrs. Keene the she Bishop of Chester,
            Mrs. Keene 1.

Bite.
Soon a King shall bite the ground.   *F. S.* 44.

Biting. *See* **Sheep-biting.**

Bitter.
To bitter Scorn a sacrifice,   *Eton* 73.

Bitterness.
The Bitterness of Death, I shall unfold. *Dante* 20.

Black. *See also* **Coal-black.**
black Misfortune's baleful train!   *Eton* 57.
in black clouds of slumber   *P. P. MS.* 23.
Mista black,   *F. S.* 17.
Black and huge along they sweep,   *Owen* 17.

Blacken.
blacken round our weary way,   *Vic.* 35.

Blacker.
the blacker his ingratitude.   *Agr.* 173.

Blade.
Blade, that once a Monarch bore, *F. S.* Whar. 15.
Blade [Sword, Whar.] with clattering buckler
    meet,   *F. S.* 23.

Blast.
blast the vernal Promise of the Year. *E. G.* 21.
†Or Poppy-thoughts blast all the shoots. *Ode* 12.

Blasted.
blasted with excess of light,   *P. P.* 101.
of Jove, and Phlegra's blasted Plain; *Prop.³* 56.

Blaze. *See* **Sapphire-blaze.**
to bear the blaze of greatness;   *Agr.* 45.
How shall the spark . . . Blaze into freedom,
            Agr. 129.
in the diamond's blaze,   *Bent.* 21.

Blazing.
no more the blazing hearth shall burn, *El.* 21.
When blazing 'gainst the sun   *Stat.¹* 30.

Bleak.
desart-beach Pent within its bleak domain, *F. S.* 38.
the rigour Of bleak Germania's snows. *Agr.* 110.

Bled.
Though by me ye bled, He was the cause. *Agr.* 180.

Bleeding.
Chatillon . . . That wept her bleeding Love,
            Inst. 42.

Blended.
And blended form, with artful strife, *Vic.* 43.

Bless.
Than Pow'r and Genius e'er conspir'd to bless.
            El. Mas. 76.
a glance . . . They send . . . To bless the place,
            Inst. 21.

Blessed. *See also* **Blest.**
Our mother-church, . . . Blush'd as she bless'd
    her griesly proselyte;   *Toph.* 6.

Blest. *See also* **Blessed.**
While spirits blest above . . . Join with glad
    voice   *Inst.* 87.
Far better scenes than these had blest [grac'd,
    Nich.] our view,   *View* 19.

Blighting.
Here reign the blustering North and blighting
    East,   *View* 9.

Bliss.
A momentary bliss bestow,   *Eton* 16.
where ignorance is bliss,   *Eton* 99.
The hues of Bliss more brightly glow, *Vic.* 41.

Blood.
keen Remorse with blood defil'd,   *Eton* 78.
By whom shall *Hoder's* blood be spilt ? *Odin* 62.

Check'd by the torrent-tide of blood,   *Owen* 27.
Cromwell guiltless of his country's blood. *El.* 60.
the blood Of Agrippina's race,   *Agr.* 37.
its will seem'd wrote in lines of blood, *Agr.* 70.
the genuine blood Of our imperial house.
                                         Agr. 104.
If murder cries for murder, blood for blood,
                                         Agr. 185.
Force and hardy Deeds of Blood prevail. *E. G.* 44.
There first in blood his infant honour seal'd;
                                         Williams 6.

Bloody.
And weave with bloody hands   *Bard* 48.
Bursting through the bloody throng   *Hoel* 22.
chas'd by Hell-hounds gaunt and bloody
                                         Dante 30.

Bloom.
The bloom of young Desire,   *P. P.* 41.
A fairer flower will never bloom again: *Child* 4.
There bloom the vernal rose's earliest pride;
                                         Prop.[2] 10.

Blooming.
A Voice, . . . Gales from blooming Eden bear;
                                         Bard 132.
Lo! Granta waits to lead her blooming band,
                                         Inst. 77.

Blossoms.
trusts her Blossoms to the churlish Skies. *E. G.* 8.

Blot.
Clouds of carnage blot [veil, Whar.] the sun.
                                         F. S. 50.

Blow.
The azure flowers, that blow;   *Cat* 3.
I feel the gales, that from ye blow,   *Eton* 15.
flowers, that round them blow,   *P. P.* 5.
†Or, soon as they begin to blow   *Ode* 5.

Blows.
soft the Zephyr blows,   *Bard* 71.

Blue.
Zephyrs thro' the clear blue sky   *Spring* 9.
With bonnet blue . . . they hid their armour,
                                         L. S. 37.
And rubies flame, with sapphire's heavenly blue,
                                         Tasso 68.

Blue-eyed.
With antic Sports, and blue-eyed Pleasures,
                                         P. P. 30.
The blue-eyed Myriads from the Baltic coast.
                                         E. G. 51.

Blush.
many a flower is born to blush unseen,   *El.* 55.
But with a blush on recollection Own'd, *L. S.* 94.
Oft at the blush of dawn I trod   *Inst.* 30.

Blushed.
Our mother-church, . . . Blush'd   *Toph.* 6.

Blushes.
quench the blushes of ingenuous shame,   *El.* 70.

Blushing.
Twined with her blushing foe,   *Bard* 92.
The fragrance of its blushing head: *Inst.* 74.
Half pleas'd, half blushing,   *Bent.* 2.

Blustering.
Here reign the blustering North and blighting
East,   *View* 9.

Boar.
The bristled Boar in infant-gore Wallows
                                         Bard 93.
Have ye seen the dusky boar,   *Caradoc* 1.

Board.
For whom yon glitt'ring board is spread, *Odin* 41.
partake His hospitable board: *Agr.* 20.

Boast.
Hie thee hence, and boast at home,   *Odin* 87.
The boast of heraldry,   *El.* 33.
theirs, who boast the genuine blood   *Agr.* 104.
The schoolman's glory, and the churchman's
boast.   *Ign.* 32.
Let him stand forth his brawny arm to boast.
                                         Stat.[1] 3.
†these Flies . . . Can boast of one good Quality;
                                         Ode 50.

Boasted.
Her boasted Titles and her golden Fields; *E. G.* 53.

Boding.
and Birds of boding cry,   *P. P.* 50.
No boding Maid of skill divine Art thou, *Odin* 84.

Boiled.
The river boil'd beneath,   *Tasso* 24.

Bold.
be with caution bold.   *Cat* 39.
Some bold adventurers disdain   *Eton* 35.
Girt with many a Baron bold   *Bard* 111.
'T is the drink of *Balder* bold: *Odin* 46.

Bolt.
To aim the forked bolt;   *Agr.* 31.

Bolts.
the dreadful Clash of Bars, And fast'ning Bolts:
                                         Dante 52.

Bonds.
lord, That broke the bonds of Rome.   *Inst.* 47.

Bones.
Long on these mould'ring bones   *Odin* 31.
these bones from insult to protect   *El.* 77.

Bonnet.
With bonnet blue . . . they hid   *L. S.* 37.
†a Sonnet On Chloe's Fan, or Cælia's Bonnet.
                                         Ode 36.

Book.
'T is just like the picture in Rochester's book;
                                         C. C. 12.
Though now a book, and interleaved you see.
                                         Shak. 4.
'T is ample Matter for a Lover's Book; *Prop.*[3] 28.

Books.
Papers and books, a huge Imbroglio! *L. S.* 66.

Bootes'.
And what Bootes' lazy waggon tires; *Prop.*[2] 36.

Border.
chains invisible [form'd] the border.   *L. S.* 84.
A shining border round the margin roll'd,
                                         Stat.[2] 26.

Borders.

Hosannas rung through hell's tremendous borders,   *Toph.* 7.

Bore.

thy rigid lore With patience . . . she bore:
     Adv. 14.

Sword, that once a Monarch bore,   *F. S.* 15.

So Caràdoc bore his lance.   *Caradoc* 4.

The pond'rous brass in exercise he bore; *Stat.*[1] 37.

A tiger's pride the victor bore away,   *Stat.*[2] 24.

His head a chaplet bore,   *Tasso* 16.

Boreas'.

As on the Rhine, when Boreas' fury reigns,
     Tasso 17.

Born. *See also* High-born, New-born.

And lively chear of vigour born;   *Eton* 47.

She-Wolf . . . From thee be born,   *Bard* 59.

that in thy noon-tide beam were born? *Bard* 69.

born of Arthur's line   *Bard Lett.*[2] 116.

many a flower is born to blush unseen, *El.* 55.

thro' the church-way path we saw him born. —
     El. 114.

two youths advance, Achaians born, *Stat.*[1] 10.

Borne. *See also* Born.

so was she borne By the young Trojan *Agr.* 195.

Much have I borne from canker'd critic's spite,
     Shak. 5.

may my pale Coarse be borne.   *Prop.*[3] 78.

Bosom.

O'er her warm cheek, and rising bosom, *P. P.* 40.

The bosom of his Father and his God. *El.* 128.

a niggard Earth, Whose flinty Bosom *E. G.* 2.

From his broad bosom life and verdure flings
     E. G. 102.

And to this bosom give its wonted Peace,
     Prop.[3] 88.

Bosomed. *See* Rosy-bosomed.

Bosoms.

You whose young bosoms feel a nobler flame
     Prop.[2] 53.

Bottom.

Better to bottom tarts   *Shak.* 17.

Bounce.

But bounce into the parlour enter'd.   *L. S.* 56.

Bound.

Bound in thy adamantine chain,   *Adv.* 5.

The orb . . . Far overleaps all bound, *Stat.*[2] 12.

My soul in Bacchus' pleasing fetters bound;
     Prop.[2] 8.

†Then to sever what is bound,   *Rond.* 31.

Boundless.

the od'rous shade Of Chili's boundless forests
     P. P. 59.

They perish in the boundless deep.   *Vic.* 60.

Bounds.

the flaming bounds of Place and Time: *P. P.* 98.

either Pole, and Life's remotest Bounds, *E. G.* 25.

How the rude surge its sandy Bounds control;
     Prop.[2] 37.

The torrent-stream his ancient bounds disdains,
     Tasso 9.

Bounty.

Large was his bounty,   *El.* 121.

Rich streams of regal bounty pour'd,   *Inst.* 52.

Bow.

Made huge Plinlimmon bow his cloud-top'd head.
     Bard 34.

The thoughtless World to Majesty may bow,
     El. Mas. 73.

bow the supple knee, and court the times *Agr.* 101.

I saw them bow,   *Toph.* 3.

Bowed.

How bow'd the woods beneath their . . . stroke!
     El. 28.

While frighted prelates bow'd   *Toph.* 2.

Bowels.

That tear'st the bowels of thy mangled Mate,
     Bard 58.

Bower.

wand'ring near her secret bow'r,   *El.* 11.

Bowers.

in these consecrated bowers,   *Inst.* 7.

ye ever gloomy bowers, Ye gothic fanes, *Ign.* 1.

Bowl.

Fill high the sparkling bowl,   *Bard* 77.

they are aware Of th' unpledg'd bowl, *Agr.* 21.

Give me to send the laughing bowl around,
     Prop.[2] 7.

Bows.

When Pindus' self . . . bows his hundred heads;
     Prop.[2] 32.

Boy.

Thine too these golden keys, immortal Boy!
     P. P. 91.

Yet thou, proud boy,   *Bard MS.* 75.

A wond'rous Boy shall *Rinda* bear,   *Odin* 65.

unus'd to shake When a boy frowns, *Agr.* 18.

a puny boy,   *Agr.* 36.

we may meet, ungrateful boy, we may! *Agr.* 140.

Boys.

they wept, unhappy Boys!   *Dante* 54.

Brace.

issues A brace of Warriors, not in buff, *L. S.* 23.

Braced.

Brac'd all his nerves,   *Stat.*[2] 7.

Bradshaw's.

Nor Mungo's, Rigby's, Bradshaw's [Calcraft's, MS.] friendship vain,   *View* 18.

Branches.

Where'er the oak's thick branches stretch
     Spring 11.

Brass.

A slipp'ry weight, and form'd of polish'd brass.
     Stat.[1] 8.

The pond'rous brass in exercise he bore; *Stat.*[1] 37.

the nations . . . Their cymbals toss, and sounding brass explore;   *Stat.*[1] 57.

Brave.

Brave Urien sleeps upon his craggy bed: *Bard* 31.

Exalt the brave, and idolize Success; *El. Mas.* 74.

Four, not less brave, That in Armenia quell
     Agr. 110.

brave the savage rushing from the wood, *E. G.* 93.
But none . . . return, Save Aëron brave, *Hoel* 21.

Brawling.
so grinned the brawling fiend,   *Toph.* 1.

Brawls.
My grave Lord-Keeper led the Brawls; *L. S.* 11.

Brawny.
Let him stand forth his brawny arm to boast.
                                                Stat.[1] 3.

Bray.
Heard ye the din of battle bray,   *Bard* 83.

Bread.
I heard 'em wail for Bread.   *Dante* 45.

Break.
To break the quiet of the tomb?   *Odin* 28.
Enquirer come To break my iron-sleep again;
                                                Odin 89.
If any spark . . . Break out,   *Ign.* 20.
Dismiss'd at length, they break through all delay
                                                Tasso 1.
Here gems break through the night   *Tasso* 63.

Breast. *See also* **Red-breast.**
The sunshine of the breast,   *Eton* 44.
Thou Tamer of the human breast,   *Adv.* 2.
Tyrant of the throbbing breast.   *Bard* 130.
that chills the throbbing breast. *Bard Lett.*[2] 130.
Some village-Hampden,. . .with dauntless breast
                                                El. 57.
On some fond breast the parting soul relies, *El.* 89.
in my Breast the imperfect Joys expire. *West* 8.
if to some feeling breast   *Bent.* 25.
With eyes of flame, and cool undaunted breast,
                                                Williams 9.
the Mistress of my faithful breast,   *Prop.*[3] 71.

Breasts.
the spark . . . that glows within their breasts,
                                                Agr. 128.

Breath. *See also* **Breathe.**
yon sanguine cloud, Rais'd by thy breath,
                                                Bard 136.
There . . . Agony, that pants for breath,
                                                Owen 39.
Back to its mansion call the fleeting breath? *El.* 42
Sweet is the breath of vernal shower,   *Inst.* 61.
Few were the days allotted to his breath; *Child* 5.
my Fates that breath they gave shall claim,
                                                Prop.[3] 99.

Breathe.
To breathe a second spring.   *Eton* 20.
Thoughts, that breath, and words, that burn.
                                                P. P. 110.
Revenge on thee in hoarser murmurs breath;
                                                Bard 26.
They breathe a soul to animate thy clay. *Bard* 122.
And breathe and walk again: *Vic.* 48.

Breathed.
Inspiration breath'd around: *P. P.* 74.
Slowly breath'd a sullen sound.   *Odin* 26.
thee, whose influence breathed from high *Ign.* 7.
Has Scythia breath'd the . . . Cloud of War;
                                                E. G. 47.

Breathing. *See also* **Incense-breathing,**
Solemn-breathing.
the new Fragrance of the breathing Rose, *E. G.* 56.

Breeding.
†In Episode, to show my breeding: *Ode* 28.

Breezes.
†Purling streams and cooling breezes   *Ode* 20.

Breezy.
The breezy call of incense-breathing Morn,
                                                El. 17.

Bribe.
Too poor for a bribe,   *Char.* 1.

Bridal.
on her bridal morn   *Inst.* 41.

Bridget.
Jesu-Maria! Madam Bridget,   *L. S.* 133.

Brief.
In brief whate'er she do, or say, or look, *Prop.*[3] 27.

Bright. *See also* **Silver-bright.**
In yon bright track [clouds, MS.],   *Bard* 103.
Bright Rapture calls, and . . . Waves *Bard* 123.
they . . . veil'd their weapons bright and keen
                                                L. S. 39.
What the bright reward we gain?   *Inst.* 59.
If bright ambition from her craggy seat, *Agr.* 51.
Pert barristers, and parsons nothing bright,
                                                Shak. 7.
As bright and huge the spacious circle lay,
                                                Stat.[1] 26.
Why does yon Orb, so exquisitely bright,
                                                Prop.[2] 33.
†Bright beaming, as the Evening-star, *Ch. Cr.* 8.

Brighter.
the Brood of Winter view A brighter Day, *E. G.* 55.

Bright-eyed.
Bright-eyed [Full-plumed, MS.] Fancy *P. P.* 108.
While bright-eyed Science watches round:
                                                Inst. 11.

Brightly.
The hues of Bliss more brightly glow, *Vic.* 41.

Brightness.
dazzled with its brightness?   *Agr.* 32.

Bring.
hours, that bring constraint   *Eton* 33.
bring the buried ages back to view.   *Ign.* 35.
Art he invokes new horrors still to bring. *View* 12.

Brings.
The laureate wreath, that Cecil wore she brings,
                                                Inst. 84.
new-born Pleasure brings to happier men: *West* 10.
That Slumber brings to aid my Poetry. *Prop.*[3] 20.
†And brings all Womankind before your view;
                                                Ch. Cr. 59.

Brink.
Beside some water's rushy brink   *Spring* 15.

Brisk.
To brisk notes in cadence beating,   *P. P.* 34.

Bristled.
The bristled Boar in infant-gore Wallows *Bard* 93.

Britain.
And scorn'd repose when Britain took the field.
          Williams 8.

Britain's.
Owen . . . Britain's gem.   *Owen* 4.
In Britain's Isle, . . . An ancient pile . . .
  stands: *L. S.* 1.

Britannia's.
ye genuine Kings, Britannia's Issue, hail!
          Bard 110.

Britannicus.
To hear the spirit of Britannicus *Agr.* 14.

Briton-line.
Her eye proclaims her of the Briton-Line;
          Bard 116.

Broad.
From his broad bosom life and verdure flings
          E. G. 102.
Where broad and turbulent it grows *Vic.* 58.

Broader.
branches stretch A broader browner shade;
          Spring 12.

Broke.
The Muse has broke the twilight-gloom *P. P.* 56.
Their furrow oft the stubborn glebe has broke:
          El. 26.
lord, That broke the bonds of Rome. *Inst.* 47.
As when from Ætna's smoking summit broke,
          Stat.[2] 18.

Broken.
strive to mend A broken character *View* 4.

Brood. *See also* **Giant-brood, Monster-brood.**
fly Self-pleasing Folly's idle brood, *Adv.* 18.
the Brood of Winter view A brighter Day, *E. G.* 54.

Brooded.
He nor heaps his brooded stores, *Owen* 5.

Broods.
sacred Calm, that broods around, *El. Mas.* 81.
broods o'er Egypt with his wat'ry wings, *E. G.* 103.

Brook.
pore upon the brook that babbles by. *El.* 104.

Broom.
At Broom, Pendragon, Appleby and Brough.
         Par. on Ep. 3.

Brother.
His Brother sends him to the tomb. *Odin* 56.

Brothers.
Brothers, . . . Stamp we our vengeance deep,
          Bard 95.

Brough.
At Broom, Pendragon, Appleby and Brough.
         Par. on Ep. 3.

Brow.
from the stately brow Of WINDSOR's heights
          Eton 5.
a rock, whose haughty brow Frowns *Bard* 15.
Virgins . . . That bend to earth their solemn
  brow,   *Odin* 77.
the high brow of yonder hanging lawn.
          El. Mas. 116.
Edward, with the lilies on his brow *Inst.* 39.

to grace thy youthful brow, The laureate wreath,
          Inst. 83.
Let majesty sit on thy awful brow, *Agr.* 145.
things, that . . . Have arch'd the hearer's brow,
          Agr. 169.
the . . . cloud That hangs on thy clear brow.
          Agr. 194.
Smiles on past Misfortune's brow . . . Reflection's hand can trace;   *Vic.* 29.

Brown.
Ye brown o'er-arching groves, *Inst.* 27.

Browner.
A broader browner shade; *Spring* 12.

Brunswick.
The star of Brunswick smiles serene, *Inst.* 93.

Brush.
With hasty footsteps brush the dews away.
          El. Mas. 115.

Brushed.
Brush'd by the hand of rough Mischance,
          Spring 38.

Brushing.
Brushing with hasty steps the dews away *El.* 99.

Bubbles.
Whate'er . . . Floats into Lakes, and bubbles
  into rills;   *Tasso* 54.

Buckler.
Blade with clattering buckler meet, *F. S.* 23.

Buds.
And the buds that deck the thorn! *Song* 4.
†My cold soil nips the Buds with Snow. *Ode* 6.

Buff.
issues A brace of Warriors, not in buff, *L. S.* 23.

Build.
The Red-breast loves to build,
     El. Pem. 119; Mas. 139.
Build to him the lofty verse, *Conan* 2.

Buildings.
An ancient pile of buildings stands: *L. S.* 2.

Builds.
Humble quiet builds her cell, *Vic.* 53.

Built. *See* **Ice-built, Straw-built.**

Bulk.
Scarce to nine acres Tityus' bulk confined,
          Prop.[2] 43.

Bull.
Have ye seen . . . the bull, . . . advance?
          Caradoc 2.

Bullen's.
gospel-light first dawn'd from Bullen's eyes.
          E. G. 109.

Bumper.
with bumper in hand,   *C. C.* 21.

Burdens.
Burthens of the angry deep. *Owen* 18.

Buried.
the buried Natives dull abode. *P. P. MS.* 57.
buried ashes glow with social fires. *El. Mas.* 108.
Again the buried Genius of old Rome *Agr.* 141.
bring the buried ages back to view. *Ign.* 35.

Burn.

Thoughts, that breath, and words, that burn.
P. P. 110.
Thousand Banners round him burn: *Owen* 32.
no more the blazing hearth shall burn, *El.* 21.
Burn incense kindled at the Muse's flame.
El. Mas. 72.
Flush'd with mirth and hope they burn: *Hoel* 19.
†I burn to write; *Ode* 27.

Burns.

inspiration . . . That burns in Shakespeare's . . .
page, *Bent.* 19.

Burrhus.

dress thy plea, and Burrhus strengthen it *Agr.*150.

Burrows.

†With Rooks and Rabbit burrows *Ch. Cr.* 56.

Burst.

Till *Lok* has burst his tenfold chain; *Odin* 90.
the deluge burst, with sweepy sway *E. G.* 48.

Bursting.

Bursting through the bloody throng *Hoel* 22.

Bursts.

Bursts on my ear th' indignant lay: *Inst.* 14.
†the rolling Sun Bursts the inactive Shell, *Ode* 44.

Burthens. *See* Burdens.

Bushy.

His bushy beard, and shoe-strings green, *L. S.* 13.

Business.

While some on earnest business bent *Eton* 31.

Buskined.

In buskin'd measures move Pale Grief, *Bard* 128.
†Tragick Numbers, buskin'd Strains, *Ode* 31.

Buss.

Come buss me — *C. C.* 32.

Bust.

Can storied urn or animated bust *El.* 41.

Busy.

The busy murmur glows! *Spring* 24.
Alike the Busy and the Gay *Spring* 35.
shall . . . busy housewife ply *El.* 22.
Morning smiles the busy Race to chear, *West* 9.

But, *omitted.*

Bute.

had Bute been true, *View* 17.

Butter.

Without design to hurt the butter, *L. S.* 123.

Butterflies.

†Like Butterflies, their Prison shun *Ode* 45.

Buxom.

Theirs buxom health of rosy hue, *Eton* 45.

Buzzing.

†Buzzing with all their parent Faults; *Ode* 46.

By, *omitted.*

C—'s.

nor C—'s, nor B—d's promises *View* Nich. 18.

Cadence.

To brisk notes in [the, MS.] cadence beating,
P. P. 34.

Cadmus'.

And batter Cadmus' walls with stony showers,
Stat.[1] 18.

Cadwallo's.

Cold is Cadwallo's tongue, *Bard* 29.

Cælia's.

†a Sonnet On Chloe's Fan, or Cælia's Bonnet.
Ode 36.

Cæsar.

Cæsar guiltless of his country's blood. *El. Mas.* 60.

Cæsars.

wife, And mother of their Cæsars. *Agr.* 119.

Calcraft's.

nor Shelburne's, Rigby's, Calcraft's friendship
vain, *View* MS. 18.

Call.

What call [voice, MS.] unknown, what charms
presume *Odin* 27.
Once again my call obey, *Odin* 51.
Yet awhile my call obey; *Odin* 73.
lurk'd A wicked Imp they call a Poet, *L. S.* 44.
The breezy call of incense-breathing Morn,
El. 17.
Back to its mansion call the fleeting breath?
El. 42.
You bade the Magi call the . . . powers, *Agr.* 64.
a call, Like mine, might serve . . . to wake
Agr. 102.
around thee call The gilded swarm *Agr.* 146.
Weddell attends your call, *Com. Lines* 1.
†the Pisgys call him Puck, *Ch. Cr.* 31.

Called.

bow'd and called him friend; *Toph.* 2.
Phlegyas . . . call'd forth all the man. *Stat.*[1] 33.

Callimachus'.

But nor Callimachus' enervate Strain *Prop.*[3] 55.

Calling.

Nor thou my gentle Calling disapprove, *Prop.*[3] 63.
often calling On their dear Names, *Dante* 79.

Calls.

Bright Rapture calls, and . . . Waves *Bard* 123.
That calls me from the bed of rest? *Odin* 36.
A Traveller, . . . Is he that calls, *Odin* 38.
calls around The sleeping fragrance *Vic.* 5.

Calm.

the sacred Calm, that broods around, *El. Mas.* 81.

Calmed.

calm'd the terrors of his claws in gold. *Stat.*[2] 27.

Cambria's.

From Cambria's curse, from Cambria's tears!
Bard 8.
Vocal no more, since Cambria's fatal day, *Bard* 27.
From Cambria's thousand hills *Bard* MS. 109.

Cambridge.

O Cambridge, attend To the Satire I 've pen'd
Satire 1.

Came.

No Dolphin came, *Cat* 34.
Squadrons three against him came; *Owen* 10.
Another came; nor yet beside the rill, *El.* 111.

The first came cap-a-pee from France *L. S.* 25.
By acclamations roused, came tow'ring *Stat.*¹ 14.
Third in the labours of the disc come [came] on,
*Stat.*² 1.
Yet a fourth Day came   *Dante* 72.

Camp.
the Prætorian camp have long rever'd *Agr.* 117.

Camus.
willowy Camus lingers with delight!   *Inst.* 29.

Camus'.
rushy Camus' slowly-winding flood   *Ign.* 3.

Can.
This can unlock the gates of Joy;   *P. P.* 92.
never can he fear a vulgar fate, *P. P.* MS. 122.
Pain can reach the Sons of Heav'n!   *Odin* 48.
Can storied urn or animated bust   *El.* 41.
Can Honour's voice provoke the silent dust,
El. 43.
Can you do nothing but describe?   *L. S.* 20.
Why, what can the Viscountess mean? *L. S.* 134.
Go! you can paint it well   *Agr.* 12.
her nod Can rouse eight hardy legions, *Agr.* 108.
Can powers immortal feel the force of years?
Ign. 26.
Can opener skies . . . O'erpower the fire
E. G. 64.
what seasons can control, . . . the soul, *E. G.* 72.
What fancied Zone can circumscribe   *E. G.* 73.
Smiles . . . Soft Reflection's hand can trace;
Vic. 30.
Whoe'er the quoit can wield,   *Stat.*¹ 1.
What wondrous force the solid earth can move,
*Prop.*² 30.
All angry heaven inflicts, or hell can feel, *Prop.*² 45.
The Power of Herbs can other Harms remove,
*Prop.*³ 79.
The Hand that can my captive heart release,
*Prop.*³ 87.
who can probe the undiscover'd Wound?
*Prop.*³ 92.
Nor changing Skies can hurt,   *Prop.*³ 94.
†these Flies, . . . Can boast of one good Quality;
Ode 50.
†P, Proteus-like . . . all shapes can shew,
Ch. Cr. 43.

Cankered.
Much have I borne from canker'd critic's spite,
Shak. 5.

Cannot.
I fruitless mourn to him that cannot hear, *West* 13.
cannot furnish out the feast,   *View* MS. 11.

Canopies. *See* O'er-canopies.

Canst.
read (for thou can'st read) the lay,   *El.* 115.

Can't.
When she died, I can't tell,   *C. C.* 14.

Cap-a-pee. *See* Cap-a-pie.

Cap-a-pie.
The first came cap-a-pee from France *L. S.* 25.

Caps.
Better be twisted into caps for spice, *Shak.* 19.

Captive.
The captive linnet which enthral?   *Eton* 27.
For adverse fate the captive chief has hurl'd
Tasso 33.
And scepter'd Alexandria's captive Shore,
*Prop.*³ 45.
The Hand that can my captive heart release,
*Prop.*³ 87.

Capucine.
With . . . capucine . . . they hid their armour,
L. S. 37.

Car.
Has curb'd the fury of his car,   *P. P.* 18.
where Dryden's less presumptuous car, *P. P.* 103.
High on her car, behold the grandam ride *Ign.* 36.
The laurell'd Triumph and the sculptured Carr;
*Prop.*³ 34.

Caradoc.
Leave your despairing Caradoc *Bard* MS. 102.
So Caràdoc bore his lance.   *Caradoc* 4.

Care.
Still is the toiling hand of Care: *Spring* 21.
Nor care beyond to-day: *Eton* 54.
Envy wan, and faded Care,   *Eton* 68.
Be thine Despair, and scept'red Care, *Bard* 141.
busy housewife ply her evening care: *El.* 22.
craz'd with care, or cross'd in . . . love. *El.* 108.
and thus relieved their care: *Tasso* 26.
And thou Mecænas, be my second Care;
*Prop.*³ 42.
nor the leeche's Care,   *Prop.*³ 93.

Careless.
Where once my careless childhood stray'd, *Eton* 13.
but, careless grown, Lethargic nods   *Ign.* 23.
And sing with what a careless Grace she flings
*Prop.*³ 15.
†And careless spares to weed the Plain: *Ode* 10.

Cares.
the sullen Cares And frantic Passions hear *P. P.* 15.
anxious Cares and endless Wishes   *El.* Mas. 86.
Antium; there to tend Her household cares,
Agr. 8.
unfriended, by those kindly Cares,   *E. G.* 10.

Carnage.
Clouds of carnage blot the sun.   *F. S.* 50.
his jaws, with carnage fill'd,   *Odin* 7.

Carry.
Carry to him thy timid counsels.   *Agr.* 87.

Carthage.
Nor lofty Carthage struggleing with her Fate.
*Prop.*³ 40.

Case.
To Phœbus he prefer'd his case,   *L. S.* 91.

Cassius.
Cassius; Vetus too, and Thrasea,   *Agr.* 125.

Cast.
cast one longing ling'ring look behind? *El.* 88.
minds of the antique cast,   *Agr.* 126.
cast me forth in duty to their lord.   *Agr.* 157.
Pursu'd his cast, and hurl'd the orb on high;
*Stat.*² 9.

Castalia's.
Me may Castalia's sweet recess detain, *Prop.*[2] 2.

Catch.
Norman sails afar Catch the winds, *Owen* 16.
Catch the new Fragrance of the . . . Rose,
E. G. 56.
catch a lustre from his genuine flame. *Bent.* 12.
could they catch his strength, *Bent.* 13.

Catches.
Why, David lov'd catches, *C. C.* 24.

Catherine.
The Master of Catherine Takes them all for his
pattern; *Satire* 19.

Cato.
Some village Cato, . . . with dauntless breast
El. Mas. 57.

Cat 's.
What Cat 's averse to fish? *Cat* 24.

Cattraeth's.
To Cattraeth's vale . . . Thrice two hundred
warriors go: *Hoel* 11.
But none from Cattraeth's vale return, *Hoel* 20.

Cause.
a cause To arm the hand of childhood, *Agr.* 138.
Though by me ye bled, He was the cause. *Agr.* 181.
Th' Event presages, and explores the Cause.
E. G. 33.
To weep without knowing the cause of my an-
guish: *Am. Lines* 2.
That first, eternal, universal Cause; *Prop.*[2] 18.

Caution.
be with caution bold. *Cat* 39.

Cautious.
I must be cautious, *Agr.* 85.

Cave.
each giant-oak, and desert cave, Sighs *Bard* 23.

Caverns.
In the caverns of the west, *Odin* 63.

Caves.
The dark unfathom'd caves of ocean *El.* 54.
Earth's inmost cells, and caves of deep descent;
Tasso 50.

Cease.
Sisters, cease, the work is done. *F. S.* 52.
Cease, my doubts, my fears to move, *Song* 11.
Bids ev'ry . . . Passion cease; *El.* Mas. 82.

Ceaseless.
whom thus I ceaseless gnaw insatiate; *Dante* 8.

Cecil.
The laureate wreath, that Cecil wore *Inst.* 84.

Ceiling's.
To raise the cieling's fretted height, *L. S,* 5.

Celebrate.
To celebrate her eyes, her air — *L. S.* 33.

Celestial.
Murmur'd a celestial sound. *P. P.* MS. 76.
once pregnant with celestial fire; *El.* 46.
Rapt in celestial transport they: *Inst.* 18.

Cell.
Each in his narrow cell for ever laid, *El.* 15.
Humble quiet builds her cell, *Vic.* 53.
A heart, within whose sacred cell *Clerke* 3.

Cells.
Earth's inmost cells, and caves of deep descent;
Tasso 50.

Censure.
To censure cold, and negligent of fame, *Bent.* 10.

Centering.
†Cent'ring, rivets heart to heart, *Rond.* 30.

Ceres.
Thro' verdant vales, and Ceres' golden reign:
P. P. 9.

Chain.
Bound in thy adamantine chain, *Adv.* 5.
Till *Lok* has burst his tenfold chain; *Odin* 90.
Servitude that hugs her chain, *Inst.* 6.

Chains.
Vice, that revels in her chains. *P. P.* 80.
And chains invisible the border. *L. S.* 86.
Every warrior's manly neck Chains of regal hon-
our deck, *Hoel* 14.
And winter binds the floods in icy chains, *Tasso* 18.
In golden Chains should loaded Monarchs bend,
Prop.[3] 48.

Chair.
Close by the regal chair *Bard* 80.
She curtsies, as she takes her chair, *L. S.* 111.

Chamber.
they explore, Each . . . cranny of his chamber,
L. S. 62.

Champagne.
Very good claret and fine Champaign.
Impr. Vane 2.

Champaign. *See* **Champagne.**

Champions.
the champions, trembling at the sight, Prevent
disgrace, *Stat.*[1] 22.

Chance.
If chance, . . . Some kindred spirit shall inquire
El. 95.
If chance that e'er some pensive spirit
El. Mas. 109.
two youths advance, . . . to try the glorious
chance; *Stat.*[1] 10.

Changed.
When my changed head these locks no more shall
know, *Prop.*[2] 13.

Changing.
Nor changing Skies can hurt, *Prop.*[3] 94.

Channel.
with copious train its channel fills, *Tasso* 53.

Chapel-door.
at the chappel-door stand sentry; *L. S.* 104.

Chaplet.
His head a chaplet bore, *Tasso* 16.

Chappel-door. *See* **Chapel-door.**

Character.

Then his character, *Phyzzy*,   *C. C.* 13.
strive to mend A broken character   *View* 4.

Characters.

The characters of hell to trace.   *Bard* 52.

Chariot.

Not I — for a coronet, chariot and six.   *C. C.* 18.

Charitie. *See* **Charity.**

Charity.

Warm Charity, the gen'ral Friend,   *Adv.* 30.
Their human passions now no more, Save Charity
    Inst. 50.
But stint your clack for sweet St. Charitie *Shak.* 2.

Charles.

But left church and state to Charles Townshend
    Char. 6.

Charm.

gems that singly charm the sight,   *Bent.* 22.

Charms.

what charms presume To break the quiet *Odin* 27.
barb'rous rites Of mutter'd charms,   *Agr.* 63.
Has oft the Charms of Constancy confest,
    *Prop.*³ 72.
†With Myra's charms In Episode,   *Ode* 27.

Chase.

To chase the rolling circle's speed,   *Eton* 29.
Nor long endur'd the Chase: *Dante* 37.

Chased.

chas'd by Hell-hounds gaunt and bloody *Dante* 30.

Chastening.

Dread goddess, lay thy chast'ning hand! *Adv.* 34.

Chastised.

Chastised by sabler tints of woe;   *Vic.* 42.

Chatillon.

And sad Chatillon,   *Inst.* 41.

Chaunticleer.

chaunticleer so shrill, or ecchoing horn.
    El. Mas. 19.

Chear. *See* **Cheer.**

Chearful. *See* **Cheerful.**

Check.

Did I not wish to check this . . . passion, *Agr.* 106.
check their tender Hopes with . . . Fear, *E. G.* 20.

Checked.

Check'd by the torrent-tide of blood, *Owen* 27.

Cheek. *See also* **Vermeil-cheek.**

O'er her warm cheek, and rising bosom, *P. P.* 40.
o'er the cheek of Sorrow throw . . . grace; *Vic.* 31.

Cheer.

And lively chear of vigour born;   *Eton* 47.
To chear the shiv'ring Natives dull abode. *P. P.* 57.
Morning smiles the busy Race to chear, *West* 9.
Relumes her crescent Orb to cheer the dreary
    Night: *Prop.*² 22.
Flash'd to pursue, and chear the eager Cry:
    Dante 36.

Cheerful.

Left the . . . precincts of the chearful day,
    El. 87.

Lamps, that shed at Ev'n a cheerful ray *E. G.* 66.
chearful Fields resume their green Attire: *West* 4.

Cheesecakes.

Better to bottom tarts and cheesecakes nice,
    Shak. 17.

Cherub-choir.

A Voice, as of the Cherub-Choir,   *Bard* 131.

Chester.

The Bishop of Chester,   *Ext. Keene* 1.
Here lies Edmund Keene Lord Bishop of Chester,
    Ep. Keene 1.
Here lies Mrs. Keene the she Bishop of Chester,
    Mrs. Keene 1.

Chief.

But chief, the Sky-lark warbles high *Vic.* 13.
For adverse fate the captive chief has hurl'd
    Tasso 33.
Heal the slow Chief, and send again *Prop.*³ 82.
He their Chief, the foremost He   *Dante* 35.

Chiefly.

chiefly thee, whose influence breathed *Ign.* 7.

Chiefs.

Their feather-cinctur'd Chiefs,   *P. P.* 62.

Child.

Virtue, his darling Child,   *Adv.* 10.
The dauntless Child Stretch'd forth *P. P.* 87.
What dangers *Odin's* Child await,   *Odin* 53.
There Confusion, Terror's child,   *Owen* 37.
A child, the darling of his parent's eyes: *Child* 2.

Childhood.

Where once my careless childhood stray'd, *Eton* 13.
To arm the hand of childhood,   *Agr.* 138.

Children.

No children run to lisp their sire's return, *El.* 23.
Bewitch'd the children of the peasants, *L. S.* 46.
My children (they were with me) *Dante* 42.

Children's.

then on my Children's Eyes . . . my Sight I
    fix'd,   *Dante* 52.

Chili's.

Chili's boundless forests   *P. P.* 59.

Chill.

the buried Natives chill abode.   *P. P.* MS. 57.
Chill Penury repress'd their noble rage, *El.* 51.

Chilled.

chill'd by age,   *Spring* 39.

Chilling.

check their . . . Hopes with chilling Fear,
    E. G. 20.

Chills.

that chills the throbbing breast. *Bard* Lett.² 130.

China.

Into the Drawers and China pry,   *L. S.* 65.

China's.

Where China's gayest art had dy'd   *Cat* 2.

Chiron.

To Chiron Phœnix owed his long-lost Sight,
    *Prop.*³ 83.

Chloe's.

†a Sonnet On Chloe's Fan,   *Ode* 36.

Choak. *See* **Choke.**

Choice.
On this congenial spot he fix'd his choice; *View* 5.

Choir. *See also* **Cherub-choir.**
In silent gaze the tuneful choir among,   *Bent.* 1.
Rise the rapturous choir among;   *Vic.* 18.
Owls would have hooted in St. Peter's choir,
                                           View 23.

Choke.
†Tares of Similes choak the roots,   *Ode* 11.

Choral.
as the choral warblings round him swell, *Inst.* 24.

Christ.
The Master of Christ By the rest is enticed;
                                           Satire 23.

Christ-cross.
†The Pleasantest Person in the Christ-Cross row.
                                           Ch. Cr. 44.

Christian.
They say he's no Christian,   *C. C.* 15.

Chronicle.
extends Beyond their chronicle —   *Agr.* 137.

Chrysalis.
†Part in a Chrysalis appear.   *Ode* 42.

Chrystalline. *See* **Crystalline.**

Church. *See also* **Mother-church.**
But left church and state to Charles Townshend
                                           Char. 6.

Churchman's.
The schoolman's glory, and the churchman's
    boast.   *Ign.* 32.

Church-way.
Slow thro' the church-way path   *El.* 114.

Churlish.
trusts her Blossoms to the churlish Skies. *E. G.* 8.

Cian.
my Hoel, died, Great Cian's son: *Hoel* 7.

Cieling's. *See* **Ceiling's.**

Cimbrian.
Not Marius' Cimbrian Wreaths would I relate,
                                           *Prop.*³ 39.

Cinctured. *See* **Feather-cinctured.**

Circle.
As bright and huge the spacious circle lay, *Stat.*¹ 26.
Collecting all his force, the circle sped; *Stat.*¹ 48.

Circled.
Not circled with the vengeful Band   *Adv.* 36.

Circle's.
To chase the rolling circle's speed,   *Eton* 29.

Circling.
Now in circling troops they meet: *P. P.* 33.

Circumscribe.
What fancied Zone can circumscribe the soul,
                                           E. G. 73.

Circumscribed.
nor circumscrib'd alone Their growing virtues,
                                           El. 65.

Circus.
created but to . . . bellow in the Circus *Agr.* 131.

Cities.
on frail floats to distant cities ride,   *E. G.* 106.
†Remote from cities lives   *Ch. Cr.* 55.

Civility.
Decorum 's turn'd to mere civility;   *L. S.* 137.

Clack.
But stint your clack for sweet St. Charitie *Shak.* 2.

Clad.
Not in thy Gorgon terrors clad,   *Adv.* 35.

Claim.
my Fates that breath they gave shall claim,
                                           *Prop.*³ 99.

Clamber.
And o'er the bed and tester clamber,   *L. S.* 64.

Clare.
and princely Clare,   *Inst.* 42.
The Master of Clare Hits them all to a hair;
                                           Satire 21.

Claret.
Very good claret and fine Champaign.
                                           Impr. Vane 2.

Clarion.
The cock's shrill clarion,   *El.* 19.

Clash.
I heard the dreadful Clash of Bars,   *Dante* 51.

Clashed.
And, clash'd, rebellows with the din of war.
                                           *Stat.*¹ 31.

Clattering.
Blade with clattering buckler meet,   *F. S.* 23.

Claudius.
Enshrined Claudius, with the pitied ghosts
                                           Agr. 175.

Claw.
A whisker first and then a claw,   *Cat* 20.

Claws.
And calm'd the terrors of his claws in gold.
                                           *Stat.*² 27.

Clay.
They breathe a soul to animate thy clay. *Bard* 122.
th' inferior laws that rule our clay: *E. G.* 80.

Clean.
The times are alter'd quite and clean!   *L. S.* 136.
Now clean, now hideous, mellow now, now gruff,
                                           Par. on Ep. 1.

Clear.
Zephyrs thro' the clear blue sky   *Spring* 9.
This pencil . . . , whose colours clear *P. P.* 89.
the . . . cloud That hangs on thy clear brow.
                                           Agr. 194.
She eyes the clear chrystalline well,   *Vic.* 55.

Cleave.
Who foremost now delight to cleave   *Eton* 25.

Cleaves.
and cleaves the solid ground.   *Stat.*¹ 52.

Cleaving.
The ponderous mass sinks in the cleaving ground,
                                           *Stat.*² 16.

Clews.

†All with fantastic clews, fantastic clothes,
Ch. Cr. 17.

Cliffs. *See also* Mountain-cliffs.

Till down the eastern cliffs afar   *P. P.* 52.
On yonder cliffs, . . . I see them sit,   *Bard* 44.

Climb.

No children . . . [shall] climb his knees *El.* 24.

Clime.

Facing to the northern clime, . . . he traced
Odin 21.
to shine Thro' every . . . undiscover'd clime.
Inst. 17.

Climes.

In climes beyond the solar road,   *P. P.* 54.
in Climes, where Winter holds his Reign, *E. G.* 5.
To different Climes seem different Souls assign'd ?
E. G. 39.
sultry climes, that spread   *E. G.* 100.

Cloathed. *See* Clothed.

Cloathing. *See* Clothing.

Cloisters.

In cloisters dim, far from the haunts of Folly,
Inst. 33.

Close.

Close by the regal chair   *Bard* 80.
Keep the tissue close and strong.   *F. S.* 16.
Now my weary lips I close;   *Odin* 57, 71.
To close my dull eyes when I see it returning;
Am. Lines 4.
she seem to close Her languid Lids, *Prop.*³ 17.

Closed.

Closed his eyes in endless night.   *P. P.* 102.

Closet.

The Muses, . . . Convey'd him . . . To a small
closet   *L. S.* 72.
Steal to his closet at the hour of prayer; *Shak.* 14.

Closing.

pious drops the closing eye requires;   *El.* 90.
†Is to tear the closing wound.   *Rond.* 32.

Clothed.

With necks in thunder cloath'd,   *P. P.* 106.
These miserable Limbs with Flesh you cloath'd;
Dante 67.

Clothes.

†All with fantastic clews, fantastic clothes,
Ch. Cr. 17.

Clothing.

Each pannel in achievements cloathing, *L. S.* 6.

Clottered.

Lips, which on the clotter'd Locks . . . he
wiped,   *Dante* 2.

Cloud.

yon sanguine cloud, . . . has quench'd the Orb
of day?   *Bard* 135.
leaning from her golden cloud The venerable
Marg'ret see!   *Inst.* 65.
the tim'rous cloud That hangs on thy . . . brow.
Agr. 193.
Scythia breath'd the living Cloud of War; *E. G.* 47.

Clouds.

In yon bright clouds,   *Bard MS.* 103.
Quench'd in dark clouds of slumber lie   *P. P.* 23.
Clouds of carnage blot the sun.   *F. S.* 50.
It towers to cut the clouds;   *Stat.*¹ 49.

Cloud-topped.

Made huge Plinlimmon bow his cloud-top'd head.
Bard 34.

Cloudy.

the cloudy Magazines maintain Their wintry war,
*Prop.*² 25.

Clouet.

So York shall taste what Clouet never knew,
Shak. 21.

Clues. *See* Clews.

Coal-black.

saddled strait his coal-black steed;   *Odin* 2.

Coan.

If the thin Coan Web her Shape reveal, *Prop.*³ 9.

Coarse. *See also* Corse.

Coarse panegyricks would but teaze her. *L. S.* 34.

Coast.

thy sea-encircled coast.   *P. P.* 82.
blue-eyed Myriads from the Baltic coast.
E. G. 51.

Coat.

Her coat, She saw;   *Cat* 10.

Cobbled.

cobbled in one's grave.   *Shak.* 20.

Cobham.

But Cobham had the polish given   *L. S.* 31.

Cock's.

The cock's shrill clarion,   *El.* 19.

Cold.

Cold is Cadwallo's tongue,   *Bard* 29.
soothe the dull cold ear of death?   *El.* 44.
With damp, cold touch forbid it to aspire, *Ign.* 21.
To censure cold, and negligent of fame, *Bent.* 10.
among their cold Remains   *Dante* 78.
†My cold soil nips the Buds with Snow. *Ode* 6.
†I told Of Phœbus' heat and Daphne's cold. *Ode* 24.

Collected.

The bee's collected treasures sweet,   *Inst.* 62.

Collecting.

Collecting all his force, the circle sped; *Stat.*¹ 48.

Colored. *See* Many-colored.

Coloring.

in fancy's airy colouring wrought   *Bent.* 7.

Colors.

In fortune's varying colours drest: *Spring* 37.
This pencil . . . whose colours clear   *P. P.* 89.
What colours paint the vivid arch   *Prop.*² 29.

Colour. *See* Color.

Comb.

Who ne'er shall comb his raven-hair, *Odin* 66.

Combine.

The parts combine and harden into Ore:
Tasso 62.

Combined.

Amazement in his van, with Flight combined,
Bard 61.

Come.

No sense have they of ills to come,   *Eton* 53.
never shall Enquirer come To break   *Odin* 88.
Such as . . . Come (sweep) along some winding
    entry   *L. S.* 102.
She smiled, and bid him come to dinner. *L. S.* 132.
To hail their Fitzroy's festal morning come;
                                          Inst. 54.
ere mid-day, Nero will come to Baiæ.   *Agr.* 159.
Come buss me —   *C. C.* 32.
†Great D draws near — the Dutchess sure is
    come,   *Ch. Cr.* 1.
†in Pond you see him come,   *Ch. Cr.* 39.

Comes.

sorrow never comes too late,   *Eton* 96.
The Peeress comes.   *L. S.* 109.
Anon, with slacken'd rage comes quiv'ring down,
                                         Stat.[1] 51.

Comfort.

Approaching Comfort view: *Vic.* 40.

Comfortless.

Grim-visag'd, comfortless Despair,   *Eton* 69.

Coming.

climb his knees the coming kiss to share.
                                         El. Mas. 24.

Command.

drop'd a thirsty lance at thy command. *P. P.* 19.
Th' applause of list'ning senates to command,
                                         El. 61.
Yielding due reverence to his . . . command:
                                         Agr. 4.
Command the Winds, and tame the . . . Deep.
                                         E. G. 43.

Commanding. *See* **Awe-commanding.**

Commenced.

The Morn had scarce commenc'd, when I awoke:
                                         Dante 41.

Commend.

Commend me to her affability!   *L. S.* 139.

Comment.

The message needs no comment.   *Agr.* 2.

Commission.

She'd issue out her high commission   *L. S.* 51.

Commissioned.

And when, our flames commission'd to destroy,
                                         Prop.[2] 11.

Common.

The common Sun, the air, the skies,   *Vic.* 51.
No common helps, no common guide ye need,
                                         Tasso 29.

Commoner.

Speak to a Commoner and Poet!   *L. S.* 140.

Companion.

Spite of her frail companion dauntless goes
                                         E. G. 76.

Companions.

Dear lost companions of my tuneful art, *Bard* 39.

Complain.

The mopeing owl does to the moon complain
                                         El. 10.
To warm their little Loves the Birds complain:
                                         West 12.

Complaint.

The fond complaint, my Song, disprove, *P. P.* 46.

Compressed.

By *Odin's* fierce embrace comprest,   *Odin* 64.

Comprest. *See* **Compressed.**

Comus.

Comus, and his midnight crew,   *Inst.* 2.

Conan.

But none . . . return, Save . . . Conan strong,
                                         Hoel 21.
Did the sword of Conan mow The crimson har-
    vest   *Conan* 9.

Conan's.

Conan's name, my lay, rehearse,   *Conan* 1.

Conceal.

And half disclose those Limbs it should conceal;
                                         Prop.[3] 10.

Concealed.

Discover'd half, and half conceal'd their way;
                                         Tasso 46.

Condemned.

men, Condemn'd alike to groan,   *Eton* 92.
The ghostly Prudes . . . Already had con-
    demn'd the sinner.   *L. S.* 130.

Condemns.

Condemns her fickle Sexe's fond Mistake,
                                         Prop.[3] 73.

Condition.

She curtsies, . . . To all the People of condi-
    tion.   *L. S.* 112.

Confess.

The stubborn elements confess her sway, *E. G.* 81.

Confessed.

all shall be confess'd, Whate'er   *Agr.* 166.
Has oft the Charms of Constancy confest,
                                         Prop.[3] 72.

Confest. *See* **Confessed.**

Confidence.

lawless force from confidence will grow *E. G.* 98.

Confine.

To Cynthia all my Wishes I confine;   *Prop.*[3] 68.

Confined.

Their lot . . . their crimes confin'd;   *El.* 66.
thro' Ages by what Fate confin'd   *E. G.* 38.
Scarce to nine acres Tityus' bulk confined,
                                         Prop.[2] 43.

Confines.

Beyond the confines of our narrow world: *Tasso* 34.

Confirmed.

these, by ties confirm'd, Of old respect *Agr.* 113.

Conflict.

Where our Friends the conflict share,   *F. S.* 27.
There . . . Conflict fierce, and Ruin wild,
                                         Owen 38.

Confusion.

Confusion on thy banners wait, *Bard* 2.
There Confusion, Terror's child, *Owen* 37.
with dire confusion hurl'd, *Prop.*² 27.

Congenial.

On this congenial spot he fix'd his choice; *View* 5.

Congregated.

the seven Sisters' congregated fires, *Prop.*² 35.

Conjurer.

He ne'er was for a conj'rer taken. *L. S.* 128.

Connected.

Words . . . by no meaning connected! *Am. Lines* 6.

Conquering.

Her conqu'ring destiny fulfilling, *L. S.* 26.

Conqueror.

Mighty Conqueror, *Bard MS.* 63.

Conquest's.

Tho' fann'd by Conquest's crimson wing *Bard* 3.

Conscious.

Her conscious tail her joy declar'd; *Cat* 7.
The struggling pangs of conscious truth *El.* 69.
the soul, Who conscious of the source *E. G.* 74.
These conscious shame withheld, *Stat.*¹ 25.

Consecrate.

Half of thy heart we consecrate. *Bard* 99.
Thee too the Muse should consecrate to Fame, *Prop.*³ 53.

Consecrated.

in these consecrated bowers, *Inst.* 7.

Consort's.

Revere his Consort's faith, *Bard* 89.

Conspired.

Than Pow'r and Genius e'er conspir'd to bless. *El. Mas.* 76.

Conspiring.

conspiring in the diamond's blaze *Bent.* 21.

Constancy.

Has oft the Charms of Constancy confest, *Prop.*³ 72.

Constitution.

A broken character and constitution. *View* 4.

Constraint.

hours, that bring constraint *Eton* 33.

Construed.

For Anguish, which they construed Hunger; *Dante* 64.

Consulate.

to soar High as the consulate, *Agr.* 43.

Consuming. *See* **Slow-consuming.**

Contemplation.

By Night and lonely Contemplation led *El. Mas.* 79.
by lonely contemplation led, *El.* 95.
groves, That contemplation loves, *Inst.* 28.

Contemplation's.

To Contemplation's sober eye Such is the race of Man: *Spring* 31.

Control.

frantic Passions hear thy soft controul. *P. P.* 16.
what seasons can control, . . . the soul, *E. G.* 72.
How the rude surge its sandy Bounds control; *Prop.*² 37.
let her ever my Desires control, *Prop.*³ 76.

Conveyed.

Convey'd him underneath their hoops *L. S.* 71.

Conway's.

o'er old Conway's foaming flood, *Bard* 16.

Cool.

Cool Zephyrs thro' the clear blue sky *Spring* 9.
Fields, that cool Ilissus laves, *P. P.* 68.
the cool sequester'd vale of life *El.* 75.
reflection Pours its cool dictates *Agr.* 83.
The cool injurious eye of frozen kindness. *Agr.* 162.
With eyes of flame, and cool undaunted breast, *Williams* 9.

Cooling.

†Purling streams and cooling breezes *Ode* 20.

Copies.

Copies them in all things; *Satire* 18.

Copious.

Whate'er with copious train its channel fills, *Tasso* 53.
And many a copious Narrative you'll see *Prop.*³ 29.
†Copious numbers, swelling grain; *Ode* 8.

Corbulo.

Under the warlike Corbulo, *Agr.* 112.

Cords.

Shafts . . . Shoot the trembling cords along. *F. S.* 14.

Cormorants.

Here sea-gulls scream, and cormorants rejoice, *View* 7.

Coronet.

My Lady . . . Swore by her coronet *L. S.* 50.
Not I — for a coronet, chariot and six. *C. C.* 18.

Corse.

Till he on *Hoder's* corse shall smile *Odin* 69.
may my pale Coarse be borne. *Prop.*³ 78.

Costly.

And paint the margin of the costly stream, *Tasso* 64.

Couch.

Low on his funeral couch he lies! *Bard* 64.

Couched.

"To arms!" cried Mortimer, and couch'd his quiv'ring lance. *Bard* 14.

Could.

Tho' Pope and Spaniard could not trouble it. *L. S.* 16.
And all that *Groom* could [might, MS.] urge against him. *L. S.* 116.
we could not have beguil'd . . . the . . . sight *Agr.* 190.
love could teach a monarch to be wise, *E. G.* 108.
could they catch his strength, *Bent.* 13.
Could love, and could hate, *Char.* 3.

Yet Nature could not [cannot, MS.] furnish out the feast,   *View* 11.

He eat a fat goose, and could not digest her.   *Ep. Keene* 2.

The Melian's Hurt Machaon could repair,   *Prop.*³ 81.

The fourth, what Sorrow could not, Hunger did.   *Dante* 81.

†But their love could not be *strong*.   *Rond.* 16.

Could'st.

oh Earth! could'st thou not gape   *Dante* 71.

Counsels.

Carry to him thy timid counsels.   *Agr.* 87.

Count.

Know, thou seest In me Count Ugolino,   *Dante* 13.

Country.

who o'er thy country hangs The scourge of Heav'n.   *Bard* 59.

Imp . . . Who prowl'd the country   *L. S.* 45.

Country-farmer.

veil'd their weapons . . . In pity to the country-farmer.   *L. S.* 40.

Country's.

Ye died amidst your dying country's cries —   *Bard* 42.

Cromwell guiltless of his country's blood.   *El.* 60.

Course.

Years of havock urge their destined course,   *Bard* 85.

Thy steady course of honour keep,   *Inst.* 91.

His . . . Sons with nearer Course surrounds   *E. G.* 24.

See, in their course, each transitory thought   *Bent.* 5.

As the whirlwind in its course;   *Conan* 6.

The orb on high tenacious of its course,   *Stat.*² 10.

a River . . . all further course withstood;   *Tasso* 8.

His course he turn'd, and thus relieved their care: *Tasso* 26.

The birth of rivers riseing to their course, *Tasso* 52.

Courser's.

Thy passing Courser's slacken'd Speed restrain;   *Prop.*³ 102.

Coursers.

Two Coursers of ethereal race,   *P. P.* 105.

Court.

The Court was sate,   *L. S.* 97.

court the times With shows   *Agr.* 101.

With a lick of court white-wash, and pious grimace,   *C. C.* 2.

Courtly.

with courtly tongue refin'd, Profane   *Inst.* 80.

Covers.

Horror covers all the heath,   *F. S.* 49.

And mimic desolation covers all.   *View* 16.

Coward.

coward Vice, that revels in her chains.   *P. P.* 80.

Cows.

Dried up the cows, and lam'd the deer,   *L. S.* 47.

Craggy.

Brave Urien sleeps upon his craggy bed: *Bard* 31.

ambition from her craggy seat   *Agr.* 51.

The eyeless Cyclops heav'd the craggy rock;   *Stat.*² 19.

Cranny.

they explore, Each creek and cranny   *L. S.* 62.

Crash.

Hauberk crash, and helmet ring.   *F. S.* 24.

Crassus.

Redeem, what Crassus lost,   *Prop.*² 54.

Crazed.

craz'd with care, or cross'd in . . . love. *El.* 108.

Creased.

he might lie, . . . creased, . . . in a folio.   *L. S.* 68.

Created.

created but to stare,   *Agr.* 130.

Creation.

shake her own creation   *Agr.* 91.

could they catch . . . His quick creation, *Bent.* 14.

Creek.

they explore, Each creek and cranny   *L. S.* 62.

Creep.

they that creep, and they that fly,   *Spring* 33.

In lingering Lab'rinths creep,   *P. P.* 70.

Creeping.

Forth from their gloomy mansions creeping   *L. S.* 98.

nor creeping Gain, Dare the Muse's walk to stain,   *Inst.* 9.

Crescent.

The uncertain Crescent gleams a sickly light.   *Tasso* 48.

with silver light Relumes her crescent Orb   *Prop.*² 22.

Crest.

High he rears his ruby crest.   *Owen* 22.

Crested.

o'er the crested pride Of the first Edward *Bard* 9.

Crevice.

Thro' a small crevice opening,   *Dante* 22.

Crew.

Comus, and his midnight crew,   *Inst.* 2.

Cried.

"To arms!" cried Mortimer,   *Bard* 14.

Cried the square Hoods in woful fidget   *L. S.* 135.

you cried   *Agr.* 68.

first my little dear Anselmo Cried,   *Dante* 56.

straight Ariseing all they cried,   *Dante* 65.

Cries.

ye died amidst your dying country's cries —   *Bard* 42.

from the tomb the voice of Nature cries,   *El.* 91.

she cries aloud   *Inst.* 67.

If murder cries for murder, blood for blood,   *Agr.* 185.

I heard Their doleful Cries;   *Dante* 77.

Crimes.

Their lot . . . their crimes confin'd; *El.* 66.
unavailing horrors, fruitless crimes! *Agr.* 177.

Crimson.

Tho' fann'd by Conquest's crimson wing *Bard* 3.
Weave the crimson web of war *F. S.* 25, 36.
The crimson harvest of the foe. *Conan* 10.

Critic's.

Much have I borne from canker'd critic's spite, *Shak.* 5.

Cromwell.

Some Cromwell [Cæsar, *Mas.*] guiltless of his country's blood. *El.* 60.

Crop.

†If a plenteous Crop arise, *Ode* 7.

Cross. *See* **Christ-cross.**

Crossed.

or cross'd in hopeless love. *El.* 108.

Crowd.

How vain the ardour of the Crowd, *Spring* 18.
unborn Ages, crowd not on my soul! *Bard* 108.
fame Has spread among the crowd; *Agr.* 168.
Far below, the crowd. *Vic.* 57.
Suspends the crowd with expectation *Stat.*[1] 44.

Crowd's.

the madding crowd's ignoble strife, *El.* 73.

Crown.

towers, That crown the watry glade, *Eton* 2.
Isles, that crown th' Egæan deep, *P. P.* 67.
Reft of a crown, he yet may share *Bard* 79.
The rival of her crown and of her woes, *Inst.* 44.
science crown my Age, *Prop.*[2] 52.

Crowned. *See* **High - crowned, Rosy-crowned.**

Cruel.

Nor cruel *Tom*, . . . heard. *Cat* 35.
Oh! thou art cruel, *Dante* 45.
†But if my Myra cruel be *Ode* 29.

Cruelty.

froze them up with deadly cruelty. *Agr.* 183.

Crush.

not fall alone; but crush his pride, *Agr.* 186.

Cry.

With screaming Horror's funeral cry, *Adv.* 39.
and Birds of boding cry, *P. P.* 50.
Mad Sedition's cry profane, *Inst.* 5.
chear the eager cry: *Dante* 36.

Crystalline.

She eyes the clear chrystalline well, *Vic.* 55.

Cuckoo's.

Responsive to the cuckow's note, *Spring* 6.

Cuckow's. *See* **Cuckoo's.**

Culprit.

The Court was sate, the Culprit there, *L. S.* 97.

Cunning.

So cunning was the Apparatus, *L. S.* 85.

Cup. *See also* **Teacup.**

From the golden cup they drink *Hoel* 16.

Cupboard.

Each hole and cupboard they explore, *L. S.* 61.

Curbed.

Has curb'd the fury of his car, *P. P.* 18.

Cure.

And find a Cure for every Ill, *Prop.*[3] 80.

Curfew.

The Curfew [Curfeu, *Dods.*, *Pem.*] tolls the Knell of parting day, *El.* 1.

Curls.

If the loose Curls around her Forehead play, *Prop.*[3] 7.
Of those loose Curls, that Ivory front I write; *Prop.*[3] 11.

Current.

Some lightly o'er the current skim, *Spring* 28.
the genial current of the soul. *El.* 52.

Curse.

From Cambria's curse, from Cambria's tears! *Bard* 8.

Curtsies.

She curtsies, as she takes her chair, *L. S.* 111.

Customed.

I [we, *Mas.*] miss'd him on the custom'd hill, *El.* 109.
rev'r'd With custom'd awe, the daughter, *Agr.* 118.

Cut.

And Glyn cut Phizzes, *Com. Lines* 3.
Nor stopp'd till it had cut the further strand. *Stat.*[1] 40.
It towers to cut the clouds; *Stat.*[1] 49.

Cyclops.

The eyeless Cyclops heav'd the craggy rock; *Stat.*[2] 19.

Cymbals.

the nations with officious fear Their cymbals toss, *Stat.*[1] 57.

Cynthia.

Oft woo'd the gleam of Cynthia silver-bright *Inst.* 32.
Wars hand to hand with Cynthia let me wage. *Prop.*[1] 4.
From Cynthia all that in my numbers shines; *Prop.*[3] 3.
To Cynthia all my Wishes I confine; *Prop.*[3] 68.

Cytherea.

Loves are seen On Cytherea's day *P. P.* 29.

D.

†Great D draws near — the Dutchess sure is come, *Ch. Cr.* 1.
†The Dowager grows a perfect double D. *Ch. Cr.* 4.

Daily.

rolling, side by side, Their dull, but daily round. *Vic.* 63.

Daintily.

†Her daughters deck'd most daintily I see, *Ch. Cr.* 3.

Dalliance.

The silken son of dalliance,   *Agr.* 98.

Dames.

gorgeous Dames, and Statesmen old . . . appear.
                                        Bard 113.
High Dames of honour once,   *L. S.* 107.
High potentates, and dames of royal birth,
                                        Inst. 37.

Damp.

With damp, cold touch forbid it to aspire, *Ign.* 21.

Dance.

their airy dance They leave,   *Spring* 39.
Thee the voice, the dance, obey,   *P. P.* 25.
New-born flocks, in rustic dance,   *Vic.* 9.
I'd in the ring knit hands, and joyn the Muses'
dance.   *Prop.²* 6.

Danced.

The Seal, and Maces, danc'd before him. *L. S.* 12.

Danger.

Spite of danger he shall live.   *F. S.* 35.
your servant's fears, who sees the danger *Agr.* 24.
dost thou talk to me . . . of danger, *Agr.* 27.
the time To shrink from danger;   *Agr.* 48.

Dangerous.

grasp the dangerous honour.   *Agr.* 53.
wish to check this dangerous passion, *Agr.* 106.
huddle up in fogs the dang'rous fire. *Ign.* 22.
foremost in the dangerous paths of fame,
                                        Williams 1.

Dangers.

What dangers *Odin*'s Child await,   *Odin* 53.
To tempt the dangers of the doubtful way;
                                        Tasso 2.

Danubius'.

The Po was there to see, Danubius' bed, *Tasso* 55.

Daphne's.

†I told Of Phœbus' heat and Daphne's cold.
                                        Ode 24.

Dare.

And unknown regions dare descry: *Eton* 37.
Nor Envy . . . Dare the Muse's walk to stain,
                                        Inst. 10.

Dared.

scarcely dar'd . . . to soar   *Agr.* 41.
Nor envy dar'd to view him with a frown.
                                        Williams 4.

Dares.

Scarce Religion dares supply Her mutter'd Requiems,   *Bard* Lett.¹ 73.
Nor dares . . . Profane thy inborn royalty
                                        Inst. 80.

Daring.

what daring Spirit Wakes thee   *P. P.* 112.

Dark.

in dark [black, MS.] clouds of slumber *P. P.* 23.
The dark unfathom'd caves of ocean   *El.* 54.
road That to the grotto leads, my dark abode."
                                        Tasso 38.
Oped the dark Veil of Fate.   *Dante* 28.

Darkened.

Iron-sleet . . . Hurtles in the darken'd air.
                                        F. S. 4.

Darkness.

Him the Dog of Darkness spied,   *Odin* 5.
leaves the world to darkness and to me. *El.* 4.
the native darkness of the sky;   *Ign.* 8.

Darling.

Virtue, his darling Child,   *Adv.* 10.
In thy green lap was Nature's Darling laid,
                                        P. P. 84.
A child, the darling of his parents' eyes: *Child* 2.

Dart.

Sorrow's piercing dart.   *Eton* 70.
gems . . . Together dart their intermingled rays,
                                        Bent. 23.
†But when once the potent dart   *Rond.* 29.

Dash.

Yet 't would dash his joy To hear   *Agr.* 13.

Dashing.

Where Ocean frets beneath the dashing oar,
                                        Stat.² 20.

Dates.

from that auspicious Night Dates the long Iliad
                                        Prop.³ 26.

Daughter.

Daughter of Jove, relentless Power,   *Adv.* 1.
As fits the daughter of Germanicus.   *Agr.* 6.
long rever'd . . . the daughter, sister, wife,
                                        Agr. 118.

Daughters.

†Her daughters deck'd most daintily I see,
                                        Ch. Cr. 3.

Daunt.

The trembling family they daunt,   *L. S.* 57.

Dauntless.

The dauntless Child Stretch'd forth   *P. P.* 87.
Low the dauntless Earl is laid,   *F. S.* 41.
Dauntless . . . The Dragon-Son of Mona stands;
                                        Owen 19.
Some village-Hampden . . . with dauntless breast
                                        El. 57.
With watchful eye and dauntless mien, *Inst.* 90.
dauntless goes O'er Libya's deserts.   *E. G.* 76.

David.

Why, David lov'd catches,   *C. C.* 24.

Dawdling.

The Master of Maudlin In the same dirt is
dawdling;   *Satire* 8.

Dawn.

at the peep of dawn   *El.* 98.
Oft at the blush of dawn I trod   *Inst.* 30.
already 'gan the Dawn To send: *Dante* 25.

Dawned.

gospel-light first dawn'd from Bullen's eyes.
                                        E. G. 109.
e'er the sixth Morn Had dawn'd,   *Dante* 75.

Day.

the Gay . . . flutter thro' life's little day,
                                        Spring 36.
The thoughtless day,   *Eton* 48.

Darkness.

The sun's pale sister, . . . Deserts precipitant
her darken'd sphere: *Stat.¹* 55.

Loves are seen On Cytherea's day *P. P.* 29.
they first were open'd on the day *P. P.* MS. 118.
Vocal no more, since Cambria's fatal day,
Bard 27.
Gone to salute the rising Day. *Bard* MS. 70.
sanguine cloud, . . . has quench'd the Orb of day? *Bard* 136.
The Curfew tolls the knell of parting day, *El.* 1.
Left the . . . precincts of the chearful day,
El. 87.
And beg'd his aid that dreadful day. *L. S.* 92.
From yonder realms of empyrean day *Inst.* 13.
Break out, and flash a momentary day, *Ign.* 20.
the rolling Orb, that gives the Day, *E. G.* 23.
the Brood of Winter view A brighter Day,
E. G. 55.
expire beneath the eye of day? *E. G.* 67.
Hope . . . Gilds with a gleam of distant day.
Vic. 36.
With double light it beam'd against the day:
Stat.[1] 27.
The watery glimmerings of a fainter day *Tasso* 45.
Each in his proper Art should waste the Day:
Prop.[3] 62.
All that whole Day, or the succeeding Night
Dante 58.
That Day, and yet another, mute we sate,
Dante 70.
yet a fourth Day came *Dante* 72.

Days.
Along the lonely vale of days? *Clerke* 12.
Few were the days allotted to his breath; *Child* 5.
Thou envied Honour of thy Poet's Days,
Prop.[3] 103.
for three days more I grop'd *Dante* 77.

Dazzle.
dazzle with a luxury of light. *Bent.* 24.

Dazzled.
dazzled with its brightness? *Agr.* 32.
the dazzled sight Of wakeful jealousy. *Agr.* 191.
lessening from the dazzled sight, Melts into air
Vic. 15.

Dazzling.
barons bold With dazzling helm, *Bard* MS. 112.

De. *See* **Nom de Guerre.**

Dead.
He rests among the Dead. *Bard* 68.
The thrilling verse that wakes the Dead: *Odin* 24.
mindful of th' unhonour'd Dead, *El.* 93; *Mas.* 77.
in a secret and dead hour of night, *Agr.* 61.
and while they wished him dead, *Toph.* 3.

Deadliest.
headed by this The deadliest. *Dante* 35.

Deadly.
not the basilisk More deadly to the sight, *Agr.* 161.
froze them up with deadly cruelty. *Agr.* 183.
rode Amain, my deadly Foes! *Dante* 34.

Dear.
Dear lost companions of my tuneful art, *Bard* 39.
Dear, as the light that visits these sad eyes,
Bard 40.

Dear, as the ruddy drops that warm my heart,
Bard 41.
A pang, to secret sorrow dear; *Clerke* 13.
No — at our time of life 't would be silly, my dear." *C. C.* 10.
Of the dear Web whole Volumes I indite:
Prop.[3] 12.
They wept, and first my little dear Anselmo Cried, *Dante* 55.
often calling On their dear names, *Dante* 80.
†But, my Dear, these Flies, they say, *Ode* 49.

Death.
The painful family of Death, *Eton* 83.
Death, sad refuge from the storms of Fate!
P. P. 45.
Severn shall re-eccho . . . The shrieks of death,
Bard 55.
Lo! liberty and death are mine. *Bard* Lett.[3] 142.
Sisters, weave the web of death; *F. S.* 51.
Balder's head to death is giv'n. *Odin* 47.
There . . . Despair and honourable Death.
Owen 40.
the dull cold ear of death? *El.* 44.
the Syllani, doom'd to early death, *Agr.* 176.
in death resign'd, *Clerke* 7; MS. 9.
sleep in peace his night of death. *Child* 6.
The Bitterness of Death, I shall unfold. *Dante* 20.
†Queen Esther next — how fair e'en after death,
Ch. Cr. 9.

Debt.
How vast the debt of gratitude *Agr.* 57.

Deck.
Every warrior's manly neck Chains of regal honour deck, *Hoel* 14.
And the buds that deck the thorn! *Song* 4.

Decked.
With . . . shapeless sculpture deck'd [deckt, Mas.], *El.* 79.
Deck'd with no other lustre, *Agr.* 37.
†Her daughters deck'd most daintily I see,
Ch. Cr. 3.

Deckt. *See* **Decked.**

Declare.
Slow melting strains their Queen's approach declare: *P. P.* 36.
"Lord! sister," says PHYSIC to Law, "I declare,
C. C. 5.

Declared.
Her conscious tail her joy declar'd *Cat* 7.

Declares.
a Florentine my Ear, . . . declares thee. *Dante* 12.

Decline.
All but two youths th' enormous orb decline,
Stat.[1] 24.

Decorum.
Decorum 's turn'd to mere civility; *L. S.* 137.

Deeds.
Thou the deeds of light shalt know; *Odin* 39.
Force and hardy Deeds of Blood prevail. *E. G.* 44.

Deep.
Deep, majestic, smooth, and strong. *P. P.* 8.
Isles, that crown th' Egæan deep, *P. P.* 67.

Murmur'd deep a solemn sound: *P. P.* 76.
Thro' the azure deep of air: *P. P.* 117.
Struck the deep sorrows of his lyre. *Bard* 22.
Stamp we our vengeance deep, *Bard* 96.
Deep in the roaring tide he plung'd *Bard* 144.
Burthens of the angry deep. *Owen* 18.
And gilds the horrors of the deep. *Inst.* 94.
tame th' unwilling Deep. *E. G.* 43.
They perish in the boundless deep. *Vic.* 60.
Where lie th' eternal fountains of the deep,
*Prop.*² 24.
Earth's inmost cells, and caves of deep descent;
Tasso 50.
Would'st thou revive the deep Despair, *Dante* 4.

Deeper.
Those in the deeper vitals rage: *Eton* 87.
the deeper My guilt, the blacker *Agr.* 172.

Deepest.
Or deepest shades, . . . Gilds with a gleam
Vic. 34.

Deep-toned.
'T was Milton struck the deep-ton'd shell, *Inst.* 23.

Deer.
Dried up the cows, and lam'd the deer, *L. S.* 47.

Defects.
Exact my own defects to scan, *Adv.* 47.

Defiled.
keen Remorse with blood defil'd *Eton* 78.

Deigns.
She deigns to hear the savage Youth *P. P.* 60.

Deïra's.
Upon Deïra's squadrons hurl'd *Hoel* 3.

Dejected.
Sighs sudden and frequent, looks ever dejected —
Am. Lines 5.

Delaval.
Weddell attends your call, and Palgrave proud,
and Delaval the loud. *Com. Lines* 1.

Delay.
Dismiss'd at length, they break through all delay
Tasso 1.

Delayed.
By sympathetic musings here delayed,
El. Mas. 110.

Delia.
— Sure Delia will tell me! *Am. Lines* 8.

Delight.
Who foremost now delight to cleave *Eton* 25.
Where willowy Camus lingers with delight!
Inst. 29
With grim Delight the Brood of Winter view
E. G. 54.
Sailors to tell of Winds and Seas delight,
*Prop.*³ 59.

Delphi's.
Woods, that wave o'er Delphi's steep, *P. P.* 66.

Delude.
Unpeopled monast'ries delude our eyes, *View* 15.

Deluge.
the deluge burst, with sweepy sway *E. G.* 48.

Delusive.
If any spark of wit's delusive ray *Ign.* 19.

Demand.
your injur'd shades demand my fate, *Agr.* 184.

Demands.
Fate demands a nobler head; *F. S.* 43.
Owen's praise demands my song, *Owen* 1.

Demurest.
Demurest of the tabby kind, *Cat* 4.

Denying.
Her sisters denying, and Jemmy proposing:
C. C. 20.

Depressed.
†Not like yon Dowager deprest with years;
Ch. Cr. 6.

Deprest. *See* **Depressed.**

Desart-beach. *See* **Desert-beach.**

Descant.
The Birds in vain their amorous Descant joyn;
West 3.

Descends.
†H mounts to Heaven, and H descends to Hell.
Ch. Cr. 24.

Descending. *See also* **Late-descending, Swift-descending.**
Descending slow their glitt'ring skirts unroll?
Bard 106.

Descent.
Earth's inmost cells, and caves of deep descent;
Tasso 50.

Describe.
Can you do nothing but describe? *L. S.* 20.

Descries.
'T is man alone that Joy descries *Vic.* 27.

Descry.
And unknown regions dare descry: *Eton* 37.
thy judging eye, The flow'r unheeded shall descry,
Inst. 72.

Desert.
each giant-oak, and desert cave, Sighs *Bard* 23.
waste its sweetness on the desert air. *El.* 56.

Desert-beach.
the desart-beach Pent within its bleak domain,
F. S. 37.

Deserted.
this long deserted shade. *El. Mas.* 112.

Deserts.
dauntless goes O'er Libya's deserts *E. G.* 77.

Deserts, *vb.*
The sun's pale sister, . . . Deserts precipitant her
darken'd sphere: *Stat.*¹ 55.

Design.
Without design to hurt the butter, *L. S.* 123.

Designed.
thy Sire to send on Earth Virtue, . . . design'd,
Adv. 10.

Desire.
The bloom of young Desire, *P. P.* 41.
A place or a pension he did not desire, *Char.* 5.

Desires.

Their little wants, their low desires refine, *E. G.* 82.

When, less averse, and yielding to Desires,

Prop.[3] 21.

let her ever my Desires control, *Prop.*[3] 76.

Desolation.

And mimic desolation covers all. *View* 16.

Despair.

Grim-visag'd comfortless Despair, *Eton* 69.

Despair, and fell Disease, and ghastly Poverty:

Adv. 40.

Be thine Despair, and scept'red Care, *Bard* 141.

There . . . Despair and honourable Death.

Owen 40.

Would'st thou revive the deep Despair, *Dante* 4.

in four Faces saw my own Despair reflected,

Dante 63.

Despaired.

the champions, . . . the palm despair'd resign;

Stat.[1] 23.

Despairing.

Leave your despairing Caradoc to mourn:

Bard MS. 102.

Despise.

What female heart can gold despise? *Cat* 23.

The threats of pain and ruin to despise, *El.* 62.

Destined.

Years of havock urge their destined course,

Bard 85.

Destiny.

Their homely joys, and destiny obscure; *El.* 30.

Her conqu'ring destiny fulfilling, *L. S.* 26.

Destroy.

Thought would destroy their paradise. *Eton* 98.

And when, our flames commission'd to destroy,

Prop.[2] 11.

Destroyer.

The prostrate South to the Destroyer yields

E. G. 52.

Detain.

Me may Castalia's sweet recess detain, *Prop.*[2] 2.

Devil.

He went, as if the Devil drove him. *L. S.* 88.

Devour.

could'st thou not gape Quick to devour me?

Dante 72.

Devoured.

Locks Of th' half devoured Head *Dante* 3.

Devouring.

As the flame's devouring force; *Conan* 5.

Dew.

scarce religion does supply . . . her holy dew.

Bard MS. 74.

Dew-bespangled.

Morn . . . Waves her dew-bespangled wing,

Vic. 2.

Dews.

Night, and all her sickly dews, *P. P.* 49.

The drenching dews, and driving rain! *Odin* 33.

Brushing . . . the dews away *El.* 99.

dews Lethean through the land dispense *Ign.* 17.

Diadem.

Shall raise . . . gem To glitter on the diadem.

Inst. 76.

Dialogue.

†In pretty Dialogue I told *Ode* 23.

Diamond.

The diamond there attracts the wondrous sight,

Tasso 69.

Proud of its diamond dies, *Tasso* 70.

Diamond's.

conspiring in the diamond's blaze, *Bent.* 21.

Dictates.

Pours its cool dictates in the madding ear *Agr.* 83.

Did.

To Him the mighty Mother did unveil *P. P.* 86.

Oft did the harvest to their sickle yield, *El.* 25.

How jocund did they drive their team *El.* 27.

Knowledge . . . her ample page, . . . did ne'er

unroll; *El.* 50.

Heav'n did a recompence . . . send: *El.* 122.

The powerful pothooks did so move him,

L. S. 86.

Did I not wish to check this . . . passion, *Agr.* 106.

A place or a pension he did not desire, *Char.* 5.

Did the sword of Conan mow The crimson har-

vest *Conan* 9.

Did not Israel filch from the Egyptians of old

C. C. 25.

He drinks — so did Noah; *C. C.* 28.

a bad face which did sadly molest her.

Mrs. Keene 2.

That I did trust him, that I was betray'd *Dante* 16.

The fourth, what Sorrow could not, Hunger did.

Dante 81.

Die.

To triumph, and to die, are mine. *Bard* 142.

Lo! to be free to die, are mine. *Bard* Lett.[3] 142.

Where they triumph, where they die. *F. S.* 24.

teach the rustic moralist to die. *El.* 84.

Tell them, tho' 't is an awful thing to die, *Stanza* 1.

To die is glorious in the Bed of Love. *Prop.*[3] 64.

the quicker let me die: *Prop.*[3] 70.

†Twenty more in Embrio dye; *Ode* 38.

Died.

Ye died amidst your dying country's cries —

Bard 42.

By them, my friend, my Hoel, died, *Hoel* 6.

When she died, I can't tell, *C. C.* 14.

and when she frown'd, he died. *Prop.*[3] 108.

my other three before my Eyes Died *Dante* 76.

Dies.

Proud of its diamond dies, and luxury of light.

Tasso 70.

Difference.

†And seems small difference the sounds between;

Ch. Cr. 46.

Different.

The different doom our Fates assign. *Bard* 140.

A different Object do these Eyes require: *West* 6.

To different Climes seem different Souls assign'd?

E. G. 39.

†while different far, Rests in Retirement, *Ch. Cr.* 53.

Difficult.

Vast, oh my friends, and difficult the toil *Tasso* 27.

Digest.

He eat a fat goose, and could not digest her.
Ep. Keene 2.

Dim.

In cloisters dim, far from the haunts of Folly,
Inst. 33.

Dimly.

deepest shades, that dimly lower *Vic.* 34.

Din.

Heard ye the din of battle bray, *Bard* 83.
Hoarse he bays with hideous din, *Odin* 9.
There the press, and there the din; *Owen* 24.
He heard the distant din of war. *L. S.* 76.
And, clash'd, rebellows with the din of war,
*Stat.*¹ 31.

Dinner.

She smiled, and bid him come to dinner. *L. S.* 132.
When you rise from your Dinner as light as before,
Couplet 1.

Dipped.

Shafts for shuttles, dipt in gore, *F. S.* 13.

Dipt. *See* **Dipped.**

Dire.

How flames perhaps, with dire confusion hurl'd,
*Prop.*² 27.
From his dire Food the griesly Fellon raised
Dante 1.

Direful.

with direful Hand Oped the dark Veil of Fate.
Dante 27.

Dirges.

with dirges due in sad array *El.* 113.

Dirt.

The Master of Maudlin In the same dirt is
dawdling; *Satire* 8.

Disapprove.

Nor thou my gentle Calling disapprove, *Prop.*³ 63.

Disc.

Young Pterelas . . . drew, Labouring, the disc,
*Stat.*¹ 6.
Sure flew the disc from his unerring hand,
*Stat.*¹ 39.
Third in the labours of the disc come on, *Stat.*² 1.

Disclose.

Disclose the long-expecting flowers, *Spring* 3.
No farther seek his merits to disclose, *El.* 125.
Th' unthought event disclose a whiter meaning.
Agr. 71.
And half disclose those Limbs it should conceal;
*Prop.*³ 10.

Discovered.

Discover'd half, and half conceal'd their way;
Tasso 46.

Disdain.

Some bold adventurers disdain *Eton* 35.

Disdainful.

Disdainful Anger, pallid Fear, *Eton* 63.
Nor Grandeur hear with a disdainful smile *El.* 31.

Disdains.

The torrent-stream his ancient bounds disdains,
Tasso 9.

Disease.

Despair, and fell Disease, and ghastly Poverty:
Adv. 40.
Disease, and Sorrow's weeping train, *P. P.* 44.

Disgrace.

the champions, trembling at the sight, Prevent
disgrace, *Stat.*¹ 23.

Dismay.

the sounds, that . . . scatter'd wild dismay,
Bard 10.

Dismiss.

but first dismiss your fears; *Tasso* 36.

Dismissed.

Dismiss'd at length, they break through all delay
Tasso 1.

Disorder.

The Poet felt a strange disorder: *L. S.* 82.

Disparted.

When mountain-high the waves disparted rise;
Tasso 40.

Dispel.

Dispel, my fair, with smiles, the tim'rous cloud
Agr. 193.

Dispense.

dews Lethean through the land dispense *Ign.* 17.

Disperse.

Light they disperse, and with them go *Adv.* 21.

Display.

No painted plumage to display: *Spring* 47.
Ambition . . . Display the radiant prize,
Agr. 52.
A milder Warfare I in Verse display; *Prop.*³ 61.

Displease.

the Master of Jesus Does hugely displease us;
Satire 6.

Disporting.

Disporting on thy margent green *Eton* 23.

Disprove.

The fond complaint, my Song, disprove, *P. P.* 46.

Disproved.

The bard, . . . Had . . . Disprov'd the arguments of *Squib*, *L. S.* 115.

Distance.

haply eyed at distance Some edileship, *Agr.* 39.
And to small distance threw, *Stat.*¹ 6.

Distant.

Ye distant spires, *Eton* 1.
Yet shall he mount, and keep his distant way
P. P. 121.
distant warblings lessen on my ear, *Bard* 133.
drowsy tinklings lull the distant folds. *El.* 8.
He heard the distant din of war. *L. S.* 76.
on frail floats to distant cities ride *E. G.* 106.
Gilds with a gleam of distant day. *Vic.* 36.
Nor yet in prospect rose the distant shore;
Tasso 5.
To seek your Hero in a distant soil! *Tasso* 28.

Distilled.

from his jaws, . . . Foam and human gore distill'd: *Odin* 8.

Diverted.

†They 're all diverted into H and B. *Ch. Cr.* 14.

Divine.

Oh! Lyre divine, *P. P.* 112.
In the midst a Form divine! *Bard* 115.
No boding Maid of skill divine Art thou, *Odin* 84.
There sit the sainted sage, the bard divine, *Inst.* 15.
tenacious of thy right divine, *Ign.* 15.
raise the mortal to a height divine. *E. G.* 83.
Back to it's Source divine the Julian Race.
*Prop.*³ 58.

Diviner.

Is that diviner inspiration giv'n, *Bent.* 18.

Divinity.

DIVINITY heard, between waking and dozing,
C. C. 19.

Do. *See also* **Don't.**

How do your tuneful Echo's languish, *P. P.* 71.
They do not sleep. *Bard* 43.
Can you do nothing but describe? *L. S.* 20.
why do I waste the fruitless hours *Agr.* 154.
A different Object do these Eyes require: *West* 6.
— he swears — so do I: *C. C.* 28.
In brief whate'er she do, or say, or look, *Prop.*³ 27.
Father, why, why do you gaze so sternly?
Dante 56.

Does.

scarce religion does [dares, *Lett.*¹] supply Her
mutter'd requiems, *Bard* MS. 73.
The mopeing owl does to the moon complain
El. 10.
Why yet does Asia dread a Monarch's nod,
E. G. 59.
the Master of Jesus Does hugely displease us;
Satire 6.
For thee does Powell squeeze, *Com. Lines* 2.
Why does yon Orb, . . . Obscure his radiance
*Prop.*² 33.
†Queer Queensbury only does refuse to wait.
Ch. Cr. 52.

Doff.

The Audience . . . doff their hats *L. S.* 110.

Dog.

Him the Dog of Darkness spied, *Odin* 5.
The triple dog that scares the shadowy kind,
*Prop.*² 44.

Dog's-ears.

creased, like dogs-ears, in a folio. *L. S.* 68.

Dogs-ears. *See* **Dog's-ears.**

Doleful.

I heard Their doleful Cries; *Dante* 77.

Dolphin.

No Dolphin came, *Cat* 34.

Domain.

desart-beach Pent within its bleak domain,
F. S. 38.

Dominion.

Sailing with supreme dominion *P. P.* 116.

Done.

The work is done. *Bard* 100.
Sisters, cease, the work is done. *F. S.* 52.
Tell me what is done below, *Odin* 40.
we hied, our Labours done, *El.* Mas. 118.

Dons.

The Master of St. John's Like the rest of the
Dons. *Satire* 34.

Don't.

"I don't know," says LAW, *C. C.* 11.

Doom.

regardless of their doom *Eton* 51.
Stamp we our vengeance deep, and ratify his
doom. *Bard* 96.
The different doom our Fates assign. *Bard* 140.
Weaving many a Soldier's doom, *F. S.* 7.
In *Hoder's* hand the Heroe's doom: *Odin* 55.
the silent Tenour of thy Doom. *El.* Mas. 88.

Doomed.

the Syllani, doom'd to early death, *Agr.* 176.

Door. *See also* **Chapel-door.**

Rap'd at the door, nor stay'd to ask, *L. S.* 55.
But that they left the door a-jarr, *L. S.* 74.
From her loved Door *Prop.*³ 78.

Doors.

†Open the *d*oors of the with*d*rawing-room;
Ch. Cr. 2.

Dost.

who . . . Dost . . . their artless tale relate;
El. 94; Mas. 78.
dost thou talk to me . . . of danger, *Agr.* 27.
successful dost thou still oppose *Ign.* 13.
Or thou dost mourn to think, *Dante* 46.

Double.

With double light it beam'd against the day:
*Stat.*¹ 27.
†The Dowager grows a perfect double D. *Ch. Cr.* 4.

Doublet. *See* **Satin-doublet.**

Doubt.

Nor doubt with me to tread the downward road
Tasso 37.

Doubtful.

To tempt the dangers of the doubtful way;
Tasso 2.

Doubts.

Cease, my doubts, my fears to move, *Song* 11.

Dove-like.

Was fashion'd fair in meek and dove-like guise;
Shak. 10.

Dowager.

†The Dowager grows a perfect double D. *Ch. Cr.* 4.
†Not like yon Dowager deprest with years;
Ch. Cr. 6.

Down.

Now rowling down the steep amain, *P. P.* 10.
Till down the eastern cliffs afar *P. P.* 52.
down the steep of Snowdon's shaggy side *Bard* 11.
Down the yawning steep he rode, *Odin* 3.
And strok'd down her band — *C. C.* 22.
Never hang down your head, *C. C.* 31.

Anon, with slacken'd rage comes quiv'ring down,
Stat.[1] 51.
And down the steep he led *Tasso* 43.
I swallow'd down My struggling Sorrow, *Dante* 68.
†slow down the Silver stream. *Ch. Cr.* 57.

Downward.
Nor doubt with me to tread the downward road
Tasso 37.

Dozing.
DIVINITY heard, between waking and dozing,
C. C. 19.

Dragon-son.
The Dragon-Son of Mona stands; *Owen* 20.

Drags.
Who . . . drags me from the realms of night?
Odin 30.

Draw.
draw his frailties from their dread abode,
El. 126 ; *Mas.* 150.
draw Mankind in vain the vital Airs, *E. G.* 9.
Then to my quiet Urn awhile draw near,
Prop.[3] 105.

Drawers.
Into the Drawers and China pry, *L. S.* 65.

Drawing-room.
visages . . . that garnish'd The drawing-room
L. S. 108.
†Q draws her train along the Drawing-room,
Ch. Cr. 50.

Drawn. See also **Long-drawn.**
The sun's pale sister, drawn by magic strain,
Stat.[1] 54.

Draws.
draws his humid train of mud: *Ign.* 4.
mends the Plan their Fancy draws, *E. G.* 32.
†Great D draws near — the Dutchess sure is come,
Ch. Cr. 1.
†Q draws her train along the Drawing-room,
Ch. Cr. 50.

Dread.
Dread goddess, lay thy chast'ning hand! *Adv.* 34.
Thrice pronounc'd, in accents dread, *Odin* 23.
draw his frailties from their dread abode, *El.* 126.
Why yet does Asia dread a Monarch's nod,
E. G. 59.
And mariners, though shipwreck'd, dread [fear,
Nich.] to land. *View* 8.
yet the dread path once trod, *Stanza* 2.

Dreaded.
This mighty emperor, this dreaded hero, *Agr.* 93.

Dreadful.
in dreadful harmony they join, *Bard* 47.
And beg'd his aid that dreadful day. *L. S.* 92.
bade the Magi call the dreadful powers, *Agr.* 64.
so 't be strange, and dreadful. — Sorceries,
Agr. 171.
Th' Æmonian hag enjoys her dreadful hour,
Stat.[1] 58.
I heard the dreadful Clash of Bars, *Dante* 51.

Dreads.
When Pindus' self approaching ruin dreads,
Prop.[2] 31.

Dream.
Each dream, in fancy's airy colouring. *Bent.* 7.
Or are our fears th' enthusiast's empty dream,
Prop.[2] 48.

Dreaming.
avaunt, . . . dreaming Sloth of pallid hue,
Inst. 4.

Drear.
steep . . . That leads to HELA's drear abode.
Odin 4.

Dreary.
He gives to range the dreary sky: *P. P.* 51.
On dreary Arvon's shore they lie, *Bard* 35.
Relumes her crescent Orb to cheer the dreary
Night: *Prop.*[2] 22.

Drenching.
The drenching dews, and driving rain! *Odin* 33.

Dress.
In gorgeous phrase . . . To dress thy plea,
Agr. 150.

Dressed.
In fortune's varying colours drest: *Spring* 37.
Truth severe, by fairy Fiction drest. *Bard* 127.
Drest for whom yon golden bed. *Odin* 42.
In glitt'ring arms and glory drest, *Owen* 21.
†Prince, in pompous Purple drest, *Ch. Cr.* 35.

Drest. See **Dressed.**

Drew.
At Aix, his voluntary sword he drew, *Williams* 5.
Young Pterelas with strength unequal drew,
Stat.[1] 5.

Dried.
Dried up the cows, and lam'd the deer, *L. S.* 47.
My love . . . Dried the soft springs of pity
Agr. 182.

Drink.
flowers, . . . Drink life and fragrance *P. P.* 6.
'T is the drink of *Balder* bold: *Odin* 46.
From the golden cup they drink *Hoel* 16.

Drinking.
They say he's no Christian, loves drinking and
whoring, *C. C.* 15.

Drinks.
He drinks — so did Noah; *C. C.* 28.

Drive.
How jocund did they drive their team afield!
El. 27.
The dusky people drive before the gale; *E. G.* 105.
Or drive the infernal Vulture *Prop.*[3] 90.

Driving.
The drenching dews, and driving rain! *Odin* 33.

Droning.
Save where the beetle wheels his droning flight,
El. 7.

Drooping.
The Herd stood drooping by: *Vic.* 24.

Drop.
while o'er the Place You drop the Tear,
Prop.[3] 106.

Dropped.

And drop'd his thirsty lance   *P. P.* 19.
a tear . . . would have dropp'd,   *Agr.* 11.

Dropping.

Pity, dropping soft the sadly-pleasing tear.
    Adv. 32.

Drops.

Dear, as the ruddy drops that warm my heart,
    Bard 41.
pious drops the closing eye requires;   *El.* 90.

Drowns.

The . . . tide, that drowns her lessening lands,
    E. G. 61.

Drowsier.

to wake pretensions Drowsier than theirs, *Agr.* 104.

Drowsy.

drowsy tinklings lull the distant folds :   *El.* 8.

Dryden's.

where Dryden's less presumptuous car, *P. P.* 103.
Dryden's harmony submit to mine.   *Bent.* 16.

Duchess.

Great D *d*raws near — the *D*utchess sure is come,
    Ch. Cr. 1.

Ductile.

In ductile Lines of Foolery: *Ode* 40.

Due.

with dirges due [meet, Mas.] in sad array *El.* 113.
And doff their hats with due submission: *L. S.* 110.
Yielding due reverence to his . . . command:
    Agr. 4.
Due sacrifice perform'd with barb'rous rites
    Agr. 62.
While Nancy earns the praise to Shakespeare due,
    Shak. 23.

Dull.

To chear the shiv'ring Natives dull [chill, MS.]
abode.   *P. P.* 57.
soothe the dull cold ear of death?   *El.* 44.
rolling, side by side, Their dull, but daily round.
    Vic. 63.
To close my dull eyes when I see it returning;
    Am. Lines 4.

Dumb.

to dumb Forgetfulness a prey,   *El.* 85.

Dusky.

Their feather-cinctur'd Chiefs, and dusky Loves.
    P. P. 62.
the loom, Where the dusky warp we strain, *F. S.* 6.
The dusky people drive before the gale; *E. G.* 105.
Have ye seen the dusky boar,   *Caradoc* 1.
As when athwart the dusky woods by night
    Tasso 47.

Dust.

their . . . dance They leave, in dust to rest.
    Spring 40.
The dust of the prophetic Maid.   *Odin* 20.
Can Honour's voice provoke the silent dust,
    El. 43.
Genius of old Rome Shall from the dust *Agr.* 142.
And now in dust the polish'd ball he roll'd,
    Stat.[1] 41.

Dutchess. *See* **Duchess.**

Duty.

cast me forth in duty to their lord.   *Agr.* 157.

Dwell.

within whose sacred cell . . . virtues lov'd to
dwell.   *Clerke* 4.
†But why on such *mock* grandeur should we
dwell,   *Ch. Cr.* 23.

Dwindled.

†Elizabeths all dwindled into Betties; *Ch. Cr.* 12.

Dye. *See* **Die.**

Dyed. *See* **Gore-dyed.**

Dying.

Ye died amidst your dying country's cries —
    Bard 42.

E.

†E enters next, and with her Eve appears, *Ch. Cr.* 5.
†in vain you think to find them under E, *Ch. Cr.* 13.

Each.

To each his suff'rings: *Eton* 91.
Where each old poetic Mountain   *P. P.* 73.
each giant-oak, and desert cave, Sighs *Bard* 23.
Each a gasping Warriour's head.   *F. S.* 12.
thro' each winding vale . . . the notes prolong.
    F. S. 59.
Each her thundering faulchion wield; *F. S.* 62.
Each bestride her sable steed.   *F. S.* 63.
Each in his narrow cell for ever laid,   *El.* 15.
Each pannel in achievements cloathing, *L. S.* 6.
Each hole and cupboard they explore, *L. S.* 61.
they explore, Each creek and cranny *L. S.* 62.
steep in slumbers each benighted sense? *Ign.* 18.
She bids each slumb'ring energy awake, *E. G.* 78.
See . . . each transitory thought   *Bent.* 5.
Each dream, in fancy's airy colouring *Bent.* 7.
His mind each Muse . . . adorn'd *Williams* 3.
Each Grace adorn'd his frame,   *Williams* 3.
Old, and abandon'd by each venal friend, *View* 1.
Firmly he plants each knee,   *Stat.*[1] 47.
Each in his proper Art should waste the Day:
    Prop.[3] 62.

Eager.

Eager to taste the honied spring,   *Spring* 26.
The words too eager to unriddle,   *L. S.* 81.
Flash'd to pursue, and chear the eager Cry:
    Dante 36.

Eagle.

That the Theban Eagle bear   *P. P.* 115.
The famish'd Eagle screams,   *Bard* 38.

Ear.

distant warblings lessen on my ear, *Bard* 133.
the dull cold ear of death?   *El.* 44.
Bursts on my ear th' indignant lay: *Inst.* 14.
cool dictates in the madding ear   *Agr.* 83.
Knows his soft ear the trumpet's . . . voice,
    Agr. 95.
a Florentine my Ear, . . . declares thee.
    Dante 11.

Earl.

Low the dauntless Earl is laid,   *F. S.* 41.
Earl Goodwin trembled for his neighbouring sand;
    View 6.

Earliest.
There scatter'd oft, the earliest of the Year,
El. Pem. 117 ; *Mas.* 137.
There bloom the vernal rose's earliest pride;
Prop.[2] 10.

Early.
the Syllani, doom'd to early death,   *Agr.* 176.

Earnest.
While some on earnest business bent   *Eton* 31.
A grateful Earnest of eternal Peace. *El. Mas.* 84.

Earns.
While Nancy earns the praise to Shakespeare due,
Shak. 23.

Ears. *See also* **Dog's-ears.**
Her ears of jet, . . . She saw;   *Cat* 11.
ears to own Her spirit-stirring voice;   *Agr.* 123.
These Ears, alas! for other Notes repine, *West* 5.
Great things . . . in your ears I shall unfold;
Tasso 35.

Earth.
thy Sire to send on earth Virtue, . . . design'd,
Adv. 9.
The groaning earth beneath him shakes, *Odin* 14.
Virgins . . . That bend to earth their solemn
brow,   *Odin* 76.
rests his head upon the lap of Earth   *El.* 117.
Shall raise from earth the latent gem *Inst.* 75.
the spirit of Britannicus Yet walks on earth:
Agr. 15.
The riches of the earth,   *Agr.* 78.
sickly Plants betray a niggard Earth,   *E. G.* 1.
Imbibes a flavour of its parent earth, *E. G.* 85.
What wondrous force the solid earth can move,
Prop.[2] 30.
oh Earth! could'st thou not gape   *Dante* 71.

Earth's.
Earth's inmost cells, and caves of deep descent;
Tasso 50.
Earth's monster-brood stretch'd on their iron bed,
Prop.[2] 41.

Ease.
At ease reclin'd in rustic state   *Spring* 17.
nurs'd in ease And pleasure's flow'ry lap?
Agr. 98.
measured Laws and philosophic Ease *E. G.* 40.
†What Ease and Elegance her person grace,
Ch. Cr. 7.

East.
Here reign the blustering North and blighting East,
View 9.

Eastern.
Till down the eastern cliffs afar   *P. P.* 52.
Right against the eastern gate,   *Odin* 17.

Easy.
The thoughtless day, the easy night,   *Eton* 48.
she wins her easy way: *P. P.* 39.
could they catch . . . his easy grace, *Bent.* 13.
She tunes my easy Rhime,   *Prop.*[3] 6.

Eat.
'T is a sign you have eat just enough *Couplet* 2.
He eat a fat goose,   *Ep. Keene* 2.

Ebon.
Lethargic nods upon her ebon throne. *Ign.* 24.

Echo. *See* **Re-echo.**

Echoes.
How do your tuneful Echo's languish, *P. P.* 71.

Echoing.
thro' each echoing vale   *F. S. Whar.* 59.
shore Echoing to the battle's roar.   *Owen* 26.
the echoing [ecchoing, *Mas.*] horn,   *El.* 19.
While vales and woods and echoing hills rebound.
Stat.[2] 17.

Ecstasy.
warbles high His trembling thrilling ecstasy;
Vic. 14.
Upon the seraph-wings of Extasy,   *P. P.* 96.
wak'd to extasy the living lyre.   *El.* 48.
riveted His eyes in fearful extasy: *Agr.* 170.

Ecstatic.
drink Nectar . . . Or the grape's extatic juice.
Hoel 18.

Eden.
A Voice, . . . Gales from blooming Eden bear;
Bard 132.

Edileship.
eyed at distance Some edileship,   *Agr.* 40.

Edmund.
Here lies Edmund Keene Lord Bishop of Chester,
Ep. Keene 1.

Edward.
o'er the crested pride Of the first Edward *Bard* 10.
Edward, lo! . . . Half of thy heart we consecrate.   *Bard* 97.
Great Edward, with the lilies on his brow *Inst.* 39.

Edward's.
The winding-sheet of Edward's race. *Bard* 50.

E'en. *See also* **Even.**
E'en from the tomb the voice of Nature *El.* 91.
E'en in our Ashes live their wonted Fires *El.* 92.
Tell them, . . . 'T was e'en to thee; *Stanza* 2.
e'en Magic here must fail,   *Prop.*[3] 85.
†Queen Esther next — how fair e'en after death,
Ch. Cr. 9.

E'er.
all that wealth e'er gave,   *El.* 34.
Than Pow'r and Genius e'er conspir'd to bless.
El. Mas. 76.
who . . . This . . . being e'er resign'd, *El.* 86.
How rude so e'er th' exterior Form   *E. G.* 26.
Love, gentle Power! to Peace was e'er a friend;
Prop.[1] 1.
e'er the sixth Morn Had dawn'd,   *Dante* 74.

Efface.
The energy of Pope they might efface, *Bent.* 15.

Egæan.
Isles, that crown the Egæan deep,   *P. P.* 67.

Eggs.
And suck'd the eggs, and kill'd the pheasants.
L. S. 48.

Egypt.
the Masians too, and those of Egypt, *Agr.* 115.
broods o'er Egypt with his wat'ry wings,*E. G.*103.

Egyptians.

Did not Israel filch from the Egyptians of old
                       C. C. 25.

Eight.

Eight times emerging from the flood   *Cat* 31.
her nod Can rouse eight hardy legions, *Agr.* 108.

Eighth's.

†Henry the Eighth's most monstrous majesty,
                       Ch. Cr. 22.

Eirin.

Long his loss shall Eirin weep,   *F. S.* 45.
This the force of Eirin hiding,   *Owen* 11.

Either.

And either Henry there,   *Inst.* 45.
with nearer Course surrounds To either Pole,
                       E. G. 25.
The flood on either hand its billows rears,
                       Tasso 41.
either Hand I gnaw'd For Anguish,   *Dante* 63.

Elegance.

†What Ease and Elegance her person grace,
                       Ch. Cr. 7.

Elegy.

The place of fame and elegy [epitaph, MS.]
    supply :   *El.* 82.
†I tell her so in Elegy.   *Ode* 30.

Elements.

The stubborn elements confess her sway, *E. G.* 81.

Elf.

Never hang down your head, you poor penitent
    elf,   *C. C.* 31.

Elizabeth.

†Then one faint glimpse of Queen Elizabeth;
                       Ch. Cr. 10.

Elizabeths.

†Elizabeths all dwindled into Betties; *Ch. Cr* 12.

Elms.

Beneath those rugged elms,   *El.* 13

Eloquence.

gorgeous phrase of labour'd eloquence *Agr.* 149.

Else.

No Phœbus else, no other Muse I know, *Prop.*³ 5.

Elude.

By Fraud elude, by Force repel the Foe, *E. G.* 35.
And struggles to elude my longing Eyes, *Prop.*³ 24.

Elusive.

To chase the hoop's elusive speed *Eton* MS. 29.
beguil'd With more elusive speed the . . . sight
                       Agr. 191.
Then grasp'd its weight, elusive of his hold;
                     *Stat.*¹ 42.
'T is hard th' elusive Symptoms to explore:
                       *Prop.*³ 95.

'Em.

Yet see how all around 'em wait   *Eton* 55.
He Perchance may heed 'em: *Agr.* 88.
And shake 'em at the name of liberty, *Agr.* 132.
I heard 'em wail for Bread.   *Dante* 45.
too soon they had aroused 'em   *Dante* 48.
I saw 'em fall;   *Dante* 76.
†Still to ripen 'em is wanted;   *Ode* 4.

Embrace.

By *Odin's* fierce embrace comprest,   *Odin* 64.
weeping I forsook thy fond embrace.   *Ign.* 12.

Embrio. *See* **Embryo.**

Embrued.

The hungry Pack their sharp-set Fangs embrued.
                       Dante 40.

Embryo.

†Twenty more in Embrio dye;   *Ode* 38.

Embryon.

And embryon metals undigested glow, *Tasso* 58.

Emerald.

Emerald eyes, She saw: *Cat* 11.
Here the soft emerald smiles   *Tasso* 67.

Emerging.

Eight times emerging from the flood   *Cat* 31.

Emits.

Emits the mass, a prelude of his might; *Stat.*¹ 46.

Emmanuel.

But the Master of Emmanuel Follows them like
    a spaniel;   *Satire* 25.

Emperor.

This mighty emperor, this dreaded hero, *Agr.* 93.

Empire.

the rod of empire   *El.* 47.
Shew'd him where empire tower'd,   *Agr.* 46.
gloomy Sway have fix'd her Empire there,
                       E. G. 19.

Empires.

Her native plains, and empires once her own.
                       E. G. 63.

Employed.

The Huntingdons . . . employ'd the power of
    Fairy hands   *L. S.* 4.

Employment.

Her household cares, a woman's best employ-
    ment.   *Agr.* 8.

Empty.

empty shade Of long-forgotten liberty: *Agr.* 43.
Or are our fears th' enthusiast's empty dream,
                       *Prop.*² 48.

Empyrean.

From yonder realms of empyrean day   *Inst.* 13.

Emulate.

that to avoid, and this to emulate.   *Stat.*² 5.

Enamelling.

†Vainly enamelling the Green.   *Ode* 18.

Enchanting.

Sovereign of the willing soul, . . . Enchanting
    shell !   *P. P.* 15.

Enchantress.

Me from myself the soft Enchantress stole;
                       *Prop.*³ 75.

Encircled. *See* **Sea-encircled.**

Encounter.

While Prows, that late in fierce Encounter mett,
                       *Prop.*³ 51.

Encroaching.
Th' encroaching tide, that drowns her . . . lands,   *E. G.* 61.

End.
they that fly, Shall end where they began.
    Spring 34.
envy oft thy happy grandsire's end.
    Bard MS. 76.

Endear.
mutual Wishes, mutual Woes endear   *E. G.* 36.

Endless.
Closed his eyes in endless night.   *P. P.* 102.
headlong . . . he plung'd [sunk, Lett.²] to endless night.   *Bard* 144.
anxious Cares and endless Wishes   *El.* Mas. 86.

Endured.
Nor long endur'd the Chase: *Dante* 37.

Energy.
She bids each slumb'ring energy awake,   *E. G.* 78.
The energy of Pope they might efface,   *Bent.* 15.

Enervate.
But nor Callimachus' enervate Strain   *Prop.*³ 55.

Enforce.
various tracts enforce a various toil,   *E. G.* 86.

Engage.
Still may his Bard in softer fights engage;
    *Prop.*¹ 3.
These soft inglorious joys my hours engage;
    *Prop.*² 51.

England's.
Mov'd the stout heart of England's Queen,
    L. S. 15.
Young Williams fought for England's fair renown;   *Williams* 2.

Enjoys.
Th' Æmonian hag enjoys her dreadful hour,
    *Stat.*¹ 58.

Enormous.
All but two youths th' enormous orb decline,
    *Stat.*¹ 24.

Enough.
Give ample room, and verge enough   *Bard* 51.
Enough for me: With joy I see   *Bard* 139.
Enough for me, with joy I see
    Bard Lett.¹, Lett.² 139.
A House there is, (and that 's enough)   *L. S.* 21.
Sour visages, enough to scare ye,   *L. S.* 106.
Enough for me,   *Bent.* 25.
'T is a sign you have eat just enough   *Couplet* 2.

Enquire.
Some kindred Spirit shall enquire thy Fate;
    El. Pem. 96.

Enquirer.
never shall Enquirer come To break   *Odin* 88.

Enquiry.
vain tho' kind enquiry   *El.* Mas. 111.

Ensanguined.
Wading through th' ensanguin'd field,   *F. S.* 30.
And there the ensanguined Wave of Sicily,
    *Prop.*³ 44.

Enshrined.
Enshrined Claudius, with the pitied ghosts
    Agr. 175.

Ensigns.
with ensigns wide unfurl'd, She rode   *Ign.* 27.

Entered.
But bounce into the parlour enter'd.   *L. S.* 56.

Enters.
†E enters next, and with her Eve appears, *Ch. Cr.* 5.

Enthral.
The captive linnet which enthral?   *Eton* 27.

Enthusiast's.
Or are our fears th' enthusiast's empty dream,
    *Prop.*² 48.

Enticed.
The Master of Christ By the rest is enticed;
    Satire 24.

Entrails.
'T is of human entrails made   *F. S.* 10.

Entrance.
such as mought entrance find within   *Dante* 60.

Entry.
Such as . . . Come (sweep) along some winding entry   *L. S.* 102.

Envied.
the envied [coming, Mas.] kiss to share.   *El.* 24.
Oh, might that envied Happiness be mine!
    *Prop.*³ 67.
Thou envied Honour of thy Poet's Days,
    *Prop.*³ 103.

Envious.
While to retain the envious Lawn she tries,
    *Prop.*³ 23.

Envy.
Envy wan, and faded Care,   *Eton* 68.
envy oft thy happy grandsire's end.
    Bard MS. 76.
Nor Envy base, nor creeping Gain,   *Inst.* 9.
Nor envy dar'd to view him with a frown.
    Williams 4.

Ephyre.
Of Pisa one, and one from Ephyre;   *Stat.*¹ 12.

Episode.
†with Myra's charms In Episode,   *Ode* 28.

Epitaph.
The Place of Fame and Epitaph supply;
    El. Pem. 82; Mas. 98.

Equal.
With equal power resume that gift,   *Agr.* 90.
If equal Justice . . . Smile not indulgent
    E. G. 15.
with fleet and equal Speed   *Dante* 31.

Ere. *See also* **E'er.**
Ere the ruddy sun be set,   *F. S.* 21.
ere mid-day, Nero will come to Baiæ.   *Agr.* 159.
ere it precipitates its fall;   *Stat.*² 15.
Ere the spring he would return —   *Song* 2.

Erected.
frail memorial still erected nigh,   *El.* 78.

Ermine.

My Lady . . . Swore by her coronet and ermine,
                                                       L. S. 50.

Errand.

your errand is perform'd,   *Agr.* 1.
nor on what Errand Sent hither: *Dante* 10.

Escaped.

And scarce Ulysses 'scap'd his giant arm.
                                                       *Stat.*² 23.

Essence.

Fix'd by his touch a lasting essence take; *Bent.* 6.

Esther.

Tho' wiser than Nestor And fairer than Esther,
                                                       Ext. Keene 3.
†Queen Esther next — how fair e'en after death,
                                                       Ch. Cr. 9.

Esthers.

†No more, our Esthers now are nought but Hetties,
                                                       Ch. Cr. 11.

Eternal.

A grateful Earnest of eternal Peace. *El. Mas.* 84.
That first, eternal, universal Cause;   *Prop.*² 18.
Where lie th' eternal fountains of the deep,
                                                       *Prop.*² 24.

Eternity.

Lubbers, That to eternity would sing, *L. S.* 143.

Ethereal.

Two Coursers of ethereal race,   *P. P.* 105.

Etough.

Thus Etough look'd;   *Toph.* 1.

Euphrates'.

Euphrates' font, and Nile's mysterious head.
                                                       Tasso 56.

European.

European Freedom still withstands   *E. G.* 60.

Eve.

†E enters next, and with her Eve appears,
                                                       Ch. Cr. 5.

Even. *See also* **E'en.**

Nor even thy virtues, Tyrant, shall avail *Bard* 6.
ev'n these bones from insult to protect *El.* 77.
Ev'n when its will seem'd wrote   *Agr.* 70.
Even in the servile senate,   *Agr.* 123.
lamps, that shed at Ev'n a cheerful ray *E. G.* 66.

Evening.

busy housewife ply her evening care: *El.* 22.

Evening-prey.

That, . . . expects his evening-prey, *Bard* 76.

Evening-star.

†Bright beaming, as the Evening-star, her face;
                                                       Ch. Cr. 8.

Event.

Th' unthought event disclose a whiter meaning
                                                       Agr. 71.
Th' Event presages, and explores the Cause.
                                                       E. G. 33.

Ever. *See also* **E'er.**

Each in his narrow cell for ever laid, *El.* 15.
The rude Forefathers . . . For ever sleep:
                                                       El. Mas. 17.

Thus ever grave and undisturbed reflection
                                                       Agr. 82.
ye ever gloomy bowers, Ye gothic fanes, *Ign.* 1.
Oh! times for ever lost!   *Ign.* 31.
For ever gone — yet still to fancy new, *Ign.* 33.
Sighs sudden and frequent, looks ever dejected —
                                                       Am. Lines 5.
Pangs without respite, fires that ever glow,
                                                       *Prop.*² 40.
let her ever my Desires control,   *Prop.*³ 76.

Ever-faithful.

weave thy ever-faithful Name.   *Prop.*³ 54.

Everlasting.

Heaven lifts its everlasting portals high, *Stanza* 3.

Ever-melting.

Whence the soft Strain and ever-melting Verse?
                                                       *Prop.*³ 2.

Ever-new.

Theirs . . . invention ever-new,   *Eton* 46.

Every.

She mew'd to every watry God,   *Cat* 32.
a voice in every wind,   *Eton* 39.
every labouring sinew strains,   *Eton* 86.
Ev'ry shade and hallow'd Fountain   *P. P.* 75.
Lord of every regal art,   *Owen* 7.
ev'ry fierce tumultuous Passion   *El. Fr.* 82.
to shine Thro' every unborn age,   *Inst.* 17.
languid Pleasure sighs in every Gale. *E. G.* 45.
Till time shall every grief remove,   *Clerke* 15.
Every warrior's manly neck Chains of regal hon-
       our deck,   *Hoel* 13.
Brac'd all his nerves, and every sinew strung;
                                                       *Stat.*² 7.
And find a Cure for every Ill,   *Prop.*³ 80.

Evil.

in Greece's evil hour,   *P. P.* 77.

Exact.

Exact my own defects to scan,   *Adv.* 47.

Exalt.

Exalt the brave, and idolize Success; *El.* *Mas.* 74.

Excess.

blasted with excess of light,   *P. P.* 101.

Exclude.

Rich windows that exclude the light, *L. S.* 7.

Excursion.

Fearless in long excursion loves to glide, *Tasso* 21.

Exercise.

The pond'rous brass in exercise he bore; *Stat.*¹ 37.

Expand.

†Expand their wings of flimzey Gold. *Ode* 48.

Expanse.

th' expanse below . . . survey,   *Eton* 6.

Expectation.

On expectation's strongest wing to soar *Agr.* 42.
Suspends the crowd with expectation warm;
                                                       *Stat.*¹ 44.

Expected. *See* **Long-expected.**

Expecting. *See* **Long-expecting.**

Expects.

That, . . . expects his evening-prey,   *Bard* 76.

Experienced.

All eyes were bent on his experienced hand,
         Stat.[1] 34.

Expire.

warblings . . . That lost in long futurity expire.
         Bard 134.

in my Breast the imperfect Joys expire.   *West* 8.

As Lamps, . . . Fade and expire   *E. G.* 67.

Expired.

imploreing In vain my Help, expir'd: *Dante* 74.

Expiring.

Your helpless, old, expiring master view!
         Bard MS. 72.

Explore.

Hark, his hands the lyre explore!   *P. P.* 107.

shall explore, Thy once loved haunt, *El.* Mas. 111.

Each hole and cupboard they explore,   *L. S.* 61.

the nations . . . Their cymbals toss, and sounding brass explore;   *Stat.*[1] 57.

'T is hard th' elusive Symptoms to explore:
         Prop.[3] 95.

Explores.

Th' Event presages, and explores the Cause.
         E. G. 33.

Exquisitely.

Why does yon Orb, so exquisitely bright,
         Prop.[2] 33.

Extasy. *See* **Ecstasy.**

Extatic. *See* **Ecstatic.**

Extend.

Whose walls along the neighbouring Sea extend,
         Tasso 4.

Extends.

but when, extends Beyond their chronicle —
         Agr. 137.

Exterior.

How rude so e'er th' exterior Form   *E. G.* 26.

Extinct.

The gen'rous spark extinct revive,   *Adv.* 45.

Eye.

To Contemplation's sober eye   *Spring* 31.

hard Unkindness' alter'd eye,   *Eton* 76.

With leaden eye, that loves the ground,   *Adv.* 28.

lie . . . light'nings of his eye.   *P. P.* 24.

No pitying heart, no eye, afford A tear *Bard* 65.

Her eye proclaims her of the Briton-Line;
         Bard 116.

Rapture . . . Waves in the eye of Heav'n
         Bard 124.

Marking with indignant eye   *Owen* 35.

pious drops the closing eye requires;   *El.* 90.

Whom meaner Beauties eye askance,   *L. S.* 27.

thy judging eye, The flow'r unheeded shall descry,
         Inst. 71.

With watchful eye and dauntless mien.   *Inst.* 90.

you spied a tear stand in her eye,   *Agr.* 10.

Oped his young eye to bear . . . greatness;
         Agr. 45.

the eye of Rome, And the Prætorian camp
         Agr. 116.

Let majesty . . . lighten from thy eye: *Agr.* 146.

cool injurious eye of frozen kindness. *Agr.* 10.

yielding modesty, And oft reverted eye, *Agr.* 198.

expire beneath the eye of day ?   *E. G.* 67.

Then, with a tempest whirl, and wary eye, *Stat.*[2] 8.

Then with unrelenting Eye   *Dante* 82.

Eye-balls.

Where his glowing eye-balls turn,   *Owen* 31.

Eyed. *See also* **Blue-eyed, Bright-eyed, Soft-eyed.**

haply eyed at distance Some edileship,   *Agr.* 39.

Eyeless.

The eyeless Cyclops heav'd the craggy rock;
         Stat.[2] 19.

Eyes.

emerald eyes, She saw;   *Cat* 11.

Presumptuous Maid ! with eyes intent
         Cat Whar. 25.

Not all that tempts your wand'ring eyes *Cat* 40.

Closed his eyes in endless night.   *P. P.* 102.

Yet oft before his infant eyes   *P. P.* 118.

Before his visionary eyes   *P. P. MS.* 118.

With haggard eyes the Poet stood;   *Bard* 18.

Dear, as the light that visits these sad eyes,
         Bard 40.

They melt, they vanish from my eyes. *Bard* 104.

Eyes that glow, and fangs, that grin;   *Odin* 10.

Till full before his fearless eyes   *Odin* 15.

Knowledge to their eyes her ample page *El.* 49.

read their hist'ry in a nation's eyes,   *El.* 64.

With whistful eyes pursue the setting sun.
         El. Mas. 120.

To celebrate her eyes, her air —   *L. S.* 33.

'Gainst four such eyes were no protection.
         L. S. 96.

riveted His eyes in fearful extasy: *Agr.* 170.

A different Object do these Eyes require: *West* 6.

gospel-light first dawn'd from Bullen's eyes.
         E. G. 109.

descries With forward and reverted eyes. *Vic.* 28.

She eyes the clear chrystalline well,   *Vic.* 55.

A child, the darling of his parents' eyes: *Child* 2.

With eyes of flame, and cool undaunted breast,
         Williams 9.

— and his eyes are so lewd!   *C. C.* 8.

By residence, by marriage, and sore eyes? *Shak.* 12.

Unpeopled monast'ries delude our eyes, *View* 15.

To close my dull eyes when I see it returning;
         Am. Lines 4.

All eyes were bent on his experienced hand,
         Stat.[1] 34.

before the warriors' eyes . . . the waves disparted rise;   *Tasso* 39.

And struggles to elude my longing Eyes, *Prop.*[3] 24.

then on my Children's Eyes . . . my Sight I fix'd,   *Dante* 52.

my other three before my Eyes Died *Dante* 75.

Eyesight.

for then Hunger had reft my Eye-sight *Dante* 79.

F.

†F follows fast the fair —   *Ch. Cr.* 15.

Fable.

The power of Magick was no fable.   *L. S.* 78.

Fabled.

If realms beneath those fabled torments know,
                                                    Prop.[2] 39.

Fabric.

Sinks the fabric of the world.   *Odin* 94.
the human fabric from the birth Imbibes *E. G.* 84.
How flames . . . Shall sink this beauteous fabric
    of the world;   *Prop.*[2] 28.

Face.

The fair round face,   *Cat* 8.
did unveil Her aweful face: *P. P.* 87.
Her lyon-port, her awe-commanding face,
                                                    Bard 117.
The ghostly Prudes with hagged face   *L. S.* 129.
face the rigour Of bleak Germania's snows.
                                                    Agr. 109.
equal Justice with unclouded Face   *E. G.* 15.
where the face of nature laughs around, *E. G.* 70.
When sly Jemmy Twitcher had smugg'd up his
    face,   *C. C.* 1.
She had a bad face   *Mrs. Keene* 2.
How riseing winds the face of Ocean sweep,
                                                    Prop.[2] 23.
†Bright beaming, as the Evening-star, her face;
                                                    Ch. Cr. 8.
†the perks upon your face,   *Ch. Cr.* 33.

Faces.

in four Faces saw my own Despair reflected,
                                                    Dante 62.

Facing.

Facing to the northern clime, . . . he traced
                                                    Odin 21.

Fade.

As Lamps, . . . Fade and expire   *E. G.* 67.

Faded.

Envy wan, and faded Care,   *Eton* 68.
with Flight combined, And sorrow's faded form,
                                                    Bard 62.

Fades.

Now fades the glimmering landscape   *El.* 5.

Fail.

resentment cannot fail to raise   *Agr.* 25.
e'en Magic here must fail,   *Prop.*[3] 85.

Faint.

†Then one faint glimpse of Queen Elizabeth;
                                                    Ch. Cr. 10.

Fainter.

The watery glimmerings of a fainter day *Tasso* 45.

Fair.

Fair Venus' train appear,   *Spring* 2.
The fair round face,   *Cat* 8.
Fair laughs the Morn,   *Bard* 71.
Fair Science frown'd not on his . . . birth,
                                                    El. 119.
With shows of fair obeisance;   *Agr.* 102.
fair befall the victors.   *Agr.* 153.

Dispel, my fair, with smiles, the tim'rous cloud
                                                    Agr. 193.
Young Williams fought for England's fair renown;
                                                    Williams 2.
our master's temper natural Was fashion'd fair
                                                    Shak. 10.
Love and the Fair were   *Prop.*[3] 107.
†Queen Esther next — how fair e'en after death,
                                                    Ch. Cr. 9.
†F follows fast the fair —   *Ch. Cr.* 15.

Fairer.

A fairer flower will never bloom again: *Child* 4.
Tho' wiser than Nestor And fairer than Esther,
                                                    Ext. Keene 3.

Fairest.

Owen . . . Fairest flower of Roderic's stem,
                                                    Owen 3.

Fairy.

Truth severe, by fairy Fiction [Fairy-Fiction,
    Lett.[1]] drest.   *Bard* 127.
The Huntingdons . . . Employ'd the power of
    Fairy hands   *L. S.* 4.

Faith.

Revere his Consort's faith,   *Bard* 89.
Affection warm, and faith sincere, . . . were
    there.   *Clerke* 5.

Faithful. *See also* **Ever-faithful.**

Fierce War, and faithful Love,   *Bard* 126.
faithful to her wonted Fires.   *El.* Dods. 92.
the Mistress of my faithful breast,   *Prop.*[3] 71.

Falchion. *See* **Faulchion.**

Fall.

Sweet music's melting fall,   *Inst.* 63.
Let me not fall alone; but crush   *Agr.* 186.
And I, . . . That live to . . . sing their fall.
                                                    Hoel 24.
Turrets and arches nodding to their fall, *View* 14.
ere it precipitates its fall   *Stat.*[2] 15.
Or if I fall the Victim   *Prop.*[3] 77.
I saw 'em fall;   *Dante* 76.

Fallen. *See* **New-fallen.**

False.

one false step is ne'er retriev'd,   *Cat* 38.

Falsehood.

The stings of Falshood those shall try, *Eton* 75.

Fame.

Revere his Consort's faith, his Father's fame,
                                                    Bard 89.
The place of fame and elegy supply: *El.* 82.
to Fortune and to Fame unknown.   *El.* 118.
Fame, in the shape of Mr. Purt, Had told *L. S.* 41.
he liv'd unknown To fame, or fortune: *Agr.* 39.
the frivolous tongue of giddy fame   *Agr.* 167.
To censure cold, and negligent of fame, *Bent.* 10.
foremost in the dangerous paths of fame,
                                                    Williams 1.
Thee too the Muse should consecrate to Fame,
                                                    Prop.[3] 53.
Happy the Youth, and not unknown to Fame,
                                                    Prop.[3] 65.

Family.

The painful family of Death,	*Eton* 83.
The trembling family they daunt,	*L. S.* 57.

Famine.

Fell Thirst and Famine scowl	*Bard* 81.
Famine at feasts, and thirst amid the stream;	*Prop.*[2] 47.
Here Mutina from flames and famine free,	*Prop.*[3] 43.
the Tower of Famine hight	*Dante* 24.

Famished.

The famish'd Eagle screams,	*Bard* 38.

Fan.

†a Sonnet On Chloe's Fan, or Cælia's Bonnet.	*Ode* 36.

Fancied.

What fancied Zone can circumscribe the soul,	*E. G.* 73.

Fancies.

Mutt'ring his wayward fancies	*El.* 106.

Fancy.

Gay hope is theirs by fancy fed,	*Eton* 41.
Bright-eyed Fancy hov'ring o'er	*P. P.* 108.
yet still to fancy new,	*Ign.* 33.
mends the Plan their Fancy draws,	*E. G.* 32.

Fancy's.

dream, in fancy's airy colouring wrought	*Bent.* 7.
†And variegated Fancy's seen	*Ode* 17.

Fanes.

And bad these awful fanes and turrets rise,	*Inst.* 53.
Ye gothic fanes, and antiquated towers,	*Ign.* 2.
Here mouldering fanes and battlements arise,	*View* 13.

Fangs.

with unrelenting fangs, That tear'st	*Bard* 57.
Eyes that glow, and fangs, that grin;	*Odin* 10.
The hungry Pack their sharp-set Fangs embrued.	*Dante* 40.

Fanned.

Tho' fann'd by Conquest's crimson wing	*Bard* 3.

Fans.

†With Fans and Flounces, Fringe and Furbelows.	*Ch. Cr.* 18.

Fantastic.

beech That wreathes its old fantastic roots	*El.* 102.
†All with fantastic clews, fantastic clothes,	*Ch. Cr.* 17.

Far.

Till o'er the eastern cliffs from far	*P. P. MS.* 52.
Far from the sun and summer gale,	*P. P.* 83.
Beneath the Good how far — but far above the Great.	*P. P.* 123.
Far, far aloof th' affrighted ravens sail;	*Bard* 37.
Far and wide the notes prolong.	*F. S.* 60.
Far from the madding crowd's ignoble strife,	*El.* 73.
Imp . . . Who prowled the country far and near,	*L. S.* 45.
In cloisters dim, far from the haunts of Folly,	*Inst.* 33.

Thus far we're safe.	*Agr.* 188.
sees far off with an indignant groan,	*E. G.* 62.
Far below, the crowd.	*Vic.* 57.
Far better scenes than these had blest our view,	*View* 19.
When blazing 'gainst the sun it shines from far,	*Stat.*[1] 30.
The orb . . . Far overleaps all bound,	*Stat.*[2] 12.
Scarce the hoarse waves from far were heard to roar,	*Tasso* 6.
far less shall be Our Suffering,	*Dante* 65.
†while different far, Rests in Retirement,	*Ch. Cr.* 53.

Farewell.

the Woodlark piped her farewell Song,	*El. Mas.* 119.

Farmer. *See* **Country-farmer.**

Farther.

No farther seek his merits to disclose,	*El.* 125.

Fasces.

Submits the fasces of her sway,	*Inst.* 86.

Fashion.

†See Folly, Fashion, Foppery, straight appear,	*Ch. Cr.* 16.

Fashioned.

our master's temper natural Was fashion'd fair	*Shak.* 10.

Fast.

Fast by th' umbrageous vale lull'd to repose,	*Prop.*[2] 3.
†F follows fast the fair	*Ch. Cr.* 15.

Fastening.

the dreadful Clash of Bars, And fast'ning Bolts:	*Dante* 52.

Fat.

For thee fat Nanny sighs,	*Com. Lines* 6.
He eat a fat goose,	*Ep. Keene* 2.

Fatal.

Vocal no more, since Cambria's fatal day,	*Bard* 27.
House . . . From whence one fatal morning issues	*L. S.* 22.

Fate.

Malignant Fate sat by, and smil'd	*Cat* 28.
The Ministers of human fate,	*Eton* 56.
why should they know their fate?	*Eton* 95.
sad refuge from the storms of Fate!	*P. P.* 45.
Beyond the limits of a vulgar fate,	*P. P.* 122.
Secure of Fate, the Poet stood,	*Bard Lett.*[1] 18.
to sudden fate . . . Half of thy heart we consecrate.	*Bard* 97.
As the paths of fate we tread,	*F. S.* 29.
Fate demands a nobler head;	*F. S.* 43.
say, . . . Who the Author of his fate.	*Odin* 54.
linger in the gloomy Walks of Fate:	*El. Mas.* 80.
Some kindred spirit . . . inquire thy fate,	*El.* 96.
to know the fate Impending o'er your son:	*Agr.* 65.
your injur'd shades demand my fate,	*Agr.* 184.
thro' Ages by what Fate confin'd	*E. G.* 38.
fir'd by Mnestheus' fate,	*Stat.*[2] 4.
For adverse fate the captive chief has hurl'd	*Tasso* 33.

Nor lofty Carthage struggleing with her Fate.
*Prop.*³ 40.
Or if, alas! it be my Fate			*Prop.*³ 69.
Oped the dark Veil of Fate.			*Dante* 28.

Fates.
The different doom our Fates assign.	*Bard* 140.
When then my Fates			*Prop.*³ 99.

Father.
Say, father Thames,			*Eton* 21.
The Father of the powerful spell.		*Odin* 12.
The bosom of his Father and his God. *El.* 128.
Father, why, why do you gaze so sternly ? *Dante* 56.

Father's.
Revere his Consort's faith, his Father's fame,
Bard 89.
Her infant image . . . Sits smiling on a father's
woe:				*Clerke* 10.

Fathers.
And mitred fathers in long order go:	*Inst.* 38.

Faulchion.
Each her thundering faulchion wield;	*F. S.* 62.

Fault.
Nor you, ye Proud, impute to These the fault,
El. 37.
Forgive, ye Proud, th' involuntary Fault,
El. Dods., Pem., Eg., Mas. 37.

Faults.
†Buzzing with all their parent Faults;	*Ode* 46.

Favor.
in the sunshine Of thy full favour;	*Agr.* 148.
I favour her repose.			*Prop.*³ 18.

Favorite.
A Fav'rite has no friend !			*Cat* 36.
What favourite has a friend ? *Cat* Wal., Dods. 36.
near his fav'rite tree;			*El.* 110.

Favour, Favourite. *See* **Favor, Favorite.**

Fear.
Disdainful Anger, pallid Fear,		*Eton* 63.
never can he fear a vulgar fate, *P. P.* MS. 122.
Marking . . . Fear to stop,		*Owen* 36.
For folks in fear are apt to pray		*L. S.* 90.
Nor fear the rocks, nor seek the shore: *Inst.* 92.
school'd by fear To bow the supple knee, *Agr.* 100.
check their . . . Hopes with chilling Fear,
E. G. 20.
Then he shambles and straddles so oddly — I
fear —				*C. C.* 9.
mariners, though shipwreck'd, fear to land.
View Nich. 8.
In vain the nations with officious fear Their cym-
bals toss,				*Stat.*¹ 56.

Feared.
Whether she fear'd, or wish'd to be pursued.
Agr. 199.

Fearful.
And snatch a fearful joy.			*Eton* 40.
riveted His eyes in fearful extasy:	*Agr.* 170.

Fearless.
Till full before his fearless eyes		*Odin* 15.
Fearless in long excursion loves to glide, *Tasso* 21.

Fears.
Of Horrour . . . and thrilling Fears,	*P. P.* 93.
To save thy secret soul from nightly fears,
Bard 7.
Forgive your servant's fears,		*Agr.* 24.
Hence rise my fears.			*Agr.* 56.
My love, my fears for him,		*Agr.* 181.
alas, my fears! Can powers immortal	*Ign.* 25.
Cease, my doubts, my fears to move,	*Song* 11.
but first dismiss your fears;		*Tasso* 36.
Or are our fears th' enthusiast's empty dream,
*Prop.*² 48.
Sad with the Fears of Sleep,		*Dante* 49.

Feast.
he yet may share the feast:		*Bard* 79.
Yet Nature could not furnish out the feast,
View 11.
hasty to renew The hellish Feast,	*Dante* 84.

Feasts.
Famine at feasts, and thirst amid the stream;
*Prop.*² 47.

Feather-cinctured.
Their feather-cinctur'd Chiefs,		*P. P.* 62.

Feathered.
thy magic lulls the feather'd king	*P. P.* 21.

Fed.
Gay hope is theirs by fancy fed,		*Eton* 41.
With many a foul and midnight murther fed,
Bard 88.

Feeble.
Man's feeble race what Ills await,	*P. P.* 42.
Frisking ply their feeble feet,		*Vic.* 10.
permit me raise My feeble Voice,		*Prop.*³ 32.

Feed.
genial Juice retains Their Roots to feed, *E. G.* 4.

Feel.
I feel the gales,				*Eton* 15.
What others are, to feel,			*Adv.* 48.
Let him feel Before he sees me.		*Agr.* 163.
Can powers immortal feel the force of years?
Ign. 26.
With Sense to feel, with Mem'ry	*E. G.* 30.
All angry heaven inflicts, or hell can feel,
*Prop.*² 45.
You whose young bosoms feel a nobler flame
*Prop.*² 53.

Feeling.
if to some feeling breast			*Bent.* 25.

Feels.
the fire it feels not.			*Agr.* 84.
The Widow feels thee in her aching hip;
Com. Lines 5.

Feet.
The slipp'ry verge her feet beguil'd,	*Cat* 29.
glance their many-twinkling feet.	*P. P.* 35.
heap'd his master's feet around,		*Owen* 29.
Frisking ply their feeble feet;		*Vic.* 10.
low as his feet there flows A vestment *Tasso* 13.
When Gaddo, at my Feet out-stretch'd, *Dante* 73.

Feign.
And realis'd the beauties which we feign: *View* 20.

Fell.

Despair, and fell Disease, and ghastly Poverty:
Adv. 40.
Fell Thirst and Famine scowl *Bard* 81.

Fellow-swains.

Ah! say, Fellow-swains, how these symptoms befell me? *Am. Lines* 7.

Felon.

From his dire Food the griesly Fellon raised
Dante 1.

Felt.

The Poet felt a strange disorder: *L. S.* 82.
She felt the wound she left behind, *Clerke* 8.
agony of mind Was felt for him *Clerke* MS. 11.
Whose heart has never felt a second flame.
*Prop.*³ 66.
†They who just have felt the flame *Rond.* 21.

Female.

Thy Joys no glittering female meets, *Spring* 45.
What female heart can gold despise? *Cat* 23.
†In shriller notes Q like a female squeaks;
Ch. Cr. 48.

Fenced.

The bard, . . . Had in imagination fenc'd him,
L. S. 114.

Fertile.

Soil, tho' fertile, will not teem in vain, *E. G.* 6.

Festal.

rise, To hail their Fitzroy's festal morning *Inst.* 54.

Fester.

The Bishop of Chester, . . . If you scratch him
will fester. *Ext. Keene* 4.

Fetters.

My soul in Bacchus' pleasing fetters bound;
*Prop.*² 8.

Few.

There sit . . . The few, whom genius gave to
shine *Inst.* 16.
Few were the days allotted to his breath; *Child* 5.
resolution To smuggle a few [some, MS.] years,
View 3.

Fib.

with many an artful fib, *L. S.* 113.

Fickle.

her fickle Sexe's fond Mistake, *Prop.*³ 73.
†but fickle throw my trains . . . into the Fire:
Ode 33.

Fiction.

Truth severe, by fairy Fiction drest. *Bard* 127.

Fidget.

Cried the square Hoods in woful fidget *L. S.* 135.

Field.

Wading through th' ensanguin'd field, *F. S.* 30.
Hurry, hurry To the field. *F. S.* 64.
And scorn'd repose when Britain took the field.
Williams 8.
And furthest send its weight athwart the field,
*Stat.*¹ 2.
With such a gleam affrights Pangæa's field,
*Stat.*¹ 29.

Fields.

Ah, fields belov'd in vain, *Eton* 12.
Fields, that cool Ilissus laves, *P. P.* 68.
Wide o'er the fields of Glory *P. P.* 104.
The little Tyrant of his fields *El.* 58.
chearful Fields resume their green Attire: *West* 4.
The Fields to all their wonted Tribute bear
West 11.
Her boasted Titles and her golden Fields; *E. G.* 53.

Fiend.

so grinned the brawling fiend, *Toph.* 1.

Fierce.

Till fierce Hyperion from afar *P. P.* MS. 51.
Fierce War, and faithful Love, *Bard* 126.
By *Odin's* fierce embrace comprest, *Odin* 64.
There . . . Conflict fierce, and Ruin wild,
Owen 38.
ev'ry fierce tumultuous Passion *El. Mas.* 82.
The drawing-room of fierce Queen Mary.
L. S. 108.
fierce resentment cannot fail to raise *Agr.* 25.
Fierce nations own'd her . . . might, *Ign.* 29.
While Prows, that late in fierce Encounter mett,
*Prop.*³ 51.

Fiercer.

opener skies, and Suns of fiercer flame *E. G.* 64.

Fiery.

As the thunder's fiery stroke, *Conan* 7.

Fifty.

When he had fifty winters o'er him, *L. S.* 10.

Fight.

the long Iliad of the amorous Fight. *Prop.*³ 26.
the Soldier of the Fight, *Prop.*³ 60.

Fights.

Still may his Bard in softer fights engage;
*Prop.*¹ 3.

Filch.

Did not Israel filch from the Egyptians of old
C. C. 25.

Filching.

And filching and lying, and Newgate-bird tricks;
C. C. 17.

Filial.

Prostrate with filial reverence I *Ign.* 10.

Fill.

Poverty, to fill the band, *Eton* 88.
Fill high the sparkling bowl, *Bard* 77.
and fill their verdant Veins. *E. G.* 4.

Filled.

his jaws, with carnage fill'd, *Odin* 7.

Fills.

Whate'er with copious train its channel fills,
Tasso 53.

Find.

How rude so e'er th' exterior Form we find,
E. G. 26.
And find a Cure for every Ill, *Prop.*³ 80.
such as mought entrance find within *Dante* 60.
†Late to find it: — and, again,
Rond. 3, 11, 19, 27, 35.
†in vain you think to find them *Ch. Cr.* 13.

Fine.
Very good claret and fine Champaign.
Impr. Vane 2.

Finished.
He finish'd: Then with unrelenting Eye *Dante* 82.

Fire.
with a Master's hand, and Prophet's fire, *Bard* 21.
Some heart once pregnant with celestial fire;
El. 46.
in thy lineaments we trace A Tudor's fire, *Inst.* 70.
bid it fire A thousand haughty hearts, *Agr.* 16.
glows with the pure Julian fire, *Agr.* 50.
thinks to quench the fire *Agr.* 84.
redning Phœbus lifts his golden Fire: *West* 2.
huddle up in fogs the dang'rous fire. *Ign.* 22.
the fire that animates our frame; *E. G.* 65.
Rise, my soul! on wings of fire, *Vic.* 17.
Better the roast meat from the fire to save,
Shak. 18.
Purg'd by the sword, and purified by fire,
View 21.
†throw . . . half an act into the Fire: *Ode* 34.

Fired.
By Phlegyas warn'd, and fir'd by Mnestheus' fate,
*Stat.*² 4.

Fires.
this fires the veins, *Eton* 85.
bright track, that fires the western skies,
Bard 103.
in our Ashes live [glow, Pem., Eg.] their wonted
Fires. *El.* 92.
buried ashes glow with social fires. *El. Mas.* 108.
That monthly waning hides her paly fires,
*Prop.*² 20.
Whence the seven Sisters' congregated fires,
*Prop.*² 35.
Pangs without respite, fires that ever glow,
*Prop.*² 40.
She half accepts, and half rejects, my Fires,
*Prop.*³ 22.

Firmly.
Firmly he plants each knee, *Stat.*¹ 47.

First.
A whisker first and then a claw, *Cat* 20.
When first thy Sire to send on earth Virtue . . .
design'd *Adv.* 9.
when they first were open'd *P. P. MS.* 118.
gospel-light first dawn'd from Bullen's eyes.
E. G. 109.
o'er the crested pride Of the first Edward
Bard 10.
What, in the very first beginning! *L. S.* 17.
The first came cap-a-pee from France *L. S.* 25.
On the first marching *L. S.* 69.
where . . . First the genuine ardour stole. *Inst.* 22.
There first in blood his infant honour seal'd;
Williams 6.
And first to Ascalon their steps they bend,
Tasso 3.
but first dismiss your fears; *Tasso* 36.
That first, eternal, universal Cause; *Prop.*² 18.
They wept, and first my little dear Anselmo
Cried, *Dante* 55.

†First when Pastorals I read, *Ode* 19.
†Whose influence first bid it live. *Ode* 54.
†First to love, — and then to part, *Rond.* 1.

Fish.
What Cat's averse to fish? *Cat* 24.

Fit.
A sudden fit of ague shook him, *L. S.* 119.

Fits.
As fits the daughter of Germanicus. *Agr.* 6.

Fitting.
Now fitting to his gripe and nervous arm,
*Stat.*¹ 43.

Fitzroy's.
rise, To hail their Fitzroy's festal morning *Inst.* 54.

Fix.
Fix and improve the . . . Arts of Peace: *E. G.* 41.

Fixed.
gloomy Sway have fix'd her Empire there,
E. G. 19.
transitory thought Fix'd by his touch *Bent.* 6.
On this congenial spot he fix'd his choice;
View 5.
Where fix'd in wonder stood the warlike pair,
Tasso 25.
Speechless my Sight I fix'd, nor wept, *Dante* 53.

Flagging.
With ruffled plumes, and flagging wing: *P. P.* 22.

Flame.
and Freedom's holy flame. *P. P.* 65.
incense kindled at the Muse's flame. *El.* 72.
opener skies, and suns of fiercer flame *E. G.* 64.
catch a lustre from his genuine flame. *Bent.* 12.
With eyes of flame, and cool undaunted breast,
Williams 9.
And rubies flame, with sapphire's heavenly blue,
Tasso 68.
You whose young bosoms feel a nobler flame
*Prop.*² 53.
Whose heart has never felt a second flame.
*Prop.*³ 66.
†They who just have felt the flame *Rond.* 21.

Flame's.
As the flame's devouring force; *Conan* 5.

Flames.
wrapt in flames, . . . Sinks the fabric of the
world. *Odin* 93.
And when, our flames commission'd to destroy,
*Prop.*² 11.
How flames . . . Shall sink this beauteous fabric
*Prop.*² 27.
Here Mutina from flames and famine free,
*Prop.*³ 43.

Flaming.
the flaming bounds of Place and Time: *P. P.* 98.
corse . . . Flaming on the fun'ral pile. *Odin* 70.

Flanks.
and in their trembling Flanks *Dante* 39.

Flash.
Break out, and flash a momentary day, *Ign.* 20.

Flashed.

The foremost He Flash'd to pursue,   *Dante* 36.

Flattering.

The summer Friend, the flatt'ring Foe; *Adv.* 22.

Flattery.

Can . . . Flatt'ry soothe the dull . . . ear of
death?   *El.* 44.

Nor . . . Let painted Flatt'ry hide her serpent-
train.   *Inst.* 8.

Flattery's.

the grateful steam Of flattery's incense, *Agr.* 35.

Flavor.

Imbibes a flavour of its parent earth, *E. G.* 85.

Flavour. *See* **Flavor.**

Flaxen.

their flaxen tresses tear, And snowy veils, *Odin* 77.

Fled.

Is the sable Warriour fled?   *Bard* 67.

Fleet.

with fleet and equal Speed   *Dante* 31.

Fleeting.

Back to its mansion call the fleeting breath?
                                       El. 42.

Flesh.

These miserable Limbs with Flesh you cloath'd;
                                       Dante 67.

Flew.

Out of the window, whisk, they flew, *L. S.* 79.

From fortune, pleasure, science, love, he flew,
                                       Williams 7.

Sure flew the disc from his unerring hand,
                                       Stat.[1] 39.

Flies.

happiness too swiftly flies,   *Eton* 97.

Sings in its rapid way, and strengthens as it flies;
                                       Stat.[1] 50.

†Judgment from the Harvest flies   *Ode* 9.

†But, my Dear, these Flies, they say, *Ode* 49.

Flight.

Amazement in his van, with Flight combined,
                                       Bard 61.

Save where the beetle wheels his droning flight,
                                       El. 7.

Flimsy.

†Expand their wings of flimzey Gold.   *Ode* 48.

Flimzey. *See* **Flimsy.**

Fling.

Their gather'd fragrance fling.   *Spring* 10.

Flings.

she . . . no venal incense flings;   *Inst.* 79.

From his . . . bosom life and verdure flings
                                       E. G. 102.

And sing with what a careless Grace she flings
                                       Prop.[3] 15.

Flinty.

a niggard Earth, Whose flinty Bosom   *E. G.* 2.

With . . . plough to quell the flinty ground,
                                       E. G. 91.

Flirt.

They flirt, they sing, they laugh, they tattle,
                                       L. S. 58.

Float.

Eager to . . . float amid the liquid noon:
                                       Spring 27.

arms sublime, that float upon the air, *P. P.* 38.

snowy veils, that float in air.   *Odin* 78.

Floats.

on frail floats to distant cities ride, *E. G.* 106.

Whate'er . . . Floats into Lakes,   *Tasso* 54.

Flocks.

New-born flocks . . . ply . . . feeble feet; *Vic.* 9.

The Shepherd of his flocks,   *Prop.*[3] 60.

Flood.

Eight times emerging from the flood,   *Cat* 31.

o'er old Conway's foaming flood,   *Bard* 16.

To-morrow he repairs the golden flood, *Bard* 137.

Backward Meinai rolls his flood;   *Owen* 28.

rushy Camus' slowly-winding flood   *Ign.* 3.

the torrent's swift-descending flood, *E. G.* 92.

When thwart the road a River roll'd its flood
                                       Tasso 7.

The flood on either hand its billows rears,
                                       Tasso 41.

Of many a flood they view'd the secret source,
                                       Tasso 51.

Floods.

And winter binds the floods in icy chains,
                                       Tasso 18.

Floor.

they . . . Run hurry-skurry round the floor,
                                       L. S. 63.

Florentine.

but a Florentine my Ear, . . . declares thee.
                                       Dante 11.

Flounces.

†With Fans and Flounces, Fringe and Furbelows.
                                       Ch. Cr. 18.

Flourish.

†Bids the poetick Spirit flourish;   *Ode* 14.

Flow.

the tear it forc'd to flow;   *Eton* 77.

a thousand rills . . . as they flow.   *P. P.* 6.

Their raptures now that wildly flow, *No* . . .
    morrow know;   *Vic.* 25.

Further they pass, where ripening minerals flow,
                                       Tasso 57.

She . . . gives the Lay to flow.   *Prop.*[3] 6.

Flowed.

Where flow'd the widest stream he took his stand;
                                       Stat.[1] 38.

Flower.

Owen . . . Fairest flower of Roderic's stem,
                                       Owen 3.

many a flower is born to blush unseen, *El.* 55.

thy judging eye, The flow'r unheeded shall descry,   *Inst.* 72.

A fairer flower will never bloom again: *Child* 4.

Ah! what means yon violet flower !   *Song* 3.

Ye Argive flower, ye warlike band,   *Stat.*[1] 16.

Floweret. *See* Flowret.

Flowers.

The long-expecting flowers, *Spring* 3.
China's . . . art had dy'd The azure flowers,
         Cat 3.
whose flowers among Wanders the . . . Thames
 along   *Eton* 8.
The laughing flowers, that round them blow,
         P. P. 5.
Flatt'ry hide her serpent-train in flowers. *Inst.* 8.
Let on this head unfadeing flowers reside,
         Prop.[2] 9.
†But, tho' Flowers his ardour raise, *Ode* 15.

Flowery.

nurs'd in ease And pleasure's flow'ry lap?
         Agr. 99.

Flown.

On hasty wings thy youth is flown; *Spring* 48.

Flowret.

The meanest flowret of the vale, *Vic.* 49.

Flows.

Near the source whence Pleasure flows; *Vic.* 54.
low as his feet there flows A vestment *Tasso* 13.
Where Aganippe warbles as it flows; *Prop.*[2] 4.

Flung.

and scornful flung th' unheeded weight *Stat.*[1] 21.
His vigorous arm he tried before he flung, *Stat.*[2] 6.

Flushed.

Flush'd with mirth and hope they burn: *Hoel* 19.

Flutter.

The Gay . . . flutter thro' life's little day,
         Spring 36.

Fly.

what art thou? A solitary fly! *Spring* 44.

Fly, *vb.*

Whisp'ring pleasure as they fly, *Spring* 8.
they that creep, and they that fly, *Spring* 33.
the slumbers . . . That fly *Eton* 50.
fly Self-pleasing Folly's idle brood, *Adv.* 17.
Let us go, and let us fly, *F. S.* 26.
Marking . . . shame to fly, *Owen* 36.
fly These hated walls that seem to mock *Agr.* 155.
They follow Pleasure, and they fly from Pain;
         E. G. 31.
Must sick'ning virtue fly the tainted ground?
         E. G. 71.
Saw the snowy whirlwind fly; *Vic.* 22.

Flying.

Hurls at their flying rear, his . . . shafts of war,
         P. P. MS. 53.
Or urge the flying ball? *Eton* 30.

Foam.

from his jaws, . . . Foam and human gore distill'd: *Odin* 8.

Foaming.

o'er old Conway's foaming flood, *Bard* 16.

Foe.

What Cat 's a foe to fish? *Cat* Dods. 24.
The summer Friend, the flatt'ring Foe; *Adv.* 22.
Twined with her blushing foe, *Bard* 92.

By Fraud elude, by Force repel the Foe,
         E. G. 35.
The crimson harvest of the foe. *Conan* 10.

Foes.

Thy leaden ægis 'gainst our ancient foes? *Ign.* 14.
Foes to the gentler genius of the plain: *E. G.* 89.
the bull, . . . On surrounding foes advance?
         Caradoc 3.
rode Amain, my deadly Foes! *Dante* 34.

Fogs.

huddle up in fogs the dang'rous fire. *Ign.* 22.

Folds.

drowsy tinklings lull the distant folds: *El.* 8.

Folio.

creased, like dogs-ears, in a folio. *L. S.* 68.

Folks.

For folks in fear are apt to pray *L. S.* 90.

Follow.

They follow Pleasure, and . . . fly from Pain;
         E. G. 31.
†Slow follow all the quality of State, *Ch. Cr.* 51.

Follows.

But the Master of Emmanuel Follows them like
 a spaniel;   *Satire* 26.
†F follows fast the fair — ₀*Ch. Cr.* 15.

Folly.

'T is folly to be wise. *Eton* 100.
In cloisters dim, far from the haunts of Folly,
         Inst. 33.
†See Folly, Fashion, Foppery, straight appear,
         Ch. Cr. 16.

Folly's.

fly Self-pleasing Folly's idle brood *Adv.* 18.

Fond.

The fond complaint, my Song, disprove, *P. P.* 46.
Fond impious Man, think'st thou, *Bard* 135.
On some fond breast the parting soul relies,
         El. 89.
With fond reluctance, yielding modesty, *Agr.* 197.
weeping I forsook thy fond embrace. *Ign.* 12.
fond Instruction on the growing Powers *E. G.* 13.
Condemns her fickle Sexe's fond Mistake,
         Prop.[3] 73.

Font.

Euphrates' font, and Nile's mysterious head.
         Tasso 56.

Food.

From his dire Food the griesly Fellon raised
         Dante 1.
now the Hour Of timely Food approach'd;
         Dante 50.

Foolery.

†In ductile Lines of Foolery: *Ode* 40.

Foot.

at the foot of yonder nodding beech, *El.* 101.

Footsteps.

little Footsteps lightly print the Ground.
     El. Pem. 120; Mas. 140.
With hasty footsteps brush the dews away
         El. Mas. 115.

Foppery.

†See Folly, Fashion, Foppery, straight appear,
       Ch. Cr. 16.

For, *omitted.*

Forbad.

Their lot forbad: *El.* 65.
Forbad to wade through slaughter   *El.* 67.

Forbade. *See* **Forbad.**

Forbid.

With damp, cold touch forbid it to aspire, *Ign.* 21.

Forbids.

The Soil, . . . Forbids her Gems to swell, *E. G.* 7.

Force.

This the force of Eirin hiding,   *Owen* 11.
in Armenia quell the Parthian force   *Agr.* 111.
Can powers immortal feel the force of years?
       Ign. 26.
by Force repel the Foe,   *E. G.* 35.
Force and hardy Deeds of Blood   *E. G.* 44.
As lawless force from confidence will grow
       E. G. 98.
As the flame's devouring force;   *Conan* 5.
Collecting all his force, the circle sped; *Stat.*[1] 48.
True to the mighty arm that gave it force,
       Stat.[2] 11.
Swoll'n with new force,   *Tasso* 10.
What wondrous force the solid earth can move,
       Prop.[2] 30.

Forced.

the tear it forc'd to flow;   *Eton* 77.

Forefathers.

The rude Forefathers of the hamlet   *El.* 16.

Forehead.

If the loose Curls around her Forehead play,
       Prop.[3] 7.

Foreknew.

what my poor Heart Foresaw, foreknew: *Dante* 47.

Foremost.

Who foremost now delight to cleave   *Eton* 25.
Foremost . . . The venerable Marg'ret see!
       Inst. 65.
foremost in the dangerous paths of fame,
       Williams 1.
He their Chief, the foremost He   *Dante* 35.

Foresaw.

what my poor Heart Foresaw, foreknew: *Dante* 47.

Forests.

Chili's boundless forests   *P. P.* 59.

For ever. *See* **Ever.**

Forgetful.

Forgetful of their wintry trance, The Birds . . .
   greet: *Vic.* 11.

Forgetfulness.

to dumb Forgetfulness a prey,   *El.* 85.

Forgive.

Teach me to love and to forgive,   *Adv.* 46.
Forgive, ye Proud, th' involuntary Fault,
     El. Dods., Pem., Eg., Mas. 37.
Forgive your servant's fears,   *Agr.* 24.

Forgot.

The tear forgot   *Eton* 43.
'T is like, thou hast forgot,   *Agr.* 33.
those of Egypt, Have not forgot your sire:
       Agr. 116.

Forgotten. *See* **Long-forgotten.**

Forked.

taught . . . To aim the forked bolt;   *Agr.* 31.

Forlorn.

nor thus forlorn Leave me unbless'd, *Bard* 101.
woeful-wan, like one forlorn,   *El.* 107.

Form.

he . . . bad to form her infant mind. *Adv.* 12.
Thy form benign, oh Goddess, wear, *Adv.* 41.
with Flight combined, And sorrow's faded form,
       Bard 62.
In the midst a Form divine!   *Bard* 115.
How rude so e'er th' exterior Form   *E. G.* 26.
And blended form, with artful strife, *Vic.* 43.
†Maggots too will form and nourish; *Ode* 16.
†In form of Parrot, Pye, or Popinjay. *Ch. Cr.* 42.

Formed.

Transparent birdlime form'd the middle, *L. S.* 83.
Here Holland form'd [took, MS.] the pious resolution   *View* 2.
form'd of polish'd brass.   *Stat.*[1] 8.

Forms.

Two angel forms were seen to glide   *Cat* 14.
shaggy forms o'er ice-built mountains roam,
       P. P. 55.
Such forms, as glitter in the Muse's ray,
       P. P. 119.

Forsook.

But soon his rhetorick forsook him, *L. S.* 117.
weeping I forsook thy fond embrace. *Ign.* 12.

Forth.

Stretch'd forth his little arms,   *P. P.* 88.
Forth from their gloomy mansions creeping
       L. S. 98.
pacing forth With solemn steps   *Inst.* 35.
cast me forth in duty to their lord.   *Agr.* 157.
Let him stand forth   *Stat.*[1] 3.
Phlegyas . . . Call'd forth all the man. *Stat.*[1] 33.

Fortune.

to Fortune and to Fame unknown.   *El.* 118.
he liv'd unknown To fame, or fortune; *Agr.* 39.
He had not the method of making a fortune:
       Char. 2.
From fortune, pleasure, science, love, he flew,
       Williams 7.

Fortune's.

In fortune's varying colours drest: *Spring* 37.

Forward.

descries With forward and reverted eyes. *Vic.* 28.

Fought.

Young Williams fought for England's fair renown;   *Williams* 2.

Foul.

With many a foul and midnight murther fed,
       Bard 88.

Found.

Scatter'd oft . . . are Show'rs of Violets found;
  El. Pem. 118 ; *Mas.* 138.
where unwearied sinews must be found *E. G.* 90.
For Ills unseen what Remedy is found?
  *Prop.*³ 91.
†As H the Hebrew found, *Ch. Cr.* 25.

Fountain.

Ev'ry shade and hallow'd Fountain *P. P.* 75.

Fountains.

Where lie th' eternal fountains of the deep,
  *Prop.*² 24.

Four.

'Gainst four such eyes were no protection.
  L. S. 96.
Four, not less brave, That in Armenia *Agr.* 110.
in four Faces saw my own Despair reflected,
  Dante 62.

Fourth.

yet à fourth Day came *Dante* 72.
The fourth, what Sorrow could not, Hunger did.
  Dante 81.

Foxes.

And foxes stunk and litter'd in St. Paul's.
  View 24.

Fragrance.

Their gather'd fragrance fling. *Spring* 10.
flowers, . . . Drink life and fragrance *P. P.* 6.
The fragrance of its blushing head: *Inst.* 74.
the new Fragrance of the breathing Rose,
  E. G. 56.
The sleeping fragrance from the ground; *Vic.* 6.

Frail.

Some frail memorial . . . erected nigh, *El.* 78.
Spite of her frail companion dauntless goes
  E. G. 76.
on frail floats to distant cities ride, *E. G.* 106.

Frailties.

draw his frailties from their dread abode,
  El. 126.
his frailties there in trembling hope repose,
  El. Mas. 15.

Frame.

the fire that animates our frame; *E. G.* 65.
each Grace adorn'd his frame, *Williams* 3.
†Lightly lambent o'er their frame, *Rond.* 22.

France.

She-Wolf of France, . . . That tear'st *Bard* 57.
The first came cap-a-pee from France *L. S.* 25.

Frantic.

frantic Passions hear thy soft controul. *P. P.* 16.

Fraud.

By Fraud elude, by Force repel the Foe. *E. G.* 35.

Free.

Lo! to be free to die, are mine *Bard* Lett.³ 142.
scatter with a free, though frugal, Hand *E. G.* 17.
Here Mutina from flames and famine free,
  *Prop.*³ 43.

Freed.

Here, freed from pain, . . . lies A child, *Child* 1.

Freedom.

With Freedom by my side, *Inst.* 34.
How shall the spark . . . Blaze into freedom,
  Agr. 129.
European Freedom still withstands *E. G.* 60.

Freedom's.

and Freedom's holy flame. *P. P.* 65.

Frequent.

Sighs sudden and frequent, *Am. Lines* 5.

Fresh.

As waving fresh their gladsome wing, *Eton* 17.

Freshest.

Scatters his freshest, tenderest green. *Vic.* 8.

Frets.

Where Ocean frets beneath the dashing oar,
  *Stat.*² 20.

Fretted.

through the long-drawn isle and fretted vault
  El. 39.
To raise the cieling's fretted height, *L. S.* 5.

Friend.

A Fav'rite has no friend ! *Cat* 36.
The summer Friend, the flatt'ring Foe; *Adv.* 22.
Warm Charity, the gen'ral Friend, *Adv.* 30.
He gain'd from Heav'n . . . a friend. *El.* 124.
A friend, a wife, a mother sleeps: *Clerke* 2.
By them, my friend, my Hoel, died, *Hoel* 6.
Old, and abandon'd by each venal friend,
  View 1.
While frighted prelates bow'd and called him
  friend; *Toph.* 2.
Love, gentle Power! to Peace was e'er a friend;
  *Prop.*¹ 1.

Friends.

Where our Friends the conflict share, *F. S.* 27.
Sylla has his friends, though school'd *Agr.* 100.
Vast, oh my friends, and difficult the toil
  Tasso 27.
A train of mourning Friends attend his Pall,
  *Prop.*³ 97.

Friendship.

Where melancholy friendship bends, and weeps.
  Williams 12.
Nor Mungo's, Rigby's, Bradshaw's friendship
  vain, *View* 18.

Frighted.

While frighted prelates bow'd *Toph.* 2.

Fringe.

†With Fans and Flounces, Fringe and Furbelows.
  Ch. Cr. 18.

Frisking.

Frisking light in frolic measures; *P. P.* 31.
Frisking ply their feeble feet; *Vic.* 10.

Frivolous.

the frivolous tongue of giddy fame *Agr.* 167.

Frolic.

Frisking light in frolic measures; *P. P.* 31.

From, *omitted.*

Front.

the glittering front of war?   *Agr.* 94.
Of those loose Curls, that Ivory front I write;
          *Prop.*³ 11.

Fronts.

Sublime their starry fronts they rear;   *Bard* 112.

Frown.

Scared at thy frown terrific,   *Adv.* 17.
Nor envy dar'd to view him with a frown.
          Williams 4.

Frowned.

and when she frown'd, he died.   *Prop.*³ 108.

Frowning.

now frowning as in Scorn,   *El. Dods.* 105.

Frowns.

a rock, whose haughty brow Frowns   *Bard* 16.
When a boy frowns,   *Agr.* 18.

Froze.

Penury . . . froze the genial current of the soul.
          El. 52.
froze them up with deadly cruelty.   *Agr.* 183.

Frozen.

cool injurious eye of frozen kindness. *Agr.* 162.
And sports and wantons o'er the frozen tide.
          Tasso 22.

Frugal.

scatter with a free, though frugal, Hand
          E. G. 17.

Fruitful.

All that on Granta's fruitful plain . . . bounty
pour'd,   *Inst.* 51.
The fruitful Muse from that auspicious Night
          *Prop.*³ 25.

Fruitless.

long pursues, with fruitless yell, The Father
          Odin 11.
why do I waste the fruitless hours   *Agr.* 154.
Ye unavailing horrors, fruitless crimes ! *Agr.* 177.
I fruitless mourn to him that cannot hear,
          West 13.

Fulfilling.

Her conqu'ring destiny fulfilling,   *L. S.* 26.

Full.

Full many a sprightly race   *Eton* 22.
Till full before his fearless eyes   *Odin* 15.
Full many a gem of purest ray serene,   *El.* 53.
Full many a flower is born   *El.* 55.
Full oft . . . he . . . led the Brawls;   *L. S.* 9.
in the sunshine Of thy full favour;   *Agr.* 148.
Great things and full of wonder . . . I shall un-
fold;   *Tasso* 35.

Full-grown.

A Wolf full-grown;   *Dante* 31.

Full-plumed.

Full-plumed Fancy hov'ring o'er *P. P. MS.* 108.

Fumbling.

From fumbling baronets and poets small,
          Shak. 6.

Fumes.

So from our works sublimer fumes shall rise;
          Shak. 22.

Funeral.

With screaming Horror's funeral cry,   *Adv.* 39.
Low on his [the, MS.] funeral couch he lies!
          Bard 64.
corse . . . Flaming on the fun'ral pile. *Odin* 70.
And wonder at the sudden Funeral. *Prop.*³ 98.

Furbelows.

†With Fans and Flounces, Fringe and Furbelows.
          Ch. Cr. 18.

Furnish.

Nature could not furnish out the feast, *View* 11.

Furrow.

Their furrow oft the stubborn glebe has broke:
          El. 26.

Further.

Nor stopp'd till it had cut the further strand.
          *Stat.*¹ 40.
a River . . . all further çourse withstood;
          Tasso 8.
Further they pass,   *Tasso* 57.

Furthest.

And furthest send its weight   *Stat.*¹ 2.

Fury.

These shall the fury Passions tear,   *Eton* 61.
Has curb'd the fury of his car,   *P. P.* 18.
with fury pale,   *Bard Lett.*¹ 17.
As on the Rhine, when Boreas' fury reigns,
          Tasso 17.

Futurity.

warblings . . . That lost in long futurity expire.
          Bard 134.
the dreadful powers, That read futurity, *Agr.* 65.

Gaddo.

When Gaddo, at my Feet out-stretch'd, *Dante* 73.

Gain.

nor creeping Gain, Dare the Muse's walk to stain,
          Inst. 9.
What the bright reward we gain?   *Inst.* 59.
heart . . . Gain the rough heights,   *Agr.* 53.
Industry and Gain their Vigils keep,   *E. G.* 42.

Gained.

He gain'd from Heav'n . . . a friend. *El.* 124.
They guard . . . what by strength they gain'd?
          E. G. 95.

'Gainst. *See also* Against.

'Gainst graver hours,   *Eton* 33.
'Gainst four such eyes were no protection.
          L. S. 96.
Thy leaden ægis 'gainst our ancient foes? *Ign.* 14.
blazing 'gainst the sun it shines   *Stat.*¹ 30.

Gale. *See also* Summer-gale.

languid Pleasure sighs in every Gale. *E. G.* 45.
The dusky people drive before the gale; *E. G.* 105.
The simplest note that swells the gale, *Vic.* 50.

Gales.

I feel the gales,   *Eton* 15.
A Voice, . . . Gales from blooming Eden bear;
          Bard 132.
Western gales . . . Speak not always winter
past.   *Song* 9.

Gall.

sweets of kindness . . . Rankle to gall; *Agr.* 74.

But may not honey's self be turn'd to gall
Shak. 11.

Gallant.

In gallant trim the gilded Vessel goes; *Bard* 73.

Ah, gallant youth! this marble tells the rest,
Williams 11.

Gallery.

And from the gallery stand peeping: *L. S.* 100.

Gallia.

lilies . . . From haughty Gallia torn, *Inst.* 40.

'Gan. *See also* **Began.**

already 'gan the Dawn To send: *Dante* 25.

Gape.

oh Earth! could'st thou not gape *Dante* 71.

Gaping.

Gor'd with many a gaping wound: *F. S.* 42.

Garb.

Wisdom in sable garb array'd *Adv.* 25.

Robed in the sable garb of woe, *Bard* 17.

Garden.

To a small closet in the garden. *L. S.* 72.

Garlands.

And with her Garlands weave *Prop.*³ 54.

Garnish'd.

visages . . . that garnish'd The drawing-room
L. S. 107.

Gasping.

Each a gasping Warriour's head. *F. S.* 12.

Gate.

Right against the eastern gate, *Odin* 17.

when at the Gate Below I heard *Dante* 50.

Gates.

This can unlock the gates of Joy; *P. P.* 92.

shut the gates of mercy on mankind, *El.* 68.

Gathered.

Their gather'd fragrance fling. *Spring* 10.

Gaunt.

chas'd by Hell-hounds gaunt and bloody *Dante* 30.

Gave.

To thee he gave the heav'nly Birth, *Adv.* 11.

all that wealth e'er gave, *El.* 34.

He gave to Mis'ry all he had, *El.* 123.

There sit . . . The few, whom genius gave to
shine *Inst.* 16.

To her that gave it being, *Agr.* 29.

the world, you gave him, *Agr.* 58.

True to the mighty arm that gave it force, *Stat.*² 11.

my Fates that breath they gave shall claim,
*Prop.*³ 99.

Gave not to know their Sum of Misery, *Dante* 43.

Gay.

Alike the Busy and the Gay *Spring* 35.

Gay hope is theirs *Eton* 41.

On her shadow long and gay Lochlin plows
Owen 13.

Be gay securely; *Agr.* 192.

With native spots and artful labour gay, *Stat.*² 25.

Gayest.

Where China's gayest art had dy'd *Cat* 2.

Gayly-gilded.

Some shew their gayly-gilded trim *Spring* 29.

Gaze.

Where Angels tremble, while they gaze,
P. P. 100.

In silent gaze the tuneful choir among, *Bent.* 1.

Father, why, why do you gaze so sternly?
Dante 56.

Gazed.

The pensive Selima . . . Gazed on the lake
Cat 6.

Still had she gaz'd; *Cat* 13.

Gazetteer.

†All, all, but Grannam Osborne's Gazetteer.
Ch. Cr. 20.

Gazing.

Swift at the word, from out the gazing host,
*Stat.*¹ 4.

Geese.

†Here Grub-street Geese presume to joke and jeer,
Ch. Cr. 19.

Geira.

Gondula, and *Geira*, spread . . . your shield.
F. S. 31.

Gem.

Britain's gem. *Owen* 4.

many a gem of purest ray serene, *El.* 53.

Shall raise from earth the latent gem *Inst.* 75.

Gems.

The Soil . . . Forbids her Gems to swell,
E. G. 7.

meaner gems that . . . charm the sight, *Bent.* 22.

General.

Warm Charity, the gen'ral Friend, *Adv.* 30.

nature . . . leads the general song: *Vic.* 20.

Generous.

The gen'rous spark extinct revive, *Adv.* 45.

Glory pursue, and generous Shame, *P. P.* 64.

flinty Bosom starves her generous Birth, *E. G.* 2.

Genial.

the genial current of the soul. *El.* 52.

Nor genial Warmth, nor genial Juice *E. G.* 3.

†But the genial Hand of Time *Ode* 3.

Genii.

The Genii of the stream: *Cat* 15.

Genius.

Than Pow'r and Genius e'er conspir'd to bless.
El. Mas. 76.

There sit . . . The few, whom genius gave to
shine *Inst.* 16.

Again the buried Genius of old Rome *Agr.* 141.

Foes to the gentler genius of the plain: *E. G.* 89.

She is my Genius, she inspires the Lines;
*Prop.*³ 4.

Gentle.

And to . . . thy gentle hand, Submits the fasces
Inst. 86.

A moment's patience, gentle Mistress Anne:
Shak. 1.

Love, gentle Power! to Peace was e'er a friend;
Prop.[1] 1.

Nor thou my gentle Calling disapprove,
Prop.[3] 63.

Gentler.

Foes to the gentler genius of the plain: *E. G.* 89.

A gentler Lamb ne'er sported on the plain,
Child 3.

Gently.

Oh, gently on thy Suppliant's head,   *Adv.* 33.

Genuine.

All hail, ye genuine Kings,   *Bard* 110.

where . . . First the genuine ardour stole.
Inst. 22.

catch a lustre from his genuine flame. *Bent.* 12.

Germania's.

the rigour Of bleak Germania's snows. *Agr.* 110.

Germanicus.

As fits the daughter of Germanicus.   *Agr.* 6.

Gestures.

With gestures quaint, now smiling as in scorn,
El. Mas. 125.

Ghastly.

Despair, and fell Disease, and ghastly Poverty:
Adv. 40.

Smear'd with gore, and ghastly pale: *Bard* 36.

Ghostly.

The ghostly Prudes . . . Already had condemn'd
the sinner.   *L. S.* 129.

Ghosts.

pitied ghosts Of the Syllani,   *Agr.* 175.

Giant.

A giant Boy shall *Rinda* bear,   *Odin* MS. 65.

And scarce Ulysses 'scaped his giant arm.
Stat.[2] 23.

No Giant Race, no Tumult of the Skies, *Prop.*[3] 35.

Giant-brood.

Mother of the giant-brood!   *Odin* 86.

Giant-oak.

each giant-oak, and desert cave, Sighs *Bard* 23.

Giddy.

the frivolous tongue of giddy fame   *Agr.* 167.

Gift.

These were your gift,   *Agr.* 80.

With equal power resume that gift,   *Agr.* 90.

if you resume your Gift;   *Dante* 66.

Gilded. *See also* Gayly-gilded.

In gallant trim the gilded Vessel goes; *Bard* 73.

around thee call The gilded swarm   *Agr.* 147.

to his gilded bark With fond reluctance,*Agr.* 196.

Gilds.

star . . . gilds the horrors of the deep. *Inst.* 94.

Hope . . . Gilds with a gleam of distant day.
Vic. 36.

Girt.

Girt with many a baron bold   *Bard* 111.

Give.

give to rapture all thy trembling strings. *P. P.* 2.

Give ample room, and verge enough   *Bard* 51.

We the reins to slaughter give,   *F. S.* 33.

Give anxious Cares and . . . Wishes room;
El. Mas. 86.

Numbers would give their oaths upon it,
L. S. 127.

liberal power to give,   *Agr.* 89.

Give me to send the laughing bowl around,
Prop.[2] 7.

And to this bosom give its wonted Peace,
Prop.[3] 88.

At once give loose to Utterance, and to Tears.
Dante 9.

†So I to you this Trifle give,   *Ode* 53.

Given.

Say, has he giv'n in vain   *P. P.* 48.

Balder's head to death is giv'n.   *Odin* 47.

But Cobham had the polish given   *L. S.* 31.

Sparks of Truth and Happiness has given.
E. G. 29.

Is that diviner inspiration giv'n,   *Bent.* 18.

Gives.

He gives to range the dreary sky: *P. P.* 51.

the rolling Orb, that gives the Day,   *E. G.* 23.

She . . . gives the Lay to flow.   *Prop.*[3] 6.

Glad.

While spirits . . . Join with glad voice *Inst.* 88.

Glad I revisit thy neglected reign,   *Ign.* 5.

Glade.

The . . . beech O'er-canopies the glade;
Spring 14.

towers, That crown the watry glade.   *Eton* 2.

Gladsome.

As waving fresh their gladsome wing,   *Eton* 17.

Glance.

Glance their many-twinkling feet.   *P. P.* 35.

a glance from high They send   *Inst.* 19.

Glancing. *See also* Quick-glancing.

thunder's fiery stroke, Glancing on the shiver'd
oak;   *Conan* 8.

Glassy.

Who . . . delight   to   cleave . . . thy   glassy
wave?   *Eton* 26.

Gleam.

Betray'd a golden gleam.   *Cat* 18.

I . . . Oft woo'd the gleam of Cynthia *Inst.* 32.

Hope . . . Gilds with a gleam of distant day.
Vic. 36.

With such a gleam affrights Pangæa's field,
Stat.[1] 29.

Till a new Sun arose with weakly Gleam,
Dante 59.

Gleams.

The uncertain Crescent gleams a sickly light.
Tasso 48.

Glebe.

Their furrow oft the stubborn glebe has broke:
El. 26.

Glide.

Two angel forms were seen to glide,   *Cat* 14.

Fearless in long excursion loves to glide,
Tasso 21.

Gliding.
In gliding state she wins her easy way: *P. P.* 39.

Glimmering.
Now fades the glimmering landscape   *El.* 5.

Glimmerings.
The watery glimmerings of a fainter day
        Tasso 45.

Glimpse.
†Then one faint glimpse of Queen Elizabeth;
        Ch. Cr. 10.

Glisters.
Nor all, that glisters, gold.   *Cat* 42.

Glitter.
Such forms, as glitter in the Muse's ray, *P. P.* 119.
Shall raise . . . gem To glitter on the diadem.
        Inst. 76.
distant cities . . . That rise and glitter *E. G.* 107.

Glittering.
Thy Joys no glittering female meets, *Spring* 45.
and glitt'ring shafts of war.   *P. P.* 53.
solemn scenes . . . their glitt'ring [golden, MS.]
   skirts unroll?   *Bard* 106.
Glitt'ring lances are the loom,   *F. S.* 5.
For whom yon glitt'ring board is spread,
        Odin 41.
In glitt'ring arms and glory drest, *Owen* 21.
Has he beheld the glittering front of war?
        Agr. 94.
in glitt'ring row Thrice two hundred warriors go:
        Hoel 11.
So glittering shows the Thracian Godhead's
   shield,   *Stat.*[1] 28.
Here gems break through the night with glitt'ring
   beam,   *Tasso* 63.

Gloom. *See* **Twilight-gloom.**

Gloomy.
linger in the gloomy Walks of Fate: *El. Mas.* 80.
Forth from their gloomy mansions creeping
        L. S. 98.
ye ever gloomy bowers, Ye gothic fanes, *Ign.* 1.
gloomy Sway have fix'd her Empire there,
        E. G. 19.

Glories.
To mourn the Glories of his sevenfold Stream,
        Prop.[3] 50.

Glorious.
For glorious puddings and immortal pies.
        Shak. 24.
two youths advance, . . . to try the glorious
   chance;   *Stat.*[1] 10.
To die is glorious in the Bed of Love. *Prop.*[3] 64.

Glory.
Awake, my lyre: my glory, wake,   *P. P.* MS. 1.
Glory pursue, and generous Shame,   *P. P.* 64.
Wide o'er the fields of Glory   *P. P.* 104.
Visions of glory, spare my aching sight,
        Bard 107.
In glitt'ring arms and glory drest, *Owen* 21.
The paths of glory lead but to the grave. *El.* 36.
The schoolman's glory, and the churchman's
   boast,   *Ign.* 32.

Gloucester.
Stout Glo'ster stood aghast in speechless trance:
        Bard 13.

Glow.
Eyes that glow, and fangs, that grin;   *Odin* 10.
in our Ashes glow their wonted Fires.
        El. Pem., Eg. 92.
buried ashes glow with social fires. *El. Mas.* 108.
The hues of Bliss more brightly glow,   *Vic.* 41.
And embryon metals undigested glow, *Tasso* 58.
Pangs without respite, fires that ever glow,
        Prop.[2] 40.

Glowing.
Where his glowing eye-balls turn,   *Owen* 31.

Glows.
The busy murmur glows!   *Spring* 24.
Charity, that glows beyond the tomb. *Inst.* 50.
A heart that glows with . . . fire,   *Agr.* 50.
the spark . . . that glows within their breasts,
        Agr. 128.

Gnaw.
Prostrate warriors gnaw the ground. *Owen* 30.
whom thus I ceaseless gnaw insatiate; *Dante* 8.

Gnawed.
either Hand I gnaw'd For Anguish, *Dante* 63.

Gnaws.
Jealousy . . . that inly gnaws   *Eton* 67.

Go.
Light they disperse, and with them go *Adv.* 21.
Let us go, and let us fly,   *F. S.* 26.
And mitred fathers in long order go: *Inst.* 38.
Go! you can paint it well   *Agr.* 12.
'T is time to go, the sun is high   *Agr.* 158.
Thrice two hundred warriors go: *Hoel* 12.

Goblet.
Mantling in the goblet see The pure bev'rage
        Odin 43.

God.
She mew'd to ev'ry watry God,   *Cat* 32.
The bosom of his Father and his God. *El.* 128.
And so God save our noble King, *L. S.* 141.
he believed in a God: *Char.* 4.
— for he talks about God —   *C. C.* 30.
And bids the pure in heart behold their God.
        Stanza 4.

Goddess.
Dread Goddess, lay thy chast'ning hand! *Adv.* 34.
Thy form benign, oh Goddess, wear,   *Adv.* 41.
where'er the Goddess roves,   *P. P.* 63.
Goddess! awake, arise!   *Ign.* 25.

Goddess'.
Before the Goddess' shrine we . . . bend,
        Prop.[1] 2.

Godhead.
The Godhead would have back'd his quarrel,
        L. S. 93.

Godhead's.
So glittering shows the Thracian Godhead's shield,
        Stat.[1] 28.

Gods.
Gods! then was the time To shrink   *Agr.* 47.
their Kings, their Gods were roll'd away. *E. G.* 49.

Goes.

In gallant trim the gilded Vessel goes; *Bard* 73.
dauntless goes O'er Libya's deserts *E. G.* 76.
And tastes it as it goes. *Vic.* 56.

Gold.

What female heart can gold despise? *Cat* 23.
Nor all, that glisters, gold. *Cat* 42.
O'er it hangs the shield of gold; *Odin* 45.
He ask'd no heaps of hoarded gold; *Hoel* 8.
Their jewels of silver and jewels of gold? *C. C.* 26.
And calm'd the terrors of his claws in gold.
 *Stat.*² 27.
†Expand their wings of flimzey Gold. *Ode* 48.

Golden.

Betray'd a golden gleam. *Cat* 18.
Thro' verdant vales, and Ceres' golden reign:
 P. P. 9.
Thine too these golden keys, *P. P.* 91.
their golden skirts unroll? *Bard* MS. 106.
To-morrow he repairs the golden flood, *Bard* 137.
Drest for whom yon golden bed. *Odin* 42.
leaning from her golden cloud The venerable
 Marg'ret see! *Inst.* 65.
redning Phœbus lifts his golden Fire: *West* 2.
Light golden Showers of Plenty *E. G.* 18.
Her boasted Titles and her golden Fields; *E. G.* 53.
Now the golden Morn aloft Waves . . . wing,
 Vic. 1.
Chains . . . Wreath'd in many a golden link:
 Hoel 15.
From the golden cup they drink *Hoel* 16.
In golden Chains should loaded Monarchs bend,
 *Prop.*³ 48.

Gondula.

Gondula, . . . , spread O'er the youthful King
 your shield. *F. S.* 31.

Gone.

Thy spring is gone — *Spring* 49.
Thy son is gone. *Bard* 68.
Gone to salute the rising Morn. *Bard* 70.
He 's gone: and much I hope *Agr.* 22.
Yes, I will be gone, But not to Antium — *Agr.* 165.
For ever gone — yet still to fancy new, *Ign.* 33.

Good.

leave us leisure to be good. *Adv.* 20.
Beneath the Good how far — *P. P.* 123.
No boding Maid . . . nor Prophetess of good;
 Odin 85.
The grateful memory of the good. *Inst.* 60.
Very good claret and fine Champaign.
 Impr. Vane 2.
†these Flies . . . can boast of one good Quality;
 Ode 50.

Good-nature.

Cobham had . . . tip'd her arrows with good-
nature. *L. S.* 32.

Goodwin.

Earl Goodwin trembled for his neighbouring sand;
 View 6.

Goose.

He eat a fat goose, *Ep. Keene* 2.

Gore. *See also* **Infant-gore.**

Smear'd with gore, and ghastly pale: *Bard* 36.
Shafts for shuttles, dipt in gore, *F. S.* 13.
from his jaws, . . . Foam and human gore distill'd. *Odin* 8.
And sad Philippi, red with Roman Gore: *Prop.*³ 46.

Gored.

gor'd with many a gaping wound: *F. S.* 42.

Gore-dyed.

the griesly Fellon raised His Gore-dyed Lips,
 Dante 2.

Gorgeous.

gorgeous Dames, and Statesmen old . . . appear.
 Bard 113.
In gorgeous phrase of labour'd eloquence
 Agr. 149.

Gorgon.

Not in thy Gorgon terrors clad, *Adv.* 35.

Gospel-light.

gospel-light first dawn'd from Bullen's eyes.
 E. G. 109.

Gothic.

Ye gothic fanes, and antiquated towers, *Ign.* 2.

Grace. *See also* **Virgin-grace.**

afford A tear to grace his obsequies. *Bard* 66.
no sign of grace, *L. S.* 89.
My Lady rose, and with a grace — *L. S.* 131.
in thy lineaments we trace . . . a Beaufort's
 grace. *Inst.* 70.
to grace thy youthful brow, The laureate wreath,
 Inst. 83.
could they catch . . . his easy grace, *Bent.* 13.
throw A melancholy grace; *Vic.* 32.
each Grace adorn'd his frame, *Williams* 3.
And sing with what a careless Grace she flings
 *Prop.*³ 15.
†What Ease and Elegance her person grace,
 Ch. Cr. 7.

Graced.

better scenes . . . had grac'd our view,
 View Nich. 19.

Graces.

the Graces homage pay. *P. P.* 37.

Grain.

†Copious numbers, swelling grain; *Ode* 8.

Grandam.

High on her car, behold the grandam ride *Ign.* 36.

Grandchildren.

Wrinkled beldams Teach it their grandchildren,
 Agr. 135.

Grandeur.

Nor Grandeur hear with a disdainful smile *El.* 31.
What is grandeur, what is power? *Inst.* 57.
†But why on such *mock* grandeur should we dwell,
 Ch. Cr. 23.

Grandsire's.

envy oft thy happy grandsire's end. *Bard* MS. 76.

Grannam.

†All, all, but Grannam Osborne's Gazetteer.
 Ch. Cr. 20.

Granta.

Lo! Granta waits to lead her blooming band,
Inst. 77.

Granta's.

All that on Granta's fruitful plain . . . bounty
pour'd, *Inst.* 51.

Grape's.

drink Nectar . . . Or the grape's extatic juice.
Hoel 18.

Grasp.

A heart that . . . will . . . grasp the dangerous
honour. *Agr.* 53.

Grasped.

Then grasp'd its weight, *Stat.*[1] 42.

Grateful.

Where grateful science still adores *Eton* 3.
A grateful Earnest of eternal Peace. *El. Mas.* 84.
The grateful memory of the good. *Inst.* 60.
the grateful steam Of flattery's incense, *Agr.* 34.

Gratefully.

†gratefully they pay Their little Songs, *Ode* 51.

Gratitude.

sweeter yet The still small voice of gratitude.
Inst. 64.
How vast the debt of gratitude *Agr.* 57.
ties . . . Of old respect and gratitude, *Agr.* 114.
The soft Returns of Gratitude *E. G.* 34.

Grave.

Hear from the grave, great Taliessin, *Bard* 121.
The paths of glory lead but to the grave. *El.* 36.
save His all from an untimely grave.
Clerke MS. 12.
Than thus be patch'd and cobbled in one's grave.
Shak. 20.

Grave, *adj.*

My grave Lord-Keeper led the Brawls; *L. S.* 11.
grave and undisturbed reflection *Agr.* 82.

Graved.

the lay, Grav'd [Wrote, Mas.] on the stone
El. 116.

Graver.

'Gainst graver hours, *Eton* 33.

Grave's.

And all the scenes, that hurt the grave's repose,
Prop.[2] 49.

Grease.

Grease his best pen, *Shak.* 16.

Great.

How indigent the great! *Spring* 20.
How little are the great! *Spring* Dods. 20.
but far above the Great. *P. P.* 123.
Hear from the grave, great Taliessin, *Bard* 121.
Great Edward, with the lilies on his brow
Inst. 39.
benefits too great To be repaid, *Agr.* 74.
My great revenge shall rise; *Agr.* 121.
No very great wit, *Char.* 4.
my Hoel, died, Great Cian's son: *Hoel* 7.
Great things and full of wonder . . . I shall
unfold; *Tasso* 35.

Here should Augustus great in Arms appear,
Prop.[3] 41.
†Great D *draws* near — the *D*utchess sure is come,
Ch. Cr. 1.
†Thus great R reigns in town, *Ch. Cr.* 53.

Great-house.

to the Great-house He went, *L. S.* 87.

Greatness.

to bear the blaze of greatness; *Agr.* 45.

Greece's.

in Greece's evil hour, *P. P.* 77.

Green. *See also* **Velvet-green.**

Disporting on thy margent green *Eton* 23.
In thy green lap was Nature's Darling laid,
P. P. 84.
His bushy beard, and shoe-strings green, *L. S.* 13.
chearful Fields resume their green Attire: *West* 4.
Scatters his freshest, tenderest green. *Vic.* 8.
Idle notes! untimely green! *Song* 7.
The theatre's green height and woody wall
Tremble *Stat.*[2] 14.
†Vainly enamelling the Green. *Ode* 18.

Greenwood.

the Greenwood Side along, *El. Mas.* 117.

Greet.

The Birds his presence greet: *Vic.* 12.

Grew.

She swept, she hiss'd, she ripen'd and grew
rough, *Par. on Ep.* 2.

Grief.

In buskin'd measures move Pale Grief, *Bard* 129.
See a kindred Grief pursue; *Vic.* 38.
Till time shall every grief remove, *Clerke* 15.

Griesly. *See* **Grisly.**

Grim.

That, hush'd in grim repose, expects his evening-
prey. *Bard* 76.
Grim Towers of Julius, *Bard MS.* 87.
With grim Delight the Brood of Winter view
E. G. 54.
That grim and antique Tower admitted
Dante 23.

Grimace.

With a lick of court white-wash, and pious
grimace, *C. C.* 2.
†ponders, with profound grimace, *Ch. Cr.* 34.

Grim-visaged.

Grim-visag'd comfortless Despair, *Eton* 69.

Grin.

Eyes that glow, and fangs, that grin; *Odin* 10.

Grinned.

so grinned the brawling fiend, *Toph.* 1.

Grinning.

And grinning Infamy. *Eton* 74.

Gripe.

Now fitting to his gripe and nervous arm,
Stat.[1] 43.

Grisly.

A griesly troop are seen, *Eton* 82.
a griesly band, I see them sit, *Bard* 44.
See the griesly texture grow! *F. S.* 9.
Our mother-church, . . . Blush'd as she bless'd
  her griesly proselyte; *Toph.* 6.
From his dire Food the griesly Fellon raised
Dante 1.

Groan.

Condemn'd alike to groan, *Eton* 92.
sees far off with an indignant groan, *E. G.* 62.

Groaning.

The groaning earth beneath him shakes,
Odin 14.

Groom.

And all that *Groom* could urge against him.
L. S. 116.

Groped.

for three days more I grop'd *Dante* 77.

Grotto.

road That to the grotto leads, *Tasso* 38.

Ground.

With leaden eye, that loves the ground, *Adv.* 28.
Soon a King shall bite the ground. *F. S.* 44.
Till from out the hollow ground *Odin* 25.
Prostrate warriors gnaw the ground. *Owen* 30.
Accents whisp'ring from the Ground, *El.* Mas. 83.
Footsteps lightly print the Ground.
El. Pem. 120 ; Mas. 140.
Hence, avaunt, ('t is holy ground) *Inst.* 1.
Hence, away, 't is holy ground! *Inst.* 12.
sick'ning virtue fly the tainted ground? *E. G.* 71.
With . . . plough to quell the flinty ground,
E. G. 91.
The sleeping fragrance from the ground; *Vic.* 6.
and cleaves the solid ground. *Stat.*[1] 52.
The ponderous mass sinks in the cleaving ground,
Stat.[2] 16.

Grove.

th' expanse below Of grove . . . survey, *Eton* 7.

Groves.

The rocks and nodding groves rebellow *P. P.* 12.
Ye brown o'er-arching groves, *Inst.* 27.

Grow.

See the griesly texture grow! *F. S.* 9.
As lawless force from confidence will grow
E. G. 98.

Growing.

nor circumscrib'd alone Their growing virtues,
El. 66.
the growing Powers Of Nature *E. G.* 13.

Grown. *See also* **Full-grown, Moss-grown.**

careless grown, Lethargic nods *Ign.* 23.

Grows.

quaff the pendent Vintage as it grows. *E. G.* 57.
Where broad and turbulent it grows *Vic.* 58.
†The Dowager grows a perfect double D.
Ch. Cr. 4.

Grub-street.

†Here Grub-street Geese presume to joke and jeer,
Ch. Cr. 19.

Gruff.

Now clean, now hideous, mellow now, now gruff,
Par. on Ep. 1.

Gualandi.

Lanfranc there And Sigismundo, and Gualandi
rode *Dante* 33.

Guard.

And guard us from long-winded Lubbers,
L. S. 142.
They guard with spirit what . . . they gain'd?
E. G. 95.

Guerre. *See* **Nom de guerre.**

Guest.

A baleful smile upon their baffled Guest. *Bard* 82.

Guilt.

say, Who th' Avenger of his guilt, *Odin* 61.
the deeper My guilt, the blacker *Agr.* 173.

Guiltless.

Cromwell guiltless of his country's blood. *El.* 60.

Guise.

Was fashion'd fair in meek and dove-like guise;
Shak. 10.

Gulf.

Nor knew the gulf between. *Cat* 27.

Gulls. *See* **Sea-gulls.**

Gunna.

Gunna, and *Gondula,* spread . . . your shield.
F. S. Pem. 31.

Guttle.

In harmless society guttle and scold. *C. C.* 4.

Gwyneth's.

Gwyneth's shield. *Owen* 4.

H.

†They 're all diverted into H and B. *Ch. Cr.* 14.
†High heaves his hugeness H, *Ch. Cr.* 21.
†H mounts to Heaven, and H descends to Hell.
Ch. Cr. 24.
†As H the Hebrew found, *Ch. Cr.* 25.

Ha.

Ha! no Traveller art thou, *Odin* 81.
Ha! by Juno, It bears a noble semblance, *Agr.* 119.

Had.

Latium had her lofty spirit lost, *P. P.* 81.
all he had, a tear, *El.* 123.
When he had fifty winters o'er him, *L. S.* 10.
kind Heaven Had arm'd with spirit, *L. S.* 30.
But Cobham had the polish given *L. S.* 31.
Had told . . . there lurk'd . . . a Poet,
L. S. 43.
The bard, . . . Had in imagination fenc'd him,
L. S. 114.
When he the solemn hall had seen; *L. S.* 118.
He once or twice had pen'd a sonnet; *L. S.* 125.
Already had condemn'd the sinner. *L. S.* 130.
one Who had such liberal power *Agr.* 89.
had her wanton son Lent us his wings, *Agr.* 189.
He had not the method of making a fortune:
Char. 2.

Had I but the torrent's might,   *Hoel* 1.
He ask'd and had the lovely maid.   *Hoel* 10.
When sly Jemmy Twitcher had smugg'd up his
   face,   *C. C.* 1.
— but he once had a wife;   *C. C.* 14.
"Ah!" said the sighing peer, "had Bute been
   true,   *View* 17.
Far better scenes than these had blest our view,
                                                    View 19.
Then had we seen proud London's hated walls;
                                                    View 22.
And Satan's self had thoughts of taking orders.
                                                    Toph. 8.
She had a bad face   *Mrs. Keene* 2.
Nor stopp'd till it had cut the further strand.
                                                    Stat.[1] 40.
Scarce had he said,   *Tasso* 39.
The Morn had scarce commenc'd, when I awoke:
                                                    Dante 41.
too soon they had aroused 'em   *Dante* 48.
e'er the sixth Morn Had dawn'd,   *Dante* 75.
for then Hunger had reft my Eye-sight *Dante* 79.

Hag.
Th' Æmonian hag enjoys her dreadful hour,
                                                    Stat.[1] 58.

Haggard.
With haggard eyes the Poet stood;   *Bard* 18.

Hagged.
The ghostly Prudes with hagged face *L. S.* 129.

Hail.
All hail, ye genuine Kings, Britannia's Issue,
   hail!   *Bard* 110.
Hail the task, and hail the hands!   *F. S.* 53.
To hail their Fitzroy's festal morning   *Inst.* 54.
Hail, horrors, hail!   *Ign.* 1.

Hair. *See also* Raven-hair.
Loose his beard, and hoary hair Stream'd, *Bard* 19.
The Master of Clare Hits them all to a hair;
                                                   Satire 22.

Half.
Half of thy heart we consecrate.   *Bard* 99.
Half pleas'd, half blushing,   *Bent.* 2.
Discover'd half, and half conceal'd their way;
                                                   Tasso 46.
And half disclose those Limbs it should conceal;
                                                   Prop.[3] 10.
She half accepts, and half rejects, my Fires,
                                                   Prop.[3] 22.
Locks Of th' half devoured Head   *Dante* 3.
†throw . . . half an act into the Fire: *Ode* 34.

Half-averted.
Our mother-church, with half-averted sight,
   Blush'd   *Toph.* 5.

Half-devoured. *See* Half *and* Devoured.

Hall.
When he the solemn hall had seen;   *L. S.* 118.
As to Trinity Hall We say nothing at all. *Satire* 36.

Hallowed.
Evr'y shade and hallow'd Fountain   *P. P.* 75.
spare the meek Usurper's hallow'd head.
                                                 Bard MS. 90.

Hamlet.
The rude Forefathers of the hamlet   *El.* 16.

Hampden. *See* Village-Hampden.

Hand.
Still is the toiling hand of Care: *Spring* 21.
Brushed by the hand of . . . Mischance,
                                                  Spring 38.
Dread goddess, lay thy chast'ning hand ! *Adv.* 34.
numbs the soul with icy hand,   *Eton* 89.
Perching on the scept'red hand   *P. P.* 20.
with a Master's hand, and Prophet's fire,
                                                  Bard 21.
In *Hoder's* hand the Heroe's doom: *Odin* 55.
OWEN . . . Lord of . . . Liberal hand, *Owen* 8.
And to . . . thy gentle hand, Submits the fasces
                                                  Inst. 85.
her that . . . taught his novice hand   *Agr.* 30.
To arm the hand of childhood,   *Agr.* 138.
scatter with a free, though frugal, Hand *E. G.* 17.
Soft Reflection's hand can trace;   *Vic.* 30.
From table she rose, and with bumper in hand,
                                                  C. C. 21.
Another orb upheaved his strong right hand,
                                                  Stat.[1] 15.
All eyes were bent on his experienced hand,
                                                  Stat.[1] 34.
Sure flew the disc from his unerring hand,
                                                  Stat.[1] 39.
His head a chaplet bore, his hand a Rod.
                                                  Tasso 16.
The flood on either hand its billows rears, *Tasso* 41.
Wars hand to hand with Cynthia let me wage.
                                                  Prop.[1] 4.
Her artful hand across the sounding Strings.
                                                  Prop.[3] 16.
The Hand that can my captive heart release,
                                                  Prop.[3] 87.
with direful Hand Oped the dark Veil of Fate.
                                                  Dante 27.
either Hand I gnaw'd For Anguish,   *Dante* 63.
†But the genial Hand of Time   *Ode* 3.

Hands.
Hark, his hands the lyre explore!   *P. P.* 107.
And weave with bloody hands   *Bard* 48.
Hail the task, and hail the hands!   *F. S.* 53.
Hands, that the rod of empire might have sway'd,
                                                  El. 47.
scatter'd oft . . . By Hands unseen,
                                     El. Pem. 118; *Mas.* 138.
The Huntingdons . . . Employ'd the power of
   Fairy hands   *L. S.* 4.
Their hands he seized,   *Tasso* 43.
I 'd in the ring knit hands,   *Prop.*[2] 6.

Handy.
For thee fat Nanny sighs, and handy Nelly,
                                             Com. Lines 6.

Hang.
Never hang down your head,   *C. C.* 31.

Hanging.
the high brow of yonder hanging lawn.
                                             El. Mas. 116.

Hangs.

who o'er thy country hangs The scourge of
Heav'n.   *Bard* 59.

O'er it hangs the shield of gold;   *Odin* 45.

the . . . cloud That hangs on thy clear brow.
                                             Agr. 194.

†He in plantations hangs   *Ch. Cr.* 40.

Hapless.

The hapless Nymph with wonder saw: *Cat* 19.

Haply.

Haply some . . . Swain may say,   *El.* 97.

haply eyed at distance Some edileship, *Agr.* 39.

Happier.

new-born Pleasure brings to happier Men:
                                           West 10.

While Hope prolongs our happier hour, *Vic.* 33.

Happiness.

happiness too swiftly flies,   *Eton* 97.

The Sparks of Truth and Happiness *E. G.* 29.

Oh, might that envied Happiness be mine!
                                          *Prop.*³ 67.

Happy.

Ah, happy hills,   *Eton* 11.

and envy oft thy happy grandsire's end.
                                        Bard MS. 76.

Happy the Youth, and not unknown to Fame,
                                          *Prop.*³ 65.

Hard.

And hard Unkindness' alter'd eye,   *Eton* 76.

Hard by yon wood,   *El.* 105.

'T is hard th' elusive Symptoms to explore:
                                          *Prop.*³ 95.

Harden.

The parts combine and harden into Ore: *Tasso* 62.

Hardened.

So mov'd the Seer, but on no harden'd plain;
                                         Tasso 23.

Hardy.

her nod Can rouse eight hardy legions, *Agr.* 108.

Force and hardy Deeds of Blood prevail.
                                          E. G. 44.

Hark.

Hark, how thro' the peopled air   *Spring* 23.

Hark, his hands the lyre explore!   *P. P.* 107.

Hark, how each giant-oak, and desert cave, Sighs
                                          Bard 23.

Hark! how the sacred Calm   *El. Mas.* 81.

But hark! the portals sound,   *Inst.* 35.

Hark! 't is nature strikes the lyre, *Vic.* 19.

Harm.

'T was there he aim'd the meditated harm,
                                         *Stat.*² 22.

Harmless.

In harmless society guttle and scold. *C. C.* 4.

Harmonious.

From Helicon's harmonious springs   *P. P.* 3.

Harmony.

The untaught harmony of spring: *Spring* 7.

in dreadful harmony they join,   *Bard* 47.

Dryden's harmony submit to mine.   *Bent.* 16.

The strength and harmony of Life.   *Vic.* 44.

Harms.

The Power of Herbs can other Harms remove,
                                         *Prop.*³ 79.

Harness.

Have his limbs Sweat under iron harness?
                                          Agr. 97.

Harnessed.

a team of harness'd monarchs bend   *Ign.* 38.

Harp.

Vocal no more, . . . To high-born Hoel's harp,
                                           Bard 28.

Harry.

nor *Harry* heard,   *Cat* Wal., Whar., Dods. 35.

Here lives Harry Vane,   *Impr. Vane* 1.

Harvest.

Oft did the harvest to their sickle yield, *El.* 25.

The crimson harvest of the foe.   *Conan* 10.

†Judgment from the Harvest flies   *Ode* 9.

Has.

A Fav'rite has no friend !   *Cat* 36.

Has curb'd the fury of his car,   *P. P.* 18.

has he giv'n in vain the heav'nly Muse? *P. P.* 48.

The Muse has broke the twilight-gloom *P. P.* 56.

has quench'd the Orb of day?   *Bard* 136.

Till *Lok* has [have, MS.] burst his tenfold chain;
                                          Odin 90.

till substantial Night Has reassum'd her ancient
right;   *Odin* 92.

Styack has often seen the sight   *L. S.* 103.

who oft has bade,   *Agr.* 69.

The very power he has   *Agr.* 81.

Has he beheld the glittering front of war?
                                           Agr. 94.

Sylla has his friends,   *Agr.* 100.

giddy fame Has spread among the crowd;
                                          Agr. 168.

The Sparks of Truth . . . has given. *E. G.* 29.

See the Wretch, that long has tost   *Vic.* 45.

The Master of Pembroke Has from them his
system took;   *Satire* 30.

The Master of Peter's Has all the same features;
                                         Satire 32.

For adverse fate the captive chief has hurl'd
                                          Tasso 33.

Whose heart has never felt a second flame.
                                          *Prop.*³ 66.

Has oft the Charms of Constancy confest,
                                          *Prop.*³ 72.

†yet has not a pain;   *Ch. Cr.* 29.

Hast.

No hive hast thou of hoarded sweets, *Spring* 46.

thou hast seen   *Eton* 21.

'T is like, thou hast forgot,   *Agr.* 33.

Haste.

Haste, the loom of Hell prepare,   *F. S.* 2.

Haste thee, fly These hated walls   *Agr.* 155.

Why this unavailing haste?   *Song* 8.

Hasty.

On hasty wings thy youth is flown;   *Spring* 48.

Hasty, hasty Rout is there,   *Owen* 34.

with hasty steps . . . To meet the sun *El.* 99.

Hat

With hasty footsteps brush the dews away
El. Mas. 115.
hasty to renew The hellish Feast, *Dante* 83.

Hat.
His high-crown'd hat, and sattin-doublet, *L. S.* 14.

Hate.
Could love, and could hate, *Char.* 3.

Hated.
These hated walls that seem to mock my shame,
Agr. 156.
Then had we seen proud London's hated walls;
View 22.

Hates.
And hates the Tale of Troy *Prop.*³ 74.

Hath.
Thrice hath Hyperion roll'd his . . . race, *Ign.* 11.

Hats.
The Audience . . . doff their hats *L. S.* 110.

Hattons.
The Huntingdons and Hattons there *L. S.* 3.

Hauberk.
Helm, nor Hauberk's twisted mail, *Bard* 5.
Hauberk crash, and helmet ring. *F. S.* 24.

Haughty.
a rock, whose haughty brow Frowns *Bard* 15.
Haughty knights and barons bold, *Bard* Lett.² 111.
lilies . . . From haughty Gallia torn, *Inst.* 40.
A thousand haughty hearts, *Agr.* 17.
haughty youth[,] and irritated power.[.]
Agr. 26, 28.

Haunt.
Thy once loved haunt, this . . . shade.
El. Mas. 112.

Haunts.
In cloisters dim, far from the haunts of Folly,
Inst. 33.

Have.
on these mould'ring bones have beat The winter's
snow, *Odin* 31.
Till *Lok* have burst his tenfold chain;
Odin MS. 90.
The Godhead would have back'd his quarrel,
L. S. 93.
I have pursued your steps, Have seen your soul,
Agr. 54, 55.
the phantom I have raised? *Agr.* 86.
Have his limbs Sweat under iron harness? *Agr.* 96.
those of Egypt, Have not forgot your sire:
Agr. 116.
the Prætorian camp have long rever'd *Agr.* 117.
things, that . . . Have arch'd the hearer's brow,
Agr. 169.
have beguil'd . . . the dazzled sight *Agr.* 190.
gloomy Sway have fix'd her Empire there,
E. G. 19.
As oft have issued, *E. G.* 50.
Have ye seen the dusky boar, *Caradoc* 1.
Much have I borne from canker'd critic's spite,
Shak. 5.
Owls would have hooted in St. Peter's choir,
View 23.

'T is a sign you have eat just enough *Couplet* 2.
Attend, and say if he have injured me. *Dante* 21.
What would you have? yet wept I not, *Dante* 57.
†Some have loved, and loved (they say) *Rond.* 5.
†Then have left, to love anew: *Rond.* 7.
†Some have lov'd, to pass the time, *Rond.* 13.
†And have loved their love in rhyme: *Rond.* 14.
†They who just have felt the flame *Rond.* 21.

Havoc.
Years of havock urge their destined course,
Bard 85.
We the reins to havock give, *F. S.* Pem. 33.

Havock. *See* **Havoc.**

He, *omitted.*

Head.
Oh, gently on thy Suppliant's head, *Adv.* 33.
Made huge Plinlimmon bow his cloud-top'd head.
Bard 34.
spare the meek Usurper's holy head. *Bard* 90.
Each a gasping Warriour's head. *F. S.* 12.
Fate demands a nobler head; *F. S.* 43.
Balder's head to death is giv'n. *Odin* 47.
rests his head upon the lap of Earth *El.* 117.
nods his hoary head, and listens to the rhyme.
Inst. 26.
The fragrance of its blushing head: *Inst.* 74.
from the dust uprear his reverend head, *Agr.* 142.
Never hang down your head, *C. C.* 31.
With servile simper nod the mitred head.
Toph. 4.
and o'er his head, . . . the circle sped; *Stat.*¹ 47.
His head a chaplet bore, *Tasso* 16.
Euphrates' font, and Nile's mysterious head.
Tasso 56.
Let on this head unfadeing flowers reside,
*Prop.*² 9.
When my changed head these locks no more shall
know, *Prop.*² 13.
The hissing terrors round Alecto's head,
*Prop.*² 42.
Locks Of th' half devoured Head *Dante* 3.
†and my head Rhimed on, *Ode* 21.
†P pokes his head out, *Ch. Cr.* 29.

Headed. *See also* **Hoary-headed.**
headed by this The deadliest. *Dante* 34.

Headlong.
She tumbled headlong in. *Cat* 30.
Headlong, impetuous, see it pour; *P. P.* 11.
headlong from the mountain's height . . . he
plung'd *Bard* 143.
With headlong rage and wild affright *Hoel* 2.

Heads.
On the Heads of thy Houses, *Satire* 3.
When Pindus' self . . . bows his hundred heads;
*Prop.*² 32.

Heal.
Heal the slow Chief, and send again *Prop.*³ 82.

Health.
Theirs buxom health *Eton* 45.
Cares, That Health and Vigour to the Soul im-
part, *E. G.* 11.

Heap.

heaves the turf in many a mould'ring heap,

El. 14.

heap [at, Mas.] the shrine of Luxury   *El.* 71.

Heaped.

heap'd his master's feet around,   *Owen* 29.

Heaps.

Owen . . . nor heaps his brooded stores,

Owen 5.

He ask'd no heaps of hoarded gold;   *Hoel* 8.

Hear.

Methinks I hear in accents low   *Spring* 41.
They hear a voice   *Eton* 39.
frantic Passions hear thy soft controul. *P. P.* 16.
to hear the savage Youth repeat   *P. P.* 60.
They hear not,   *Bard* MS. 73.
Hear from the grave, great Taliessin, hear;

Bard 121.

Nor Grandeur hear with a disdainful smile

El. 31.

To hear the spirit of Britannicus Yet walks on
earth: *Agr.* 14.
If . . . my voice ye hear,   *Agr.* 178.
I fruitless mourn to him that cannot hear,

West 13.

now hear My Wrongs,   *Dante* 14.

Heard.

Nor *Susan* heard.   *Cat* 35.
But ah! 't is heard no more —   *P. P.* 111.
Heard ye the din of battle bray,   *Bard* 83.
My Lady heard their joint petition,   *L. S.* 49.
He heard the distant din of war.   *L. S.* 76.
Yet something he was heard to mutter,

L. S. 121.

Divinity heard, between waking and dozing,

C. C. 19.

No tree is heard to whisper,   *View* 10.
Scarce the hoarse waves from far were heard to
roar,   *Tasso* 6.
I heard 'em wail for Bread.   *Dante* 45.
I heard the dreadful Clash of Bars,   *Dante* 51.
I heard Their doleful Cries;   *Dante* 76.
that heard me now no more: *Dante* 80.

Hearer's.

things, that . . . Have arch'd the hearer's brow,

Agr. 169.

Hearest.

Mortal, thou that hear'st the tale,   *F. S.* 57.
when thou hear'st the organ piping shrill

Shak. 15.

Hears.

she hears me not, but, careless grown,   *Ign.* 23.

Heart.

What female heart can gold despise?   *Cat* 23.
To soften, not to wound my heart.   *Adv.* 44.
Jealousy . . . That inly gnaws the secret heart,

Eton 67.

Dear, as the ruddy drops that warm my heart,

Bard 41.

No pitying heart, . . . afford A tear   *Bard* 65.
Half of thy heart we consecrate.   *Bard* 99.
Liberal hand, and open heart.   *Owen* 8.

Some heart once pregnant with celestial fire;

El. 46.

Large was his bounty, and his heart sincere,

El. Mas. 145.

Mov'd the stout heart of England's Queen,

L. S. 15.

Thy liberal heart, . . . The flow'r unheeded
shall descry,   *Inst.* 71.
a heart like mine, A heart that glows *Agr.* 49, 50.
the soft springs of pity in my heart,   *Agr.* 182.
My lonely Anguish melts no Heart but mine;

West 7.

warm the opening Heart.   *E. G.* 12.
A heart, within whose sacred cell   *Clerke* 3.
And bids the pure in heart behold their God.

Stanza 4.

Whose heart has never felt a second flame.

Prop.[3] 66.

The Hand that can my captive heart release,

Prop.[3] 87.

that unutter'd nathless wrings My inmost Heart?

Dante 6.

to think, what my poor Heart Foresaw, *Dante* 46.
†Long to seek a mutual heart,

Rond. 2, 10, 18, 26, 34.

†Cent'ring, rivets heart to heart,   *Rond.* 30.

Hearth.

no more the blazing hearth shall burn,   *El.* 21.

Hearts.

Not all that tempts your . . . heedless hearts,

Cat 41.

A thousand haughty hearts,   *Agr.* 17.
steel our hearts to war?   *E. G.* 69.

Heat.

The winter's snow, the summer's heat, *Odin* 32.
†I told Of Phœbus' heat and Daphne's cold.

Ode 24.

Heath.

Horror covers all the heath,   *F. S.* 49.
Along the heath, and near his . . . tree; *El.* 110.
While o'er the Heath we hied,   *El.* Mas. 118.

Heaved.

The eyeless Cyclops heav'd the craggy rock;

Stat.[2] 19.

Heaven.

The scourge of Heav'n.   *Bard* 60.
what [solemn, Lett.[1]] scenes of Heaven on Snowdon's height   *Bard* MS. 105.
Rapture . . . Waves in the eye of Heav'n

Bard 124.

Pain can reach the Sons of Heav'n!   *Odin* 48.
Heav'n did a recompence . . . send!   *El.* 122.
He gain'd from Heav'n . . . a friend.   *El.* 124.
kind Heaven Had arm'd with spirit,   *L. S.* 29.
to all the Kind impartial Heaven . . . has given.

E. G. 28.

pomp and prodigality of heav'n.   *Bent.* 20.
Heaven lifts its everlasting portals high, *Stanza* 3.
All angry heaven inflicts, or hell can feel,

Prop.[2] 45.

†H mounts to Heaven, and H descends to Hell.

Ch. Cr. 24.

Heavenly.
To thee he gave the heav'nly Birth,   *Adv.* 11.
has he giv'n in vain the heav'nly Muse? *P. P.* 48.
And rubies flame, with sapphire's heavenly blue,
           Tasso 68.

Heaven's.
round heav'n's altars shed The fragrance *Inst.* 73.
the rest is heav'n's;   *Agr.* 69.

Heaves.
Where heaves the turf in many a mould'ring heap,
           El. 14.
†High heaves his hugeness H,   *Ch. Cr.* 21.

Heavier.
Heavier toil, superior pain.   *Inst.* 58.

Heavy.
benefits . . . sit heavy on the soul,   *Agr.* 75.
Comes quiv'ring down Heavy and huge, *Stat.*¹ 52.

Hebrew.
†As H the Hebrew found,   *Ch. Cr.* 25.

Heed.
He Perchance may heed 'em: *Agr.* 88.

Heedless.
Not all that tempts your . . . heedless hearts,
           Cat 41.

Height.
what solemn scenes on Snowdon's height
           Bard 105.
headlong from the mountain's height . . . he
   plung'd   *Bard* 143.
To raise the cieling's fretted height,   *L. S.* 5.
raise the mortal to a height divine.   *E. G.* 83.
The theatre's green height and woody wall
   Tremble   *Stat.*² 14.

Heighten.
My struggling Sorrow, nor to heighten theirs:
           Dante 69.

Heights.
the stately brow Of WINDSOR's heights *Eton* 6.
heart . . . Gain the rough heights,   *Agr.* 53.

Hela's.
steep . . . That leads to HELA's drear abode.
           Odin 4.

Helen.
So Helen look'd, So her white neck reclin'd,
           Agr. 194.

Helen's.
hates the Tale of Troy for Helen's Sake.
           *Prop.*³ 74.

Helicon's.
From Helicon's harmonious springs *P. P.* 3.

Hell.
The characters of hell to trace.   *Bard* 52.
Haste, the loom of Hell prepare,   *F. S.* 2.
The portals nine of hell arise.   *Odin* 16.
All angry heaven inflicts, or hell can feel,
           *Prop.*² 45.
†H mounts to Heaven, and H descends to Hell.
           Ch. Cr. 24.

Hell-hounds.
chas'd by Hell-hounds gaunt and bloody *Dante* 30.

Hellish.
hasty to renew The hellish Feast   *Dante* 84.

Hell's.
Hosannas rung through hell's tremendous borders,   *Toph.* 7.

Helm.
Helm, nor Hauberk's twisted mail,   *Bard* 5.
and Pleasure at the helm;   *Bard* 74.
With dazzling helm, and horrent spear.
          Bard MS. 112.

Helmet.
Hauberk crash, and helmet ring.   *F. S.* 24.

Help.
imploreing In vain my Help,   *Dante* 74.

Helpless.
Your helpless, old, expiring master view !
          Bard MS. 72.
his helpless offspring soon O'erta'en beheld,
          Dante 38.

Helps.
No common helps, no common guide ye need,
          Tasso 29.

Hence.
From hence, ye Beauties,   *Cat* 37.
Sisters, hence with spurs of speed: *F. S.* 61.
Hie thee hence, and boast at home,   *Odin* 87.
Hence, avaunt, ('t is holy ground)   *Inst.* 1.
Hence, away, 't is holy ground!   *Inst.* 12.
Hence rise my fears.   *Agr.* 56.

Henry.
And either Henry there,   *Inst.* 45.
†Henry the Eighth's most monstrous majesty,
          Ch. Cr. 22.

Henry's.
Science still adores Her Henry's holy shade;
          Eton 4.

Her, *omitted.*

Heraldry.
The boast of heraldry,   *El.* 33.

Herbs.
The Power of Herbs can other Harms remove,
          *Prop.*³ 79.

Herd.
The lowing herd wind slowly o'er the lea, *El.* 2.
when the idle herd . . . yet will start *Agr.* 129.
The Herd stood drooping by: *Vic.* 24.

Herds.
The panting herds repose: *Spring* 22.

Here.
Leave me unbless'd, unpitied, here to mourn:
          Bard 102.
nor here forlorn   *Bard MS.* 101.
Some mute inglorious Milton here may rest,
          El. 59.
By sympathetic musings here delayed,
          El. Mas. 110.
Here rests his head upon the lap of Earth *El.* 117.
Here measured Laws and philosophic Ease
          E. G. 40.
Here Force and hardy Deeds of Blood prevail.
          E. G. 44.

Her infant image here below, Sits smiling
Clerke 9.

Here, lies . . . A child,   *Child* 1.

Here, . . . Williams fought for England's fair renown;   *Williams* 1.

What a pother is here about wenching and roaring!   *C. C.* 23.

Here Holland form'd the pious resolution *View* 2.

Here sea-gulls scream,   *View* 7.

Here reign the blustering North and blighting East,   *View* 9.

Here [Now, MS.] mouldering fanes and battlements arise,   *View* 13.

Here lives Harry Vane,   *Impr. Vane* 1.

Here lies Edmund Keene Lord Bishop of Chester,   *Ep. Keene* 1.

Here lies Mrs. Keene   *Mrs. Keene* 1.

Here gems break through the night   *Tasso* 63.

Here the soft emerald smiles of verdant hue,
Tasso 67.

Here should Augustus great in Arms appear,
Prop.[3] 41.

Here Mutina from flames and famine free,
Prop.[3] 43.

Here Arts are vain,   *Prop.*[3] 85.

†Here Grub-street Geese presume to joke and jeer,
Ch. Cr. 19.

Hero.

This mighty emperor, this dreaded hero,
Agr. 93.

difficult the toil To seek your Hero   *Tasso* 28.

Heroe's. *See* **Hero's.**

Heroic.

†If heroïc Verse I 'm reading   *Ode* 26.

Heroine.

And Anjou's heroine,   *Inst.* 43.

Heroines.

The Heroines undertook the task,   *L. S.* 53.

Hero's.

In *Hoder's* hand the Heroe's doom: *Odin* 55.

Verse, the hero's sole reward.   *Conan* 4.

To paint the Hero's Toil,   *Prop.*[3] 33.

Herself.

Justice to herself severe,   *Adv.* 31.

She reveres herself and thee.   *Inst.* 82.

Hetties.

†No more, our Esthers now are nought but Hetties,
Ch. Cr. 11.

Hid.

With . . . aprons long they hid their armour,
L. S. 38.

Hidden.

Some hidden Spirit shall inquire thy Fate,
El. Dods. 96.

Hide.

The struggling pangs of conscious truth to hide,
El. 69.

Nor . . . Let painted Flatt'ry hide her serpent-train   *Inst.* 8.

To hide her cares her only art,   *Clerke* MS. 7.

Hideous.

More hideous than their Queen: *Eton* 84.

Hoarse he bays with hideous din,   *Odin* 9.

Now clean, now hideous, mellow now, now gruff,
Par. on Ep. 1.

Hides.

That monthly waning hides her paly fires,
Prop.[2] 20.

Hiding.

This the force of Eirin hiding,   *Owen* 11.

Hie.

Hie thee hence, and boast at home,   *Odin* 87.

Hied.

While o'er the Heath we hied,   *El. Mas.* 118.

High. *See also* **Mountain-high.**

Then whirl the wretch from high.   *Eton* 72.

Fill high the sparkling bowl,   *Bard* 77.

High he rears his ruby crest.   *Owen* 22.

beech, That wreathes its . . . roots so high,
El. 102.

the high brow of yonder hanging lawn.
El. Mas. 116.

She 'd issue out her high commission   *L. S.* 51.

High Dames of honour once,   *L. S.* 107.

a glance from high They send   *Inst.* 19.

High potentates, and dames of royal birth,
Inst. 37.

due reverence to his high command: *Agr.* 4.

To soar High as the consulate,   *Agr.* 43.

before His high tribunal thou and I   *Agr.* 144.

the sun is high advanc'd,   *Agr.* 158.

thee, whose influence breathed from high
Ign. 7.

High on her car, behold the grandam ride
Ign. 36.

But chief, the Sky-lark warbles high   *Vic.* 13.

Heaven lifts its everlasting portals high, *Stanza* 3.

Pursu'd his cast, and hurl'd the orb on high,
Stat.[2] 9.

The orb on high tenacious of its course, *Stat.*[2] 10.

†High heaves his hugeness H,   *Ch. Cr.* 21.

High-born.

Vocal no more, . . . To high-born Hoel's harp,
Bard 28.

High-crowned.

His high-crown'd hat, and sattin-doublet, *L. S.* 14.

Hight.

the Tower of Famine hight,   *Dante* 24.

Hilda.

Sangrida, and *Hilda* see, Join . . . to aid:
F. S. 18.

Hill.

I [we, Mas.] miss'd him on the custom'd hill,
El. 109.

Hills.

Ah, happy hills.   *Eton* 11.

On Thracia's hills the Lord of War   *P. P.* 17.

From Cambria's thousand hills   *Bard* MS. 109.

While vales and woods and echoing hills rebound.
Stat.[2] 17.

Him, omitted.

Hippomedon.

Nor more, for now Nesimachus's son, — (*Hippomedon,*) *Stat.*[1] 13.

come on, With sturdy step and slow, Hippomedon; *Stat.*[2] 2.

His, *omitted.*

Hissed.

She swept, she hiss'd, she ripen'd and grew rough, *Par. on Ep.* 2.

Hissing.

The hissing terrors round Alecto's head, *Prop.*[2] 42.

History.

read their hist'ry in a nation's eyes. *El.* 64.

Your Hist'ry whither are you spinning? *L. S.* 19.

Big with the important Nothing's History. *Prop.*[3] 30.

Hither.

Yet hither oft a glance . . . They send *Inst.* 19.

nor on what Errand Sent hither: *Dante* 11.

Hits.

The Master of Clare Hits them all to a hair; *Satire* 22.

Hive.

No hive hast thou of hoarded sweets, *Spring* 46.

Hoarded.

No hive hast thou of hoarded sweets, *Spring* 46.

He ask'd no heaps of hoarded gold; *Hoel* 8.

Hoarse.

Hoarse he bays with hideous din, *Odin* 9.

Scarce the hoarse waves from far were heard to roar, *Tasso* 6.

Hoarser.

Revenge on thee in hoarser murmurs breath; *Bard* 26.

†K, as a man, with hoarser accent speaks, *Ch. Cr.* 47.

Hoary.

Wanders the hoary Thames along *Eton* 9.

Loose his beard, and hoary hair Stream'd, *Bard* 19.

And hoary Nile with pensive Aspect seem *Prop.*[3] 49.

Hoary-headed.

some hoary-headed Swain may say, *El.* 97.

Hoder's.

In *Hoder's* hand the Heroe's doom: *Odin* 55.

By whom shall *Hoder's* blood be spilt? *Odin* 62.

Till he on *Hoder's* corse shall smile *Odin* 69.

Hoel.

By them, my friend, my Hoel, died, *Hoel* 6.

Hoel's.

Vocal no more, . . . To high-born Hoel's harp, *Bard* 28.

Hold.

Then grasp'd its weight, elusive of his hold; *Stat.*[1] 42.

Holds.

all the air a solemn stillness holds, *El.* 6.

Climes, where Winter holds his Reign, *E. G.* 5.

Hole.

Each hole and cupboard they explore, *L. S.* 61.

Holland.

Here Holland form'd the pious resolution *View* 2.

Hollow.

Till from out the hollow ground *Odin* 25.

To taste of hollow kindness, *Agr.* 19.

Holy.

Science still adores Her Henry's holy Shade; *Eton* 4.

and Freedom's holy flame. *P. P.* 65.

her holy dew. *Bard* MS. 74.

spare the meek Usurper's holy [hallow'd, MS.] head. *Bard* 90.

many a holy text around she strews, *El.* 83.

Hence, avaunt, ('t is holy ground) *Inst.* 1.

Hence, away, 't is holy ground! *Inst.* 12.

Homage.

the Graces homage pay. *P. P.* 37.

The willing homage Of prostrate Rome, *Agr.* 76.

Home.

Hie thee hence, and boast at home, *Odin* 87.

Homely.

Their homely joys, and destiny obscure; *El.* 30.

Homeward.

The plowman homeward plods his weary way, *El.* 3.

Honest.

his plain soldier's oath, and honest seeming. *Agr.* 151.

Honeyed. See **Honied.**

Honey's.

But may not honey's self be turn'd to gall *Shak.* 11.

Honied.

Eager to taste the honied spring, *Spring* 26.

Honor.

High Dames of honour once, *L. S.* 107.

Thy steady course of honour keep, *Inst.* 91.

grasp the dangerous honour. *Agr.* 53.

There first in blood his infant honour seal'd; *Williams* 6.

Every warrior's manly neck Chains of regal honour deck, *Hoel* 14.

Spare the honour of my love. *Song* 12.

The love of honour bade two youths advance, *Stat.*[1] 9.

Thou envied Honour of thy Poet's Days, *Prop.*[3] 103.

Honorable.

There . . . Despair and honourable Death. *Owen* 40.

Honor's.

Can Honour's voice provoke the silent dust? *El.* 43.

Honors.

And all its jetty honours turn to snow; *Prop.*[2] 14.

Honour. See **Honor.**

Honourable. See **Honorable.**

Hoods.

In peaked hoods and mantles tarnish'd, *L. S.* 105.
Cried the square Hoods in woful fidget *L. S.* 135.

Hoops.

To chase the hoop's elusive speed, *Eton MS.* 29.
Convey'd him underneath their hoops *L. S.* 71.

Hooted.

Owls would have hooted in St. Peter's choir,
View 23.

Hope.

Gay hope is theirs *Eton* 41.
. . . they alike in trembling hope repose, *El.* 127.
much I hope these walls alone *Agr.* 22.
While Hope prolongs our happier hour, *Vic.* 33.
Flush'd with mirth and hope they burn: *Hoel* 19.

Hoped.

Yet hop'd, that he might save his bacon: *L. S.* 126.

Hopeless.

cross'd in hopeless love. *El.* 108.
The Muses, hopeless of his pardon, Convey'd him
L. S. 70.

Hopes.

check their tender Hopes with . . . Fear,
E. G. 20.

Horn.

the echoing horn, *El.* 19.

Horrent.

With dazzling helm, and horrent spear.
Bard MS. 112.

Horrid.

That which yet remains . . . (a horrid Tale)
Dante 19.

Horror.

Of Horrour [Terror, MS.] that, *P. P.* 93.
A smile of horror *Bard MS.* 82.
Horrour, Tyrant of the throbbing breast.*Bard* 130.
With horror wild that chills the throbbing breast.
Bard Lett.[2] 130.
Horror covers all the heath, *F. S.* 49.
But pictured horrour and poëtic woes. *Prop.*[2] 50.

Horror's.

With screaming Horror's funeral cry, *Adv.* 39.

Horrors.

gilds the horrors of the deep. *Inst.* 94.
Ye unavailing horrors, fruitless crimes! *Agr.* 177.
Hail, horrors, hail! *Ign.* 1.
new horrors [terrors, Nich.] still to bring. *View* 12.
the horrors which we feign: *View Nich.* 20.

Horrour. *See* **Horror.**

Horse.

Lance to lance, and horse to horse? *Bard* 84.

Hosannas.

Hosannas rung through hell's tremendous borders,
Toph. 7.

Hospitable.

partake His hospitable board: *Agr.* 20.

Host.

oft have issued, Host impelling Host, *E. G.* 50.
Swift at the word, from out the gazing host,
Stat.[1] 4.

Hosts.

Big with hosts . . . Squadrons . . . came;
Owen 9.

Hounds. *See* **Hell-hounds.**

Hour.

Whose iron scourge and tort'ring hour *Adv.* 3.
in Greece's evil hour, *P. P.* 77.
Awaits alike th' inevitable hour. *El.* 35.
a secret and dead hour of night, *Agr.* 61.
While Hope prolongs our happier hour, *Vic.* 33.
Steal to his closet at the hour of prayer; *Shak.* 14.
Th' Æmonian hag enjoys her dreadful hour,
Stat.[1] 58.
now the Hour Of timely Food approach'd;
Dante 49.

Hours.

Lo! where the rosy bosom'd Hours, *Spring* 1.
'Gainst graver hours, *Eton* 33.
why do I waste the fruitless hours *Agr.* 154.
Long as of youth the joyous hours remain,
Prop.[2] 1.
These soft inglorious joys my hours engage;
Prop.[2] 51.

House. *See also* **Great-house.**

A House there is, (and that's enough) *L. S.* 21.
the genuine blood Of our imperial house.
Agr. 105.
within That House of Woe. *Dante* 61.

Household.

there to tend Her household cares, *Agr.* 8.

Houses.

On the Heads of thy Houses, *Satire* 3.

Housewife.

Or busy housewife [Hus-wife, Mas.] ply her evening care : *El.* 22.

Hovered.

that hover'd in thy noontide ray? *Bard MS.* 69.

Hovering.

Bright-eyed Fancy hov'ring o'er *P. P.* 108.

How.

How vain the ardour of the Crowd, *Spring* 18.
How low, how little are the Proud, *Spring* 19.
How indigent the Great [proud, Dods.]! *Spring* 20.
Yet hark, how thro' the peopled air *Spring* 23.
Yet see how all around 'em wait *Eton* 55.
How do your tuneful Echo's languish, *P. P.* 71.
Beneath the Good how far — *P. P.* 123.
Hark, how each giant-oak, and desert cave, Sighs
Bard 23.
How jocund did they drive their team *El.* 27.
How bow'd the woods beneath their sturdy stroke!
El. 28.
how the sacred Calm, that broods around,
El. Mas. 81.
How in the park . . . He . . . had pen'd a
sonnet; *L. S.* 122.
What if you add, how she turn'd pale *Agr.* 9.
How vast the debt of gratitude *Agr.* 57.
how oft in weak and sickly minds *Agr.* 72.
How shall the spark . . . Blaze *Agr.* 128.
How rude so e'er th' exterior Form *E. G.* 26.

Ah! say, . . . how these symptoms befell me?
Am. Lines 7.

How riseing winds the face of Ocean sweep,
Prop.[2] 23.

How flames . . . Shall sink this beauteous fabric   *Prop.*[2] 27.

How the rude surge its sandy Bounds control;
Prop.[2] 37.

Nor how the Persian trod the indignant Sea;
Prop.[3] 38.

†Queen Esther next — how fair e'en after death,
Ch. Cr. 9.

Howe'er.

Howe'er Opinion tinge the . . . Mind, *E. G.* 27.

Huddle.

huddle up in fogs the dang'rous fire.   *Ign.* 22.

Hue.

Their scaly armour's Tyrian hue   *Cat* 16.

Theirs buxom health of rosy hue,   *Eton* 45.

avaunt, . . . dreaming Sloth of pallid hue,
Inst. 4.

A brighter Day, and Skies of azure Hue;
E. G. 55.

Here the soft emerald smiles of verdant hue,
Tasso 67.

Hues.

With orient hues, unborrow'd of the Sun:
P. P. 120.

The hues of Bliss more brightly glow,   *Vic.* 41.

Huge.

Made huge Plinlimmon bow his cloud-top'd head.   *Bard* 34.

Black and huge along they sweep,   *Owen* 17.

Papers and books, a huge Imbroglio! *L. S.* 66.

As bright and huge the spacious circle lay,
Stat.[1] 26.

comes quiv'ring down, Heavy and huge, *Stat.*[1] 51.

Hugely.

the Master of Jesus Does hugely displease us;
Satire 6.

Hugeness.

†High heaves his hugeness H,   *Ch. Cr.* 21.

Hugs.

Servitude that hugs her chain,   *Inst.* 6.

Human.

Thou Tamer of the human breast,   *Adv.* 2.

The Ministers of human fate,   *Eton* 56.

'T is of human entrails made   *F. S.* 10.

from his jaws, . . . Foam and human gore distill'd: *Odin* 8.

Their human passions now no more,   *Inst.* 49.

the human fabric from the birth Imbibes *E. G.* 84.

Humanity.

faith sincere, And soft humanity were there.
Clerke 6.

Humble.

Humble quiet builds her cell,   *Vic.* 53.

Science frown'd not on his humble birth, *El.* 119.

Humid.

draws his humid train of mud: *Ign.* 4.

Hundred.

their hundred arms they wave,   *Bard* 25.

Thrice two hundred warriors go: *Hoel* 12.

When Pindus' self . . . bows his hundred heads;
Prop.[2] 32.

Hunger.

For Anguish, which they construed Hunger;
Dante 64.

for then Hunger had reft my Eye-sight *Dante* 79.

The fourth, what Sorrow could not, Hunger did.
Dante 81.

Hungry.

The hungry Pack their sharp-set Fangs embrued.
Dante 40.

Huntingdons.

The Huntingdons and Hattons there   *L. S.* 3.

Hurled.

in ruin hurl'd, Sinks the fabric of the world.
Odin 93.

Upon Deïra's squadrons hurl'd   *Hoel* 3.

but hurl'd upright, Emits the mass,   *Stat.*[1] 45.

Pursu'd his cast, and hurl'd the orb on high;
Stat.[2] 9.

For adverse fate the captive chief has hurl'd
Tasso 33.

How flames perhaps, with dire confusion hurl'd,
Prop.[2] 27.

Hurls.

Hurls . . . his glitt'ring shafts of war.
P. P. MS. 52.

Hurry.

Hurry, hurry to the field.   *F. S.* 64.

Hurry-skurry.

Run hurry-skurry round the floor,   *L. S.* 63.

Hurt.

Without design to hurt the butter,   *L. S.* 123.

And all the scenes, that hurt the grave's repose,
Prop.[2] 49.

The Melian's Hurt Machaon could repair,
Prop.[3] 81.

Nor changing Skies can hurt,   *Prop.*[3] 94.

Hurtles.

Iron-sleet . . . Hurtles in the darken'd air.
F. S. 4.

Hushed.

tongue, That hush'd the stormy main: *Bard* 30.

That, hush'd in grim repose, expects his evening-prey.   *Bard* 76.

Hyperion.

Till fierce Hyperion from afar   *P. P. MS.* 52.

Hyperion hurls around his glitt'ring shafts
P. P. MS. 53.

Thrice hath Hyperion roll'd his . . . race,
Ign. 11.

Hyperion's.

Hyperion's march they spy,   *P. P.* 53.

I.

†As H the Hebrew found, so I the Jew, *Ch. Cr.* 25.

I, *pron., omitted.*

Ice-built.

shaggy forms o'er ice-built mountains roam,
P. P. 55.

Icy.

numbs the soul with icy hand, *Eton* 89.
And winter binds the floods in icy chains, *Tasso* 18.

I'd. *See also* **Would.**

I'd in the ring knit hands, *Prop.*² 6.
To Providence, to Him my thoughts I'd raise,
*Prop.*² 16.

Idalia.

O'er Idalia's velvet-green *P. P.* 27.

Idiom.

The manners speak the idiom of their soil.
E. G. 87.

Idle.

What idle progeny succeed *Eton* 28.
Self-pleasing Folly's idle brood, *Adv.* 18.
They mock the air with idle state. *Bard* 4.
when the idle herd . . . yet will start, *Agr.* 129.
Idle notes! untimely green! *Song* 7.

Idly.

Instruction . . . idly lavishes her Stores,
E. G. 14.

Idolize.

Exalt the brave, and idolize Success; *El. Mas.* 74.

If.

If Mem'ry o'er their Tomb no Trophies raise,
El. 38.
If chance . . . Some kindred spirit *El.* 95.
If chance that e'er some pensive spirit.
El. Mas. 109.
He went, as if the Devil drove him. *L. S.* 88.
What if you add, how she turn'd pale *Agr.* 9.
If bright ambition from her craggy seat *Agr.* 51.
If the son reign, the mother perishes. *Agr.* 67.
If from the realms of night *Agr.* 178.
if your injur'd shades demand my fate, *Agr.* 184.
If murder cries for murder, *Agr.* 185.
as if she knew not Whether she fear'd, *Agr.* 198.
If any spark of wit's delusive ray *Ign.* 19.
If equal Justice . . . Smile not indulgent
E. G. 15.
What wonder, if to patient valour train'd
E. G. 94.
If with adventrous oar and ready sail *E. G.* 104.
if to some feeling breast *Bent.* 25.
If then he wreak on me his wicked will, *Shak.* 13.
The Bishop of Chester, . . . If you scratch him
will fester. *Ext. Keene* 4.
If realms beneath those fabled torments know,
*Prop.*² 39.
If the loose Curls around her Forehead play,
*Prop.*³ 7.
If the thin Coan Web her shape reveal, *Prop.*³ 9.
Or if to Musick she the Lyre awake, *Prop.*³ 13.
If sinking into Sleep she seem to close *Prop.*³ 17.
Or if, alas! it be my Fate *Prop.*³ 69.
Or if I fall the Victim *Prop.*³ 77.
yet if the telling may Beget *Dante* 6.
Attend, and say if he have injured me. *Dante* 21.
oh! if thou weep not now, *Dante* 47.

if you resume your Gift; *Dante* 66.
†If a plenteous Crop arise, *Ode* 7.
†If heroïc Verse I'm reading *Ode* 26.
†But if my Myra cruel be *Ode* 29.
†buskin'd Strains, If Melpomene inspire, *Ode* 32.

Ignoble.

the madding crowd's ignoble strife, *El.* 73.

Ignorance.

where ignorance is bliss, *Eton* 99.
And Ignorance with looks profound, *Inst.* 3.
ignorance! soft salutary power! *Ign.* 9.
all was ignorance, and all was night. *Ign.* 30.

Ile. *See also* **Isle.**

through the long-drawn Ile *El. Pem., Mas.* 39.

Iliad.

the long Iliad of the amorous Fight. *Prop.*³ 26.

Ilissus.

Fields, that cool Ilissus laves, *P. P.* 68.

Ilium.

Nor Tale of Thebes, nor Ilium *Prop.*³ 37.

I'll.

I'll be Mrs. *Twitcher* myself. *C. C.* 32.

Ill.

And find a Cure for every Ill, *Prop.*³ 80.

Ills.

No sense have they of ills to come, *Eton* 53.
Man's feeble race what Ills await, *P. P.* 42.
For Ills unseen what Remedy is found? *Prop.*³ 91.

I'm.

You know I'm no prude, *C. C.* 7.
†If heroïc Verse I'm reading *Ode* 26.

Image.

Her infant image here below, Sits smiling *Clerke* 9.

Imagination.

Had in imagination fenc'd him, *L. S.* 114.

Imbibes.

Imbibes a flavour of its parent earth, *E. G.* 85.

Imbroglio.

Papers and books, a huge Imbroglio! *L. S.* 66.

Imbrued. *See* **Embrued.**

Immersed.

Immers'd in rapt'rous thought profound, *Adv.* 26.

Immortal.

Can powers immortal feel *Ign.* 26.
glorious puddings and immortal pies. *Shak.* 24.
immortal Boy! *P. P.* 91.

Immortality.

Strains of Immortality! *F. S.* 48.

Imp.

lurk'd A wicked Imp they call a Poet, *L. S.* 44.

Impart.

Thy milder influence impart, *Adv.* 42.
Health and Vigour to the Soul impart, *E. G.* 11.
Her pleasure, pleasures to impart, *Clerke MS.* 8.

Impartial.

Alike to all the Kind impartial Heav'n *E. G.* 28.

Impelling.
Oft have issued, Host impelling Host,   *E. G.* 50.

Impending.
fate Impending o'er your son: *Agr.* 66.

Imperfect.
in my Breast the imperfect Joys expire. *West* 8.

Imperial.
the genuine blood Of our imperial house. *Agr.* 105.

Impetuous.
Headlong, impetuous, see it pour;   *P. P.* 11.

Impious.
As by the Impious thou art seen   *Adv.* 37.
Fond impious Man, think'st thou,   *Bard* 135.

Implanted.
†Nature in my Soul implanted: *Ode* 2.

Imploreing. *See* **Imploring.**

Implores.
Implores the passing tribute of a sigh. *El.* 80.

Imploring.
imploreing In vain my Help,   *Dante* 73.

Important.
Big with the important Nothing's History.
     *Prop.*³ 30.

Importune.
too proud to importune;   *Char.* 1.

Improve.
Fix and improve the polish'd Arts of Peace:
     E. G. 41.

Impute.
Nor you, ye Proud, impute to These the fault,
     El. 37.

In, *omitted.*

Inactive.
†the rolling Sun Bursts the inactive Shell, *Ode* 44.

Inborn.
dares . . . Profane thy inborn royalty of mind:
     Inst. 81.

Incense.
incense kindled at the Muse's flame.   *El.* 72.
she . . . no venal incense flings;   *Inst.* 79.
the grateful steam Of flattery's incense, *Agr.* 35.

Incense-breathing.
The breezy call of incense-breathing [*om.* Mas.]
 Morn,   *El.* 17.

Indies.
Not I for the Indies!   *C. C.* 7.

Indigent.
how indigent the proud,   *Spring* Dods. 19.
How indigent the Great!   *Spring* 20.

Indignant.
Marking with indignant eye   *Owen* 35.
Bursts on my ear th' indignant lay: *Inst.* 14.
sees far off with an indignant groan,   *E. G.* 62.
Nor how the Persian trod the indignant Sea;
     *Prop.*³ 38.

Indite.
Of the dear Web whole Volumes I indite:
     *Prop.*³ 12.

Indolence.
Mark where Indolence and Pride,   *Vic.* 61.

Indulged.
sweets of kindness lavishly indulg'd   *Agr.* 73.

Industry.
Industry and Gain their Vigils keep,   *E. G.* 42.

Inevitable.
Awaits alike th' inevitable hour.   *El.* 35.

Infamy.
And grinning Infamy.   *Eton* 74.
the telling may Beget the Traitour's Infamy,
     Dante 7.

Infant.
he . . . bad to form her infant mind.   *Adv.* 12.
before his infant [visionary, MS.] eyes *P. P.* 118.
Her infant image here below, Sits smiling
     Clerke 9.
There first in blood his infant honour seal'd;
     Williams 6.

Infant-gore.
The bristled Boar in infant-gore Wallows
     Bard 93.

Inferior.
th' inferior laws that rule our clay: *E. G.* 80.

Infernal.
Or drive the infernal Vulture   *Prop.*³ 90.

Inflicts.
All angry heaven inflicts, or hell can feel,
     *Prop.*² 45.

Influence.
Thy milder influence impart,   *Adv.* 42.
thee, whose influence breathed from high *Ign.* 7.
the influence of the northern star   *E. G.* 68.
as their pleasing influence   *Bent.* 27.
†Whose influence first bid it live.   *Ode* 54.

Ingenuous.
quench the blushes of ingenuous shame, *El.* 70.

Inglorious.
Some mute inglorious Milton   *El.* 59.
These soft inglorious joys my hours engage;
     *Prop.*² 51.

Ingratitude.
the blacker his ingratitude.   *Agr.* 173.

Inherit.
tho' he inherit Nor the pride, nor ample pinion,
     P. P. 113.

Inhospitable.
Oceans unknown, inhospitable Sands ! *Tasso* 32.

Injured.
your injur'd shades demand my fate,   *Agr.* 184.
Attend, and say if he have injured me. *Dante* 21.

Injurious.
The cool injurious eye of frozen kindness.
     Agr. 162.

Inly.
Jealousy . . . that inly gnaws   *Eton* 67.

Inmost.
Beneath the obedient river's inmost bed;
     Tasso 44.

Earth's inmost cells, and caves of deep descent;
Tasso 50.
that unutter'd nathless wrings My inmost Heart?
Dante 6.

Innocence.
More to Innocence their Safety owe *El. Mas.* 75.

Inquire. *See* **Enquire.**

Inquirer. *See* **Enquirer.**

Inquiry. *See* **Enquiry.**

Insatiate.
I ceaseless gnaw insatiate; *Dante* 8.

Insect.
The insect youth are on the wing, *Spring* 25.

Inspiration.
Inspiration breath'd around: *P. P.* 74.
Is that diviner inspiration giv'n, *Bent.* 18.

Inspire.
†buskin'd Strains, If Melpomene inspire, *Ode* 32.

Inspires.
She is my Genius, she inspires the Lines;
*Prop.*³ 4.

Instruction.
fond Instruction . . . idly lavishes her Stores,
E. G. 13.

Insult.
these bones from insult to protect *El.* 77.
Insult the plenty of the vales below? *E. G.* 99.

Intent.
Presumptuous Maid! with looks intent *Cat* 25.

Intercept.
Age step 'twixt love and me, and intercept the joy;
*Prop.*² 12.

Intercepts.
Pisa's Mount, that intercepts the View Of Lucca,
Dante 29.

Interleaved.
Though now a book, and interleaved [interleav'd,
Lett.⁴] you see. *Shak.* 4.

Intermingled.
dart their intermingled rays, *Bent.* 23.

Into.
But bounce into the parlour enter'd. *L. S.* 56.
Into the Drawers and China pry, *L. S.* 65.
How shall the spark . . . Blaze into freedom,
Agr. 129.
Better be twisted into caps for spice, *Shak.* 19.
Whate'er . . . Floats into Lakes, and bubbles
into rills; *Tasso* 54.
The parts combine and harden into Ore:
Tasso 62.
If sinking into Sleep she seem to close *Prop.*³ 17.
†throw . . . half an act into the Fire: *Ode* 34.
†Elizabeths all dwindled into Betties; *Ch. Cr.* 12.
†They're all diverted into H and B. *Ch. Cr.* 14.

Invention.
Theirs . . . invention ever-new, *Eton* 46.

Invisible.
chains invisible the border. *L. S.* 84.

Invocation.
charms, and solemn invocation, *Agr.* 63.

Invokes.
Art he invokes new horrors still to bring.
View 12.

Involuntary.
Forgive, ye Proud, th' involuntary Fault,
El. Dods., Pem., Eg., Mas. 37.

Ios.
Then, while the vaulted Skies loud Ios rend,
*Prop.*³ 47.

Iron.
Whose iron scourge and tort'ring hour *Adv.* 3.
Have his limbs Sweat under iron harness?
Agr. 97.
Earth's monster-brood stretch'd on their iron bed,
*Prop.*² 41.

Iron-race.
An Iron-race the mountain-cliffs maintain,
E. G. 88.

Iron-sleep.
Enquirer come To break my iron-sleep again;
Odin 89.

Iron-sleet.
Iron-sleet of arrowy shower Hurtles *F. S.* 3.

Irresolute.
Irresolute they stand; *Tasso* 11.

Irritated.
haughty youth[,] and irritated power.[,]
Agr. 26, 28.

Is, *omitted.*

Isaac.
†See Isaac, Joseph, Jacob, pass in view;
Ch. Cr. 26.

Isle. *See also* **Isle.**
through the long-drawn isle *El.* 39.
In Britain's Isle, . . . An ancient pile . . . stands:
L. S. 1.

Isles.
Isles, that crown the Egæan deep, *P. P.* 67.

Israel.
Did not Israel filch from the Egyptians of old
C. C. 25.
†See Israel, and all Judah thronging there.
Ch. Cr. 28.

Issue.
ye genuine Kings, Britannia's Issue, hail!
Bard 110.
Swore . . . She'd issue out her high commission
L. S. 51.

Issued.
oft have issued, Host impelling Host, *E. G.* 50.

Issues.
House . . . From whence one fatal morning
issues *L. S.* 22.

It, *omitted.*

Its.
desart-beach Pent within its bleak domain,
F. S. 38.
The fragrance of its blushing head: *Inst.* 74.
soul, and wonder'd at its daring: *Agr.* 55.

its will seem'd wrote in lines of blood, *Agr.* 70.
reflection Pours its cool dictates *Agr.* 83.
shake . . . To its original atoms — *Agr.* 92.
I will not meet its poison. *Agr.* 163.
a flavour of its parent earth, *E. G.* 85.
As the whirlwind in its course; *Conan* 6.
Heaven lifts its everlasting portals high, *Stanza* 3.
And furthest send its weight *Stat.*[1] 2.
Then grasp'd its weight, *Stat.*[1] 42.
through the skies Sings in its rapid way, *Stat.*[1] 50.
The orb on high tenacious of its course, *Stat.*[2] 10.
The orb . . . joys to see Its ancient lord secure
of victory. *Stat.*[2] 13.
ere it precipitates its fall *Stat.*[2] 15.
When thwart the road a River roll'd its flood
Tasso 7.
The flood on either hand its billows rears,
Tasso 41.
Whate'er with copious train its channel fills,
Tasso 53.
Proud of its diamond dies, *Tasso* 70.
And all its jetty honours turn to snow; *Prop.*[2] 14.
Who taught this vast machine its steadfast laws,
Prop.[2] 17.
How the rude surge its sandy Bounds control;
Prop.[2] 37.
Back to it's Source divine the Julian Race.
Prop.[3] 58.
And to this bosom give its wonted Peace,
Prop.[3] 88.

Ivory.
Or lawless, o'er their Ivory Margin stray:
Prop.[3] 8.
Of those loose Curls, that Ivory front I write;
Prop.[3] 11.

Ivy-mantled.
from yonder ivy-mantled tow'r *El.* 9.

Ixion's.
The pendent rock, Ixion's whirling wheel,
Prop.[2] 46.

Jacob.
†See Isaac, Joseph, Jacob, pass in view;
Ch. Cr. 26.

Janes.
The lady *Janes* and *Joans* repair, *L. S.* 99.

Javelins.
Pikes must shiver, javelins sing, *F. S.* 22.

Jaws.
from his jaws, . . . Foam and human gore distill'd: *Odin* 7.

Jealousy.
Jealousy with rankling tooth, *Eton* 66.
the dazzled sight Of wakeful jealousy. *Agr.* 192.

Jeer.
†Here Grub-street Geese presume to joke and jeer,
Ch. Cr. 19.

Jemmy.
When sly Jemmy Twitcher had smugg'd up his
face, *C. C.* 1.

Jerusalem.
†The walls of old Jerusalem appear, *Ch. Cr.* 27.

Jesu-Maria.
Jesu-Maria! Madam Bridget, *L. S.* 133.

Jesus.
Know the Master of Jesus Does hugely displease
us; *Satire* 5.

Jet.
Her ears of jet . . . she saw; *Cat* 11.

Jetty.
And all its jetty honours turn to snow; *Prop.*[2] 14.

Jew.
†As H the Hebrew found, so I the Jew, *Ch. Cr.* 25.

Jewels.
Their jewels of silver and jewels of gold? *C. C.* 26.

Joans.
The lady *Janes* and *Joans* repair, *L. S.* 99.

Jocund.
How jocund did they drive their team afield!
El. 27.

John's.
The Master of St. John's *Satire* 33.

Join.
in dreadful harmony they join, *Bard* 47.
Join the wayward work to aid: *F. S.* 19.
Norman sails afar . . . join the war: *Owen* 16.
While spirits . . . Join with glad voice *Inst.* 88.
The Birds in vain their amorous Descant joyn;
West 3.
I'd in the ring knit hands, and joyn the Muses'
dance. *Prop.*[2] 6.

Joint.
My Lady heard their joint petition, *L. S.* 49.
the senate's joint applause, *Agr.* 77.

Joints.
This racks the joints, *Eton* 85.

Joke.
†Here Grub-street Geese presume to joke and jeer,
Ch. Cr. 19.

Joseph.
†See Isaac, Joseph, Jacob, pass in view;
Ch. Cr. 26.

Jove.
Daughter of Jove, relentless Power, *Adv.* 1.
on the scept'red hand Of Jove, *P. P.* 21.
justify the laws of Jove. *P. P.* 47.
her that arm'd This painted Jove, *Agr.* 30.
What colours paint the vivid arch of Jove;
Prop.[2] 29.
nor Callimachus' enervate Strain May tell of
Jove, *Prop.*[3] 56.

Joy.
Her conscious tail her joy declar'd; *Cat* 7.
redolent of joy and youth, *Eton* 19.
And snatch a fearful joy. *Eton* 40.
Laughter, Noise, and thoughtless Joy, *Adv.* 19.
This can unlock the gates of Joy; *P. P.* 92.
With joy I see The different doom *Bard* 139.
Songs of joy and triumph sing! *F. S.* 54.
Joy to the victorious bands; *F. S.* 55.
Short was his joy. *L. S.* 77.

't would dash his joy To hear the spirit *Agr.* 13.
'T is man alone that Joy descries *Vic.* 27.
Age step 'twixt love and me, and intercept the joy;
Prop.² 12.

Joyous.
Long as of youth the joyous hours remain,
Prop.² 1.

Joys.
Thy Joys no glittering female meets, *Spring* 45.
Their homely joys, and destiny obscure; *El.* 30.
in my Breast the imperfect Joys expire. *West* 8.
The orb . . . joys to see Its ancient lord secure
of victory, *Stat.² 12.*
These soft inglorious joys my hours engage;
Prop.² 51.

Judah.
†See Israel, and all Judah thronging there.
Ch. Cr. 28.

Judge.
power To judge of weights and measures;
Agr. 41.
My Wrongs, and from them judge of my Revenge. *Dante* 15.

Judging.
thy judging eye, The flow'r unheeded shall descry, *Inst.* 71.

Judgment.
Their Judgment mends the Plan *E. G.* 32.
†Judgment from the Harvest flies *Ode* 9.

Juice.
Nor genial Warmth, nor genial Juice *E. G.* 3.
drink Nectar . . . Or the grape's extatic juice.
Hoel 18.

Julian.
glows with the pure Julian fire, *Agr.* 50.
Back to it's Source divine the Julian Race.
Prop.³ 58.

Julius.
Ye Towers of Julius, London's lasting shame,
Bard 87.

Juno.
By Juno, It bears a noble semblance. *Agr.* 119.

Just.
And to thy just, . . . hand, Submits the fasces
Inst. 85.
'T is just like the picture in Rochester's book;
C. C. 12.
'T is a sign you have eat just enough *Couplet* 2.
†They who just have felt the flame *Rond.* 21.

Justice.
With Justice to herself severe, *Adv.* 31.

Justify.
justify the laws of Jove. *P. P.* 47.

K.
†As K a King, Q represents a Queen,
Ch. Cr. 45.
†K, as a man, with hoarser accent speaks,
Ch. Cr. 47.
†Behold K struts, *Ch. Cr.* 49.

Keen.
keen Remorse with blood defil'd, *Eton* 78.
they . . . veil'd their weapons bright and keen
L. S. 39.

Keene.
Here lies Edmund Keene Lord Bishop of Chester,
Ep. Keene 1.
Here lies Mrs. Keene *Mrs. Keene* 1.

Keep.
Yet shall he mount, and keep his distant way
P. P. 121.
Keep the tissue close and strong. *F. S.* 16.
And keep my Lady from her Rubbers. *L. S.* 144.
Thy steady course of honour keep, *Inst.* 91.
Industry and Gain their Vigils keep, *E. G.* 42.

Keeper. *See* **Lord-keeper.**

Kept.
They kept the noiseless tenor of their way. *El.* 76.

Keys.
Thine too these golden keys, *P. P.* 91.
As the Master of Keys *Satire* 13.

Kidney.
Is of the same kidney; *Satire* 10.

Kill.
Ours to kill, and ours to spare: *F. S.* 34.

Killed.
And suck'd the eggs, and kill'd the pheasants.
L. S. 48.

Killing.
meaner Beauties . . . ape her art of killing.
L. S. 28.

Kind.
The sportive kind reply: *Spring* 42.
Demurest of the tabby kind, *Cat* 4.
vain tho' kind enquiry *El. Mas.* 111.
The other Amazon kind Heaven Had arm'd
L. S. 29.
Alike to all the Kind *E. G.* 28.
The triple dog that scares the shadowy kind,
Prop.² 44.
He lived, while she was kind; *Prop.³ 108.*

Kindled.
incense kindled at the Muse's flame. *El.* 72.

Kindly.
unfriended, by those kindly Cares, *E. G.* 10.

Kindness.
lured . . . To taste of hollow kindness, *Agr.* 19.
The sweets of kindness . . . Rankle *Agr.* 73.
cool injurious eye of frozen kindness. *Agr.* 162.

Kindred.
thro' the kindred squadrons mow their way.
Bard 86.
Some kindred spirit shall inquire *El.* 96.
Welcome, . . . To this, thy kindred train, and
me: *Inst.* 68.
See a kindred Grief pursue; *Vic.* 38.

King.
thy magic lulls the feather'd king *P. P.* 21.
Ruin seize thee, ruthless King! *Bard* 1.

O'er thee, oh King! their hundred arms they
   wave,   *Bard* 25.
Shrieks of an agonizing King!   *Bard* 56.
spread O'er the youthful King your shield.
                                 F. S. 32.
Soon a King shall bite the ground.   *F. S.* 44.
Triumph to the younger King.   *F. S.* 56.
Uprose the King of Men with speed, *Odin* 1.
King of Men, I know thee now;   *Odin* 82.
And so God save our noble King,   *L. S.* 141.
Then thus the King: —   *Stat.*[1] 1.
†As K a King, Q represents a Queen, *Ch. Cr.* 45.
†as might a King become,   *Ch. Cr.* 49.

King's
The Master of King's   *Satire* 17.

Kings.
All hail, ye genuine Kings,   *Bard* 110.
Their Arms, their Kings, their Gods *E. G.* 49.

Kiss.
climb his knees the envied kiss to share. *El.* 24.

Knee.
bow the supple knee,   *Agr.* 101.
Firmly he plants each knee,   *Stat.*[1] 47.

Knees.
No children . . . climb his knees   *El.* 24.

Knell.
The Curfew tolls the knell of parting day, *El.* 1.
†Light to them the parting knell: *Rond.* 23.

Knew.
Nor knew the gulf between.   *Cat* 27.
He little knew   *L. S.* 77.
as if she knew not Whether she fear'd, *Agr.* 198.
what Clouet never knew,   *Shak.* 21.

Knights.
Youthful knights, and barons bold *Bard* MS. 111.

Knit.
I 'd in the ring knit hands,   *Prop.*[2] 6.

Know.
Know, one false step is ne'er retriev'd, *Cat* 38.
why should they know their fate? *Eton* 95.
What sorrow was, thou bad'st her know, *Adv.* 15.
know myself a Man.   *Adv.* 48.
Thou the deeds of light shalt know; *Odin* 39.
King of Men, I know thee now;   *Odin* 82.
By this time all the Parish know it *L. S.* 42.
who know Without a spell to raise, *Agr.* 15.
to know the fate Impending   *Agr.* 65.
The soft Returns of Gratitude they know,
                             E. G. 34.
Their raptures . . . No yesterday, nor morrow
   know;   *Vic.* 26.
You know I 'm no prude,   *C. C.* 7.
"I don't know," says LAW,   *C. C.* 11.
Know the Master of Jesus Does hugely displease
   us;   *Satire* 5.
When my changed head these locks no more
   shall know,   *Prop.*[2] 13.
If realms beneath those fabled torments know,
                          Prop.[2] 39.

no other Muse I know,   *Prop.*[3] 5.
I know not, who thou art;   *Dante* 10.
Know, thou seest In me Count Ugolino, *Dante* 12.
Gave not to know their Sum of Misery, *Dante* 43.

Knowing.
To weep without knowing the cause of my anguish: *Am. Lines* 2.

Knowledge.
Knowledge . . . her ample page . . . did ne'er
   unroll;   *El.* 49.

Known. *See also* **Well-known.**
and known To many a Wretch   *Dante* 24.

Knows.
Knows his soft ear the trumpet's thrilling voice,
                           Agr. 95.

Labor.
Labour, and Penury, the racks of Pain, *P. P.* 43.
With native spots and artful labour gay, *Stat.*[2] 25.

Labored.
gorgeous phrase of labour'd eloquence *Agr.* 149.

Laboring.
every labouring sinew strains,   *Eton* 86.
Young Pterelas . . . drew, Labouring, the disc,
                           Stat.[1] 6.
hag . . . smiles malignant on the labouring
   power.   *Stat.*[1] 59.

Labors.
some . . . Their murm'ring labours ply *Eton* 32.
we hied, our Labours done,   *El. Mas.* 118.
Third in the labours of the disc come on, *Stat.*[2] 1.

Labour. *See* **Labor.**

Laboured. *See* **Labored.**

Labouring. *See* **Laboring.**

Labours. *See* **Labors.**

Labyrinths.
In lingering Lab'rinths creep,   *P. P.* 70.

Lady.
My Lady heard their joint petition, *L. S.* 49.
The lady *Janes* and *Joans* repair, *L. S.* 99.
My Lady rose,   *L. S.* 131.
And keep my Lady from her Rubbers. *L. S.* 144.

Laid.
Of Chili's boundless forests laid, *P. P.* 59.
In thy green lap was Nature's Darling laid,
                             P. P. 84.
Low the dauntless Earl is laid,   *F. S.* 41.
was laid The dust of the prophetic Maid. *Odin* 19.
Each in his narrow cell for ever laid, *El.* 15.
in this neglected spot is laid Some heart *El.* 45.

Lake.
The pensive Selima . . . Gazed on the lake
                             Cat 6.

Lakes.
Whate'er . . . Floats into Lakes, *Tasso* 54.

Lamb.
A gentler Lamb ne'er sported on the plain, *Child* 3.

Lambent.

†Lightly lambent o'er their frame, *Rond.* 22.

Lamed.

Dried up the cows, and lam'd the deer, *L. S.* 47.

Lamps.

Lamps, that shed at Ev'n a cheerful ray *E. G.* 66.

Lance.

drop'd his thirsty lance at thy command. *P. P.* 19.

" To arms! " cried Mortimer, and couch'd his quiv'ring lance. *Bard* 14.

Lance to lance, and horse to horse? *Bard* 84.

So Caràdoc bore his lance. *Caradoc* 4.

Lances.

Glitt'ring lances [launces, MS.] are the loom, *F. S.* 5.

Land.

Avengers of their native land: *Bard* 46.

scatter plenty o'er a smiling land, *El.* 63.

dews Lethean through the land dispense *Ign.* 17.

scatter . . . Showers of Plenty o'er the Land. *E. G.* 18.

And mariners, though shipwreck'd, dread to land. *View* 8.

his native land Admired that arm, *Stat.*¹ 35.

Lands.

The . . . tide, that drowns her lessening lands, *E. G.* 61.

What length of sea remains, what various lands, *Tasso* 31.

Landscape.

fades the glimmering landscape on the sight, *El.* 5.

Lanes.

Thro' lanes unknown, o'er stiles they ventur'd, *L. S.* 54.

Lanfranc.

Lanfranc there And Sigismundo, *Dante* 32.

Language.

they speak . . . The liquid language of the skies: *Inst.* 56.

Languid.

languid Pleasure sighs in every Gale. *E. G.* 45.

she seem to close Her languid Lids, *Prop.*³ 18.

Languish.

How do your tuneful Echo's languish, *P. P.* 71.

With beauty, with pleasure surrounded, to languish — *Am. Lines* 1.

Lap.

In thy green lap was Nature's Darling laid, *P. P.* 84.

rests his head upon the lap of Earth *El.* 117.

nurs'd in ease And pleasure's flow'ry lap? *Agr.* 99.

Large.

Large was his bounty, *El.* 121.

Largely.

Heav'n did a recompence as largely send: *El.* 122.

Lark. *See also* **Sky-lark, Woodlark.**

'T was the Lark that upward sprung! *Song* 5.

Lasting.

Ye Towers of Julius, London's lasting shame, *Bard* 87.

Fix'd by his touch a lasting essence take; *Bent.* 6.

Late.

sorrow never comes too late, *Eton* 96.

While Prows, that late in fierce Encounter mett, *Prop.*³ 51.

†Late to find it: — and, again, *Rond.* 3, 11, 19, 27, 35.

Late-descending.

Swoll'n with new force, and late-descending rains. *Tasso* 10.

Latent.

Shall raise from earth the latent gem *Inst.* 75.

Latest.

Her latest agony of mind *Clerke* MS. 10.

Latian.

Left their Parnassus for the Latian plains. *P. P.* 78.

Latium.

Latium had her lofty spirit lost, *P. P.* 81.

Laugh.

they sing, they laugh, they tattle, *L. S.* 58.

Laughing.

moody Madness laughing wild *Eton* 79.

The laughing flowers, that round them blow, *P. P.* 5.

safe and laughing in his sleeve, *L. S.* 75.

Give me to send the laughing bowl around, *Prop.*² 7.

Laughs.

Fair laughs the Morn, *Bard* 71.

where the face of nature laughs around, *E. G.* 70.

Laughter.

Wild Laughter, Noise, and thoughtless Joy, *Adv.* 19.

Launces. *See* **Lances.**

Laureate.

The laureate wreath, that Cecil wore *Inst.* 84.

Laurel.

Own'd . . . his quiver and his laurel . . . no protection. *L. S.* 95.

Laurelled.

The laurell'd Triumph and the sculptured Carr, *Prop.*³ 34.

Laves.

Fields, that cool Ilissus laves, *P. P.* 68.

Lavishes.

Instruction . . . idly lavishes her Stores, *E. G.* 14.

Lavishly.

The sweets of kindness lavishly indulg'd *Agr.* 73.

Law.

"Lord! sister," says PHYSIC to LAW, *C. C.* 5.

"I don't know," says LAW, *C. C.* 11.

Lawful.

Not all that tempts . . . is lawful prize, *Cat* 41.

Lawless.

As lawless force from confidence will grow
E. G. 98.

Or lawless, o'er their Ivory Margin stray: *Prop.*³ 8.

Lawn.

th' expanse below . . . of lawn . . . survey,
Eton 7.

meet the sun upon the upland lawn. *El.* 100.

Nor up the lawn, nor at the wood *El.* 112.

the high brow of yonder hanging lawn.
El. Mas. 116.

I trod your level lawn, *Inst.* 31.

While to retain the envious Lawn she tries,
*Prop.*³ 23.

Laws.

justify the laws of Jove. *P. P.* 47.

measured Laws and philosophic Ease *E. G.* 40.

th' inferior laws that rule our clay: *E. G.* 80.

Who taught this vast machine its steadfast laws,
*Prop.*² 17.

Lay.

Dread goddess, lay thy chast'ning hand! *Adv.* 34.

Temper'd to thy warbled lay. *P. P.* 26.

Vocal no more, . . . To . . . soft Llewellyn's
lay, *Bard* 28.

Approach and read . . . the lay, *El.* 115.

Bursts on my ear th' indignant lay: *Inst.* 14.

Join with glad voice the loud symphonious lay,
Inst. 88.

Conan's name, my lay, rehearse, *Conan* 1.

As bright and huge the spacious circle lay,
*Stat.*¹ 26.

She . . . gives the Lay to flow *Prop.*³ 6.

the whilst I slumb'ring lay, *Dante* 26.

Lazy.

And what Bootes' lazy waggon tires; *Prop.*² 36.

Lea.

The lowing herd wind slowly o'er the lea, *El.* 2.

Lead.

The paths of glory lead but to the grave. *El.* 36.

And passages, that lead to nothing. *L. S.* 8.

Lo! Granta waits to lead her blooming band,
Inst. 77.

Leaden.

With leaden eye, that loves the ground, *Adv.* 28.

Thy leaden ægis 'gainst our ancient foes? *Ign.* 14.

Leader.

by you Mark'd for their leader: *Agr.* 113.

Leads.

steep . . . That leads to HELA's drear abode.
Odin 4.

Bentley leads her sister-art along, *Bent.* 3.

nature . . . leads the general song: *Vic.* 20.

where rosy Pleasure leads, *Vic.* 37.

road That to the grotto leads, *Tasso* 38.

Leaning.

leaning from her golden cloud The venerable
Marg'ret see! *Inst.* 65.

Learn.

Learn the tenour of our song. *F. S.* 58.

Nor am I yet to learn *Agr.* 56.

Learned.

she learn'd to melt at others' woe. *Adv.* 16.

Their sober wishes never learn'd to stray; *El.* 74.

Least.

at least there are who know *Agr.* 15.

Leave.

their airy dance They leave, *Spring* 40.

leave us leisure to be good. *Adv.* 20.

Leave me unbless'd, unpitied, here to mourn:
Bard 102.

Leave me, leave me to repose. *Odin* 50, 58, 72.

Then I leave thee to repose. *Odin* 80.

†Leave, and lose it, — oh the pain!
Rond. 4, 12, 20, 28, 36.

Leaves.

leaves the world to darkness and to me. *El.* 4.

Led.

by lonely contemplation led, *El.* 95; *Mas.* 79.

My grave Lord-Keeper led the Brawls;
L. S. 11.

and down the steep he led *Tasso* 43.

Leeche's. *See* **Leech's.**

Leech's.

nor the leeche's Care, *Prop.*³ 93.

Left.

Left their Parnassus for the Latian plains.
P. P. 78.

Left the warm precincts of the . . . day, *El.* 87.

But that they left the door a-jarr, *L. S.* 74.

But left a spell upon the table. *L. S.* 80.

She felt the wound she left behind, *Clerke* 8.

But left church and state to Charles Townshend
Char. 6.

†Then have left, to love anew: *Rond.* 7.

Legions.

her nod Can rouse eight hardy legions, *Agr.* 108.

Leisure.

leave us leisure to be good. *Adv.* 20.

Length.

His listless length . . . would he stretch,
El. 103.

See the Wretch, . . . At length repair his vigour
lost, *Vic.* 47.

Dismiss'd at length, they break through all delay
Tasso 1.

What length of sea remains, *Tasso* 31.

Lent.

had her wanton son Lent us his wings, *Agr.* 190.

Less.

Less pleasing when possest; *Eton* 42.

where Dryden's less presumptuous car, *P. P.* 103.

Four, not less brave, That in Armenia quell
Agr. 110.

When, less averse, and yielding to Desires,
*Prop.*³ 21.

far less shall be Our Suffering, *Dante* 65.

Lessen.

distant warblings lessen on my ear, *Bard* 133.

Lessening.

The . . . tide, that drowns her lessening lands,
E. G. 61.

lessening from the dazzled sight, Melts into air
Vic. 15.

Let.

Let us go, and let us fly,   *F. S.* 26.

Let me, let me sleep again.   *Odin* 34.

Let not Ambition mock their . . . toil, *El.* 29.

Nor . . . Let painted Flatt'ry hide her serpent-train   *Inst.* 8.

Let majesty sit on thy awful brow, *Agr.* 145.

Let him feel Before he sees me.   *Agr.* 163.

Let me not fall alone; but crush his pride, *Agr.* 186.

let the Muse admire,   *Bent.* 2.

Now let him sleep in peace   *Child* 6.

Let him stand forth   *Stat.*[1] 3.

yon puny ball Let youngsters toss: *Stat.*[1] 20.

Wars hand to hand with Cynthia let me wage.
Prop.[1] 4.

Let on this head unfadeing flowers reside,
Prop.[2] 9.

Then let me rightly spell of nature's ways;
Prop.[2] 15.

the quicker let me die: *Prop.*[3] 70.

let her ever my Desires control, *Prop.*[3] 76.

Lethargic.

Lethargic nods upon her ebon throne. *Ign.* 24.

Lethean.

dews Lethean through the land dispense *Ign.* 17.

Level.

I trod your level lawn,   *Inst.* 31.

Lewd.

and his eyes are so lewd!   *C. C.* 8.

Liberal.

OWEN . . . Lord of . . . Liberal hand, *Owen* 8.

Thy liberal heart, . . . The flow'r unheeded shall
descry,   *Inst.* 71.

Who had such liberal power   *Agr.* 89.

Liberty.

constraint To sweeten liberty: *Eton* 34.

Lo! liberty and death are mine. *Bard* Lett.[3] 142.

empty shade Of long-forgotten liberty: *Agr.* 44.

say we sound The trump of liberty; *Agr.* 122.

shake 'em at the name of liberty, *Agr.* 132.

Against thee, liberty and Agrippina: *Agr.* 152.

The rough abode of want and liberty, *E. G.* 97.

Libya's.

dauntless goes O'er Libya's deserts   *E. G.* 77.

Lick.

With a lick of court white-wash, and pious grimace,   *C. C.* 2.

Lictor.

Alone, unguarded and without a lictor; *Agr.* 5.

Lids.

she seem to close Her languid Lids, *Prop.*[3] 18.

Lie.

Quench'd in dark clouds of slumber lie *P. P.* 23.

On dreary Arvon's shore they lie, *Bard* 35.

Under a tea-cup he might lie, *L. S.* 67.

The prophet of Bethel, we read, told a lie:
C. C. 27.

Where lie th' eternal fountains of the deep,
Prop.[2] 24.

Lies.

Low on his funeral couch he lies!   *Bard* 64.

Here, . . . lies A child,   *Child* 1.

Here lies Edmund Keene   *Ep. Keene* 1.

Here lies Mrs. Keene   *Mrs. Keene* 1.

Lieu.

In lieu of penitence, and vain remorse, *Agr.* 179.

Life.

Drink life and fragrance   *P. P.* 6.

the cool sequester'd vale of life   *El.* 75.

Through various life I have pursued *Agr.* 54.

From his broad bosom life and verdure flings
E. G. 102.

To local symmetry and life awake! *Bent.* 8.

The strength and harmony of Life. *Vic.* 44.

With life, with memory, and with love.
Clerke 16.

No — at our time of life 't would be silly, *C. C.* 10.

Then his character, *Phyzzy,* — his morals — his
life —   *C. C.* 13.

were of his Life the Pride; *Prop.*[3] 107.

Life's.

The Gay . . . flutter thro' life's little day,
Spring 36.

either Pole, and Life's remotest Bounds, *E. G.* 25.

Lifts.

redning Phœbus lifts his golden Fire : *West* 2.

Heaven lifts its everlasting portals high, *Stanza* 3.

Light. See also **Gospel-light.**

The spirits pure, the slumbers light, *Eton* 49.

Light they disperse, and with them go *Adv.* 21.

Frisking light in frolic measures; *P. P.* 31.

purple light of Love.   *P. P.* 41.

blasted with excess of light,   *P. P.* 101.

Dear, as the light that visits these sad eyes,
Bard 40.

Thou the deeds of light shalt know; *Odin* 39.

Rich windows that exclude the light, *L. S.* 7.

Light golden Showers of Plenty *E. G.* 18.

By reason's light on resolution's wings, *E. G.* 75.

dazzle with a luxury of light.   *Bent.* 24.

Melts into air and liquid light.   *Vic.* 16.

When you rise from your Dinner as light as before,   *Couplet* 1.

With double light it beam'd against the day:
Stat.[1] 27.

The uncertain Crescent gleams a sickly light.
Tasso 48.

Proud of its diamond dies, and luxury of light.
Tasso 70.

with silver light Relumes her crescent Orb
Prop.[2] 21.

Phœbus' Son recall'd Androgeon to the Light.
Prop.[3] 84.

what scant Light That . . . Tower admitted
Dante 22.

†Light to them the parting knell: *Rond.* 23.

Lighten.

Let majesty . . . lighten from thy eye: *Agr.* 146.

Lightly.

Some lightly o'er the current skim, *Spring* 28.

little Footsteps lightly print the Ground.

El. Pem. 120; *Mas.* 140.

And lightly . . . Scatters his freshest, tenderest
green. *Vic.* 7.

†Lightly lambent o'er their frame, *Rond.* 22.

Lightnings.

light'nings of his eye. *P. P.* 24.

Like. *See* **Dove-like, Proteus-like.**

Stream'd, like a meteor, to the troubled air
Bard 20.

woeful-wan, like [as, *Mas.*] one forlorn, *El.* 107.

creased, like dogs-ears, in a folio. *L. S.* 68.

'T is like, thou hast forgot, *Agr.* 33.

a heart like mine, *Agr.* 49.

a call, Like mine, might serve . . . to wake
Agr. 103.

Like old Sesostris with barbaric pride; *Ign.* 37.

'T is just like the picture in Rochester's book;
C. C. 12.

Is as like as two pease, *Satire* 14.

Is as like as two beans; *Satire* 16.

Follows them like a spaniel; *Satire* 26.

Is of the like tenet; *Satire* 28.

Like the rest of the Dons. *Satire* 34.

†and thoughts Like Butterflies, *Ode* 45.

†Not like yon Dowager deprest with years;
Ch. Cr. 6.

†Like Punch, he peeps, *Ch. Cr.* 30.

†Like Perch or Pike, *Ch. Cr.* 39.

†hangs like Pear or Plum, *Ch. Cr.* 40.

†In shriller notes Q like a female squeaks;
Ch. Cr. 48.

Likeness.

Ne'er again his likeness see; *F. S.* 46.

Lilies.

Great Edward, with the lilies on his brow *Inst.* 39.

Limbs.

Have his limbs Sweat under iron harness? *Agr.* 96.

And half disclose those Limbs it should conceal;
Prop.[3] 10.

These miserable Limbs with Flesh you cloath'd;
Dante 67.

Limits.

The limits of their little reign, *Eton* 36.

Beyond the limits of a vulgar fate, *P. P.* 122.

Line. *See also* **Briton-line.**

weave . . . the tissue of thy line. *Bard* 48.

born of Arthur's line *Bard* Lett.[2] 116.

Mightiest of a mighty line — *Odin* 83.

The massy sceptre o'er thy slumb'ring line?
Ign. 16.

could they catch . . . his unerring line; *Bent.* 14.

pride of noble line. *Stat.*[1] 25.

Lineaments.

in thy lineaments we trace A Tudor's fire, *Inst.* 69.

Lines.

in these lines their artless tale relate; *El.* 94.

wrote in lines of blood, *Agr.* 70.

My lines a secret sympathy *Bent.* 26.

She is my Genius, she inspires the Lines;
Prop.[3] 4.

†In ductile Lines of Foolery: *Ode* 40.

Linger.

they linger yet, Avengers of their native land:
Bard 45.

linger in the gloomy Walks of Fate: *El. Mas.* 80.

rhymes that us'd to linger on, *Bent.* 9.

Lingering.

In lingering Lab'rinths creep, *P. P.* 70.

one longing ling'ring look *El.* 88.

In ling'ring pain, in death resign'd, *Clerke* MS. 9.

Lingers.

Where willowy Camus lingers with delight!
Inst. 29.

Link.

Chains . . . Wreath'd in many a golden link:
Hoel 15.

Linnet.

The captive linnet which enthral? *Eton* 27.

Lion-port.

Her [A, MS.] lyon-port, her [an, MS.] awe-commanding face, *Bard* 117.

Lips.

Unwilling I my lips unclose: *Odin* 49.

Now my weary lips I close; *Odin* 57, 71.

the griesly Fellon raised His Gore-dyed Lips,
Dante 2.

Liquid.

float amid the liquid noon: *Spring* 27.

The liquid language of the skies: *Inst.* 56.

Melts into air and liquid light, *Vic.* 16.

Lisp.

No children run to lisp their sire's return, *El.* 23.

Listening.

Th' applause of list'ning senates *El.* 61.

Listens.

nods his hoary head, and listens to the rhyme.
Inst. 26.

Listless.

His listless length . . . would he stretch, *El.* 103.

Littered.

And foxes stunk and litter'd in St. Paul's.
View 24.

Little.

how little are the Proud, *Spring* 19.

flutter thro' life's little day, *Spring* 36.

The limits of their little reign, *Eton* 36.

The little victims play! *Eton* 52.

Stretch'd forth his little arms, *P. P.* 88.

The little Tyrant of his fields *El.* 58.

little Footsteps lightly print the Ground.
El. Pem. 120 ; *Mas.* 140.

He little knew *L. S.* 77.

Their tears, their little triumphs o'er, *Inst.* 48.

To warm their little Loves the Birds complain:
West 12.

Their little wants, their low desires refine,
E. G. 82.

A little Verse my All that shall remain; *Prop.*³ 101.
They wept, and first my little dear Anselmo
Cried, *Dante* 55.
†Some spin away their little lives *Ode* 39.
†gratefully they pay Their little Songs, *Ode* 52.
†Rests in Retirement, *little* Rural R; *Ch. Cr.* 54.

Live.
Spite of danger he shall live. *F. S.* 35.
in our Ashes live their wonted Fires. *El.* 92.
And I, . . . That live to weep *Hoel* 24.
†Whose influence first bid it live. *Ode* 54.

Lived. *See also* **Short-lived.**
he liv'd unknown To fame, or fortune; *Agr.* 38.
He lived, while she was kind; *Prop.*³ 108.

Lively.
And lively chear of vigour born; *Eton* 47.

Lives.
Rubellius lives, And Sylla has his friends, *Agr.* 99.
Here lives Harry Vane, *Impr. Vane* 1.
†Some spin away their little lives *Ode* 39.
†Remote from cities lives *Ch. Cr.* 55.

Living.
The living Throne, the saphire-blaze, *P. P.* 99.
wak'd to extasy the living lyre. *El.* 48.
Scythia breath'd the living Cloud of War; *E. G.* 47.
o'er the living scene Scatters . . . green. *Vic.* 7.
Sulphureous veins and liveing silver shine, *Tasso* 59.

Llewellyn's.
Vocal no more, . . . To . . . soft Llewellyn's
lay, *Bard* 28.

Lo.
Lo! where the rosy-bosom'd Hours, *Spring* 1.
Lo, in the vale of years *Eton* 81.
Lo, Poverty, to fill the band, *Eton* 88.
Edward, lo! . . . Half of thy heart we consecrate. *Bard* 97.
Lo! liberty and death are mine. *Bard Lett.*³ 142.
Lo! to be free to die, are mine. *Bard Lett.*³ 142.
Lo! Granta waits to lead her blooming band, *Inst.* 77.
Lo! where the silent marble weeps, . . . a mother
sleeps: *Clerke* 1.
when lo! appears The wondrous Sage: *Tasso* 11.

Load.
Receive a worthier load; *Stat.*¹ 19.

Loaded.
In golden Chains should loaded Monarchs bend, *Prop.*³ 48.

Loathed.
†Loath'd the love; and loath'd the song; *Rond.* 15.

Local.
To local symmetry and life awake! *Bent.* 8.

Lochlin.
Lochlin plows the watry way; *Owen* 14.

Locks.
these locks no more shall know, *Prop.*² 13.
Lips, which on the clotter'd Locks . . . he
wiped, *Dante* 2.

Lofty.
'T was on a lofty vase's side, *Cat* 1.
Latium had her lofty spirit lost, *P. P.* 81.
Build to him the lofty verse, *Conan* 2.
Nor lofty Carthage struggleing with her Fate. *Prop.*³ 40.

Lok.
Till *Lok* has burst his tenfold chain; *Odin* 90.

London's.
Ye Towers of Julius, London's lasting shame, *Bard* 87.
Then had we seen proud London's hated walls; *View* 22.

Lone.
†lives in lone Retreat; *Ch. Cr.* 55.

Lonely.
By Night and lonely Contemplation led *El. Mas.* 79.
by lonely contemplation led, *El.* 95.
My lonely Anguish melts no Heart but mine; *West* 7.
Along the lonely vale of days? *Clerke* 12.

Long. *See also* **Side-long.**
He wound with Toilsome march his long array. *Bard* 12.
Long Years of havock urge their destined course, *Bard* 85.
warblings . . . That lost in long futurity expire. *Bard* 134.
long pursues, with fruitless yell, *Odin* 11.
long of yore to sleep was laid *Odin* 19.
Long on these mould'ring bones *Odin* 31.
Long her strains in sorrow steep: *F. S.* 47.
On her shadow long and gay Lochlin plows *Owen* 13.
this long deserted shade. *El. Mas.* 112.
With . . . aprons long they hid their armour, *L. S.* 38.
And mitred fathers in long order go: *Inst.* 38.
the Prætorian camp have long rever'd *Agr.* 117.
See the Wretch, that long has tost *Vic.* 45.
Fearless in long excursion loves to glide, *Tasso* 21.
Long as of youth the joyous hours remain, *Prop.*² 1.
from that auspicious Night Dates the long Iliad *Prop.*³ 26.
May the long Thirst of Tantalus allay, *Prop.*³ 89.
Nor long endur'd the Chase: *Dante* 37.
†Long to seek a mutual heart, *Rond.* 2, 10, 18, 26, 34.

Long-drawn.
through the long-drawn isle and fretted vault *El.* 39.

Long-expected.
Phlegyas the long-expected play began, *Stat.*¹ 32.

Long-expecting.
the long-expecting flowers, *Spring* 3.

Long-forgotten.
empty shade Of long-forgotten liberty: *Agr.* 44.

Longing.
one longing ling'ring look *El.* 88.
And struggles to elude my longing Eyes, *Prop.*³ 24.

Long-lost.

No more our long-lost Arthur we bewail.
Bard 109.

To Chiron Phœnix owed his long-lost Sight,
*Prop.*³ 83.

Long-resounding.

With . . . long-resounding pace.　*P. P.* 106.

Long-winded.

And guard us from long-winded Lubbers,
L. S. 142.

Look.

Still as they run they look behind,　*Eton* 38.

Such a sheep-biting look,　　　*C. C.* 6.

but methinks for his look, 'T is just like the picture
C. C. 11.

In brief whate'er she do, or say, or look,
*Prop.*³ 27.

Looked.

So Helen look'd, So her white neck reclin'd,
Agr. 194.

Thus Etough look'd;　　　*Toph.* 1.

Looks.

Presumptuous Maid! with looks [eyes, Whar.]
intent　　　　　　　*Cat* 25.

And Ignorance with looks profound,　*Inst.* 3.

looks ever dejected —　　　*Am. Lines* 5.

Loom.

bending o'er th' accursed loom　*Bard* 95.

Haste, the loom of Hell prepare,　*F. S.* 2.

Glitt'ring lances are the loom,　*F. S.* 5.

Loose.

In loose numbers wildly sweet　*P. P.* 61.

Loose his beard, and hoary hair Stream'd,
Bard 19.

the song-thrush there Scatters his loose notes
Birds 2.

If the loose Curls around her Forehead play,
*Prop.*³ 7.

Of those loose Curls, that Ivory front I write;
*Prop.*³ 11.

give loose to Utterance, and to Tears.　*Dante* 9.

Lord.

On Thracia's hills the Lord of War　*P. P.* 17.

Mighty Victor, mighty Lord!　*Bard* 63.

Owen . . . Lord of every regal art,　*Owen* 7.

Henry . . . the majestic lord,　*Inst.* 46.

cast me forth in duty to their Lord.　*Agr.* 157.

"Lord! sister," says PHYSIC to LAW,　*C. C.* 5.

Here lies Edmund Keene Lord Bishop of Chester,
Ep. Keene 1.

The orb . . . joys to see Its ancient lord secure
of victory.　　　　　*Stat.*² 13.

Lord-keeper.

My grave Lord-Keeper led the Brawls; *L. S.* 11.

Lore.

thy rigid lore . . . many a year she bore: *Adv.* 13.

Lose.

†Leave, and lose it, — oh the pain!
Rond. 4, 12, 20, 28, 36.

Loss.

Long his loss shall Eirin weep,　*F. S.* 45.

Lost.　*See* **Long-lost.**

Latium had her lofty spirit lost,　*P. P.* 81.

Dear lost companions of my tuneful art, *Bard* 39.

That lost in long futurity expire.　*Bard* 134.

Oh! times for ever lost!　　*Ign.* 31.

At length repair his vigour lost,　*Vic.* 47.

Redeem, what Crassus lost,　*Prop.*² 54.

Lot.

Their lot forbad: nor circumscrib'd alone *El.* 65.

Loud.

Join with glad voice the loud symphonious lay.
Inst. 88.

Weddell attends your call, . . . and Delaval the
loud.　　　　　*Com. Lines* 1.

Then, while the vaulted Skies loud Ios rend,
*Prop.*³ 47.

Love.

pineing Love shall waste their youth,　*Eton* 65.

Teach me to love and to forgive,　*Adv.* 46.

purple light of Love.　　*P. P.* 41.

Fierce War, and faithful Love,　*Bard* 126.

cross'd in hopeless love.　　*El.* 108.

That wept her bleeding Love,　*Inst.* 42.

they love not aconite.　　*Agr.* 21.

My love, my fears for him,　*Agr.* 181.

love could teach a monarch to be wise, *E. G.* 108.

With life, with memory, and with love. *Clerke* 16.

Could love, and could hate,　*Char.* 3.

From fortune, pleasure, science, love, he flew,
Williams 7.

Spare the honour of my love.　*Song* 12.

The love of honour bade two youths advance,
*Stat.*¹ 9.

Love, gentle Power! to Peace was e'er a friend;
*Prop.*¹ 1.

Age step 'twixt love and me,　*Prop.*² 12.

Be love my youth's pursuit,　*Prop.*² 52.

Yet would the Tyrant Love permit me raise
*Prop.*³ 31.

To die is glorious in the Bed of Love. *Prop.*³ 64.

it be my Fate to try Another Love,　*Prop.*³ 70.

a Cure for every Ill, but Love.　*Prop.*³ 80.

Love and the Fair were　　*Prop.*³ 107.

†to love, — and then to part,
Rond. 1, 9, 17, 25, 33.

†'Till they loved their love away ;　*Rond.* 6.

†Then have left, to love anew;　*Rond.* 7.

†And have loved their love in rhyme: *Rond.* 14.

†Loath'd the love; and loath'd the song; *Rond.* 15.

†But their love could not be *strong.*　*Rond.* 16.

†For, too sure, they love not *well.*　*Rond.* 24.

Loved.

Thy once loved haunt, this . . . shade.
El. Mas. 112.

within whose sacred cell . . . virtues lov'd to
dwell.　　　　　*Clerke* 4.

Why, David lov'd catches,　*C. C.* 24.

From her loved Door　　*Prop.*³ 78.

†Some have loved, and loved (they say) *Rond.* 5.

†'Till they loved their love away;　*Rond.* 6.

†But, I wot, they loved not *true.*　*Rond.* 8.

†Some have lov'd, to pass the time,　*Rond.* 13.

†And have loved their love in rhyme: *Rond.* 14.

Lovely.

He ask'd and had the lovely maid.   *Hoel* 10.

Lover.

To-day the Lover walks,   *Prop.³* 96.

Lover's.

'T is ample Matter for a Lover's Book; *Prop.³* 28.

Love's.

Before the Goddess' shrine we too, love's vot'ries,
bend,   *Prop.¹* 2.

Loves.

With leaden eye, that loves the ground, *Adv.* 28.

The rosy-crowned Loves are seen   *P. P.* 28.

Their feather-cinctur'd Chiefs, and dusky Loves.
      P. P. 62.

The Red-breast loves to build
      El. Pem. 119; *Mas.* 139.

groves, That contemplation loves,   *Inst.* 28.

To warm their little Loves the Birds complain:
      West 12.

They say he 's no Christian, loves drinking and
whoring,   *C. C.* 15.

Fearless in long excursion loves to glide, *Tasso* 21.

You ask, why thus my Loves I still rehearse,
      Prop.³ 1.

†Mortals he loves to prick,   *Ch. Cr.* 32.

Low.

How low, how little are the Proud, *Spring* 19.

I hear in accents low   *Spring* 41.

Low on his funeral couch he lies!   *Bard* 64.

Low the dauntless Earl is laid,   *F S.* 41.

Their little wants, their low desires refine,
      E. G. 82.

low as his feet there flows A vestment *Tasso* 13.

But yet in low and uncompleated Sounds
      Dante 44.

Lower.

Now the storm begins to lower   *F. S.* 1.

deepest shades, that dimly lower   *Vic.* 34.

Lowing.

The lowing herd wind slowly o'er the lea, *El.* 2.

Lowly.

shall rouse them from their lowly bed.   *El.* 20.

Loyalty.

Mirrors of Saxon truth and loyalty *Bard MS.* 71.

Lubbers.

And guard us from long-winded Lubbers,
      L. S. 142.

Lucca.

that intercepts the View Of Lucca,   *Dante* 30.

Lucid.

where lucid Avon stray'd,   *P. P.* 85.

Lull.

drowsy tinklings lull the distant folds: *El.* 8.

Lulled.

Fast by th' umbrageous vale lull'd to repose,
      Prop.² 3.

Lulling.

I favour her repose With lulling Notes, *Prop.³* 19.

Lulls.

thy magic lulls the feather'd king   *P. P.* 21.

Lured.

to be lured with smiles   *Agr.* 18.

Lurked.

that thereabouts there lurk'd . . . a Poet,
      L. S. 43.

Lustre.

with no other lustre, than the blood   *Agr.* 37.

catch a lustre from his genuine flame. *Bent.* 12.

All stones of lustre shoot their vivid ray, *Tasso* 65.

Luxury.

heap the shrine of Luxury and Pride   *El.* 71.

dazzle with a luxury of light.   *Bent.* 24.

Proud of its diamond dies, and luxury of light.
      Tasso 70.

Lying.

And filching and lying, and Newgate-bird tricks;
      C. C. 17.

Lyon-port. *See* **Lion-port.**

Lyre.

Awake, Æolian lyre, awake,   *P. P.* 1.

Awake, my lyre: *P. P. MS.* 1.

Hark, his hands the lyre explore!   *P. P.* 107.

Oh! Lyre divine,   *P. P.* 112.

Struck the deep sorrows of his lyre.   *Bard* 22.

wak'd to extasy the living lyre.   *El.* 48.

bids the pencil answer to the lyre.   *Bent.* 4.

Hark! 't is nature strikes the lyre,   *Vic.* 19.

Or if to Musick she the Lyre awake,   *Prop.³* 13.

Maces.

The Seal, and Maces, danc'd before him.
      L. S. 12.

Machaon.

The Melian's Hurt Machaon could repair,
      Prop.³ 81.

Machine.

Who taught this vast machine its steadfast laws,
      Prop.² 17.

Macleane.

He stood as mute as poor *Macleane*. *L. S.* 120.

Mad.

Mad Sedition's cry profane,   *Inst.* 5.

Madam.

Jesu-Maria! Madam Bridget,   *L. S.* 133.

Madding.

the madding crowd's ignoble strife,   *El.* 73.

cool dictates in the madding ear   *Agr.* 83.

Made.

Made huge Plinlimmon bow his cloud-top'd head.
      Bard 34.

'T is of human entrails made   *F. S.* 10.

Madness.

moody Madness laughing wild   *Eton* 79.

Madoc.

of Madoc old He ask'd no heaps of hoarded gold;
      Hoel 7.

Mæander's.

Or where Mæander's amber waves   *P. P.* 69.

Mæcenas.
And thou Mecænas, be my second Care;
　　　　　　　　　　　　　　*Prop.*³ 42.

Magazines.
the cloudy Magazines maintain Their wintry war,
　　　　　　　　　　　　　　*Prop.*² 25.

Maggots.
†Maggots too will form and nourish;　　*Ode* 16.

Magi.
You bade the Magi call the dreadful powers,
　　　　　　　　　　　　　　Agr. 64.

Magic.
thy magic lulls the feather'd king　　*P. P.* 21.
Modred, whose magic song Made huge Plinlim-
　　mon bow　　　　　　　　　　*Bard* 33.
The power of Magick was no fable.　*L. S.* 78.
a vain tradition, As there were magic in it?
　　　　　　　　　　　　　　Agr. 134.
The sun's pale sister, drawn by magic strain,
　　　　　　　　　　　　　　*Stat.*¹ 54.
e'en Magic here must fail,　　　　*Prop.*³ 85.

Magick. *See* **Magic.**

Maid. *See also* **Village-maid.**
Presumptuous Maid! with looks intent　*Cat* 25.
Melancholy, silent maid,　　　　　*Adv.* 27.
terrific Maid,　　　　　　　　　*F. S.* 17.
The dust of the prophetic Maid.　　*Odin* 20.
No boding Maid of skill divine Art thou,
　　　　　　　　　　　　　　Odin 84.
He ask'd and had the lovely maid.　*Hoel* 10.

Mail.
Helm, nor Hauberk's twisted mail,　*Bard* 5.

Main.
tongue, That hush'd the stormy main: *Bard* 30.
The river boil'd beneath, and rush'd toward the
　　Main,　　　　　　　　　　*Tasso* 24.

Maintain.
An Iron-race the mountain-cliffs maintain,
　　　　　　　　　　　　　　E. G. 88.
the cloudy Magazines maintain Their wintry war,
　　　　　　　　　　　　　　*Prop.*² 25.

Majestic.
Deep, majestic, smooth, and strong.　*P. P.* 8.
Henry . . . the majestic lord,　　　*Inst.* 46.

Majesty.
Statesmen old In [Of, Lett.²] bearded majesty,
　　　　　　　　　　　　　　Bard 114.
The thoughtless World to Majesty may bow,
　　　　　　　　　　　　　　El. Mas. 73.
Let majesty sit on thy awful brow,　*Agr.* 145.
†Henry the Eighth's most monstrous majesty,
　　　　　　　　　　　　　　Ch. Cr. 22.

Make.
That the soft Subject of my Song I make,
　　　　　　　　　　　　　　*Prop.*³ 14.

Making.
He had not the method of making a fortune:
　　　　　　　　　　　　　　Char. 2.

Malice.
Or any malice to the poultry,　　*L. S.* 124.

Malignant.
Malignant Fate sat by, and smil'd　*Cat* 28.
hag . . . smiles malignant on the labouring
　　power.　　　　　　　　　*Stat.*¹ 59.

Man.
Such is the race of Man　　　　*Spring* 32.
know myself a Man.　　　　　　*Adv.* 48.
Fond impious Man, think'st thou,　*Bard* 135.
'T is man alone that Joy descries　*Vic.* 27.
'T is Willy begs, once a right proper man, *Shak.* 3.
call'd forth all the man.　　　　*Stat.*¹ 33.
†K, as a man, with hoarser accent speaks,
　　　　　　　　　　　　　　Ch. Cr. 47.

Manes.
you, ye manes of ambition's victims,　*Agr.* 174.

Mangled.
That tear'st the bowels of thy mangled Mate,
　　　　　　　　　　　　　　Bard 58.

Mankind.
shut the gates of mercy on mankind,　*El.* 68.
draw Mankind in vain the vital Airs,　*E. G.* 9.

Manly.
Every warriors manly neck Chains of regal hon-
　　our deck,　　　　　　　　*Hoel* 13.

Manners.
Her air and all her manners shew it.　*L. S.* 138.
The manners speak the idiom of their soil.
　　　　　　　　　　　　　　E. G. 87.

Manor.
To rid the manour of such vermin.　*L. S.* 52.

Manour. *See* **Manor.**

Man's.
Man's feeble race what Ills await,　*P. P.* 42.

Mansion.
Back to its mansion call the fleeting breath? *El.* 42.

Mansions.
from their gloomy mansions creeping　*L. S.* 98.

Mantled. *See* **Ivy-mantled.**

Mantles.
In peaked hoods and mantles tarnish'd, *L. S.* 105.

Mantling.
Mantling in the goblet see The pure bev'rage
　　　　　　　　　　　　　　Odin 43.

Many.
With many an ardent wish,　　　*Cat* 21.
Full many a sprightly race　　　*Eton* 22.
thy rigid lore . . . many a year she bore: *Adv.* 14.
With many a foul and midnight murther fed,
　　　　　　　　　　　　　　Bard 88.
Girt with many a Baron bold　　*Bard* 111.
Weaving many a Soldier's doom,　*F. S.* 7.
Gor'd with many a gaping wound :　*F. S.* 42.
in many a mould'ring heap,　　　*El.* 14.
Full many a gem of purest ray serene,　*El.* 53.
Full many a flower is born　　　*El.* 55.
many a holy text around she strews,　*El.* 83.
with many an artful fib,　　　　*L. S.* 113.
Wreath'd in many a golden link:　*Hoel* 15.

Of many a flood they view'd the secret source,
Tasso 51.

And many a copious Narrative you 'll see
*Prop.*³ 29.

and known To many a Wretch   *Dante* 25.

Many-colored.

Waves . . . her many-colour'd wings. *Bard* 124.

Many-coloured. *See* **Many-colored.**

Many-twinkling.

Glance their many-twinkling feet.   *P. P.* 35.

Marble.

where the silent marble weeps, . . . a mother sleeps: *Clerke* 1.

Ah, gallant youth! this marble tells the rest,
Williams 11.

And the short Marble but preserve a Name,
*Prop.*³ 100.

March.

Hyperion's march they spy,   *P. P.* 53.

He wound with toilsome march   *Bard* 12.

Marching.

On the first marching of the troops   *L. S.* 69.

Margaret.

The venerable Marg'ret see!   *Inst.* 66.

Margent.

Disporting on thy margent green   *Eton* 23.

Margin.

A shining border round the margin roll'd,
*Stat.*² 26.

And paint the margin of the costly stream,
Tasso 64.

Or lawless, o'er their Ivory Margin stray:
*Prop.*³ 8.

Maria. *See* **Jesu-Maria.**

Mariners.

And mariners, though shipwreck'd, dread to land.
View 8.

Marius'.

Not Marius' Cimbrian Wreaths would I relate,
*Prop.*³ 39.

Mark.

Mark the year, and mark the night,   *Bard* 53.

Mark where Indolence and Pride,   *Vic.* 61.

Marked.

Melancholy mark'd him for her own.   *El.* 120.

by you Mark'd for their leader: *Agr.* 113.

Marking.

Marking with indignant eye   *Owen* 35.

Marriage.

By residence, by marriage, and sore eyes?
Shak. 12.

Mary.

The drawing-room of fierce Queen Mary.
L. S. 108.

Masians.

the Masians too, and those of Egypt, *Agr.* 115.

Mask.

fear might . . . have worn The mask of prudence;   *Agr.* 49.

Mass.

The band around admire the mighty mass,
*Stat.*¹ 7.

Emits the mass, a prelude of his might;
*Stat.*¹ 46.

The ponderous mass sinks in the cleaving ground,
*Stat.*² 16.

In one rich mass unite the precious store,
Tasso 61.

Massy.

The massy sceptre o'er thy slumb'ring line?
Ign. 16.

Master.

Your helpless, old, expiring master view!
Bard MS. 72.

Tell your master, His mother shall obey him.
Agr. 2.

the Master of Jesus   *Satire* 5.

The Master of Maudlin   *Satire* 7.

The Master of Sidney   *Satire* 9.

The Master of Trinity   *Satire* 11.

the Master of Keys   *Satire* 13.

the Master of Queen's   *Satire* 15.

The Master of King's   *Satire* 17.

The Master of Catherine   *Satire* 19.

The Master of Clare   *Satire* 21.

The Master of Christ   *Satire* 23.

the Master of Emmanuel   *Satire* 25.

The Master of Benet   *Satire* 27.

The Master of Pembroke   *Satire* 29.

The Master of Peter's   *Satire* 31.

The Master of St. John's   *Satire* 33.

Master's.

with a Master's hand, and Prophet's fire, *Bard* 21.

heap'd his master's feet around,   *Owen* 29.

'T is true, our master's temper natural Was fashion'd fair   *Shak.* 9.

Mate.

That tear'st the bowels of thy mangled Mate,
Bard 58.

Matter.

In Britain's Isle, no matter where,   *L. S.* 1.

no matter What; so 't be strange,   *Agr.* 170.

'T is ample Matter for a Lover's Book; *Prop.*³ 28.

Maudlin.

The Master of Maudlin In the same dirt is dawdling;   *Satire* 7.

May.

We frolick, while 't is May.   *Spring* 50.

May, *vb.*

he yet may share the feast: *Bard* 79.

Some mute inglorious Milton here may rest,
El. 59.

The thoughtless World to Majesty may bow,
El. Mas. 73.

some hoary-headed Swain may say,   *El.* 97.

He Perchance may heed 'em: *Agr.* 88.

one . . . may still With equal power resume
Agr. 89.

we may meet, ungrateful boy, we may! *Agr.* 140.

Where he so soon may —   *Agr.* 165.

But may not honey's self be turn'd to gall
                Shak. 11.
Still may his Bard in softer fights engage;
                Prop.[1] 3.
Me may Castalia's sweet recess detain, *Prop.*[2] 2.
nor Callimachus' enervate Strain May tell of Jove,
                Prop.[3] 56.
may my pale Coarse be borne.   *Prop.*[3] 78.
May the long Thirst of Tantalus allay, *Prop.*[3] 89.
yet if the telling may Beget   *Dante* 6.

Mazy.
A thousand rills their mazy progress take: *P. P.* 4.

Me, *omitted.*

Mead.
th' expanse below . . . of mead survey, *Eton* 7.

Mean.
Why, what can the Viscountess mean? *L. S.* 134.

Meaner.
Whom meaner Beauties eye askance,   *L. S.* 27.
The meaner gems that . . . charm the sight,
                Bent. 22.

Meanest.
The meanest flowret of the vale,   *Vic.* 49.
And I, the meanest of them all,   *Hoel* 23.

Meaning.
Th' unthought event disclose a whiter meaning.
                Agr. 71.
Words . . . by no meaning connected!
                Am. Lines 6.

Means.
Ah! what means yon violet flower!   *Song* 3.

Measured.
Here measured Laws and philosophic Ease
                E. G. 40.
Who measured out the year,   *Prop.*[2] 38.

Measures.
Frisking light in frolic measures;   *P. P.* 31.
In buskin'd [mystic, Lett.[2]] measures move
                Bard 128.
To judge of weights and measures;   *Agr.* 41.
In swifter measures animated run,   *Bent.* 11.

Meat.
Better the roast meat from the fire to save,
                Shak. 18.

Mecænas. *See* **Mæcenas.**

Meditated.
'T was there he aim'd the meditated harm,
                Stat.[2] 22.

Meek.
spare the meek Usurper's holy head. *Bard* 90.
Meek Newton's self bends   *Inst.* 25.
Was fashion'd fair in meek and dove-like guise;
                Shak. 10.

Meet.
Now in circling troops they meet: *P. P.* 33.
Blade with clattering buckler meet,   *F. S.* 23.
To meet the sun upon . . . the lawn.   *El.* 100.
with dirges meet in sad array   *El.* Mas. 133.
we may meet, ungrateful boy,   *Agr.* 140.
I will not meet its poison.   *Agr.* 163.

Meets.
Thy Joys no glittering female meets, *Spring* 45.

Meinai.
Backward Meinai rolls his flood;   *Owen* 28.

Melancholy.
Melancholy, silent maid,   *Adv.* 27.
Melancholy mark'd him for her own. *El.* 120.
Freedom by my side, and soft-eyed Melancholy.
                Inst. 34.
throw A melancholy grace;   *Vic.* 32.
Where melancholy friendship bends, *Williams* 12.

Melian's.
The Melian's Hurt Machaon could repair,
                Prop.[3] 81.

Melissa.
Melissa is her Nom de Guerre.   *L. S.* 35.

Mellow.
mellow now, now gruff,   *Par. on Ep.* 1.

Melody.
†Their little Songs, and Melody;   *Ode* 52.

Melpomene.
†buskin'd Strains, If Melpomene inspire, *Ode* 32.

Melt.
she learn'd to melt at others' woe.   *Adv.* 16.
They melt [sink, MS.], they vanish from my eyes.
                Bard 104.

Melting. *See also* **Ever-melting.**
Slow melting strains their Queen's approach
declare: *P. P.* 36.
Sweet music's melting fall,   *Inst.* 63.

Melts.
My lonely Anguish melts no Heart but mine;
                West 7.
Melts into air and liquid light.   *Vic.* 16.

Memorial.
Some frail memorial . . . erected nigh, *El.* 78.

Memory.
If Mem'ry [Memory, Dods., Pem., Eg., Mas.]
o'er their Tomb no Trophies raise, *El.* 38.
The grateful memory of the good. *Inst.* 60.
with Mem'ry to retain,   *E. G.* 30.
With life, with memory, and with love. *Clerke* 16.

Men.
tell them, they are men!   *Eton* 60.
To each his suff'rings: all are men, *Eton* 91.
Uprose the King of Men with speed, *Odin* 1.
King of Men, I know thee now;   *Odin* 82.
and men below Join with glad voice *Inst.* 87.
new-born Pleasure brings to happier Men:
                West 10.
†Battles, Sieges, Men, and Arms,   *Ode* 25.

Mend.
strive to mend A broken character   *View* 3.

Mends.
Their Judgment mends the Plan   *E. G.* 32.

Mercy.
shut the gates of mercy on mankind, *El.* 68.

Mere.

Decorum's turn'd to mere civility;   *L. S.* 137.

Merits.

No farther seek his merits to disclose,   *El.* 125.

Message.

The message needs no comment.   *Agr.* 2.

Met.

While Prows, that late in fierce Encounter mett,
   *Prop.*³ 51.

Metals.

And embryon metals undigested glow,   *Tasso* 58.

Meteor.

Stream'd, like a meteor, to the troubled air
   Bard 20.

Methinks.

Methinks I hear in accents low   *Spring* 41.
but methinks for his look, 'T is just like the picture   *C. C.* 11.
†methinks we see,   *Ch. Cr.* 21.

Method.

He had not the method of making a fortune:
   Char. 2.

Methought.

I saw methought Towards Pisa's Mount,
   Dante 28.

Mewed.

She mew'd to ev'ry watry God,   *Cat* 32.

Midday.

ere mid-day, Nero will come to Baiæ.   *Agr.* 159.

Middle.

Transparent birdlime form'd the middle, *L. S.* 83.

Midnight.

With many a foul and midnight murther fed,
   Bard 88.
Comus, and his midnight crew,   *Inst.* 2.
The powerful Mixture and the midnight Spell;
   *Prop.*³ 86.

Midst.

In the midst a Form divine!   *Bard* 115.
And in the midst a spacious arch appears.
   Tasso 42.

'Midst.

'Midst the tide   *Cat* 13.

Mien.

With watchful eye and dauntless mien, *Inst.* 90.
vigorous he seem'd in years, Awful his mien,
   Tasso 13.

Might. *See also* **Mought.**

the rod of empire might have sway'd,   *El.* 47.
Under a tea-cup he might lie,   *L. S.* 67.
all that *Groom* might urge   *L. S. MS.* 116.
Yet hop'd, that he might save his bacon:
   L. S. 126.
fear might then have worn The mask   *Agr.* 48.
a call, Like mine, might serve . . . to wake
   Agr. 103.
I might remind my mistress that her nod *Agr.* 107.
nations own'd her unresisted might,   *Ign.* 29.
The energy of Pope they might efface, *Bent.* 15.
Owls might have hooted   *View MS.* 23.

Had I but the torrent's might,   *Hoel* 1.
Emits the mass, a prelude of his might ;
   *Stat.*¹ 46.
Oh, might that envied Happiness be mine!
   *Prop.*³ 67.
†as might a King become,   *Ch. Cr.* 49.

Mightiest.

[The, MS.] Mightiest of a [the, MS.] mighty
   line —   *Odin* 83.

Mighty.

To Him the mighty Mother did unveil
   P. P. 86.
Mighty Victor, mighty Lord!   *Bard* 63.
Mightiest of a mighty line —   *Odin* 83.
Big with hosts of mighty name,   *Owen* 9.
This mighty emperor, this dreaded hero, *Agr.* 93.
The band around admire the mighty mass,
   *Stat.*¹ 7.
True to the mighty arm that gave it force,
   *Stat.*² 11.

Milder.

Thy milder influence impart,   *Adv.* 42.
A milder Warfare I in Verse display; *Prop.*³ 61.

Millions.

Rous'd by the shout of millions: *Agr.* 143.

Milton.

Some mute inglorious Milton [Tully, Mas.] here
   may rest,   *El.* 59.
Milton struck the deep-ton'd shell,   *Inst.* 23.

Milton's.

in Shakespeare's or in Milton's page,   *Bent.* 19.

Mimic.

And mimic desolation covers all.   *View* 16.

Mind.

The vulturs of the mind,   *Eton* 62.
Th' unconquerable Mind,   *P. P.* 65.
Profane thy inborn royalty of mind: *Inst.* 81.
Opinion tinge the varied Mind,   *E. G.* 27.
Her latest agony of mind   *Clerke MS.* 10.
His mind each Muse, . . . adorn'd *Williams* 3.

Mindful.

mindful of th' unhonour'd Dead,
   El. 93; *Mas.* 77.

Minds.

how oft in weak and sickly minds   *Agr.* 72.
Minds of the antique cast,   *Agr.* 126.

Mine.

To triumph, and to die, are mine.   *Bard* 142.
a heart like mine,. . . . that glows   *Agr.* 49.
a call, Like mine, might serve belike   *Agr.* 103.
My lonely Anguish melts no Heart but mine;
   West 7.
Dryden's harmony submit to mine.   *Bent.* 16.
Oh, might that envied Happiness be mine!
   *Prop.*³ 67.

Minerals.

Further they pass, where ripening minerals flow,
   Tasso 57.

Ministers.

The Ministers of human fate,   *Eton* 56.

Mirrors.
Mirrors of Saxon truth and loyalty *Bard* MS. 71.

Mirth.
Flush'd with mirth and hope they burn: *Hoel* 19.

Mischance.
Brush'd by the hand of rough Mischance,
Spring 38.

Miserable.
These miserable Limbs with Flesh you cloath'd;
Dante 67.

Misery.
and Misery not thine own.   *Adv.* MS. 8.
He gave to Mis'ry all he had,   *El.* 123.
Behind the steps that Misery treads,   *Vic.* 39.
Here, . . . secure from misery, lies A child,
Child 1.
Gave not to know their Sum of Misery, *Dante* 43.

Misfortune's.
black Misfortune's baleful train!   *Eton* 57.
Smiles on past Misfortune's brow . . . Reflection's
hand can trace;   *Vic.* 29.

Missed.
One morn I [we, Mas.] miss'd him   *El.* 109.

Mista.
Mista black,   *F. S.* 17.

Mistake.
Condemns her fickle Sexe's fond Mistake,
*Prop.*³ 73.

Mistress.
I might remind my mistress that her nod *Agr.* 107.
A moment's patience, gentle Mistress [Mistris,
Lett.⁴] Anne: *Shak.* 1.
the Mistress of my faithful breast,   *Prop.*³ 71.

Mistris. *See* **Mistress.**

Mitred.
And mitred fathers in long order go: *Inst.* 38.
With servile simper nod the mitred head. *Toph.* 4.

Mix.
All stones . . . mix attemper'd in a various day;
Tasso 66.

Mixture.
The powerful Mixture and the midnight Spell;
*Prop.*³ 86.

Mnestheus'.
By Phlegyas warn'd, and fir'd by Mnestheus' fate,
*Stat.*² 4.

Mock.
They mock the air with idle state.   *Bard* 4.
Let not Ambition mock their . . . toil, *El.* 29.
walls that seem to mock my shame, *Agr.* 156.
†But why on such *mock* grandeur should we dwell,
Ch. Cr. 23.

Mocks.
eye, That mocks the tear it forc'd   *Eton* 77.

Modest.
With modest pride . . . The laureate wreath,
. . . she brings,   *Inst.* 83.

Modesty.
fond reluctance, yielding modesty,   *Agr.* 197.

Modred.
Mountains, ye mourn in vain Modred, *Bard* 33.

Moiety.
†Then for a Moiety of the Year   *Ode* 41.

Molest.
such as . . . Molest her ancient solitary reign.
El. 12.
a bad face which did sadly molest her.
Mrs. Keene 2.

Momentary.
A momentary bliss bestow,   *Eton* 16.
Break out, and flash a momentary day, *Ign.* 20.

Moment's.
A moment's patience, gentle Mistress Anne:
Shak. 1.

Mona.
The Dragon-Son of Mona Stands;   *Owen* 20.

Monarch.
Sword, that once a Monarch bore,   *F. S.* 15.
love could teach a monarch to be wise, *E. G.* 108.

Monarch's.
Why yet does Asia dread a Monarch's nod,
E. G. 59.

Monarchs.
a team of harness'd monarchs bend   *Ign.* 38.
In golden Chains should loaded Monarchs bend,
*Prop.*³ 48.

Monasteries.
Unpeopled monast'ries [palaces, MS.] *View* 15.

Monster-brood.
Earth's monster-brood stretch'd on their iron bed,
*Prop.*² 41.

Monstrous.
†Henry the Eighth's most monstrous majesty,
Ch. Cr. 22.

Monthly.
That monthly waning hides her paly fires,
*Prop.*² 20.

Moody.
moody Madness laughing wild   *Eton* 79.

Moon.
The mopeing owl does to the moon complain
El. 10.

Mopeing. *See* **Moping.**

Moping.
The mopeing owl does to the moon complain
El. 10.

Moralist.
Poor moralist! and what art thou?   *Spring* 43.
teach the rustic moralist to die.   *El.* 84.

Morals.
Then his character, *Phyzzy*, — his morals —
C. C. 13.

More.
More hideous than their Queen: *Eton* 84.
No more; where ignorance is bliss,   *Eton* 99.
But ah! 'tis heard no more —   *P. P.* 111.
Vocal no more, since Cambria's fatal day,
Bard 27.
No more I weep.   *Bard* 43.

No more our long-lost Arthur we bewail.
Bard 109.
The . . . horn, No more shall rouse them
El. 20.
no more the blazing hearth shall burn,   *El.* 21.
more to Innocence their Safety owe *El.* Mas. 75.
No more, with Reason and thyself at Strife,
El. Mas. 85.
Their human passions now no more,   *Inst.* 49.
not the basilisk More deadly to the sight, *Agr.* 161.
beguil'd With more elusive speed the . . . sight
Agr. 191.
I . . . weep the more because I weep in vain.
West 14.
The hues of Bliss more brightly glow,   *Vic.* 41.
you have eat just enough and no more. *Couplet* 2.
Nor more, for now Nesimachus's son,   *Stat.*[1] 13.
Art it requires, and more than winged speed.
Tasso 30.
When my changed head these locks no more shall
know,   *Prop.*[2] 13.
to-morrow is no more;   *Prop.*[3] 96.
for three days more I grop'd   *Dante* 77.
that heard me now no more: *Dante* 80.
†Twenty more in Embrio dye;   *Ode* 38.
†No more, our Esthers now are nought but Hetties,
Ch. Cr. 11.

Morn.
That fly th' approach of morn.   *Eton* 50.
Gone to salute the rising Morn [Day, MS.].
Bard 70.
Fair laughs the Morn,   *Bard* 71.
The breezy call of incense-breathing Morn,
El. 17.
One morn I miss'd him   *El.* 109.
on her bridal morn   *Inst.* 41.
Now the golden Morn aloft Waves . . . wing,
Vic. 1.
The Morn had scarce commenc'd, when I awoke:
Dante 41.
e'er the sixth Morn Had dawn'd,   *Dante* 74.

Morning.
House . . . From whence one fatal morning is-
sues   *L. S.* 22.
To hail their Fitzroy's festal morning come;
Inst. 54.
Morning smiles the busy Race to chear, *West* 9.
To start from short slumbers, and wish for the
morning —   *Am. Lines* 3.

Mornings.
In vain to me the smileing Mornings shine,
West 1.

Morrow.
Their raptures . . . No yesterday, nor morrow
know;   *Vic.* 26.

Mortal.
Mortal, thou that hear'st the tale;   *F. S.* 57.
raise the mortal to a height divine.   *E. G.* 83.

Mortals.
†Mortals he loves to prick,   *Ch. Cr.* 32.

Mortimer.
"To arms!" cried Mortimer,   *Bard* 14.

Moss-grown.
the rude and moss-grown beech   *Spring* 13.
By the moss-grown pile he sate;   *Odin* 18.

Most.
†Her daughters deck'd most daintily I see,
Ch. Cr. 3.
†Henry the Eighth's most monstrous majesty,
Ch. Cr. 22.

Mother.
To Him the mighty Mother did unveil *P. P.* 86.
Mother of the giant-brood!   *Odin* 86.
Rummage his Mother, pinch his Aunt,   *L. S.* 59.
Tell your master, His mother shall obey him.
Agr. 3.
gratitude which Nero To such a mother owes;
Agr. 58.
If the son reign, the mother perishes.   *Agr.* 67.
Perish (you cried) the mother!   *Agr.* 68.
the daughter, sister, wife, And mother of their
Cæsars.   *Agr.* 119.
A friend, a wife, a mother sleeps: *Clerke* 2.

Mother-church.
Our mother-church, with half-averted sight,
Blush'd   *Toph.* 5.

Mother's.
sink the traitor in his mother's ruin.   *Agr.* 187.

Motionless.
mute we sate, And motionless;   *Dante* 71.

Mought. See also Might.
such as mought entrance find within   *Dante* 60.

Mould.
†And, springing from the sluggish mould, *Ode* 47.

Mouldering.
Long on these mould'ring bones   *Odin* 31.
heaves the turf in many a mould'ring heap,
El. 14.
Here mouldering fanes and battlements arise,
View 13.

Mount.
Yet shall he mount,   *P. P.* 121.
heart . . . will mount undaunted,   *Agr.* 52.
I saw methought Towards Pisa's Mount,
Dante 29.

Mountain.
Where each old poetic Mountain   *P. P.* 73.

Mountain-cliffs.
An Iron-race the mountain-cliffs maintain,
E. G. 88.

Mountain-high.
When mountain-high the waves disparted rise;
Tasso 40.

Mountain's.
headlong from the mountain's height *Bard* 143.

Mountains.
shaggy forms o'er ice-built mountains roam,
P. P. 55.
Mountains, ye mourn in vain   *Bard* 32.

Mountain-structures.
No Mountain-Structures in my Verse should rise,
Prop.[3] 36.

Mounts.

†H mounts to Heaven, and H descends to Hell.
Ch. Cr. 24.

Mourn.

Mountains, ye mourn in vain   *Bard* 32.
Leave me unbless'd, unpitied, here to mourn:
Bard 102.
I fruitless mourn to him that cannot hear,
West 13.
To mourn the Glories of his sevenfold Stream,
Prop.[3] 50.
Or thou dost mourn to think,   *Dante* 46.

Mourning.

A train of mourning Friends attend his Pall,
Prop.[3] 97.

Move.

move The bloom . . . and purple light *P. P.* 40.
In buskin'd [mystic, *Lett.*[2]] measures move
Bard 128.
The powerful pothooks did so move him, *L. S.* 86.
Cease, my doubts, my fears to move, *Song* 11.
What wondrous force the solid earth can move,
Prop.[2] 30.
Move through the Sacred Way and vainly threat,
Prop.[3] 52.

Moved.

Mov'd the stout heart of England's Queen,
L. S. 15.
So mov'd the Seer,   *Tasso* 23.

Mow.

thro' the kindred squadrons mow their way.
Bard 86.
Did the sword of Conan mow The crimson har-
vest   *Conan* 9.

Mr.

Fame, in the shape of Mr. Purt, . . . Had told,
L. S. 41.

Mrs.

Here lies Mrs. Keene   *Mrs. Keene* 1.
I'll be Mrs. *Twitcher* myself.   *C. C.* 32.

Much.

much I hope these walls alone   *Agr.* 22.
Much have I borne from canker'd critic's spite,
Shak. 5.

Mud.

draws his humid train of mud: *Ign.* 4.

Mungo's.

Nor Mungo's [Shelburne's, MS.], Rigby's, Bradshaw's friendship vain,   *View* 18.

Murder.

With many a foul and midnight murther fed,
Bard 88.
If murder cries for murder,   *Agr.* 185.

Murdered.

Henry . . . The murder'd saint   *Inst.* 46.

Murderous.

To seize their prey the murth'rous band! *Eton* 59.

Murmur.

The busy murmur glows!   *Spring* 24.

Murmured.

Murmur'd deep a solemn sound: *P. P.* 76.

Murmuring.

While some . . . Their murm'ring labours ply
Eton 32.

Murmurs.

Revenge on thee in hoarser murmurs breath;
Bard 26.
in murmurs dread,   *Odin* Whar. 23.
Thrice pronounc'd, in murmurs dread,
Odin MS. 23.

Murther. *See* Murder.

Murtherous. *See* Murderous.

Muse.

With me the Muse shall sit,   *Spring* 16.
has he giv'n in vain the heav'nly muse? *P. P.* 48.
The Muse has broke the twilight-gloom *P. P.* 56.
their years, spelt by th' unletter'd muse, *El.* 81.
let the Muse admire,   *Bent.* 2.
His mind each Muse, . . . adorn'd *Williams* 3.
no other Muse I know,   *Prop.*[3] 5.
The fruitful Muse from that auspicious Night
Prop.[3] 25.
Thee too the Muse should consecrate to Fame,
Prop.[3] 53.

Muse's.

Such forms, as glitter in the Muse's ray,
P. P. 119.
incense kindled at the Muse's flame. *El.* 72.
Nor Envy . . . Dare the Muse's walk to stain,
Inst. 10.

Muses.

The Muses, . . . Convey'd him   *L. S.* 70.
Thou Seat of the Muses!   *Satire* 4.

Muses'.

I'd in the ring knit hands, and joyn the Muses'
dance.   *Prop.*[2] 6.

Music.

the rich stream of music winds   *P. P.* 7.
Mute was the musick of the air,   *Vic.* 23.
Or if to Musick she the Lyre awake, *Prop.*[3] 13.

Musick. *See* Music.

Music's.

Sweet music's melting fall,   *Inst.* 63.

Musings.

By sympathetic musings here delayed,
El. Mas. 110.

Must.

Pikes must shiver, javelins sing,   *F. S.* 22.
Soon a King must bite the ground. *F. S.* Whar. 44.
I must be cautious, must be silent,   *Agr.* 85.
Must sick'ning virtue fly the tainted ground?
E. G. 71.
where unwearied sinews must be found *E. G.* 90.
e'en Magic here must fail,   *Prop.*[3] 85.

Mute.

Mute, but to the voice of Anguish?   *P. P.* 72.
Some mute inglorious Milton   *El.* 59.
He stood as mute as poor *Macleane.* *L. S.* 120.
these walls alone And the mute air   *Agr.* 23.
Mute was the musick of the air,   *Vic.* 23.
That Day, and yet another, mute we sate,
Dante 70.

Mutina.
Here Mutina from flames and famine free,
*Prop.*³ 43.

Mutter.
Yet something he was heard to mutter, *L. S.* 121.

Muttered.
Her mutter'd requiems, *Bard MS.* 74.
barb'rous rites Of mutter'd charms, *Agr.* 63.

Muttering.
Mutt'ring his wayward fancies *El.* 106.

Mutual.
mutual Wishes, mutual Woes endear *E. G.* 36.
†Long to seek a mutual heart,
Rond. 2, 10, 18, 26, 34.

My, *omitted.*

Myra.
†But if my Myra cruel be *Ode* 29.

Myra's.
†With Myra's charms In Episode, *Ode* 27.

Myriads.
blue-eyed Myriads from the Baltic coast.
E. G. 51.

Myself.
know myself a Man. *Adv.* 48.
I'll be Mrs. *Twitcher* myself. *C. C.* 32.
Me from myself the soft Enchantress stole;
*Prop.*³ 75.

Mysterious.
Euphrates' font, and Nile's mysterious head.
Tasso 56.

Mystic.
In mystic measures move *Bard Lett.*² 128.

Name.
Big with hosts of mighty name, *Owen* 9.
Their name . . . spelt by th' unletter'd muse,
El. 81.
shake 'em at the name of liberty, *Agr.* 132.
Conan's name, my lay, rehearse, *Conan* 1.
Redeem, what Crassus lost, and vindicate his
name. *Prop.*² 54.
weave thy ever-faithful Name. *Prop.*³ 54.
And the short Marble but preserve a Name,
*Prop.*³ 100.

Names.
often calling On their dear Names, *Dante* 80.

Nancy.
While Nancy earns the praise to Shakespeare due,
Shak. 23.

Nanny.
For thee fat Nanny sighs, *Com. Lines* 6.

Narrative.
many a copious Narrative you'll see *Prop.*³ 29.

Narrow.
Each in his narrow cell for ever laid, *El.* 15.
Beyond the confines of our narrow world:
Tasso 34.

Nathless.
The Anguish, that unutter'd nathless wrings
Dante 5.

Nation's.
read their hist'ry in a nation's eyes, *El.* 64.

Nations.
warms the nations with redoubled ray. *Bard* 138.
Fierce nations own'd her unresisted might,
Ign. 29.
o'er the trembling Nations from afar *E. G.* 46.
In vain the nations with officious fear *Stat.*¹ 56.

Native.
Avengers of their native land: *Bard* 46.
on his native sands The Dragon-Son . . . stands;
Owen 19.
the native darkness of the sky; *Ign.* 8.
sees far off . . . Her native plains, *E. G.* 63.
his native land Admired that arm, *Stat.*¹ 35.
With native spots and artful labour gay, *Stat.*² 25.

Natives.
To chear the shiv'ring Natives dull abode.
P. P. 57.

Natural.
our master's temper natural Was fashion'd fair
Shak. 9.

Nature. *See also* **Good-nature.**
the voice of Nature cries, *El.* 91.
the growing Powers Of Nature *E. G.* 14.
where the face of nature laughs around, *E. G.* 70.
Hark! 't is nature strikes the lyre, *Vic.* 19.
Yet Nature could not furnish out the feast, *View* 11.
†Nature in my Soul implanted: *Ode* 2.

Nature's.
In thy green lap was Nature's Darling laid,
P. P. 84.
Alone in nature's wealth array'd, *Hoel* 9.
Then let me rightly spell of nature's ways;
*Prop.*² 15.

Near.
wand'ring near her secret bow'r, *El.* 11.
near his fav'rite tree; *El.* 110.
Who prowl'd the country far and near, *L. S.* 45.
Near the source whence Pleasure flows; *Vic.* 54.
Then to my quiet Urn awhile draw near,
*Prop.*³ 105.
†Great D draws near — the Dutchess sure is come,
Ch. Cr. 1.

Nearer.
His . . . Sons with nearer Course surrounds
E. G. 24.

Neck.
So her white neck reclin'd, *Agr.* 195.
Every warrior's manly neck Chains of regal hon-
our deck, *Hoel* 13.

Necks.
With necks in thunder cloath'd, *P. P.* 106.

Nectar.
drink Nectar that the bees produce, *Hoel* 17.

Need.
Need we the influence of the northern star
E. G. 68.
No common helps, no common guide ye need,
Tasso 29.

Needs.

The message needs no comment. *Agr.* 2.

Ne'er. *See also* **Never.**

one false step is ne'er retrieved, *Cat* 38.
Ne'er again his likeness see; *F. S.* 46.
Who ne'er shall comb his raven-hair, *Odin* 66.
Knowledge . . . her ample page . . . did ne'er
    unroll; *El.* 50.
He ne'er was for a conj'rer taken. *L. S.* 128.
A gentler Lamb ne'er sported on the plain,
    Child 3.

Neglected.

Perhaps in this neglected spot is laid *El.* 45.
Glad I revisit thy neglected reign, *Ign.* 5.

Negligent.

To censure cold, and negligent of fame, *Bent.* 10.

Neighboring.

Earl Goodwin trembled for his neighbouring
    sand; *View* 6.
Whose walls along the neighbouring Sea extend,
    Tasso 4.

Nereid.

no Nereid stirr'd: *Cat* 34.

Nero.

the debt of gratitude which Nero . . . owes;
    Agr. 57.
ere mid-day, Nero will come to Baiæ. *Agr.* 159.

Nerves.

wont to stem With stubborn nerves the tide,
    Agr. 109.
string our nerves and steel our hearts *E. G.* 69.
Brac'd all his nerves, and every sinew strung;
    Stat.[2] 7.

Nervous.

Now fitting to his gripe and nervous arm,
    Stat.[1] 43.

Nesimachus'.

Nor more, for now Nesimachus's son, *Stat.*[1] 13.

Nestor.

The Bishop of Chester, Tho' wiser than Nestor
    Ext. Keene 2.

Never. *See also* **Ne'er.**

sorrow never comes too late, *Eton* 96.
Yet never can he fear a vulgar fate,
    P. P. MS. 122.
never shall Enquirer come To break *Odin* 88.
Never, till substantial Night Has reassum'd
    Odin 91.
Their sober wishes never learn'd to stray; *El.* 74.
A fairer flower will never bloom again: *Child* 4.
Never hang down your head, *C. C.* 31.
So York shall taste what Clouet never knew,
    Shak. 21.
Whose heart has never felt a second flame.
    Prop.[3] 66.

New. *See also* **Ever-new.**

For ever gone — yet still to fancy new, *Ign.* 33.
the new Fragrance of the breathing Rose,
    E. G. 56.
Art he invokes new horrors still to bring.
    View 12.

Swoll'n with new force, and late-descending
    rains. *Tasso* 10.
Till a new Sun arose with weakly Gleam,
    Dante 59.

New-born.

new-born Pleasure brings to happier Men:
    West 10.
New-born flocks, *Vic.* 9.

New-fallen.

A vestment unadorn'd, though white as new-
    fal'n Snows; *Tasso* 14.

Newgate-bird.

And filching and lying, and Newgate-bird tricks;
    C. C. 17.

Newton's.

Meek Newton's self bends from his state sub-
    lime, *Inst.* 25.

Next.

next thy sea-encircled coast. *P. P.* 82.
The next with dirges due *El.* 113.
†E enters next, and with her Eve appears,
    Ch. Cr. 5.
†Queen Esther next — how fair e'en after death,
    Ch. Cr. 9.

Nice.

Better to bottom tarts and cheesecakes nice,
    Shak. 17.

Niggard.

As sickly Plants betray a niggard Earth, *E. G.* 1.

Nigh.

Some frail memorial still erected nigh, *El.* 78.

Night.

the easy night, *Eton* 48.
Night, and all her sickly dews, *P. P.* 49.
Closed his eyes in endless night. *P. P.* 102.
Mark the year, and mark the night, *Bard* 53.
headlong . . . he plung'd [sunk, Lett.[2]] to endless
    night. *Bard* 144.
Who . . . drags me from the realms of night?
    Odin 30.
till substantial Night Has reassum'd *Odin* 91.
By Night and lonely Contemplation led
    El. Mas. 79.
Such as in silence of the night *L. S.* 101.
a secret and dead hour of night, *Agr.* 61.
from the realms of night my voice ye hear,
    Agr. 178.
all was ignorance, and all was night. *Ign.* 30.
sleep in peace his night of death. *Child* 6.
As when athwart the dusky woods by night
    Tasso 47.
Here gems break through the night *Tasso* 63.
to cheer the dreary Night: *Prop.*[2] 22.
Obscure his radiance in a short-liv'd night;
    Prop.[2] 34.
The fruitful Muse from that auspicious Night
    Prop.[3] 25.
All that whole Day, or the succeeding Night
    Dante 58.

Nightingale.

'T was the Nightingale that sung! *Song* 6.

Nightly.

To save thy secret soul from nightly fears,
Bard 7.

So from th' astonish'd stars, her nightly train,
Stat.[1] 53.

Nile.

Nile redundant o'er his Summer-bed *E. G.* 101.

And hoary Nile with pensive Aspect seem
Prop.[3] 49.

Nile's.

Euphrates' font, and Nile's mysterious head.
Tasso 56.

Nill. *See also* **Will.**

That will he, nill he, . . . He went, *L. S.* 87.

Nine.

Till the sad Nine in Greece's evil hour, *P. P.* 77.

The portals nine of hell arise. *Odin* 16.

Scarce to nine acres Tityus' bulk confined,
Prop.[2] 43.

Nips.

†My cold soil nips the Buds with Snow. *Ode* 6.

No.

Thy Joys no glittering female meets, *Spring* 45.

No hive hast thou of hoarded sweets, *Spring* 46.

No painted plumage to display: *Spring* 47.

No Dolphin came, no Nereid stirr'd: *Cat* 34.

A Fav'rite has no friend! *Cat* 36.

No sense have they of ills to come, *Eton* 53.

No more; where ignorance is bliss, *Eton* 99.

But ah! 't is heard no more — *P. P.* 111.

Vocal no more, since Cambria's fatal day,
Bard 27.

No more I weep. *Bard* 43.

No pitying heart, no eye, afford A tear *Bard* 65.

No more our long-lost Arthur we bewail.
Bard 109.

the echoing horn, No more shall rouse them
El. 20.

no more the blazing hearth shall burn, *El.* 21.

No children run to lisp their sire's return, *El.* 23.

If Mem'ry . . . no Trophies raise, *El.* 38.

No more, with Reason and thyself at Strife,
El. Mas. 85.

No farther seek his merits to disclose, *El.* 125.

In Britain's Isle, no matter where, *L. S.* 1.

no sign of grace, *L. S.* 89.

'Gainst four such eyes were no protection.
L. S. 96.

Their human passions now no more, *Inst.* 49.

The message needs no comment. *Agr.* 2.

Deck'd with no other lustre, *Agr.* 37.

no matter What; so 't be strange, *Agr.* 170.

My lonely Anguish melts no Heart but mine;
West 7.

Their raptures . . . No yesterday, nor morrow
know; *Vic.* 26.

No very great wit, *Char.* 4.

He ask'd no heaps of hoarded gold; *Hoel* 8.

You know I 'm no prude, *C. C.* 7.

No — at our time of life 't would be silly, *C. C.* 10.

They say he's no Christian, *C. C.* 15.

No tree is heard to whisper, *View* 10.

Words . . . by no meaning connected! *Am. Lines* 6.

you have eat just enough and no more. *Couplet* 2.

So mov'd the Seer, but on no harden'd plain;
Tasso 23.

No common helps, no common guide ye need,
Tasso 29.

When my changed head these locks no more
shall know, *Prop.*[2] 13.

No Phœbus else, no other Muse I know, *Prop.*[3] 5.

No Giant Race, no Tumult of the skies,
Prop.[3] 35.

No Mountain-Structures in my Verse should rise,
Prop.[3] 36.

to-morrow is no more; *Prop.*[3] 96.

that heard me now no more: *Dante* 80.

†No more, our Esthers now are nought but Hetties,
Ch. Cr. 11.

Noah.

He drinks — so did Noah; *C. C.* 28.

Noble.

Chill Penury repress'd their noble rage, *El.* 51.

And so God save our noble King, *L. S.* 141.

Welcome, my noble son, *Inst.* 67.

bade him strike The noble quarry. *Agr.* 47.

by Juno, It bears a noble semblance. *Agr.* 120.

These conscious Shame withheld, and pride of
noble line. *Stat.*[1] 25.

Nobler.

Fate demands a nobler head; *F. S.* 43.

You whose young bosoms feel a nobler flame
Prop.[2] 53.

Nod.

her nod Can rouse eight hardy legions, *Agr.* 107.

Why yet does Asia dread a Monarch's nod,
E. G. 59.

With servile simper nod the mitred head. *Toph.* 4.

Nodding.

The rocks and nodding groves rebellow *P. P.* 12.

the foot of yonder nodding beech, *El.* 101.

Turrets and arches nodding to their fall, *View* 14.

Nods.

nods his hoary head, and listens to the rhyme.
Inst. 26.

Lethargic nods upon her ebon throne. *Ign.* 24.

Noise.

Laughter, Noise, and thoughtless Joy, *Adv.* 19.

Noiseless.

the noiseless tenor of their way. *El.* 76.

Nom de guerre.

Melissa is her Nom de Guerre. *L. S.* 35.

None.

But none from Cattraeth's vale return, *Hoel* 20.

Noon.

float amid the liquid noon: *Spring* 27.

Noon-tide.

in thy noon-tide beam [ray, MS.] *Bard* 69.

His listless length at noontide would he stretch,
El. 103.

Nor.

Nor cruel *Tom*, nor *Susan* heard. *Cat* 35.

Nor all, that glisters, gold. *Cat* 42.

Nor second He, that rode sublime   *P. P.* 95.
Nor the pride, nor ample pinion,   *P. P.* 114.
Helm, nor Hauberk's twisted mail,   *Bard* 5.
Nor even thy virtues, Tyrant, shall avail *Bard* 6.
nor thus forlorn Leave me unbless'd,   *Bard* 101.
Nor wash his visage in the stream,   *Odin* 67.
Nor see the sun's departing beam,   *Odin* 68.
No boding Maid . . . nor Prophetess of good;
    Odin 85.
nor heaps his brooded stores,   *Owen* 5.
Nor on all profusely pours;   *Owen* 6.
Nor climb his knees   *El.* Pem., Eg., Mas. 24.
Nor Grandeur hear with a disdainful smile *El.* 31.
Nor you, ye Proud, impute to These   *El.* 37.
Their lot forbad: nor circumscrib'd alone *El.* 65.
Nor cast one longing ling'ring look   *El.* 88.
nor yet beside the rill,   *El.* 111.
Nor up the lawn, nor at the wood   *El.* 112.
Nor think to draw them from their dread abode,
    El. Mas. 150.
Rap'd at the door, nor stay'd to ask,   *L. S.* 55.
Nor . . . Let . . . Flatt'ry hide her serpent-
train   *Inst.* 7.
Nor Envy base, nor creeping Gain,   *Inst.* 9.
Nor dares . . . Profane thy inborn royalty
    Inst. 80.
Nor fear the rocks, nor seek the shore: *Inst.* 92.
unus'd to shake . . . nor to be lured   *Agr.* 18.
Nor am I yet to learn   *Agr.* 56.
Nor genial Warmth, nor genial Juice   *E. G.* 3.
Nor trusts her Blossoms to the churlish Skies.
    E. G. 8.
Their raptures . . . No yesterday, nor morrow
know ;   *Vic.* 26.
Nor envy dar'd to view him with a frown.
    Williams 4.
had Bute been true, Nor Mungo's . . . friend-
ship vain,   *View* 18.
Nor more, for now Nesimachus' son, *Stat.*¹ 13.
Nor stopp'd till it had cut the further strand,
    *Stat.*¹ 40.
Nor tempts he yet the plain,   *Stat.*¹ 45.
Nor yet in prospect rose the distant shore;
    Tasso 5.
Nor doubt with me to tread the downward road
    Tasso 37.
Nor Tale of Thebes, nor Ilium   *Prop.*³ 37.
Nor how the Persian trod the indignant Sea;
    *Prop.*³ 38.
Nor lofty Carthage struggleing with her Fate.
    *Prop.*³ 40.
But nor Callimachus' enervate Strain *Prop.*³ 55.
Nor I with unaccustom'd Vigour trace *Prop.*³ 57.
Nor thou my gentle Calling disapprove,
    *Prop.*³ 63.
nor the leeche's Care,   *Prop.*³ 93.
Nor changing Skies can hurt, nor sultry Air.
    *Prop.*³ 94.
who thou art; nor on what Errand Sent
    Dante 10.
Nor long endur'd the Chase: *Dante* 37.
Speechless my sight I fix'd, nor wept, *Dante* 53.
My struggling Sorrow, nor [not?] to heighten
theirs: *Dante* 69.

Norman.
There the Norman sails afar Catch the winds,
    Owen 15.

North.
Here reign the blustering North and blighting
East,   *View* 9.

Northern.
Facing to the northern clime, . . . he traced
    Odin 21.
the influence of the northern star   *E. G.* 68.

Nose.
But his nose is a shame,   *C. C.* 8.

Nose's.
Brown sees thee sitting on his nose's tip,
    Com. Lines 4.

Not, *omitted.* See Cannot, Don't.

Note.
Responsive to the cuckow's note,   *Spring* 6.
The pealing anthem swells the note of praise.
    El. 40.
The simplest note that swells the gale, *Vic.* 50.

Notes.
To brisk notes in cadence beating,   *P. P.* 34.
Far and wide the notes prolong.   *F. S.* 60.
in these Notes their artless Tale relate,
    El. Mas. 78.
These Ears, alas! for other Notes repine, *West* 5.
Idle notes! untimely green!   *Song* 7.
the song-thrush there Scatters his loose notes
    Birds 2.
I favour her repose With lulling Notes, *Prop.*³ 19.
†In shriller notes Q like a female squeaks;
    Ch. Cr. 48.

Nothing.
And passages, that lead to nothing.   *L. S.* 8.
Can you do nothing but describe?   *L. S.* 20.
Pert barristers, and parsons nothing bright,
    Shak. 7.

Nothing's.
Big with the important Nothing's History.
    *Prop.*³ 30.

Nought.
†No more, our Esthers now are nought but Hetties,
    Ch. Cr. 11.

Nourish.
†Maggots too will form and nourish;   *Ode* 16.

Novice.
taught his novice hand To aim   *Agr.* 30.

Now.
Who foremost now delight to cleave   *Eton* 25.
Now the rich stream of music winds along *P. P.* 7.
Now rowling down the steep amain,   *P. P.* 10.
Now pursuing, now retreating,   *P. P.* 32.
Now in circling troops they meet: *P. P.* 33.
what daring Spirit Wakes thee now? *P. P.* 113.
Now, Brothers, . . . Stamp we our vengeance
deep,   *Bard* 95.
Now the storm begins to lower   *F. S.* 1.
Now your thundering faulchion wield;
    F. S. Pem. 62.
Now your sable steed bestride.   *F. S.* Pem. 63.
Now my weary lips I close; [:]   *Odin* 57, 71.

King of Men, I know thee now;   *Odin* 82.
Now fades the glimmering landscape   *El.* 5.
Now all the air a solemn stillness holds,
   El. Mas. 6.
now smiling as in scorn,   *El.* 105.
Now drooping, woeful-wan,   *El.* 107.
Their human passions now no more,   *Inst.* 49.
Now the golden Morn aloft   *Vic.* 1.
Their raptures now that wildly flow,   *Vic.* 25.
Now let him sleep in peace   *Child* 6.
Though now a book, and interleaved you see.
   Shak. 4.
But what awaits me now is worst of all. *Shak.* 8.
Now mouldering fanes and battlements arise,
   View MS. 13.
Now clean, now hideous, mellow now, now gruff,
   Par. on Ep. 1.
Nor more, for now Nesimachus's son, *Stat.*[1] 13.
And now in dust the polish'd ball he roll'd,
   Stat.[1] 41.
Now fitting to his gripe and nervous arm,
   Stat.[1] 43.
now through the skies Sings in its rapid way,
   Stat.[1] 49.
now hear My Wrongs,   *Dante* 14.
oh! if thou weep not now,   *Dante* 47.
now the Hour Of timely Food approach'd;
   Dante 49.
that heard me now no more: *Dante* 80.
†No more, our Esthers now are nought but Hetties,
   Ch. Cr. 11.
†Now a pert Prig, he perks   *Ch. Cr.* 33.
†Now peers, pores, ponders,   *Ch. Cr.* 34.
†Now a proud Prince,   *Ch. Cr.* 35.
†And now a Player, a Peer,   *Ch. Cr.* 36.
†Now seems a Penny, and now shews a Pound;
   Ch. Cr. 38.

Numbers.
In loose numbers wildly sweet   *P. P.* 61.
Numbers would give their oaths   *L. S.* 127.
From Cynthia all that in my numbers shines;
   Prop.[3] 3.
†Copious numbers, swelling grain;   *Ode* 8.
†Tragick Numbers, buskin'd Strains,   *Ode* 31.

Numbs.
That numbs the soul with icy hand,   *Eton* 89.

Nurse.
Stern rugged Nurse! thy rigid lore   *Adv.* 13.

Nursed.
The silken son of dalliance, nurs'd in ease
   Agr. 98.

Nymph.
The hapless Nymph with wonder saw: *Cat* 19.

O, *omitted. See* **Oh.**

Oak. *See also* **Giant-oak.**
thunder's fiery stroke, Glancing on the shiver'd
   oak;   *Conan* 8.

Oak's.
Where'er the oak's thick branches stretch
   Spring 11.

Oar.
with adventrous oar and ready sail   *E. G.* 104.
Where Ocean frets beneath the dashing oar,
   Stat.[2] 20.

Oath.
strengthen it With his plain soldier's oath,
   Agr. 151.

Oaths.
Numbers would give their oaths upon it, *L. S.* 127.

Obedient.
he led Beneath the obedient river's inmost bed;
   Tasso 44.

Obeisance.
With shows of fair obeisance;   *Agr.* 102.

Obey.
Thee the voice, the dance, obey,   *P. P.* 25.
Once again my call obey,   *Odin* 51.
Prophetess, my spell obey,   *Odin* 59.
Yet awhile my call obey;   *Odin* 73.
His mother shall obey him.   *Agr.* 3.

Object.
A different Object do these Eyes require: *West* 6.

Obligation.
Suffices not to pay the obligation.   *Agr.* 59.

Obscure.
Their homely joys, and destiny obscure; *El.* 30.
Why does yon Orb, . . . Obscure his radiance
   Prop.[2] 34.

Obsequies.
afford A tear to grace his obsequies.   *Bard* 66.

Obsequious.
obsequious vows From voluntary realms, *Agr.* 35.

Obtrusive.
not obtrusive, she . . . no venal incense flings;
   Inst. 78.

Obvious.
Not obvious, . . . she . . . no venal incense
   flings;   *Inst.* 78.

Ocean.
The dark unfathom'd caves of ocean   *El.* 54.
Where Ocean frets beneath the dashing oar,
   Stat.[2] 20.
How riseing winds the face of Ocean sweep,
   Prop.[2] 23.

Oceans.
Oceans unknown, inhospitable Sands! *Tasso* 32.

Odd.
so was thought somewhat odd;   *Char.* 3.
To reject him for such peccadillos, were odd;
   C. C. 29.

Oddly.
Then he shambles and straddles so oddly —
   C. C. 9.

Odin.
Hie thee, Odin,   *Odin* MS. 87.

Odin's.
What dangers *Odin's* Child await,   *Odin* 53.
By *Odin's* fierce embrace comprest,   *Odin* 64.

Odorous.
beneath the od'rous shade   *P. P.* 58.

O'er.

O'er Idalia's velvet-green   *P. P.* 27.
O'er her warm cheek, and rising bosom, *P. P.* 40.
Hurls o'er their . . . rear,   *P. P.* MS. 52.
Till o'er the eastern cliffs from far *P. P.* MS. 52.
shaggy forms o'er ice-built mountains roam,
         P. P. 55.
Woods, that wave o'er Delphi's steep, *P. P.* 66.
Wide o'er the fields of Glory   *P. P.* 104.
Bright-eyed Fancy hov'ring o'er   *P. P.* 108.
o'er the crested pride Of the First Edward *Bard* 9.
o'er old Conway's foaming flood,   *Bard* 16.
O'er thee, oh King! their hundred arms they
   wave,   *Bard* 25.
who o'er thy country hangs The scourge of
   Heav'n.   *Bard* 59.
While proudly riding o'er the azure realm
         Bard 72.
bending o'er th' accursed loom   *Bard* 95.
spread O'er the youthful King your shield.
         F. S. 32.
shall stretch O'er the plenty of the plain. *F. S.* 40.
O'er it hangs the shield of gold;   *Odin* 45.
The lowing herd wind slowly o'er the lea, *El.* 2.
If Mem'ry o'er their Tomb no Trophies raise,
         El. 38.
While o'er the Heath we hied, *El.* Mas. 118.
When he had fifty winters o'er him, *L. S.* 10.
Thro' lanes unknown, o'er stiles they ventur'd,
         L. S. 54.
And o'er the bed and tester clamber, *L. S.* 64.
Their tears, their little triumphs o'er, *Inst.* 48.
the fate Impending o'er your son: *Agr.* 66.
The massy sceptre o'er thy slumb'ring line?
         Ign. 16.
triumphant o'er the vanquish'd world; *Ign.* 28.
o'er the trembling Nations from afar *E. G.* 46.
goes O'er Libya's deserts   *E. G.* 77.
Nile redundant o'er his Summer-bed *E. G.* 101.
broods o'er Egypt with his wat'ry wings,
         E. G. 103.
rise and glitter o'er the ambient tide *E. G.* 107.
o'er the living scene Scatters . . . green. *Vic.* 7.
o'er the cheek of Sorrow throw . . . grace;
         Vic. 31.
And o'er his head, . . . the circle sped; *Stat.*[1] 47.
And sports and wantons o'er the frozen tide.
         Tasso 22.
Or lawless, o'er their Ivory Margin stray:
         Prop.[3] 8.
while o'er the Place You drop the Tear,
         Prop.[3] 106.
†Lightly lambent o'er their frame,   *Rond.* 22.

O'er-arching.

Ye brown o'er-arching groves,   *Inst.* 27.

O'er-canopies.

The . . . beech O'er-canopies the glade;
         Spring 14.

O'erpower.

suns of fiercer flame O'erpower the fire *E. G.* 65.

O'erta'en.

his helpless offspring soon O'erta'en beheld,
         Dante 39.

Of, *omitted.*

Off.

sees far off with an indignant groan,   *E. G.* 62.

Officious.

In vain the nations with officious fear Their cymbals toss,   *Stat.*[1] 56.

Offspring.

his helpless offspring soon O'erta'en beheld,
         Dante 38.

Oft.

And oft, beneath the od'rous shade   *P. P.* 58.
Yet oft before his infant eyes   *P. P.* 118.
and envy oft thy happy grandsire's end.
         Bard MS. 76.
Oft did the harvest to their sickle yield, *El.* 25.
Their furrow oft the stubborn glebe has broke:
         El. 26.
Oft have we seen him   *El.* 98.
There scatter'd oft, the earliest of the Year,
      El. Pem. 117 ; Mas. 137.
Oft as the Woodlark piped   *El.* Mas. 119.
Oft at the foot of yonder . . . beech,
         El. Mas. 121.
Full oft . . . he . . . led the Brawls; *L. S.* 9.
Yet hither oft a glance . . . They send *Inst.* 19.
Oft at the blush of dawn I trod   *Inst.* 30.
Oft woo'd the gleam of Cynthia   *Inst.* 32.
He reigns, . . . who oft has bade, *Agr.* 69.
how oft in weak and sickly minds *Agr.* 72.
yielding modesty, And oft reverted eye, *Agr.* 198.
Oft o'er the trembling Nations from afar
         E. G. 46.
oft have issued, Host impelling Host, *E. G.* 50.
For oft . . . his native land Admired that arm,
         Stat.[1] 35.
oft on Alpheus' shore The pond'rous brass . . .
   he bore;   *Stat.*[1] 36.
Has oft the Charms of Constancy confest,
         Prop.[3] 72.

Often.

Styack has often seen the sight   *L. S.* 103.
often calling On their dear Names, *Dante* 79.

Oh.

Oh, gently on thy Suppliant's head,   *Adv.* 33.
Stay, oh stay! nor thus forlorn Leave me
         Bard 101.
But oh! what solemn scenes   *Bard* 105.
oh! 't is a cause To arm . . . childhood *Agr.* 132.
Oh take me to thy peaceful shade   *Ign.* 6.
Oh say, successful dost thou still oppose *Ign.* 13.
Oh say — she hears me not,   *Ign.* 23.
Oh! sacred age! Oh! times for ever lost! *Ign.* 31.
Vast, oh my friends, and difficult the toil
         Tasso 27.
Oh, might that envied Happiness be mine!
         Prop.[3] 67.
Oh! thou art cruel,   *Dante* 45.
oh! if thou weep not now,   *Dante* 47.
But oh! when I beheld My Sons,   *Dante* 61.
oh Earth! could'st thou not gape   *Dante* 71.
†Leave, and lose it, — oh the pain!
     Rond. 4, 12, 20, 28, 36.

Old. *See also* **Old-tree.**

Where each old poetic Mountain   *P. P.* 73.
o'er old Conway's foaming flood,   *Bard* 16.
Your helpless, old, expiring master view!
          Bard MS. 72.
gorgeous Dames, and Statesmen old . . . appear.
          Bard 113.
beech, That wreathes its old fantastic roots *El.* 102.
ties . . . Of old respect and gratitude, *Agr.* 114.
Again the buried Genius of old Rome *Agr.* 141.
Not thus of old, with ensigns wide   *Ign.* 27.
Like old Sesostris with barbaric pride;   *Ign.* 37.
of Madoc old He ask'd no heaps of hoarded gold;
          Hoel 7.
where three sisters of old In harmless society
   guttle   *C. C.* 3.
Did not Israel filch from the Egyptians of old
          C. C. 25.
Old, and abandon'd by each venal friend, *View* 1.
†The walls of old Jerusalem appear, *Ch. Cr.* 27.

Old-tree.

in the park beneath an old-tree,   *L. S.* 122.

On.

The insect youth are on the wing,   *Spring* 25.
On hasty wings thy youth is flown;   *Spring* 48.
to send on earth Virtue,   *Adv.* 9.
on thy solemn steps attend: *Adv.* 29.
gently on thy Suppliant's head,   *Adv.* 33.
On Thracia's hills the Lord of War   *P. P.* 17.
Perching on the scept'red hand   *P. P.* 20.
Pours on their scatter'd rear,   *P. P. MS.* 52.
when they first were open'd on the day
         P. P. MS. 118.
On a rock . . . the Poet stood;   *Bard* 15.
On dreary Arvon's shore they lie,   *Bard* 35.
On yonder cliffs, . . . I see them sit, *Bard* 44.
Low on his funeral couch he lies!   *Bard* 64.
Youth on the prow,   *Bard* 74.
A smile of horror on their baffled guest.
         Bard Lett.[1] 82.
unborn Ages, crowd not on my soul! *Bard* 108.
Till he on *Hoder's* corse shall smile *Odin* 69.
corse . . . Flaming on the fun'ral pile. *Odin* 70.
Nor on all profusely pours;   *Owen* 6.
On her shadow . . . Lochlin plows *Owen* 13.
on his native sands The Dragon-Son . . . stands;
         Owen 19.
fades the glimmering landscape on the sight,
         El. 5.
waste its sweetness on the desert air.   *El.* 56.
shut the gates of mercy on mankind,   *El.* 68.
On some fond breast the parting soul relies,
         El. 89.
on the custom'd hill,   *El.* 109.
Grav'd on the stone   *El.* 116.
frown'd not on his humble birth,   *El.* 119.
On the first marching . . . The Muses, . . .
   Convey'd him   *L. S.* 69.
Yet on his way . . . he prefer'd his case, *L. S.* 89.
with a blush on recollection Own'd,   *L. S.* 94.
Bursts on my ear th' indignant lay: *Inst.* 14.
where on their opening soul First . . . ardour
   stole.   *Inst.* 21.

Great Edward, with the lilies on his brow *Inst.* 39.
on her bridal morn   *Inst.* 41.
All that on Granta's fruitful plain   *Inst.* 51.
To glitter on the diadem.   *Inst.* 76.
the spirit of Britannicus Yet walks on earth:
         Agr. 15.
On expectation's strongest wing to soar *Agr.* 42.
benefits . . . sit heavy on the soul,   *Agr.* 75.
pleasures That wait on youth,   *Agr.* 79.
On this base My great revenge shall rise;
         Agr. 120.
Let majesty sit on thy awful brow,   *Agr.* 145.
the tim'rous cloud That hangs on thy clear brow.
         Agr. 194.
on the . . . Powers Of Nature idly lavishes
         E. G. 13.
Smile not indulgent on the rising Race, *E. G.* 16.
on resolution's wings, . . . dauntless goes
         E. G. 75.
on frail floats to distant cities ride, *E. G.* 106.
rhymes that us'd to linger on,   *Bent.* 9.
tost On the thorny bed of Pain,   *Vic.* 46.
Her infant image . . . Sits smiling on a father's
   woe: *Clerke* 10.
A gentler Lamb ne'er sported on the plain,
         Child 3.
Victor he stood on Bellisle's rocky steeps —
         Williams 10.
On surrounding foes advance?   *Caradoc* 3.
Glancing on the shiver'd oak;   *Conan* 8.
By acclamations roused, came tow'ring on.
         Stat.[1] 14.
All eyes were bent on his experienced hand,
         Stat.[1] 34.
oft on Alpheus' shore The pond'rous brass . . .
   he bore;   *Stat.*[1] 36.
hag . . . smiles malignant on the labouring
   power.   *Stat.*[1] 59.
Third in the labours of the disc come on, *Stat.*[2] 1.
Pursu'd his cast, and hurl'd the orb on high;
         Stat.[2] 9.
The orb on high tenacious of its course, *Stat.*[2] 10.
As on the Rhine, when Boreas' fury reigns,
         Tasso 17.
So mov'd the Seer, but on no harden'd plain;
         Tasso 23.
The flood on either hand its billows rears,
         Tasso 41.
Let on this head unfadeing flowers reside, *Prop.*[2] 9.
Earth's monster-brood stretch'd on their iron bed,
         Prop.[2] 41.
Lips, which on the clotter'd Locks . . . he
   wiped,   *Dante* 2.
on what Errand Sent hither: *Dante* 10.
then on my Children's Eyes . . . my Sight I
   fix'd,   *Dante* 52.
often calling On their dear Names, *Dante* 80.
†and my head Rhimed on,   *Ode* 22.
†a Sonnet On Chloe's Fan, or Cælia's Bonnet.
         Ode 36.
†But why on such *mock* grandeur should we dwell,
         Ch. Cr. 23.
†then perches on the spray,   *Ch. Cr.* 41.

Once.

Where once my careless childhood stray'd,
Eton 13.
Sword, that once a Monarch bore,   *F. S.* 15.
They, whom once the desart-beach Pent
F. S. 37.
Once again my call obey,   *Odin* 51.
Once again arise, and say,   *Odin* 60.
Some heart once pregnant with celestial fire;
El. 46.
explore Thy once loved haunt,   *El.* Mas. 112.
High Dames of honour once,   *L. S.* 107.
He once or twice had pen'd a sonnet; *L. S.* 125.
native plains, and empires once her own.
E. G. 63.
— but he once had a wife;   *C. C.* 14.
'T is Willy begs, once a right proper man,
Shak. 3.
yet the dread path once trod,   *Stanza* 2.
At once give loose to Utterance, and to Tears.
Dante 9.
Take back, what once was yours.   *Dante* 68.
†But when once the potent dart   *Rond.* 29.

One.

one false step is ne'er retriev'd,   *Cat* 38.
one longing ling'ring look   *El.* 88.
woeful-wan, like one forlorn,   *El.* 107.
One morn I miss'd him   *El.* 109.
From whence one fatal morning issues *L. S.* 22.
one Who had such liberal power   *Agr.* 88.
not to one in this benighted age   *Bent.* 17.
Of Pisa one, and one from Ephyre;   *Stat.*[1] 12.
In one rich mass unite the precious store,
Tasso 61.
before my Eyes Died one by one;   *Dante* 76.
†For one Silk-worm thought that thrives *Ode* 37.
†these Flies . . . can boast of one good Quality;
Ode 50.
†Then one faint glimpse of Queen Elizabeth;
Ch. Cr. 10.

One's.

Than thus be patch'd and cobbled in one's grave.
Shak. 20.

Ones.

His young ones ran beside him.   *Dante* 32.

Only.

To hide her cares her only art,   *Clerke* MS. 7.
†cooling breezes I only wrote of;   *Ode* 21.
†Queer Queensbury only does refuse to wait.
Ch. Cr. 52.

Onward.

Onward still his way he takes   *Odin* 13.

Ope.

Or ope the sacred source of sympathetic Tears.
P. P. 94.

Oped.

when I Oped his young eye   *Agr.* 45.
Oped the dark Veil of Fate.   *Dante* 28.

Open.

OWEN . . . Lord of . . . open heart.   *Owen* 8.
†Open the *d*oors of the with*d*rawing-room;
Ch. Cr. 2.

Opened.

when they first were open'd   *P. P.* MS. 118.
His shaggy throat he open'd wide,   *Odin* 6.

Opener.

Can opener skies, and suns of fiercer flame
E. G. 64.

Opening.

where on their opening soul First . . . ardour
stole.   *Inst.* 21.
warm the opening Heart.   *E. G.* 12.
skies, To him are opening Paradise.   *Vic.* 52.
Thro' a small crevice opening,   *Dante* 22.

Opinion.

Howe'er Opinion tinge the . . . Mind, *E. G.* 27.

Oppose.

dost thou still oppose Thy leaden ægis *Ign.* 13.

Or.

Or chill'd by age,   *Spring* 39.
Or urge the flying ball?   *Eton* 30.
Or where Mæander's amber waves   *P. P.* 69.
Or ope the sacred source of sympathetic Tears.
P. P. 94.
Or drowsy tinklings lull the distant folds:
El. Eg. 8.
Or swallow twitt'ring from the straw-built shed,
El. Mas. 18.
The cock's shrill clarion, or the echoing horn,
El. 19.
Or chaunticleer . . . , or ecchoing horn,
El. Mas. 19.
Or busy housewife ply her evening care: *El.* 22.
Or [Nor, Eg., Mas.] climb his knees   *El.* 24.
storied urn or animated bust   *El.* 41.
Or Flatt'ry soothe the dull cold ear of death?
El. 44.
Or wak'd to extasy the living lyre.   *El.* 48.
Or shut the gates of mercy   *El. Eg.* 68.
Or craz'd with care, or cross'd in hopeless love.
El. 108.
Or draw his frailties from their dread abode,
El. 126.
Or creased, like dogs-ears, in a folio.   *L. S.* 68.
Or at the chappel-door   *L. S.* 104.
Or any malice to the poultry,   *L. S.* 124.
To taste of hollow kindness, or partake *Agr.* 19.
unknown To fame, or fortune;   *Agr.* 39.
she fear'd, or wish'd to be pursued.   *Agr.* 199.
Or chearful Fields resume their green Attire:
West 4.
Or on frail floats to distant cities ride, *E. G.* 106,
in Shakespeare's or in Milton's page, *Bent.* 19.
Or deepest shades,   *Vic.* 34.
drink Nectar . . . Or the grape's extatic juice.
Hoel 18.
Have ye seen the dusky boar, Or the bull,
Caradoc 2.
Or roused by sprightly sounds   *Prop.*[2] 5,
All angry heaven inflicts, or hell can feel,
Prop.[2] 45.
Or are our fears th' enthusiast's empty dream,
Prop.[2] 48.
Or lawless, o'er their Ivory Margin stray: *Prop.*[3] 8.

Or if to Musick she the Lyre awake, *Prop.*³ 13.
In brief whate'er she do, or say, or look,
                                     *Prop.*³ 27.
Or if, alas! it be my Fate   *Prop.*³ 69.
Or if I fall the Victim   *Prop.*³ 77.
Or drive the infernal Vulture   *Prop.*³ 90.
Or who can probe the undiscover'd Wound?
                                     *Prop.*³ 92.
Or Thou dost mourn to think,   *Dante* 46.
yet wept I not, or answer'd   *Dante* 57.
All that whole Day, or the succeeding Night
                                      Dante 58.
†Or, soon as they begin to blow   *Ode* 5.
†Or Poppy-thoughts blast all the shoots. *Ode* 12.
†a Sonnet On Chloe's Fan, or Cælia's Bonnet.
                                      Ode 36.
†a Peer, a Pimp, or Priest;   *Ch. Cr.* 36.
†Like Perch or Pike,   *Ch. Cr.* 39.
†hangs like Pear or Plum,   *Ch. Cr.* 40.
†Pippin or Peach;   *Ch. Cr.* 41.
†In form of Parrot, Pye, or Popinjay. *Ch. Cr.* 42.

Orb.
sanguine cloud, . . . has quench'd the Orb of day?
                                      Bard 136.
the rolling Orb, that gives the Day, *E. G.* 23.
Another orb upheaved his strong right hand,
                                      *Stat.*¹ 15.
All but two youths th' enormous orb decline,
                                      *Stat.*¹ 24.
Pursu'd his cast, and hurl'd the orb on high;
                                      *Stat.*² 9.
The orb on high tenacious of its course, *Stat.*² 10.
with silver light Relumes her crescent Orb
                                      *Prop.*² 22.

Order.
And mitred fathers in long order go: *Inst.* 38.

Orders.
And Satan's self had thoughts of taking orders.
                                      Toph. 8.

Ore.
The parts combine and harden into Ore:
                                      Tasso 62.

Organ.
when thou hear'st the organ piping shrill
                                      Shak. 15.

Orient.
With orient hues, unborrow'd of the Sun:
                                      P. P. 120.

Original.
shake her own creation To its original atoms —
                                      Agr. 92.

Orkney's.
Orkney's woe, and *Randver's* bane. *F. S.* 8.

Osborne's.
†All, all, but Grannam Osborne's Gazetteer.
                                      Ch. Cr. 20.

Other.
The other Amazon kind Heaven Had arm'd
                                      L. S. 29.
Deck'd with no other lustre,   *Agr.* 37.
These Ears, alas! for other Notes repine, *West* 5.
Far other scenes than these   *View* MS. 19.

no other Muse I know,   *Prop.*³ 5.
The Power of Herbs can other Harms remove,
                                      *Prop.*³ 79.
my other three before my Eyes Died   *Dante* 75.

Others.
What others are, to feel,   *Adv.* 48.

Others'.
she learned to melt at others' woe.   *Adv.* 16.

Our, *omitted.*

Ours.
Ours to kill, and ours to spare: *F. S.* 34.

Out, *omitted.*

Outcry.
voice, And outcry of the battle?   *Agr.* 96.

Out-stretched.
at my Feet out-stretch'd,   *Dante* 73.

Over. *See* **O'er.**

Overleaps.
The orb . . . Far overleaps all bound, *Stat.*² 12.

Owe.
more to Innocence their Safety owe *El. Mas.* 75.

Owed.
To Chiron Phœnix owed his long-lost Sight,
                                      *Prop.*³ 83.

Owen.
OWEN swift, and OWEN strong;   *Owen* 2.

Owen's.
OWEN's praise demands my song,   *Owen* 1.

Owes.
Nero To such a mother owes;   *Agr.* 58.

Owl.
The mopeing owl does to the moon complain
                                      El. 10.

Owls.
Owls would have hooted   *View* 23.

Own.
Th' unfeeling for his own.   *Eton* 94.
and Misery not thine own.   *Adv.* MS. 8.
from her own she learn'd to melt at others' woe.
                                      Adv. 16.
Exact my own defects to scan,   *Adv.* 47.
Melancholy mark'd him for her own.   *El.* 120.
shake her own creation   *Agr.* 91.
ears to own Her spirit-stirring voice; *Agr.* 123.
native plains, and empires once her own.
                                      E. G. 63.
saw my own Despair reflected,   *Dante* 62.

Owned.
Own'd, . . . his quiver . . . no protection.
                                      L. S. 95.
nations own'd her unresisted might,   *Ign.* 29.

P.
†P pokes his head out,   *Ch. Cr.* 29.
†P, Proteus-like all tricks, . . . can shew,
                                      Ch. Cr. 43.

Pace.
> With necks in thunder cloath'd, and long-re-
> sounding pace.   *P. P.* 106.

Pacing.
> pacing forth With solemn steps   *Inst.* 35.

Pack.
> The hungry Pack their sharp-set Fangs embrued.
>   *Dante* 40.

Page.
> Knowledge . . . her ample page . . . did ne'er
> unroll;   *El.* 49.
> in Shakespeare's or in Milton's page,   *Bent.* 19.

Pain.
> A stranger yet to pain!   *Eton* 14.
> The tender for another's pain;   *Eton* 93.
> The Proud are taught to taste of pain,   *Adv.* 6.
> Labour, and Penury, the racks of Pain, *P. P.* 43.
> Pale Grief, and pleasing Pain,   *Bard* 129.
> Pain can reach the Sons of Heav'n!   *Odin* 48.
> The threats of pain and ruin to despise,   *El.* 62.
> Heavier toil, superior pain.   *Inst.* 58.
> They follow Pleasure, and they fly from Pain;
>   *E. G.* 31.
> tost On the thorny bed of Pain,   *Vic.* 46.
> In ling'ring pain, in death resign'd,
>   *Clerke* MS. 9.
> Here, freed from pain,   *Child* 1.
> †Leave, and lose it, — oh the pain!
>   *Rond.* 4, 12, 20, 28, 36.
> †yet has not a pain;   *Ch. Cr.* 29.

Painful.
> The painful family of Death,   *Eton* 83.

Paint.
> Richly paint the vernal year   *P. P.* 90.
> Go! you can paint it well   *Agr.* 12.
> And paint the margin of the costly stream,
>   *Tasso* 64.
> What colours paint the vivid arch of Jove;
>   *Prop.²* 29.
> To paint the Hero's Toil,   *Prop.³* 33.

Painted.
> No painted plumage to display: *Spring* 47.
> Nor . . . Let painted Flatt'ry hide her serpent-
> train   *Inst.* 8.
> her that arm'd This painted Jove,   *Agr.* 30.

Pair.
> Where fix'd in wonder stood the warlike pair,
>   *Tasso* 25.

Palaces.
> Unpeopled palaces delude his eyes, *View* MS. 15.

Pale.
> With fury pale, and pale with woe,
>   *Bard* Lett.¹ 17.
> Smear'd with gore, and ghastly pale: *Bard* 36.
> Pale Grief and pleasing Pain,   *Bard* 129.
> how she turn'd pale and trembled: *Agr.* 9.
> The sun's pale sister, drawn by magic strain,
>   *Stat.¹* 54.
> may my pale Coarse be borne.   *Prop.³* 78.

Paler.
> the paler rose, The rival of her crown   *Inst.* 43.

Palgrave.
> Weddell attends your call, and Palgrave proud,
>   *Com. Lines* 1.

Pall.
> A train of mourning Friends attend his Pall,
>   *Prop.³* 97.

Pallid.
> Disdainful Anger, pallid Fear,   *Eton* 63.
> dreaming Sloth of pallid hue,   *Inst.* 4.

Palm.
> the champions, . . . the palm despair'd resign;
>   *Stat.¹* 23.

Paly.
> That monthly waning hides her paly fires,
>   *Prop.²* 20.

Panegyricks. *See* **Panegyrics.**

Panegyrics.
> Coarse Panegyricks would but teaze her.
>   *L. S.* 34.

Panel.
> Each pannel in achievements cloathing, *L. S.* 6.

Pang.
> A pang, to secret sorrow dear;   *Clerke* 13.

Pangæa's.
> With such a gleam affrights Pangæa's field,
>   *Stat.¹* 29.

Pangs.
> Tyrants . . . groan With pangs unfelt before,
>   *Adv.* 8.
> The struggling pangs of conscious truth   *El.* 69.
> Pangs without respite, fires that ever glow,
>   *Prop.²* 40.

Pannel. *See* **Panel.**

Panting.
> The panting herds repose: *Spring* 22.
> the panting Sire Of Strength bereft,   *Dante* 37.

Pants.
> Agony, that pants for breath,   *Owen* 39.

Papers.
> Papers and books, a huge Imbroglio! *L. S.* 66.

Paradise.
> Thought would destroy their paradise. *Eton* 98.
> skies, To him are opening Paradise.   *Vic.* 52.

Pardon.
> The Muses, hopeless of his pardon, Convey'd him
>   *L. S.* 70.

Parent.
> Parent of sweet and solemn-breathing airs,
>   *P. P.* 14.
> Imbibes a flavour of its parent earth,   *E. G.* 85.
> Which soon the parent sun's warm powers refine,
>   *Tasso* 60.
> †Buzzing with all their parent Faults;   *Ode* 46.

Parents'.
> the darling of his parents' eyes: *Child* 2.

Parish.
> By this time all the Parish know it   *L. S.* 42.

Park.
> How in the park beneath an old-tree, *L. S.* 122.

Parlor.
But bounce into the parlour enter'd. *L. S.* 56.

Parlour. *See* **Parlor.**

Parnassus.
Left their Parnassus for the Latian plains.
P. P. 79.

Parrot.
†In form of Parrot, Pye, or Popinjay. *Ch. Cr.* 42.

Parsons.
Pert barristers, and parsons nothing bright,
Shak. 7.

Part.
†Part in a Chrysalis appear.   *Ode* 42.
†to love, — and then to part,
Rond. 1, 9, 17, 25, 33.

Partake.
partake His hospitable board: *Agr.* 19.

Parted.
Thyrsis, when we parted, swore   *Song* 1.

Parthian.
in Armenia quell the Parthian force   *Agr.* 111.

Parting.
The Curfew tolls the knell of parting day, *El.* 1.
On some fond breast the parting soul relies,
El. 89.
And parting surges round the vessel roar; *Stat.²* 21.
†Light to them the parting knell: *Rond.* 23.

Parts.
The parts combine and harden into Ore:
Tasso 62.

Pass.
Further they pass,   *Tasso* 57.
†Some have lov'd, to pass the time, *Rond.* 13.
†See Isaac, Joseph, Jacob, pass in view;
Ch. Cr. 26.

Passages.
And passages, that lead to nothing.   *L. S.* 8.
Through subterraneous passages they went,
Tasso 49.

Passed.
He pass'd the flaming bounds of Place and Time:
P. P. 98.

Passes.
The famish'd Eagle screams, and passes by.
Bard 38.

Passing.
the passing tribute of a sigh.   *El.* 80.
Thy passing Courser's slacken'd Speed restrain;
Prop.³ 102.

Passion.
ev'ry fierce tumultuous Passion   *El. Mas.* 82.
are privy to your passion.   *Agr.* 23.
to check this dangerous passion,   *Agr.* 106.

Passions.
These shall the fury Passions tear, *Eton* 61.
frantic Passions hear thy soft controul. *P. P.* 16.
Their human passions now no more, *Inst.* 49.

Past.
Smiles on past Misfortune's brow   *Vic.* 29.
skies serene Speak not always winter past.
Song 10.

Pastorals.
†First when Pastorals I read,   *Ode* 19.

Patched.
Than thus be patch'd and cobbled in one's grave.
Shak. 20.

Path.
Slow thro' the church-way path   *El.* 114.
yet the dread path once trod,   *Stanza* 2.

Paths.
The paths of pleasure trace,   *Eton* 24.
As the paths of fate we tread,   *F. S.* 29.
The paths of glory lead but to the grave. *El.* 36.
in the dangerous paths of fame,   *Williams* 1.

Patience.
thy rigid lore With patience . . . she bore:
Adv. 14.
A moment's patience, gentle Mistress Anne:
Shak. 1.

Patient.
to patient valour train'd They guard *E. G.* 94.

Pattern.
Takes them all for his pattern;   *Satire* 20.

Paul's.
And foxes stunk and litter'd in St. Paul's.
View 24.

Paws.
The velvet of her paws,   *Cat* 9.

Pay.
the Graces homage pay.   *P. P.* 37.
Suffices not to pay the obligation.   *Agr.* 59.
†gratefully they pay Their little Songs, *Ode* 51.

Pea.
†A Pea, a Pin,   *Ch. Cr.* 37.

Peace.
A grateful Earnest of eternal Peace. *El. Mas.* 84.
improve the polish'd Arts of Peace: *E. G.* 41.
Now let him sleep in peace   *Child* 6.
Love, gentle Power! to Peace was e'er a friend;
Prop.¹ 1.
And to this bosom give its wonted Peace,
Prop.² 88.

Peaceful.
take me to thy peaceful shade again. *Ign.* 6.
The peaceful virtues lov'd to dwell. *Clerke* 4.

Peach.
†like Pear or Plum, Pippin or Peach; *Ch. Cr.* 41.

Peaked.
In peaked hoods and mantles tarnish'd, *L. S.* 105.

Pealing.
The pealing anthem swells the note of praise.
El. 40.

Pear.
†hangs like Pear or Plum,   *Ch. Cr.* 40.

Peasants.
Bewitch'd the children of the peasants, *L. S.* 46.

Pease.
As the Master of Keys Is as like as two Pease,
Satire 14.

Peccadillos.
　To reject him for such peccadillos, were odd;
　　　　　　　　　　　　　C. C. 29.
Peep.
　at the peep of dawn　　　　　　*El.* 98.
Peeping.
　And from the gallery stand peeping:　*L. S.* 100.
Peeps.
　†Like Punch, he peeps,　　　*Ch. Cr.* 30.
Peer.
　said the sighing peer,　　　　*View* 17.
Peeress.
　The Peeress comes.　　　　　*L. S.* 109.
Peers.
　†Now peers, pores, ponders,　*Ch. Cr.* 34.
Pembroke.
　The Master of Pembroke　　　*Satire* 29.
Pen.
　Grease his best pen,　　　　*Shak.* 16.
Pencil.
　This pencil Take (she said),　　*P. P.* 89.
　bids the pencil answer to the lyre.　*Bent.* 4.
Pen'd. *See* **Penned.**
Pendent.
　quaff the pendent Vintage as it grows. *E. G.* 57.
　The pendent rock, Ixion's whirling wheel,
　　　　　　　　　　　　　*Prop.*² 46.
Pendragon.
　At Broom, Pendragon, Appleby and Brough.
　　　　　　　　　　　　Par. on Ep. 3.
Penitence.
　In lieu of penitence, and vain remorse, *Agr.* 179.
Penitent.
　Never hang down your head, you poor penitent
　　elf,　　　　　　　　　　　*C. C.* 31.
Penned.
　He once or twice had pen'd a sonnet; *L. S.* 125.
　attend To the Satire I've pen'd　*Satire* 2.
Penny.
　†Now seems a Penny,　　　*Ch. Cr.* 38.
Pension.
　A place or a pension he did not desire, *Char.* 5.
Pensive.
　The pensive Selima reclin'd,　　*Cat* 5.
　If chance that e'er some pensive spirit
　　　　　　　　　　　　　El. Mas. 109.
　And hoary Nile with pensive Aspect seem
　　　　　　　　　　　　　*Prop.*³ 49.
Pent.
　desart-beach Pent within its bleak domain,
　　　　　　　　　　　　　F. S. 38.
Penury.
　Labour, and Penury, the racks of Pain, *P. P.* 43.
　Chill Penury repress'd their noble rage, *El.* 51.
People.
　She curtsies, . . . To all the People of condition.
　　　　　　　　　　　　　L. S. 112.
　The dusky people drive before the gale; *E. G.* 105.

Peopled.
　Hark, how thro' the peopled air　*Spring* 23.
Perch.
　†Like Perch or Pike,　　　　*Ch. Cr.* 39.
Perchance.
　He Perchance may heed 'em:　　*Agr.* 88.
Perches.
　†then perches on the spray,　*Ch. Cr.* 41.
Perching.
　Perching on the scept'red hand　*P. P.* 20.
Perfect.
　†The Dowager grows a perfect double D.
　　　　　　　　　　　　　Ch. Cr. 4.
Perfidious.
　Ruggieri, Pisa's perfidious Prelate this: *Dante* 14.
Performed.
　your errand is perform'd,　　　*Agr.* 1.
　Due sacrifice perform'd with barb'rous rites
　　　　　　　　　　　　　Agr. 62.
Perhaps.
　Perhaps in this . . . spot is laid Some heart
　　　　　　　　　　　　　El. 45.
　How flames perhaps, . . . Shall sink this beau-
　　teous fabric　　　　　　*Prop.*² 27.
　†Perhaps Thalia prompts a Sonnet　*Ode* 35.
Perish.
　Perish (you cried) the mother!　*Agr.* 68.
　They perish in the boundless deep.　*Vic.* 60.
Perishes.
　If the son reign, the mother perishes.　*Agr.* 67.
Perks.
　†he perks upon your face,　*Ch. Cr.* 33.
Permit.
　Yet would the Tyrant Love permit me raise
　　　　　　　　　　　　　*Prop.*³ 31.
Perpetual.
　Perpetual draws his . . . train of mud: *Ign.* 4.
　†in a perpetual round,　　　*Ch. Cr.* 37.
Persian.
　Nor how the Persian trod the indignant Sea;
　　　　　　　　　　　　　*Prop.*³ 38.
Person.
　†What Ease and Elegance her person grace,
　　　　　　　　　　　　　Ch. Cr. 7.
　†The Pleasantest Person in the Christ-Cross row.
　　　　　　　　　　　　　Ch. Cr. 44.
Pert.
　Pert barristers, and parsons nothing bright,
　　　　　　　　　　　　　Shak. 7.
　†Now a pert Prig, he perks　*Ch. Cr.* 33.
Peter's.
　The Master of Peter's Has all the same features;
　　　　　　　　　　　　　Satire 31.
　Owls would have hooted in St. Peter's choir,
　　　　　　　　　　　　　View 23.
Petition.
　My Lady heard their joint petition,　*L. S.* 49.
Phantom.
　tremble at the phantom I have raised? *Agr.* 86.

Pheasants.
And suck'd the eggs, and kill'd the pheasants.
L. S. 48.

Philippi.
And sad Philippi, red with Roman Gore:
Prop.³ 46.

Philosophic.
Thy philosophic Train be there To soften,
Adv. 43.
measured Laws and philosophic Ease *E. G.* 40.

Phizzes.
And Glyn cut Phizzes, *Com. Lines* 3.

Phlegra's.
of Jove, and Phlegra's blasted Plain; *Prop.³* 56.

Phlegyas.
Phlegyas the long-expected play began, *Stat.¹* 32.
By Phlegyas warn'd, and fir'd by Mnestheus' fate,
Stat.² 4.

Phœbus.
To Phœbus he prefer'd his case, *L. S.* 91.
redning Phœbus lifts his golden Fire: *West* 2.
No Phœbus else, no other Muse I know, *Prop.³* 5.
†To Phœbus gratefully they pay Their little Songs,
Ode 51.

Phœbus .
And Phœbus' Son recall'd Androgeon *Prop* ³ 84.
†I told Of Phœbus' heat and Daphne's cold. *Ode* 24.

Phœnix.
To Chiron Phœnix owed his long-lost Sight,
Prop.³ 83.

Phrase.
gorgeous phrase of labour'd eloquence *Agr.* 149.

Physic.
"Lord! sister," says Physic to Law, *C. C.* 5.

Phyzzy.
Then his character, *Phyzzy*, *C. C.* 13.

Pick-pocket.
such a pick-pocket air! *C. C.* 6.

Picture.
'T is just like the picture in Rochester's book;
C. C. 12.

Pictured.
Scatters from her pictur'd urn *P. P.* 109.
But pictured horrour and poëtic woes. *Prop.²* 50.

Piercing.
Sorrow's piercing dart. *Eton* 70.

Pike.
†Like Perch or Pike, *Ch. Cr.* 39.

Pikes.
Pikes must shiver, javelins sing, *F. S.* 22.

Pile.
By the moss-grown pile he sate; *Odin* 18.
corse . . . Flaming on the fun'ral pile. *Odin* 70.
An ancient pile of buildings stands: *L. S.* 2.

Pimp.
†a Peer, a Pimp, or Priest; *Ch. Cr.* 36.

Pin.
†A Pea, a Pin, *Ch. Cr.* 37.

Pinch.
Rummage his Mother, pinch his Aunt, *L. S.* 59.
†to prick, and pinch, and pluck; *Ch. Cr.* 32.

Pindus'.
When Pindus' self approaching ruin dreads,
Prop.² 31.

Pies.
For glorious puddings and immortal pies.
Shak. 24.

Pineing. *See* **Pining.**

Pining.
Or pineing Love shall waste their youth, *Eton* 65.

Pines.
When Pindus' self . . . Shakes all his Pines,
Prop.² 32.

Pinion.
Nor the pride, nor ample pinion, *P. P.* 114.

Pious.
pious drops the closing eye requires; *El.* 90.
With a lick of court white-wash, and pious
grimace, *C. C.* 2.
Here Holland form'd the pious resolution
View 2.

Piped.
the Woodlark piped her farewell Song,
El. Mas. 119.

Pipes.
There pipes the woodlark, *Birds* 1.

Piping.
when thou hear'st the organ piping shrill *Shak.* 15.

Pippin.
†like Pear or Plum, Pippin or Peach; *Ch. Cr.* 41.

Pisa.
Of Pisa one, and one from Ephyre; *Stat.¹* 12.

Pisa's.
oft in Pisa's sports, his native land Admired that
arm, *Stat.¹* 35.
Ruggieri, Pisa's perfidious Prelate this: *Dante* 14.
I saw methought Towards Pisa's Mount,
Dante 29.

Pisgys.
†the Pisgys call him Puck, *Ch. Cr.* 31.

Pitied.
pitied ghosts Of the Syllani, *Agr.* 175.

Pity.
Pity, dropping soft the sadly-pleasing tear.
Adv. 32.
In pity to the country-farmer. *L. S.* 40.
the soft springs of pity in my heart, *Agr.* 182.

Pitying.
No pitying heart, . . . afford A tear *Bard* 65.

Place.
the flaming bounds of Place and Time: *P. P.* 98.
The place of fame and elegy supply: *El.* 82.
To bless the place, *Inst.* 21.
A place or a pension he did not desire, *Char.* 5.
while o'er the Place You drop the Tear,
Prop.³ 106.

Plain.

shall stretch O'er the plenty of the plain. *F. S.* 40.

on Granta's fruitful plain,   *Inst.* 51.

strengthen it With his plain soldier's oath,
Agr. 151.

Foes to the gentler genius of the plain: *E. G.* 89.

A gentler Lamb ne'er sported on the plain,
Child 3.

Nor tempts he yet the plain,   *Stat.*¹ 45.

So mov'd the Seer, but on no harden'd plain;
Tasso 23.

of Jove, and Phlegra's blasted Plain; *Prop.*³ 56.

†careless spares to weed the Plain: *Ode* 10.

Plains.

Left their Parnassus for the Latian plains.
P. P. 78.

sees far off . . . Her native plains,   *E. G.* 63.

Plan.

mends the Plan their Fancy draws, *E. G.* 32.

Plantations.

†He in plantations hangs   *Ch. Cr.* 40.

Plants.

sickly Plants betray a niggard Earth,   *E. G.* 1.

Firmly he plants each knee,   *Stat.*¹ 47.

Play.

The little victims play!   *Eton* 52.

What strains of vocal transport round her play.
Bard 120.

And the weights, that play below,   *F. S.* 11.

Phlegyas the long-expected play began, *Stat.*¹ 32.

Swift shoots the Village-maid in rustic play
Tasso 19.

If the loose Curls around her Forehead play,
*Prop.*³ 7.

Player.

†And now a Player, a Peer,   *Ch. Cr.* 36.

Plays.

†Youth, his torrid Beams thay [that?] plays,
Ode 13.

Plea.

in gorgeous phrase . . . To dress thy plea,
Agr. 150.

Pleasantest.

†The Pleasantest Person in the Christ-Cross row.
Ch. Cr. 44.

Please.

Alas, who would not wish to please her! *L. S.* 36.

't will profit you, And please the stripling.
Agr. 13.

Pleased.

Pleas'd in thy lineaments we trace   *Inst.* 69.

Half pleas'd, half blushing,   *Bent.* 2.

†Pleased with his Pranks,   *Ch. Cr.* 31.

Pleasing. *See* Sadly-pleasing, Self-pleasing.

ah, pleasing shade,   *Eton* 11.

Less pleasing when possest;   *Eton* 42.

Pale Grief, and pleasing Pain,   *Bard* 129.

This pleasing anxious being   *El.* 86.

as their pleasing influence   *Bent.* 27.

My soul in Bacchus' pleasing fetters bound;
*Prop.*² 8.

Pleasure.

whisp'ring pleasure as they fly,   *Spring* 8.

The paths of pleasure trace,   *Eton* 24.

and Pleasure at the helm;   *Bard* 74.

new-born Pleasure brings to happier Men:
West 10.

They follow Pleasure, and they fly from Pain;
E. G. 31.

languid Pleasure sighs in every Gale. *E. G.* 45.

where rosy Pleasure leads,   *Vic.* 37.

Near the source whence Pleasure flows; *Vic.* 54.

Her pleasure, pleasures to impart, *Clerke* MS. 8.

From fortune, pleasure, science, love, he flew,
Williams 7.

With beauty, with pleasure surrounded, to languish —   *Am. Lines* 1.

Pleasure's.

nurs'd in ease And pleasure's flow'ry lap? *Agr.* 99.

Pleasures.

With antic Sports, and blue-eyed Pleasures,
P. P. 30.

pleasures That wait on youth,   *Agr.* 78.

Her pleasure, pleasures to impart, *Clerke* MS. 8.

Plenteous.

†If a plenteous Crop arise,   *Ode* 7.

Plenty.

shall stretch O'er the plenty of the plain.
F. S. 40.

scatter plenty o'er a smiling land,   *El.* 63.

scatter . . . Showers of Plenty o'er the Land.
E. G. 18.

Insult the plenty of the vales below? *E. G.* 99.

Pliant.

cleave With pliant arm thy glassy wave? *Eton* 26.

Proud of the yoke, and pliant to the rod,
E. G. 58.

Plinlimmon.

Made huge Plinlimmon bow his cloud-top'd head.   *Bard* 34.

Plods.

The plowman homeward plods his weary way,
El. 3.

Plough.

With side-long plough to quell the . . . ground,
E. G. 91.

Plow. *See* Plough.

Plowman.

The plowman homeward plods his weary way,
El. 3.

Plows.

Lochlin plows the watry way;   *Owen* 14

Pluck.

††to prick, and pinch, and pluck; *Ch. Cr.* 32.

Plum.

†hangs like Pear or Plum,   *Ch. Cr.* 40.

Plumage.

No painted plumage to display: *Spring* 47.

Plumed. *See* Full-plumed.

Plumes.

With ruffled plumes, and flagging wing: *P. P.* 22.

Plunged.
 headlong . . . he plung'd to endless night.
  Bard 144.
Ply.
 some . . . Their murm'ring labours ply *Eton* 32.
 Or busy housewife ply her evening care: *El.* 22.
 Frisking ply their feeble feet; *Vic.* 10.
Po.
 The Po was there to see, *Tasso* 55.
Pocket. *See* **Pick-pocket.**
Poet.
 With haggard eyes the Poet stood; *Bard* 18.
 A wicked Imp they call a Poet, *L. S.* 44.
 The Poet felt a strange disorder: *L. S.* 82.
 Speak to a Commoner and Poet! *L. S.* 140.
Poetic.
 Where each old poetic Mountain *P. P.* 73.
 But pictured horrour and poëtic woes. *Prop.*[2] 50.
 †Bids the poetick Spirit flourish; *Ode* 14.
Poetry.
 That Slumber brings to aid my Poetry. *Prop.*[3] 20.
 †Seeds of Poetry and Rhime *Ode* 1.
Poet's.
 Thou envied Honour of thy Poet's Days,
  Prop.[3] 103.
Poets.
 From fumbling baronets and poets small, *Shak.* 6.
Points.
 Where he points his purple spear, *Owen* 33.
Poised.
 he pois'd the well-known weight *Stat.*[2] 3.
Poison.
 I will not meet its poison. *Agr.* 163.
Poisonings.
 Sorceries, Assassinations, poisonings — *Agr.* 172.
Pokes.
 †P pokes his head out, *Ch. Cr.* 29.
Pole.
 with nearer Course surrounds To either Pole,
  E. G. 25.
Polish.
 But Cobham had the polish given *L. S.* 31.
Polished.
 improve the polish'd Arts of Peace: *E. G.* 41.
 A slipp'ry weight, and form'd of polish'd brass.
  Stat.[1] 8.
 And now in dust the polish'd ball he roll'd,
  Stat.[1] 41.
Pomfret's.
 from Pomfret's walls shall send *Bard* MS. 75.
Pomp.
 the pomp of tyrant-Power, *P. P.* 79.
 the pomp of pow'r, *El.* 33.
 The pomp and prodigality of heav'n. *Bent.* 20.
Pompous.
 †Prince, in pompous Purple drest, *Ch. Cr.* 35.
Pond.
 †in Pond you see him come, *Ch. Cr.* 39.

Ponderous.
 The pond'rous brass in exercise he bore; *Stat.*[1] 37.
 The ponderous mass sinks in the cleaving ground,
  Stat.[2] 16.
Ponders.
 †Now peers, pores, ponders, *Ch. Cr.* 34.
Poor.
 Poor moralist! and what art thou? *Spring* 43.
 The short and simple annals of the poor. *El.* 32.
 He stood as mute as poor *Macleane.* *L. S.* 120.
 Too poor for a bribe, *Char.* 1.
 Never hang down your head, you poor penitent
  elf, *C. C.* 31.
 to think, what my poor Heart Foresaw, *Dante* 46.
Pope.
 Tho' Pope and Spaniard could not trouble it.
  L. S. 16.
 The energy of Pope they might efface, *Bent.* 15.
Popinjay.
 †In form of Parrot, Pye, or Popinjay. *Ch. Cr.* 42.
Poppy-thoughts.
 †Or Poppy-thoughts blast all the shoots. *Ode* 12.
Pops.
 †but soon pops in again; *Ch. Cr.* 30.
Pore.
 pore upon the brook that babbles by. *El.* 104.
Pores.
 †Now peers, pores, ponders, *Ch. Cr.* 34.
Port. *See* **Lion-port.**
Portals.
 The portals nine of hell arise. *Odin* 16.
 But hark! the portals sound, *Inst.* 35.
 Heaven lifts its everlasting portals high, *Stanza* 3.
Possessed.
 Less pleasing when possest; *Eton* 42.
Possest. *See* **Possessed.**
Potent.
 †But when once the potent dart *Rond.* 29.
Potentates.
 High potentates, and dames of royal birth,
  Inst. 37.
Pother.
 What a pother is here about wenching and roar-
  ing! *C. C.* 23.
Pothooks.
 The powerful pothooks did so move him,
  L. S. 86.
Poultry.
 Or any malice to the poultry, *L. S.* 124.
Pound.
 †and now shews a Pound; *Ch. Cr.* 38.
Pour.
 Headlong, impetuous, see it pour; *P. P.* 11.
 the cloudy Magazines . . . pour the autumnal
  rain; *Prop.*[2] 26.
Poured.
 Rich streams of regal bounty pour'd, *Inst.* 52.

Pours.

The Attic warbler pours her throat,   *Spring* 5.
Pours on their scatter'd rear,   *P. P. MS.* 52.
Nor on all profusely pours;   *Owen* 6.
reflection Pours its cool dictates   *Agr.* 83.

Poverty.

Poverty to fill the band,   *Eton* 88.
Despair, and fell Disease, and ghastly Poverty:
   Adv. 40.

Power. *See also* **Tyrant-power.**

Love, gentle Power! to Peace was e'er a friend;
   Prop.[1] 1.
Daughter of Jove, relentless Power,   *Adv.* 1.
the pomp of pow'r,   *El.* 33.
Than Pow'r and Genius e'er conspir'd to bless.
   El. Mas. 76.
Employ'd the power of Fairy hands   *L. S.* 4.
The power of Magick was no fable.   *L. S.* 78.
What is grandeur, what is power?   *Inst.* 57.
haughty youth [,] and irritated power.[,]
   Agr. 26, 28.
the power To judge of weights and measures;
   Agr. 40.
The very power he has   *Agr.* 81.
Who had such liberal power   *Agr.* 89.
With equal power resume that gift,   *Agr.* 90.
ignorance! soft salutary power!   *Ign.* 9.
hag . . . smiles malignant on the labouring
power.   *Stat.*[1] 59.
The Power of Herbs can other Harms remove,
   Prop.[3] 79.

Powerful.

The Father of the powerful spell.   *Odin* 12.
The powerful pothooks did so move him,
   L. S. 86.
The powerful Mixture and the midnight Spell;
   Prop.[3] 86.

Powers.

bade the Magi call the dreadful powers, *Agr.* 64.
Can powers immortal feel the force of years?
   Ign. 26.
the growing Powers Of Nature   *E. G.* 13.
Which soon the parent sun's warm powers refine,
   Tasso 60.

Prætorian.

the Prætorian camp have long rever'd   *Agr.* 117.

Praise.

OWEN's praise demands my song,   *Owen* 1.
The pealing anthem swells the note of praise.
   El. 40.
she No vulgar praise, . . . flings;   *Inst.* 79.
While Nancy earns the praise to Shakespeare due,
   Shak. 23.
to sound the Victor's Praise,   *Prop.*[3] 32.
Of all our Youth the Ambition and the Praise!
   Prop.[3] 104.

Pranks.

†Pleased with his Pranks,   *Ch. Cr.* 31.

Pray.

For folks in fear are apt to pray   *L. S.* 90.

Prayer.

Steal to his closet at the hour of prayer; *Shak.* 14.

Precincts.

Left the warm precincts of the chearful day, *El.* 87.

Precious.

In one rich mass unite the precious store,
   Tasso 61.

Precipitant.

The sun's pale sister, . . . Deserts precipitant
her darken'd sphere: *Stat.*[1] 55.

Precipitates.

ere it precipitates its fall;   *Stat.*[2] 15.

Preferred.

To Phœbus he prefer'd his case,   *L. S.* 91.

Pregnant.

Some heart once pregnant with celestial fire;
   El. 46.

Prelate.

Ruggieri, Pisa's perfidious Prelate this: *Dante* 14.

Prelates.

While frighted prelates bow'd   *Toph.* 2.

Prelude.

Emits the mass, a prelude of his might; *Stat.*[1] 46.

Prepare.

The rich repast prepare,   *Bard* 78.
Haste, the loom of Hell prepare,   *F. S.* 2.

Presages.

Th' Event presages, and explores the Cause.
   E. G. 33.

Presence.

The Birds his presence greet: *Vic.* 12.

Present.

for I was present   *Agr.* 60.

Preserve.

And the short Marble but preserve a Name,
   Prop.[3] 100.

Press.

There the press, and there the din;   *Owen* 24.

Presume.

what charms presume To break the quiet *Odin* 27.
†Here Grub-street Geese presume to joke and jeer,
   Ch. Cr. 19.

Presumptuous.

Presumptuous Maid! with looks intent   *Cat* 25.
where Dryden's less presumptuous car, *P. P.* 103.

Pretensions.

to wake pretensions Drowsier than theirs,
   Agr. 103.

Pretty.

†In pretty Dialogue I told   *Ode* 23.

Prevail.

Force and hardy Deeds of Blood prevail. *E. G.* 44.

Prevent.

the champions, trembling at the sight, Prevent
disgrace,   *Stat.*[1] 23.

Prey. *See also* **Evening-prey.**

To seize their prey the murth'rous band! *Eton* 59.
to dumb Forgetfulness a prey,   *El.* 85.
Or drive the infernal Vulture from his Prey.
   Prop.[3] 90.
and rent his trembling Prey.   *Dante* 84.

Prick.
†Mortals he loves to prick,   *Ch. Cr.* 32.
Pride.
Nor the pride, nor ample pinion,   *P. P.* 114.
o'er the crested pride Of the first Edward *Bard* 9.
heap the shrine of Luxury and Pride   *El.* 71.
With modest pride . . . The laureate wreath,
   . . . she brings,   *Inst.* 83.
but that her pride restrain'd it?   *Agr.* 11.
nor fall alone; but crush his pride,   *Agr.* 186.
Like old Sesostris with barbaric pride;   *Ign.* 37.
Mark where Indolence and Pride,   *Vic.* 61.
Too, too secure in youthful pride,   *Hoel* 5.
These conscious shame withheld, and pride of
   noble line.   *Stat.*[1] 25.
A tiger's pride the victor bore away,   *Stat.*[2] 24.
There bloom the vernal rose's earliest pride;
     Prop.[2] 10.
were of his Life the Pride;   *Prop.*[3] 107.
Priest.
†a Peer, a Pimp, or Priest;   *Ch. Cr.* 36.
Prig.
†Now a pert Prig, he perks   *Ch. Cr.* 33.
Prince.
†Now a proud Prince,   *Ch. Cr.* 35.
Princely.
and princely Clare,   *Inst.* 42.
Print.
Footsteps lightly print the Ground.
     El. Pem. 120; Mas. 140.
Prison.
†and thoughts Like Butterflies, their Prison shun
     Ode 45.
Privy.
And the mute air are privy to your passion.
     Agr. 23.
Prize.
She stretch'd in vain to reach the prize. *Cat* 22.
Not all that tempts . . . is lawful prize, *Cat* 41.
ambition . . . Display the radiant prize, *Agr.* 52.
The world, the prize;   *Agr.* 153.
Probe.
who can probe the undiscover'd Wound?
     Prop.[3] 92.
Proclaims.
Her eye proclaims her of the Briton-Line;
     Bard 116.
Prodigality.
The pomp and prodigality of heav'n. *Bent.* 20.
Produce.
drink Nectar that the bees produce,   *Hoel* 17.
Profane.
Mad Sedition's cry profane,   *Inst.* 5.
dares . . . Profane thy inborn royalty of mind:
     Inst. 81.
Profit.
't will profit you,   *Agr.* 12.
Profound.
Immers'd in rapt'rous thought profound, *Adv.* 26.
avaunt, . . . Ignorance with looks profound, *Inst.* 3.
†ponders, with profound grimace,   *Ch. Cr.* 34.

Profusely.
Nor on all profusely pours;   *Owen* 6.
Progeny.
What idle progeny succeed   *Eton* 28.
Progress.
A thousand rills their mazy progress take: *P. P.* 4.
Prolong.
Far and wide the notes prolong.   *F. S.* 60.
Prolongs.
While Hope prolongs our happier hour, *Vic.* 33.
Promise.
blast the vernal Promise of the Year. *E. G.* 21.
Promises.
nor B—d's promises been vain,   *View* Nich. 18.
Prompts.
†Perhaps Thalia prompts a Sonnet   *Ode* 35.
Pronounced.
Thrice pronounc'd, . . . The thrilling verse
     Odin 23.
Proper.
'T is Willy begs, once a right proper man, *Shak.* 3.
Each in his proper Art should waste the Day:
     Prop.[3] 62.
Prophet.
The prophet of Bethel, we read, told a lie: *C. C.* 27.
Prophetess.
Prophetess, arise, and say,   *Odin* 52.
Prophetess, my spell obey,   *Odin* 59.
Prophetess, awake, and say,   *Odin* 74.
No boding Maid . . . nor Prophetess of good;
     Odin 85.
Prophetic.
The dust of the prophetic Maid.   *Odin* 20.
and Sleep Prophetic of my Woes   *Dante* 27.
Prophet's.
with a Master's hand, and Prophet's fire, *Bard* 21.
Proposing.
Her sisters denying, and Jemmy proposing:
     C. C. 20.
Proselyte.
Our mother-church, . . . Blush'd as she bless'd
   her griesly proselyte;   *Toph.* 6.
Prospect.
Nor yet in prospect rose the distant shore;
     Tasso 5.
Prosperity.
By vain Prosperity received,   *Adv.* 23.
Prostrate.
Prostrate warriors gnaw the ground. *Owen* 30.
The willing homage Of prostrate Rome, *Agr.* 77.
Prostrate with filial reverence I adore. *Ign.* 10.
The prostrate South to the Destroyer yields
     E. G. 52.
Protect.
these bones from insult to protect   *El.* 77.
Protection.
'Gainst four such eyes were no protection.
     L. S. 96.

Proteus-like.

†P, Proteus-like all tricks . . . can shew,
Ch. Cr. 43.

Proud.

how little are the Proud,   Spring 19.
how indigent the proud,   Spring Dods. 19.
The Proud are taught to taste of pain,   Adv. 6.
Yet thou, proud boy,   Bard MS. 75.
Nor you, ye Proud, impute to These the fault,
El. 37.
Forgive, ye Proud, th' involuntary Fault,
El. Dods., Pem., Eg., Mas. 37.
Proud of the yoke, and pliant to the rod,
E. G. 58.
too proud to importune;   Char. 1.
Then had we seen proud London's hated walls ;
View 22.
Weddell attends your call, and Palgrave proud,
Com. Lines 1.
Proud of its diamond dies, and luxury of light.
Tasso 70.
†Now a proud Prince,   Ch. Cr. 35.

Proudly.

While proudly riding o'er the azure realm Bard 72.
Side by side as proudly riding,   Owen 12.

Providence.

To Providence, to Him my thoughts I'd raise,
Prop.² 16.

Provoke.

Can Honour's voice provoke [awake, MS.] the
silent dust,   El. 43.

Prow.

Youth on the prow,   Bard 74.

Prowled.

Imp . . . Who prowl'd the country   L. S. 45.

Prows.

While Prows, that late in fierce Encounter mett,
Prop.³ 51.

Prude.

You know I'm no prude,   C. C. 7.

Prudence.

The mask of prudence;   Agr. 49.

Prudes.

The ghostly Prudes . . . Already had condemn'd the sinner.   L. S. 129.

Pry.

Into the Drawers and China pry,   L. S. 65.

Pterelas.

Young Pterelas with strength unequal drew,
Stat.¹ 5.

Puck.

†the Pisgys call him Puck,   Ch. Cr. 31.

Puddings.

For glorious puddings and immortal pies.
Shak. 24.

Punch.

†Like Punch, he peeps,   Ch. Cr. 30.

Puny.

a puny boy,   Agr. 36.
yon puny ball Let youngsters toss: Stat.¹ 19.

Pure.

The spirits pure,   Eton 49.
The pure bev'rage of the bee,   Odin 44.
glows with the pure Julian fire,   Agr. 50.
And bids the pure in heart behold their God.
Stanza 4.

Purest.

many a gem of purest ray   El. 53.

Purged.

Purg'd by the sword, and purified by fire,
View 21.

Purified.

Purg'd by the sword, and purified [beautified,
MS.] by fire,   View 21.

Purling.

†Purling streams and cooling breezes   Ode 20.

Purple.

And wake the purple year!   Spring 4.
Thro' richest purple . . . Betray'd a golden
gleam.   Cat 17.
purple Tyrants vainly groan   Adv. 7.
purple light of Love.   P. P. 41.
Where he points his purple spear,   Owen 33.
†Prince, in pompous purple drest,   Ch. Cr. 35.

Purred.

She saw; and purr'd applause   Cat 12.

Pursue.

Glory pursue, and generous Shame,   P. P. 64.
Pursue the silent Tenour of thy Doom.
El. Mas. 88.
With whistful eyes pursue the setting sun.
El. Mas. 120.
Her rapid wings the transient scene pursue,
Ign. 34.
See a kindred Grief pursue;   Vic. 38.
The foremost He Flash'd to pursue,   Dante 36.

Pursued.

I have pursued your steps,   Agr. 54.
she fear'd, or wish'd to be pursued. Agr. 199.
Pursu'd his cast, and hurl'd the orb on high;
Stat.² 9.

Pursues.

long pursues, with fruitless yell, The Father
Odin 11.

Pursuing.

Now pursuing, now retreating,   P. P. 32.

Pursuit.

Be love my youth's pursuit,   Prop.² 52.

Purt.

Fame, in the shape of Mr. Purt,   L. S. 41.

Pye.

†In form of Parrot, Pye, or Popinjay. Ch. Cr. 42.

Q.

†As K a King, Q represents a Queen, Ch. Cr. 45.
†In shriller notes Q like a female squeaks;
Ch. Cr. 48.
†Q draws her train along the Drawing-room,
Ch. Cr. 50.

Quaff.

quaff the pendent Vintage as it grows. *E. G.* 57.

Quaint.

With gestures quaint, now smiling as in scorn,
El. Mas. 125.

Quakes.

The groaning earth beneath him quakes,
Odin MS. 14.

Quality.

†these Flies . . . can boast of one good Quality;
Ode 50.

†Slow follow all the quality of State, *Ch. Cr.* 51.

Quarrel.

The Godhead would have back'd his quarrel,
L. S. 93.

Quarry.

bade him Strike The noble quarry. *Agr.* 46.

Queen.

More hideous than their Queen: *Eton* 84.

Mov'd the stout heart of England's Queen,
L. S. 15.

The drawing-room of fierce Queen Mary.
L. S. 108.

the rosy queen Of amorous thefts: *Agr.* 188.

†Queen Esther next — how fair e'en after death,
Ch. Cr. 9.

†Then one faint glimpse of Queen Elizabeth;
Ch. Cr. 10.

†As K a King, Q represents a Queen,
Ch. Cr. 45.

Queen's.

Slow melting strains their Queen's approach declare: *P. P.* 36.

So the Master of Queen's Is as like as two beans;
Satire 15.

Queensbury.

†Queer Queensbury only does refuse to wait.
Ch. Cr. 52.

Queer.

†Queer Queensbury only does refuse to wait.
Ch. Cr. 52.

Quell.

in Armenia quell the Parthian force *Agr.* 111.

With . . . plough to quell the flinty ground,
E. G. 91.

Quench.

To quench the blushes of ingenuous shame,
El. 70.

thinks to quench the fire *Agr.* 84.

Quenched.

Quench'd in dark clouds of slumber *P. P.* 23.

has quench'd the Orb of day? *Bard* 136.

Quick.

could they catch . . . his quick creation,
Bent. 14.

could'st thou not gape Quick to devour me?
Dante 72.

Quicker.

the quicker let me die: *Prop.*[3] 70.

Quick-glancing.

Quick-glancing to the sun. *Spring* 30.

Quiet.

To break the quiet of the tomb? *Odin* 27.

Humble quiet builds her cell, *Vic.* 53.

Then to my quiet Urn awhile draw near,
Prop.[3] 105.

Quire. *See* **Choir.**

Quite.

The times are alter'd quite and clean! *L. S.* 136.

Quiver.

Own'd, . . . his quiver . . . no protection.
L. S. 95.

Quivering.

"To arms!" cried Mortimer, and couch'd his
quiv'ring lance. *Bard* 14.

Anon, with slacken'd rage comes quiv'ring down,
Stat.[1] 51.

Quoit.

Whoe'er the quoit can wield, *Stat.*[1] 1.

R.

†Thus great R reigns in town, *Ch. Cr.* 53.

†Rests in Retirement, *little* Rural R; *Ch. Cr.* 54.

Rabbit.

†With Rooks and Rabbit burrows *Ch. Cr.* 56.

Race. *See also* **Iron-race.**

Such is the race of Man: *Spring* 32.

Full many a sprightly race *Eton* 22.

Man's feeble race what Ills await, *P. P.* 42.

Two Coursers of ethereal race, *P. P.* 105.

The winding-sheet of Edward's race. *Bard* 50.

the blood of Agrippina's race, *Agr.* 38.

Morning smiles the busy Race to chear, *West* 9.

hath Hyperion roll'd his annual race, *Ign.* 11.

Smile not indulgent on the rising Race, *E. G.* 16.

No Giant Race, no Tumult of the Skies,
Prop.[3] 35.

Back to it's Source divine the Julian Race.
Prop.[3] 58.

Racks.

This racks the joints, *Eton* 85.

Labour, and Penury, the racks of Pain, *P. P.* 43.

Radiance.

Why does yon Orb . . . Obscure his radiance
Prop.[2] 34.

Radiant.

If bright ambition . . . Display the radiant
prize, *Agr.* 52.

Rage.

Those in the deeper vitals rage: *Eton* 87.

Chill Penury repress'd their noble rage, *El.* 51.

the madding ear Of rage, *Agr.* 84.

With headlong rage and wild affright *Hoel* 2.

Anon, with slacken'd rage comes quiv'ring down,
Stat.[1] 51.

Rain.

The drenching dews, and driving rain! *Odin* 33.

pour the autumnal rain; *Prop.*[2] 26.

Rains.

Swoll'n with new force, and late-descending rains.
Tasso 10.

Raise.

If Mem'ry . . . no Trophies raise,	*El.* 38.
To raise the cieling's fretted height,	*L. S.* 5.
Shall raise from earth the latent gem	*Inst.* 75.
Without a spell to raise,	*Agr.* 16.
resentment cannot fail to raise	*Agr.* 25.
raise A tempest that shall shake	*Agr.* 90.
raise the mortal to a height divine.	*E. G.* 83.
To Providence, to Him my thoughts I'd raise,	*Prop.²* 16.
permit me raise My feeble Voice,	*Prop.³* 31.
†But, tho' Flowers his ardour raise,	*Ode* 15.

Raised.

yon sanguine cloud, Rais'd by thy breath,	*Bard* 136.
the phantom I have raised?	*Agr.* 86.
From his dire Food the griesly Fellon raised	*Dante* 1.

Ramparts.

while their rocky ramparts round they see,	*E. G.* 96.

Ran.

His young ones ran beside him.	*Dante* 32.

Randver's.

Orkney's woe, and *Randver's* bane.	*F. S.* 8.

Range.

He gives To range the dreary sky:	*P. P.* 51.

Rankle.

The sweets of kindness . . . Rankle to gall;	*Agr.* 74.

Rankling.

Jealousy with rankling tooth,	*Eton* 66.

Ranks.

To paint . . . the Ranks of War,	*Prop.³* 33.

Rapid.

Her rapid wings the transient scene pursue,	*Ign.* 34.
through the Skies Sings in its rapid way,	*Stat.¹* 50.

Rapped.

Rap'd at the door, nor stay'd to ask,	*L. S.* 55.

Rapt.

Rapt in celestial transport they:	*Inst.* 18.

Rapture.

give To rapture all thy trembling strings.	*P. P.* 2.
With torrent rapture, see it pour,	*P. P.* MS. 11.
Bright Rapture calls [wakes, *Lett.²*],	*Bard* 123.

Raptures.

Their raptures . . . No yesterday, nor morrow know;	*Vic.* 25.

Rapturous.

Immers'd in rapt'rous thought profound,	*Adv.* 26.
Rise the rapturous choir among;	*Vic.* 18.

Rare.

Teach it . . . as somewhat rare	*Agr.* 136.

Rase. *See* Raze.

Ratify.

Stamp we our vengeance deep, and ratify his doom.	*Bard* 96.

Rattle.

And up stairs in a whirlwind rattle.	*L. S.* 60.

Raven-hair.

Who ne'er shall comb his raven-hair,	*Odin* 66.

Ravens.

far aloof th' affrighted ravens sail;	*Bard* 37.

Ray.

Such forms, as glitter in the Muse's ray,	*P. P.* 119.
that hover'd in thy noontide ray?	*Bard* MS. 69.
warms the nations with redoubled ray.	*Bard* 138.
many a gem of purest ray serene,	*El.* 53.
If any spark of wit's delusive ray	*Ign.* 19.
Lamps, that shed at Ev'n a cheerful ray	*E. G.* 66.
All stones of lustre shoot their vivid ray,	*Tasso* 65.

Rays.

dart their intermingled rays,	*Bent.* 23.

Raze.

your arms shall rase the Tyrian towers,	*Stat.¹* 17.

Reach.

She stretch'd in vain to reach the prize.	*Cat* 22.
Pain can reach [touch, MS.] the Sons of Heav'n!	*Odin* 48.

Read.

read their hist'ry in a nation's eyes,	*El.* 64.
Approach and read (for thou can'st read)	*El.* 115.
dreadful powers, That read futurity,	*Agr.* 65.
The prophet of Bethel, we read, told a lie:	*C. C.* 27.
†First when Pastorals I read,	*Ode* 19.

Reading.

†If heroic Verse I'm reading	*Ode* 26.

Ready.

with adventrous oar and ready sail	*E. G.* 104.

Realised.

And realis'd the beauties which we feign:	*View* 20.

Realm.

proudly riding o'er the azure realm	*Bard* 72.

Realms.

Who . . . drags me from the realms of night?	*Odin* 30.
From yonder realms . . . Bursts . . . th' indignant lay:	*Inst.* 13.
obsequious vows From voluntary realms,	*Agr.* 36.
from the realms of night my voice ye hear,	*Agr.* 178.
If realms beneath those fabled torments know,	*Prop.²* 39.

Rear.

Pours on their scatter'd rear, [etc.]	*P. P.* MS. 52.
Sublime their starry fronts they rear;	*Bard* 112.
†F follows fast the fair — and in his rear,	*Ch. Cr.* 15.

Rears.

High he rears his ruby crest.	*Owen* 22.
The flood on either hand its billows rears,	*Tasso* 41.

Reason.

with Reason and thyself at Strife,	*El.* Mas. 85.

Reason's.
By reason's light on resolution's wings, *E. G.* 75.

Reassumed.
till substantial Night Has reassum'd [Reassumes, MS.] her ancient right;   *Odin* 92.

Reassumes.
Reassumes her ancient right;   *Odin* MS. 92.

Rebellow.
groves rebellow to the roar.   *P. P.* 12.

Rebellows.
And, clash'd, rebellows with the din of war.   *Stat.*[1] 31.

Rebound.
While vales and woods and echoing hills rebound.   *Stat.*[2] 17.

Rebrace.
rebrace The slacken'd sinews of . . . age.   *Agr.* 139.

Recalled.
And Phœbus' Son recall'd Androgeon *Prop.*[3] 84.

Receive.
Receive a worthier load;   *Stat.*[1] 19.

Received.
By vain Prosperity received,   *Adv.* 23.

Recess.
Me may Castalia's sweet recess detain, *Prop.*[2] 2.

Recks.
it rekes not That I advise thee.   *Dante* 17.

Reclined.
At ease reclin'd in rustic state   *Spring* 17.
The pensive Selima reclin'd,   *Cat* 5.
So her white neck reclin'd,   *Agr.* 195.
†reclined beneath the Tree-zes;   *Ode* 22.

Recollection.
with a blush on recollection Own'd,   *L. S.* 94.

Recompence. *See* **Recompense.**

Recompense.
Heav'n did a recompence . . . send: *El.* 122.

Red.
And sad Philippi, red with Roman Gore: *Prop.*[3] 46.

Red-breast.
The Red-breast [Redbreast, Mas.] loves to build . . . there,   *El.* Pem. 119; Mas. 138.

Reddening.
redning Phœbus lifts his golden Fire: *West* 2.

Redeem.
Redeem, what Crassus lost,   *Prop.*[2] 54.

Redning. *See* **Reddening.**

Redolent.
And, redolent of joy and youth,   *Eton* 19.

Redoubled.
warms the nations with redoubled ray. *Bard* 138.

Redundant.
Nile redundant o'er his Summer-bed   *E. G.* 101.

Re-echo.
Severn shall re-eccho with affright   *Bard* 54.

Refine.
Their little wants, their low desires refine,   *E. G.* 82.
Which soon the parent sun's warm powers refine,   *Tasso* 60.

Refined.
with courtly tongue refin'd,   *Inst.* 80.

Reflected.
in four Faces saw my own Despair reflected,   *Dante* 63.

Reflection.
grave and undisturb'd reflection   *Agr.* 82.
A sigh of soft reflection.   *Bent.* 28.

Reflection's.
Smiles . . . Soft Reflection's hand can trace;   *Vic.* 30.

Reft.
Reft of a crown, he yet may share   *Bard* 79.
for then Hunger had reft my Eye-sight *Dante* 79.

Refuge.
sad refuge from the storms of Fate!   *P. P.* 45.

Refuse.
†Queer Queensbury only does refuse to wait.   *Ch. Cr.* 52.

Regal.
Close by the regal chair   *Bard* 80.
OWEN . . . Lord of every regal art,   *Owen* 7.
Rich streams of regal bounty pour'd,   *Inst.* 52.
Chains of regal honour deck,   *Hoel* 14.

Regardless.
Regardless of the sweeping Whirlwind's sway,   *Bard* 75.
regardless of their doom   *Eton* 51.

Regions.
And unknown regions dare descry: *Eton* 37.
Search to what regions yonder Star retires,   *Prop.*[2] 19.

Rehearse.
Conan's name, my lay, rehearse,   *Conan* 1.
You ask, why thus my Loves I still rehearse,   *Prop.*[3] 31.

Reign.
The limits of their little reign,   *Eton* 36.
Thro' verdant vales, and Ceres' golden reign: *P. P.* 9.
Molest her ancient solitary reign.   *El.* 12.
If the son reign, the mother perishes.   *Agr.* 67.
reign the son!   *Agr.* 68.
Glad I revisit thy neglected reign,   *Ign.* 5.
Climes, where Winter holds his Reign, *E. G.* 5.
Here reign the blustering North and blighting East,   *View* 9.

Reigns.
Another *Arthur* reigns.   *Bard.* MS. 110.
He reigns, the rest is heav'n's;   *Agr.* 69.
when Boreas' fury reigns,   *Tasso* 17.
†Thus great R reigns in town,   *Ch. Cr.* 53.

Reins.
We the reins to slaughter give,   *F. S.* 33.
the reins of empire   *El.* Dods., Pem., Mas. 47.

Reject.
  To reject him for such peccadillos, were odd;
  C. C. 29.

Rejects.
  She half accepts, and half rejects, my Fires,
  *Prop.*³ 22.

Rejoice.
  Here . . . cormorants rejoice,   *View* 7.

Rekes. *See* Recks.

Relate.
  Dost . . . their artless tale relate; *El.* 94; *Mas.* 78.
  Not Marius' Cimbrian Wreaths would I relate,
  *Prop.*³ 39.

Release.
  The Hand that can my captive heart release,
  *Prop.*³ 87.

Relentless.
  Daughter of Jove, relentless Power,   *Adv.* 1.

Relies.
  On some fond breast the parting soul relies,
  El. 89.

Relieved.
  and thus relieved their care: *Tasso* 26.

Religion.
  scarce religion does supply Her mutter'd requiems,   *Bard* MS. 73.

Reluctance.
  With fond reluctance, yielding modesty, *Agr.* 197.

Relumes.
  with silver light Relumes her crescent Orb
  *Prop.*² 22.

Remain.
  Long as of youth the joyous hours remain,
  *Prop.*² 1.
  A little Verse my All that shall remain;
  *Prop.*³ 101.

Remains.
  What length of sea remains,   *Tasso* 31.
  That which yet remains . . . I shall unfold.
  Dante 18.
  I grop'd About among their cold Remains
  Dante 78.

Remedy.
  For Ills unseen what Remedy is found?
  *Prop.*³ 91.

Remember.
  I well remember too   *Agr.* 60.

Remind.
  I might remind my mistress   *Agr.* 107.

Remorse
  keen Remorse with blood defil'd,   *Eton* 78.
  penitence, and vain remorse,   *Agr.* 179.

Remote.
  †Remote from cities lives   *Ch. Cr.* 55.

Remotest.
  either Pole, and Life's remotest Bounds, *E. G.* 25.

Remove.
  Till time shall every grief remove,   *Clerke* 15.
  The Power of Herbs can other Harms remove,
  *Prop.*³ 79.

Rend.
  Then, while the vaulted Skies loud Ios rend,
  *Prop.*³ 47.

Renew.
  hasty to renew The hellish Feast,   *Dante* 83.

Renown.
  Young Williams fought for England's fair renown;   *Williams* 2.

Rent.
  and rent his trembling Prey.   *Dante* 84.

Repaid.
  benefits too great To be repaid,   *Agr.* 75.

Repair.
  The lady *Janes* and *Joans* repair,   *L. S.* 99.
  See the Wretch, . . . At length repair his vigour
  lost,   *Vic.* 47.
  The Melian's Hurt Machaon could repair,
  *Prop.*³ 81.

Repairs.
  To-morrow he repairs the golden flood, *Bard* 137.

Repast.
  The rich repast prepare,   *Bard* 78.

Repeat.
  To hear the savage Youth repeat   *P. P.* 60.

Repel.
  By Force repel the Foe,   *E. G.* 35.

Repents.
  Besides, he repents —   *C. C.* 30.

Repine.
  These Ears, alas! for other Notes repine, *West* 5.

Reply.
  The sportive kind reply: *Spring* 42.
  They smile, but reply not —   *Am. Lines* 8.

Repose.
  The panting herds repose: *Spring* 22.
  hush'd in grim repose, expects his evening-prey.
  Bard 76.
  Leave me, leave me to repose.   *Odin* 50, 58, 72.
  Then I leave thee to repose.   *Odin* 80.
  they alike in trembling hope repose,   *El.* 127.
  And scorn'd repose when Britain took the field.
  Williams 8.
  Fast by th' umbrageous vale lull'd to repose,
  *Prop.*² 3.
  And all the scenes, that hurt the grave's repose,
  *Prop.*² 49.
  I favour her repose.   *Prop.*³ 18.

Represents.
  †As K a King, Q represents a Queen, *Ch. Cr.* 45.

Repressed.
  Chill Penury repress'd their noble rage, *El.* 51.

Requiems.
  Her mutter'd requiems,   *Bard* MS. 74.

Require.
  A different Object do these Eyes require: *West* 6.

Requires.
  pious drops the closing eye requires;   *El.* 90.
  Art it requires, and more than winged speed.
  Tasso 30.

Resentment.
  fierce resentment cannot fail to raise   *Agr.* 25.

Reside.
  Let on this head unfadeing flowers reside,
                               *Prop.*² 9.

Residence.
  By residence, by marriage,   *Shak.* 12.

Resign.
  the palm despair'd resign;   *Stat.*¹ 23.

Resigned.
  who . . . This pleasing anxious being e'er re-
    sign'd?   *El.* 86.
  In agony, in death resign'd,   *Clerke* 7.
  In ling'ring pain, in death resign'd,
                              Clerke MS. 9.

Resistless.
  with resistless sweep   *Vic.* 59.

Resolution.
  Here Holland form'd the pious resolution
                               View 2.

Resolution's.
  By reason's light on resolution's wings, *E. G.* 75.

Resounding. *See* **Long-resounding.**

Respect.
  ties . . . Of old respect and gratitude, *Agr.* 114.

Respite.
  Pangs without respite, fires that ever glow,
                            *Prop.*² 40.

Responsive.
  Responsive to the cuckow's note,   *Spring* 6.

Rest.
  Their . . . dance They leave, in dust to rest.
                            Spring 40.
  That calls me from the bed of rest?   *Odin* 36.
  Some mute inglorious Milton here may rest,
                              El. 59.
  He reigns, the rest is heav'n's;   *Agr.* 69.
  Ah, gallant youth! this marble tells the rest,
                         Williams 11.
  The Master of Christ By the rest is enticed;
                         Satire 24.
  The Master of St. John's Like the rest of the
    Dons.   *Satire* 34.

Restrain.
  Thy passing Courser's slacken'd Speed restrain;
                         *Prop.*³ 102.

Restrained.
  but that her pride restrain'd it?   *Agr.* 12.

Rests.
  He rests among the Dead.   *Bard* 68.
  Here rests his head   *El.* 117.
  †Rests in Retirement, *little* Rural R; *Ch. Cr.* 54.

Resume.
  Fierce War and faithful Love Resume
                      Bard Lett.³ 127.
  chearful Fields resume their green Attire:
                          West 4.
  With equal power resume that gift,   *Agr.* 90.
  if you resume your Gift;   *Dante* 66.

Retain.
  with Mem'ry to retain,   *E. G.* 30.
  While to retain the envious Lawn she tries,
                            *Prop.*³ 23.

Retains.
  Nor . . . Warmth, nor genial Juice retains
                              E. G. 3.

Retired.
  Say, she retir'd to Antium;   *Agr.* 7.

Retirement.
  †Rests in Retirement, *little* Rural R; *Ch. Cr.* 54.

Retires.
  Search to what regions yonder Star retires,
                            *Prop.*² 19.

Retreat.
  †lives in lone Retreat,   *Ch. Cr.* 55.

Retreating.
  Now pursuing, now retreating,   *P. P.* 32.

Retrieved.
  One false step is ne'er retriev'd   *Cat* 38.

Return.
  No children run to lisp their sire's return, *El.* 23.
  But none from Cattraeth's vale return, *Hoel* 20.
  Ere the spring he would return —   *Song* 2.

Returning.
  To close my dull eyes when I see it returning;
                       Am. Lines 4.

Returns.
  The soft Returns of Gratitude   *E. G.* 34.

Reveal.
  If the thin Coan Web her Shape reveal, *Prop.*³ 9.

Revels.
  Vice, that revels in her chains.   *P. P.* 80.

Revenge.
  Revenge on thee in hoarser murmurs breath;
                            Bard 26.
  My great revenge shall rise;   *Agr.* 121.
  My Wrongs, and from them judge of my Revenge.
                         Dante 15.

Revere.
  Revere his Consort's faith,   *Bard* 89.

Revered.
  have long rever'd With custom'd awe, *Agr.* 117.

Reverence.
  Say you saw her Yielding due reverence *Agr.* 4.
  Prostrate with filial reverence I adore. *Ign.* 10.

Reverend.
  from the dust uprear his reverend head, *Agr.* 142.

Reveres.
  She reveres herself and thee.   *Inst.* 82.

Reverted.
  yielding modesty, And oft reverted eye, *Agr.* 198.
  descries With forward and reverted eyes. *Vic.* 28.

Revisit.
  Glad I revisit thy neglected reign,   *Ign.* 5.

Revive.
  The gen'rous spark extinct revive,   *Adv.* 45.
  Would'st thou revive the deep Despair, *Dante* 4.

Revived.

anew revived, with silver light   *Prop.*[2] 21.

Reward.

What the bright reward we gain?   *Inst.* 59.
Verse, the hero's sole reward.   *Conan* 4.

Rhetoric.

But soon his rhetorick forsook him,   *L. S.* 117.

Rhime. *See* Rime.

Rhimed. *See* Rimed.

Rhimes. *See* Rimes.

Rhine.

As on the Rhine, when Boreas' fury reigns,
    Tasso 17.

Rhyme. *See* Rime.

Rhymes. *See* Rimes.

Rich.

the rich stream of music winds along   *P. P.* 7.
The rich repast prepare,   *Bard* 78.
page Rich with the spoils of time   *El.* 50.
Rich windows that exclude the light,   *L. S.* 7.
Rich streams of regal bounty pour'd,   *Inst.* 52.
In one rich mass unite the precious store,
    Tasso 61.

Riches.

The riches of the earth,   *Agr.* 78.

Richest.

Thro' richest purple . . . Betray'd a golden
gleam.   *Cat* 17.

Richly.

Richly paint the vernal year: *P. P.* 90.

Rid.

commission To rid the manour of such vermin.
    L. S. 52.

Ride.

't is time to ride: *F. S.* Pem. 61.
High on her car, behold the grandam ride
    Ign. 36.
on frail floats to distant cities ride,   *E. G.* 106.

Riding.

While proudly riding o'er the azure realm *Bard* 72.
Side by side as proudly riding,   *Owen* 12.

Rigby's.

Nor Mungo's, Rigby's, Bradshaw's friendship
vain,   *View* 18.

Right.

Right against the eastern gate,   *Odin* 17.
till substantial Night Has reassum'd her ancient
right;   *Odin* 92.
tenacious of thy right divine,   *Ign.* 15.
'T is Willy begs, once a right proper man, *Shak.* 3.
Another orb upheaved his strong right hand,
    Stat.[1] 15.

Rightly.

Then let me rightly spell of nature's ways;
    Prop.[2] 15.

Rigid.

thy rigid lore With patience . . . she bore:
    Adv. 13.

Rigor.

face the rigour Of bleak Germania's snows.
    Agr. 109.

Rigour. *See* Rigor.

Rill.

beside the rill, Nor up the lawn,   *El.* 111.

Rills.

A thousand rills their mazy progress take:
    P. P. 4.
Whate'er . . . Floats into Lakes, and bubbles
into rills;   *Tasso* 54.

Rime.

Thrice he traced the runic rhyme;   *Odin* 22.
uncouth rhime and shapeless sculpture
    El. Mas. 79.
listens to the rhyme.   *Inst.* 26.
She tunes my easy Rhime,   *Prop.*[3] 6.
†Seeds of Poetry and Rhime   *Ode* 1.
†And have loved their love in rhyme: *Rond.* 14.

Rimed.

†and my head Rhimed on,   *Ode* 22.

Rimes.

uncouth rhimes [rhime, Mas.] and shapeless
sculpture   *El.* 79.
tardy rhymes that us'd to linger on,   *Bent.* 9.

Rinda.

A wond'rous Boy shall *Rinda* bear,   *Odin* 65.

Ring.

The shrieks of death, thro' Berkley's roofs that
ring,   *Bard* 55.
Hauberk crash, and helmet ring.   *F. S.* 24.
I'd in the ring knit hands,   *Prop.*[2] 6.

Rings.

And all the town rings of his swearing and roaring!
    C. C. 16.

Ripen.

†Still to ripen 'em is wanted;   *Ode* 4.

Ripened.

She swept, she hiss'd, she ripen'd and grew rough,
    Par. on Ep. 2.

Ripening.

Further they pass, where ripening minerals flow,
    Tasso 57.

Rise.

Ambition this shall tempt to rise,   *Eton* 71.
And bad these awful fanes and turrets rise,
    Inst. 53.
Hence rise my fears.   *Agr.* 56.
My great revenge shall rise,   *Agr.* 121.
Forbids . . . her Shades to rise,   *E. G.* 7.
distant cities . . . That rise and glitter *E. G.* 107.
Rise, my soul! on wings of fire,   *Vic.* 17.
Rise the rapturous choir among;   *Vic.* 18.
So from our works sublimer fumes shall rise;
    Shak. 22.
When you rise from your Dinner as light as before,
    Couplet 1.
When mountain-high the waves disparted rise;
    Tasso 40.
No Mountain-Structures in my Verse should rise,
    Prop.[3] 36.

Riseing. *See* **Rising.**

Rising.

O'er her warm cheek, and rising bosom, *P. P.* 40.

Gone To salute the rising Morn [Day, MS.].
Bard 70.

Smile not indulgent on the rising Race, *E. G.* 16.

The birth of rivers riseing to their course,
Tasso 52.

How riseing winds the face of Ocean sweep,
*Prop.*² 23.

Rites.

sacrifice perform'd with barb'rous rites *Agr.* 62.

Rival.

The rival of her crown and of her woes, *Inst.* 44.

River.

When thwart the road a River roll'd its flood
Tasso 7.

The river boil'd beneath,   *Tasso* 24.

River's.

he led Beneath the obedient river's inmost bed;
Tasso 44.

Rivers.

The birth of rivers riseing to their course,
Tasso 52.

Riveted.

riveted His eyes in fearful extasy: *Agr.* 169.

Rivets.

†Cent'ring, rivets heart to heart,   *Rond.* 30.

Road.

In climes beyond the solar road,   *P. P.* 54.

When thwart the road a River roll'd its flood
Tasso 7.

Nor doubt with me to tread the downward road
Tasso 37.

Roam.

shaggy forms o'er ice-built mountains roam,
P. P. 55.

Roar.

groves rebellow to the roar.   *P. P.* 12.

Echoing to the battle's roar.   *Owen* 26.

Thro' the wild waves as they roar,   *Inst.* 89.

Or the bull, with sullen roar, . . . advance?
Caradoc 2.

parting surges round the vessel roar; *Stat.*² 21.

Scarce the hoarse waves from far were heard to
roar,   *Tasso* 6.

Roaring.

Deep in the roaring tide he plung'd *Bard* 144.

the town rings of his swearing and roaring!
C. C. 16.

What a pother is here about wenching and roaring!   *C. C.* 23.

Roast.

Better the roast meat from the fire to save,
Shak. 18.

Robed.

Robed in the sable garb of woe,   *Bard* 17.

Rochester's.

'T is just like the picture in Rochester's book;
C. C. 12.

Rock.

On a rock . . . the Poet stood;   *Bard* 15.

The eyeless Cyclops heav'd the craggy rock;
*Stat.*² 19.

The pendent rock, Ixion's whirling wheel,
*Prop.*² 46.

Rocks.

The rocks and nodding groves rebellow *P. P.* 12.

Nor fear the rocks, nor seek the shore: *Inst.* 92.

Rocky.

Talymalfra's rocky shore   *Owen* 25.

while their rocky ramparts round they see,
E. G. 96.

Victor he stood on Bellisle's rocky steeps —
Williams 10.

Rod.

the rod [reins, Dods., Pem., Mas.] of empire
El. 47.

Proud of the yoke, and pliant to the rod,
E. G. 58.

His head a chaplet bore, his hand a Rod.
Tasso 16.

Rode.

Nor second He, that rode sublime   *P. P.* 95.

Down the yawning steep he rode,   *Odin* 3.

She rode triumphant o'er the . . . world; *Ign.* 28.

Lanfranc there And Sigismundo, and Gualandi
rode   *Dante* 33.

Roderic's.

OWEN . . . Fairest flower of Roderic's stem,
Owen 3.

Roll.

Who measured out the years, and bad the seasons
roll;   *Prop.*² 38.

Rolled.

hath Hyperion roll'd his annual race, *Ign.* 11.

their Kings, their Gods were roll'd away.
E. G. 49.

And now in dust the polish'd ball he roll'd,
*Stat.*¹ 41.

A shining border round the margin roll'd,
*Stat.*² 26.

When thwart the road a River roll'd its flood
Tasso 7.

Rolling.

To chase the rolling circle's speed,   *Eton* 29.

Now rowling down the steep amain,   *P. P.* 10.

the rolling Orb, that gives the Day, *E. G.* 23.

Indolence and Pride, Softly rolling, side by side,
Vic. 62.

†Till again the rolling Sun Bursts   *Ode* 43.

Rolls.

Backward Meinai rolls his flood;   *Owen* 28.

Roman.

And sad Philippi, red with Roman Gore:
*Prop.*³ 46.

Rome.

lord, That broke the bonds of Rome. *Inst.* 47.

The willing homage Of prostrate Rome *Agr.* 77.

the eye of Rome, And the Prætorian camp
Agr. 116.

Again the buried Genius of old Rome *Agr.* 141.

Roofs.
The shrieks of death, thro' Berkley's roofs that
ring,   *Bard* 55.

Rooks.
†With Rooks and Rabbit burrows   *Ch. Cr.* 56.

Room. *See also* **Drawing-room, Withdraw-
ing-room.**
Give ample room, and verge enough   *Bard* 51.
Give . . . Cares and endless Wishes room;
        El. Mas. 86.

Roots.
beech, That wreathes its old fantastic roots
        El. 102.
genial Juice retains Their Roots to feed, *E. G.* 4.
†Tares of similes choak the roots,   *Ode* 11.

Rose.
the rose of snow . . . we spread: *Bard* 91.
the new Fragrance of the breathing Rose.
        E. G. 56.
the paler rose, The rival of her crown   *Inst.* 43.

Rose, *vb.*
My Lady rose,   *L. S.* 131.
From table she rose,   *C. C.* 21.
Nor yet in prospect rose the distant shore;
        Tasso 5.
Tell me, whence their sorrows rose: *Odin* 79.

Rose's.
There bloom the vernal rose's earliest pride;
        *Prop.*² 10.

Rosy.
Theirs buxom health of rosy hue,   *Eton* 45.
the rosy queen Of amorous thefts: *Agr.* 188.
where rosy Pleasure leads,   *Vic.* 37.

Rosy-bosomed.
Lo! where the rosy-bosom'd Hours . . . appear,
        Spring 1.

Rosy-crowned.
The rosy-crowned Loves are seen   *P. P.* 28.

Rough.
Brush'd by the hand of rough Mischance,
        Spring 38.
A heart that . . . will . . . Gain the rough
heights,   *Agr.* 52.
rough, stubborn souls, That struggle with the
yoke.   *Agr.* 126.
The rough abode of want and liberty, *E. G.* 97.
She swept, she hiss'd, she ripen'd and grew rough,
        Par. on Ep. 2.

Round.
The fair round face.   *Cat* 8.
flowers, that round them blow,   *P. P.* 5.
What Terrors round him wait!   *Bard* 60.
What strains of vocal transport round her play.
        Bard 120.
Thousand Banners round him burn: *Owen* 32.
they . . . Run hurry-skurry round the floor,
        L. S. 63.
While bright-eyed Science watches round:
        Inst. 11.
as the choral warblings round him swell,
        Inst. 24.

round heav'n's altars shed The fragrance *Inst.* 73.
while their rocky ramparts round they see, *E. G.* 96.
shades, that . . . blacken round our weary way,
        Vic. 35.
rolling, side by side, Their dull, but daily round.
        Vic. 63.
And parting surges round the vessel roar;
        *Stat.*² 21.
A shining border round the margin roll'd,
        *Stat.*² 26.
The hissing terrors round Alecto's head,
        *Prop.*² 42.
†in a perpetual round,   *Ch. Cr.* 37.
†Rabbit burrows round his seat —   *Ch. Cr.* 56.

Rouse.
The . . . horn, No more shall rouse them *El.* 20.
her nod Can rouse eight hardy legions, *Agr.* 108.

Roused.
Rous'd by the shout of millions: *Agr.* 142.
By acclamations roused, came tow'ring on.
        *Stat.*¹ 14.
Or roused by sprightly sounds from out the trance,
        *Prop.*² 5.

Rout.
Hasty, hasty Rout is there,   *Owen* 34.

Rove.
Mutt'ring his . . . fancies he would rove, *El.* 106.

Roves.
where'er the Goddess roves,   *P. P.* 63.

Row.
in glitt'ring row Thrice two hundred warriors go:
        Hoel 11.
†The Pleasantest Person in the Christ-Cross row.
        Ch. Cr. 44.

Rowling. *See* **Rolling.**

Royal.
High potentates, and dames of royal birth,
        Inst. 37.

Royalty.
dares . . . Profane thy inborn royalty of mind:
        Inst. 81.

Rubbers.
And keep my Lady from her Rubbers. *L. S.* 144.

Rubellius.
Rubellius lives, And Sylla has his friends, *Agr.* 99.

Rubies.
And rubies flame, with sapphire's heavenly blue,
        Tasso 68.

Ruby.
High he rears his ruby crest.   *Owen* 22.

Ruddy.
Dear, as the ruddy drops that warm my heart,
        Bard 41.
Ere the ruddy sun be set,   *F. S.* 21.

Rude.
the rude and moss-grown beech   *Spring* 13.
The rude Forefathers of the hamlet   *El.* 16.
How rude so e'er th' exterior Form   *E. G.* 26.
How the rude surge its sandy bounds control;
        *Prop.*² 37.

Ruffled.

With ruffled plumes, and flagging wing: *P. P.* 22.

Rugged.

Stern rugged Nurse! thy rigid lore   *Adv.* 13.

Beneath those rugged elms, that yew-tree's shade,
              El. 13.

Ruggieri.

Ruggieri, Pisa's perfidious Prelate this: *Dante* 13.

Ruin.

Ruin seize thee, ruthless King!   *Bard* 1.

in ruin hurl'd, Sinks the fabric of the world.
              Odin 93.

There . . . Conflict fierce, and Ruin wild,
              Owen 38.

The threats of pain and ruin   *El.* 62.

sink the traitor in his mother's ruin.   *Agr.* 187.

When Pindus' self approaching ruin dreads,
              *Prop.*² 31.

Ruins.

the ruins that we feign: *View* MS. 20.

Rule.

th' inferior laws that rule our clay: *E. G.* 80.

Rummage.

They . . . Rummage his Mother, pinch his
Aunt,   *L. S.* 59.

Rumor.

So Rumor says.   *L. S.* 73.

Run.

Still as they run they look behind,   *Eton* 38.

Yet oft before his infant eyes would run *P. P.* 118.

No children run to lisp their sire's return, *El.* 23.

they . . . Run hurry-skurry round the floor,
              L. S. 63.

In swifter measures animated run,   *Bent.* 11.

Rung.

Hosannas rung through hell's tremendous borders.   *Toph.* 7.

Runic.

Thrice he traced the runic rhyme;   *Odin* 22.

Rural.

†Rests in Retirement, *little* Rural R;   *Ch. Cr.* 54.

Rush.

To rush, and sweep them from the world!
              Hoel 4.

Rushed.

The river boil'd beneath, and rush'd toward the
Main,   *Tasso* 24.

Rushing.

brave the savage rushing from the wood, *E. G.* 93.

Rushy.

Beside some water's rushy brink   *Spring* 15.

Where rushy Camus' slowly-winding flood, *Ign.* 3.

Rustic.

At ease reclin'd in rustic state   *Spring* 17.

teach the rustic moralist to die.   *El.* 84.

Let not Ambition mock their rustic toil,
              El. Mas. 29.

New-born flocks, in rustic dance,   *Vic.* 9.

Swift shoots the Village-maid in rustic play
              Tasso 19.

Rustling.

not in buff, But rustling in their silks   *L. S.* 24.

Ruthless.

Ruin seize thee, ruthless King!   *Bard* 1.

S.

†S, sails the Swan   *Ch. Cr.* 57.

Sable.

Wisdom in sable garb array'd   *Adv.* 25.

Robed in the sable garb of woe,   *Bard* 17.

Is the sable Warriour fled?   *Bard* 67.

Each bestride her sable steed.   *F. S.* 63.

His sable Sons with nearer Course surrounds
              E. G. 24.

Sabler.

Chastised by sabler tints of woe;   *Vic.* 42.

Sacred.   *See also* **Sacred Way.**

the sacred source of sympathetic Tears. *P. P.* 94.

such, as wand'ring near her sacred Bow'r,
              El. Dods. 11.

the sacred Calm, that broods around,
              El. Mas. 81.

sacred age! Oh! times for ever lost!   *Ign.* 31.

A heart, within whose sacred cell   *Clerke* 3.

Sacred tribute of the bard,   *Conan* 3.

Sacred Way.

Move through the Sacred Way and vainly threat,
              *Prop.*³ 52.

Sacrifice.

To bitter Scorn a sacrifice,   *Eton* 73.

sacrifice perform'd with barb'rous rites *Agr.* 62.

Sad.

sad refuge from the storms of Fate!   *P. P.* 45.

Till the sad Nine in Greece's evil hour, *P. P.* 77.

Dear, as the light that visits these sad eyes,
              Bard 40.

with dirges due in sad array   *El.* 113.

And sad Chatillon,   *Inst.* 41.

And sad Philippi, red with Roman Gore:
              *Prop.*³ 46.

Sad with the Fears of Sleep,   *Dante* 49.

Saddled.

saddled strait his coal-black steed;   *Odin* 2.

Sadly.

A bad face which did sadly molest her.
              Mrs. Keene 2.

Sadly-pleasing.

Pity, dropping soft the sadly-pleasing tear.
              Adv. 32.

Safe.

safe and laughing in his sleeve,   *L. S.* 75.

Thus far we 're safe.   *Agr.* 188.

Safety.

more to Innocence their Safety owe
              El. Mas. 75.

Sage.

There sit the sainted sage, the bard divine,
              Inst. 15.

When lo! appears The wondrous Sage: *Tasso* 12.

Said.

This pencil take (she said),   *P. P.* 89.
"Ah!" said the sighing peer,   *View* 17.
He said, and scornful flung th' unheeded weight
           Stat.[1] 21.
Scarce had he said,   *Tasso* 39.

Sail.

far aloof th' affrighted ravens sail;   *Bard* 37.
with adventrous oar and ready sail *E. G.* 104.

Sailing.

Sailing with supreme dominion   *P. P.* 116.

Sailors.

Sailors to tell of Winds and Seas delight,
           Prop.[3] 59.

Sails.

There the Norman sails afar Catch the winds,
           Owen 15.
†S, sails the Swan   *Ch. Cr.* 57.

Saint. *See also* **St.**

The murder'd saint   *Inst.* 46.

Sainted.

There sit the sainted sage, the bard divine,
           Inst. 15.

Sake.

hates the Tale of Troy for Helen's Sake.
           Prop.[3] 74.

Salutary.

ignorance! soft salutary power!   *Ign.* 9.

Salute.

Gone to salute the rising Morn.   *Bard* 70.

Same.

The Master of Maudlin In the same dirt is
dawdling;   *Satire* 8.
The Master of Sidney Is of the same kidney;
           Satire 10.
The Master of Peter's Has all the same features;
           Satire 32.

Sand.

Earl Goodwin trembled for his neighbouring
sand;   *View* 6.

Sands.

on his native sands The Dragon-Son . . . stands;
           Owen 19.
Oceans unknown, inhospitable Sands! *Tasso* 32.

Sandy.

How the rude surge its sandy Bounds control;
           Prop.[2] 37.

Sangrida.

Sangrida, terrific maid,   *F. S.* Whar. 17.
Sangrida and *Hilda* see, Join . . . to aid;
           F. S. 18.

Sanguine.

yon sanguine cloud, . . . has quench'd the Orb
of day?   *Bard* 135.

Saphire-blaze. *See* **Sapphire-blaze.**

Sapphire-blaze.

The living Throne, the saphire-blaze, *P. P.* 99.

Sapphire's.

And rubies flame, with sapphire's heavenly blue,
           Tasso 68.

Sat. *See also* **Sate.**

Malignant Fate sat by, and smil'd   *Cat* 28.

Satan's.

And Satan's self had thoughts of taking orders.
           Toph. 8.

Sate. *See also* **Sat.**

By the moss-grown pile he sate;   *Odin* 18.
The Court was sate,   *L. S.* 97.
That Day, and yet another, mute we sate,
           Dante 70.

Satin-doublet.

His high-crown'd hat, and sattin-doublet,
           L. S. 14.

Satire.

Heaven Had arm'd with spirit, wit, and satire:
           L. S. 30.
attend To the Satire I 've pen'd   *Satire* 2.

Sattin-doublet. *See* **Satin-doublet.**

Savage.

To hear the savage Youth repeat   *P. P.* 60.
brave the savage rushing from the wood, *E. G.* 93.

Save.

Save where the beetle wheels his droning flight,
           El. 7.
Save that from yonder ivy-mantled tow'r *El.* 9.
Their human passions now no more, Save Charity,
           Inst. 50.
But none . . . return, Save Aëron brave,
           Hoel 21.

Save, *vb.*

To save thy secret soul from nightly fears,
           Bard 7.
Yet hcp'd, that he might save his bacon:
           L. S. 126.
And so God save our noble King, *L. S.* 141.
could not save His all   *Clerke* MS. 11.
Better the roast meat from the fire to save,
           Shak. 18.

Saw.

Her . . . emerald eyes she saw;   *Cat* 12.
The hapless Nymph with wonder saw: *Cat* 19.
The living Throne, the saphire-blaze . . . He
saw;   *P. P.* 101.
thro' the church-way path we saw him borne —
           El. 114.
Say you saw her Yielding due reverence *Agr.* 3.
Saw the snowy whirlwind fly;   *Vic.* 22.
I saw them bow,   *Toph.* 3.
I saw methought Towards Pisa's Mount,
           Dante 28.
in four Faces saw my own Despair reflected,
           Dante 62.
I saw 'em fall;   *Dante* 76.

Saxon.

Mirrors of Saxon truth and loyalty *Bard* MS. 71.

Say.

Say, father Thames,   *Eton* 21.
Say, has he giv'n in vain   *P. P.* 48.
Prophetess, arise, and say,   *Odin* 52.
Once again arise, and say,   *Odin* 60.
Prophetess, awake, and say,   *Odin* 74.
Say from whence their sorrows rose: *Odin* MS. 79.

some hoary-headed Swain may say, *El.* 97.
Say you saw her Yielding . . . reverence *Agr.* 4.
Say, she retir'd to Antium; *Agr.* 7.
tell me! say *Agr.* 92.
say we sound The trump of liberty; *Agr.* 121.
Oh say, successful dost thou still oppose *Ign.* 13.
Oh say — she hears me not, *Ign.* 23.
Say then, . . . by what Fate confin'd *E. G.* 38.
They say he's no Christian, *C. C.* 15.
As to Trinity Hall We say nothing at all.
Satire 36.
Ah! say, Fellow-swains, how these symptoms be-
fell me? *Am. Lines* 7.
In brief whate'er she do, or say, or look,
*Prop.*³ 27.
awhile draw near, And say, *Prop.*³ 106.
Attend, and say if he have injured me. *Dante* 21.
†But, my Dear, these Flies, they say, *Ode* 49.
†Some have loved, and loved (they say) *Rond.* 5.

Sayest.
Say'st thou I must be cautious, *Agr.* 85.

Says.
So Rumor says. *L. S.* 73.
"Lord! sister," says PHYSIC to LAW, *C. C.* 5.
"I don't know," says LAW, *C. C.* 11.

Scaly.
Their scaly armour's Tyrian hue, *Cat* 16.

Scan.
Exact my own defects to scan, *Adv.* 47.

Scant.
what scant Light That . . . Tower admitted
Dante 22.

'Scaped. *See* **Escaped.**

Scarce.
scarce religion does supply Her mutter'd re-
quiems, *Bard* MS. 73.
And scarce Ulysses 'scaped his giant arm.
*Stat.*² 23.
Scarce the hoarse waves from far were heard to
roar, *Tasso* 6.
Scarce had he said, *Tasso* 39.
Scarce to nine acres Tityus' bulk confined,
*Prop.*² 43.
The Morn had scarce commenc'd, when I awoke:
Dante 41.

Scarcely.
scarcely dar'd On expectation's . . . wing to
soar *Agr.* 41.

Scare.
Sour visages, enough to scare ye, *L. S.* 106.

Scared.
Scared at thy frown terrific, *Adv.* 17.
he stood trembling, Scar'd at the sound, *Agr.* 32.

Scares.
The triple dog that scares the shadowy kind,
*Prop.*² 44.

Scatter.
scatter plenty o'er a smiling land, *El.* 63.
scatter with a free, though frugal, Hand
E. G. 17.

Scattered.
their scatter'd rear, *P. P.* MS. 52.
the sounds, that . . . scatter'd wild dismay,
Bard 10.
There scatter'd oft, the earliest of the Year,
El. Pem. 117; *Mas.* 137.

Scatters.
Scatters from her pictur'd urn Thoughts, that
breath, *P. P.* 109.
Scatters his freshest, tenderest green. *Vic.* 8.
the song-thrush there Scatters his loose notes
Birds 2.

Scene.
Her rapid wings the transient scene pursue,
Ign. 34.
This spacious animated Scene survey *E. G.* 22.
o'er the living scene Scatters . . . green. *Vic.* 7.

Scenes.
what solemn scenes on Snowdon's height
Bard 105.
what [solemn, Lett.¹] scenes of Heaven on Snow-
don's height *Bard* MS. 105.
Far better scenes than these had blest our view,
View 19.
And all the scenes, that hurt the grave's repose,
*Prop.*² 49.

Sceptered.
Perching on the scept'red hand *P. P.* 20.
Be thine Despair, and scept'red Care, *Bard* 141.
And scepter'd Alexandria's captive Shore,
*Prop.*³ 45.

Sceptre.
The massy sceptre o'er thy slumb'ring line?
Ign. 16.

Schooled.
school'd by fear To bow the supple knee,
Agr. 100.

Schoolman's.
The schoolman's glory, and the churchman's
boast. *Ign.* 32.

Science.
Where grateful Science still adores *Eton* 3.
Fair Science frown'd not on his . . . birth,
El. 119.
While bright-eyed Science watches round:
Inst. 11.
From fortune, pleasure, science, love, he flew,
Williams 7.
Be love my youth's pursuit, and science crown my
Age. *Prop.*² 52.

Scold.
In harmless society guttle and scold. *C. C.* 4.

Scorn.
To bitter scorn a sacrifice, *Eton* 73.
alike they scorn the pomp of tyrant-Power,
P. P. 79.
now smiling as in scorn, *El.* 105.
the Victim of her Scorn, *Prop.*³ 77.

Scorned.
And scorn'd repose when Britain took the field.
Williams 8.

Scornful.
And scornful flung th' unheeded weight *Stat.*[1] 21.

Scotland.
Scotland, . . . Far and wide the notes prolong.
F. S. 59.

Scourge.
Whose iron scourge and tort'ring hour   *Adv.* 3.
The scourge of Heav'n.   *Bard* 60.

Scowl.
Fell Thirst and Famine scowl   *Bard* 81.

Scratch.
The Bishop of Chester, . . . If you scratch him
will fester.   *Ext. Keene* 4.

Scream.
Here sea-gulls scream,   *View* 7.

Screaming.
With screaming Horror's funeral cry,   *Adv.* 39.

Screams.
The famish'd Eagle screams,   *Bard* 38.

Scribbles.
And all his [he, Lett.[4]] scribbles, tear. *Shak.* 16.

Sculks. *See* Skulks.

Sculpture.
With . . . shapeless sculpture deck'd,   *El.* 79.

Sculptured.
The laurell'd Triumph and the sculptured Carr;
Prop.[3] 34.

Scythia.
Has Scythia breath'd the . . . Cloud of War;
E. G. 47.

Sea.
Whose walls along the neighbouring Sea extend,
Tasso 4.
What length of sea remains,   *Tasso* 31.
Nor how the Persian trod the indignant Sea;
Prop.[3] 38.

Sea-encircled.
thy sea-encircled coast.   *P. P.* 82.

Sea-gulls.
Here sea-gulls scream,   *View* 7.

Seal.
The Seal, and Maces, danc'd before him.
L. S. 12.

Sealed.
There first in blood his infant honour seal'd;
Williams 6.

Search.
Search to what regions yonder Star retires,
Prop.[2] 19.

Seas.
Sailors to tell of Winds and Seas delight,
Prop.[3] 59.

Seasons.
what seasons can control . . . the soul, *E. G.* 72.
Who measured out the year, and bad the seasons
roll;   *Prop.*[2] 38.

Seat.
ambition from her craggy seat   *Agr.* 51.
Thou Seat of the Muses!   *Satire* 4.
†Rabbit burrows round his seat —   *Ch. Cr.* 56.

Second.
To breathe a second spring.   *Eton* 20.
Nor second He, that rode sublime   *P. P.* 95.
And thou Mecænas, be my second Care;
Prop.[3] 42.
Whose heart has never felt a second flame.
Prop.[3] 66.

Secret.
Jealousy . . . That inly gnaws the secret heart,
Eton 67.
To save thy secret soul from nightly fears, *Bard* 7.
wand'ring near her secret bow'r,   *El.* 11.
a secret and dead hour of night,   *Agr.* 61.
My lines a secret sympathy   *Bent.* 26.
A pang, to secret sorrow dear;   *Clerke* 13.
Of many a flood they view'd the secret source,
Tasso 51.

Secrets.
The secrets of the Abyss to spy.   *P. P.* 97.

Secure.
Secure of Fate, the Poet stood,   *Bard Lett.*[1] 18.
Here, . . . secure from misery, lies A child,
Child 1.
Too, too secure in youthful pride,   *Hoel* 5.
The orb . . . joys to see Its ancient lord secure
of victory.   *Stat.*[2] 13.
Against the stream the waves secure he trod,
Tasso 15.

Securely.
Be gay securely;   *Agr.* 192.

Sedition's.
Mad Sedition's cry profane,   *Inst.* 5.

See.
Yet see how all around 'em wait   *Eton* 55.
Headlong, impetuous, see it pour;   *P. P.* 11.
a griesly band, I see them sit,   *Bard* 45.
I see The different doom our Fates assign.
Bard 139.
See the griesly texture grow!   *F. S.* 9.
Sangrida, and *Hilda* see,   *F. S.* 18.
Ne'er again his likeness see;   *F. S.* 46.
see The pure bev'rage of the bee,   *Odin* 43.
Nor see the sun's departing beam,   *Odin* 68.
Foremost . . . The venerable Marg'ret see!
Inst. 66.
while their rocky ramparts round they see,
E. G. 96.
See . . . each transitory thought   *Bent.* 5.
See a kindred Grief pursue;   *Vic.* 38.
See the Wretch, that long has tost   *Vic.* 45.
Though now a book, and interleaved you see.
Shak. 4.
To close my dull eyes when I see it returning;
Am. Lines 4.
The orb . . . joys to see Its ancient lord secure of
victory.   *Stat.*[2] 12.
The Po was there to see,   *Tasso* 55.
and thousand beauties see   *Prop.*[3] 19.
And many a copious Narrative you'll see
Prop.[3] 29.
thou shalt see me . . . give loose   *Dante* 8.
†Her daughters deck'd most daintily I see,
Ch. Cr. 3.

†See Folly, Fashion, Foppery, straight appear,
                                    Ch. Cr. 16.
†methinks we see,   Ch. Cr. 21.
†See Isaac, Joseph, Jacob, pass in view;
                                    Ch. Cr. 26.
†See Israel, and all Judah thronging there.
                                    Ch. Cr. 28.
†in Pond you see him come,   Ch. Cr. 39.

Seeds.
†Seeds of Poetry and Rhime   Ode 1.

Seek.
No farther seek his merits to disclose, El. 125.
Nor fear the rocks, nor seek the shore: Inst. 92.
difficult the toil To seek your Hero Tasso 28.
†Long to seek a mutual heart,
                        Rond. 2, 10, 18, 26, 34.

Seem.
My weary soul they seem to sooth,   Eton 18.
walls that seem to mock my shame,   Agr. 156.
To different Climes seem different Souls assign'd?
                                    E. G. 39.
she seem to close Her languid Lids, Prop.³ 17.
And hoary Nile with pensive Aspect seem
                                    Prop.³ 49.

Seemed.
will seem'd wrote in lines of blood, Agr. 70.
vigorous he seem'd in years,   Tasso 12.

Seeming.
his plain soldier's oath, and honest seeming.
                                    Agr. 151.

Seems.
†Now seems a Penny,   Ch. Cr. 38.
†And seems small difference the sounds between;
                                    Ch. Cr. 46.

Seen.
Two angel forms were seen   Cat 14.
thou hast seen . . . a sprightly race Eton 21.
A griesly troop are seen,   Eton 82.
As by the Impious thou art seen   Adv. 37.
The rosy-crowned Loves are seen   P. P. 28.
Oft have we seen him   El. 97.
Him have we seen   El. Mas. 117.
Styack has often seen the sight   L. S. 103.
When he the solemn hall had seen;   L. S. 118.
I . . . Have seen your soul, and wonder'd
                                    Agr. 55.
Have ye seen the dusky boar,   Caradoc 1.
Then had we seen proud London's hated walls;
                                    View 22.
†And variegated Fancy's seen   Ode 17.

Seer.
So mov'd the Seer,   Tasso 23.

Sees.
your servant's fears, who sees the danger
                                    Agr. 24.
Let him feel Before he sees me.   Agr. 164.
sees far off with an indignant groan, E. G. 62.
Brown sees thee sitting on his nose's tip,
                                    Com. Lines 4.

Seest.
Know, thou seest In me Count Ugolino,
                                    Dante 12.

Seize.
To seize their prey the murth'rous band! Eton 59.
Ruin seize thee, ruthless King!   Bard 1.

Seized.
Their hands he seized,   Tasso 43.

Self.
Meek Newton's self bends from his state sub-
lime,   Inst. 25.
But may not honey's self be turn'd to gall
                                    Shak. 11.
And Satan's self had thoughts of taking orders.
                                    Toph. 8.
When Pindus' self approaching ruin dreads,
                                    Prop.² 31.

Self-pleasing.
Self-pleasing Folly's idle brood,   Adv. 18.

Selima.
The pensive Selima reclin'd,   Cat 5.

Semblance.
by Juno, It bears a noble semblance. Agr. 120.

Senate.
Even in the servile senate,   Agr. 123.

Senate's.
the senate's joint applause,   Agr. 77.

Senates.
Th' applause of list'ning senates   El. 61.

Send.
Some speedy aid to send.   Cat 33.
thy Sire to send on earth Virtue . . . design'd,
                                    Adv. 9.
from Pomfret's walls shall [shalt, Lett.¹] send
                                    Bard MS. 75.
Heav'n did a recompence . . . send: El. 122.
a glance . . . They send   Inst. 20.
And furthest send its weight   Stat.¹ 2.
Give me to send the laughing bowl around,
                                    Prop.² 7.
and send again to War;   Prop.³ 82.
already 'gan the Dawn to send: Dante 26.

Sends.
His Brother sends him to the tomb.   Odin 56.

Seneca.
Seneca be there In gorgeous phrase   Agr. 148.

Sense.
No sense have they of ills to come, Eton 53.
steep in slumbers each benighted sense? Ign. 18.
With Sense to feel,   E. G. 30.

Senseless.
Stung by a senseless word,   Agr. 134.

Sent.
nor on what Errand Sent hither: Dante 11.

Sentry.
Such as . . . at the chappel-door stand sentry;
                                    L. S. 104.

Sequestered.
the cool sequester'd vale of life   El. 75.

Seraph-wings.
Upon the seraph-wings of Extasy,   P. P. 96.

Serene.

many a gem of purest ray serene, *El.* 53.
The star of Brunswick smiles serene, *Inst.* 93.
skies serene Speak not always winter past.
Song 9.

Serpent-train.

Nor . . . Let painted Flatt'ry hide her serpent-train *Inst.* 8.

Servant's.

Forgive your servant's fears, *Agr.* 24.

Serve.

a call, Like mine, might serve . . . to wake
Agr. 103.

Servile.

Even in the servile senate, *Agr.* 123.
With servile simper nod the mitred head.
Toph. 4.

Servitude.

Servitude that hugs her chain, *Inst.* 6.

Sesostris.

Like old Sesostris with barbaric pride; *Ign.* 37.

Set. *See also* Sharp-set.

Thy sun is set, *Spring* 49.
Ere the ruddy sun be set, *F. S.* 21.

Setting.

With whistful eyes pursue the setting sun.
El. Mas. 120.

Seven.

Whence the seven Sisters' congregated fires,
Prop.[2] 35.

Sevenfold.

To mourn the Glories of his sevenfold Stream,
Prop.[3] 50.

Sever.

†Then to sever what is bound, *Rond.* 31.

Severe.

With Justice to herself severe, *Adv.* 31.
Truth severe, by fairy Fiction drest. *Bard* 127.

Severest.

laughing wild Amid severest woe. *Eton* 80.

Severn.

Severn shall re-eccho with affright *Bard* 54.

Sexe's. *See* Sex's.

Sex's.

Condemns her fickle Sexe's fond Mistake,
Prop.[3] 73.

Shade.

branches stretch A broader, browner shade;
Spring 12.
Science still adores Her HENRY's holy Shade;
Eton 4.
whose shade . . . Wanders the hoary Thames along *Eton* 8.
ah, pleasing shade, *Eton* 11.
beneath the od'rous shade *P. P.* 58.
Ev'ry shade and hallow'd Fountain *P. P.* 75.
Boar . . . Wallows beneath the thorny shade.
Bard 94.
Beneath . . . that yew-tree's shade, *El.* 13.
this long deserted shade. *El. Mas.* 112.

that empty shade Of long-forgotten liberty:
Agr. 43.
take me to thy peaceful shade again. *Ign.* 6.

Shades.

your injur'd shades demand my fate, *Agr.* 184.
The Soil . . . Forbids . . . her Shades to rise,
E. G. 7.
Or deepest shades . . . Gilds with a gleam
Vic. 36.

Shadow.

On her shadow . . . Lochlin plows *Owen* 13.

Shadowy.

Hurls o'er their shadowy rear, *P. P. MS.* 52.
The triple dog that scares the shadowy kind,
Prop.[2] 44.

Shafts.

glitt'ring shafts of war. *P. P.* 53; *MS.* 52.
Shafts for shuttles, dipt in gore, *F. S.* 13.

Shaggy.

shaggy forms o'er ice-built mountains roam,
P. P. 55.
down the steep of Snowdon's shaggy side
Bard 11.
His shaggy throat he open'd wide, *Odin* 6.

Shake.

haughty hearts, unus'd to shake *Agr.* 17.
A tempest that shall shake her own creation
Agr. 91.
shake 'em at the name of liberty, *Agr.* 133.

Shakes.

The groaning earth beneath him shakes [quakes, MS.], *Odin* 14.
Shakes all his Pines, *Prop.*[2] 32.

Shakespeare.

While Nancy earns the praise to Shakespeare due,
Shak. 23.

Shakespeare's.

burns in Shakespeare's . . . page, *Bent.* 19.

Shall, *omitted.*

Shalt, *omitted.*

Shambles.

Then he shambles and straddles so oddly —
C. C. 9.

Shame.

And Shame that sculks behind; *Eton* 64.
Glory pursue, and generous Shame, *P. P.* 64.
Ye Towers of Julius, London's lasting shame,
Bard 87.
Marking . . . shame to fly, *Owen* 36.
quench the blushes of ingenuous shame, *El.* 70.
Shame of the versifying tribe! *L. S.* 18.
walls that seem to mock my shame, *Agr.* 156.
But his nose is a shame, *C. C.* 8.
These conscious shame withheld, *Stat.*[1] 25.

Shape.

Fame, in the shape of Mr. Purt, *L. S.* 41.
If the thin Coan Web her Shape reveal, *Prop.*[3] 9.

Shapeless.

uncouth rhimes and shapeless sculpture *El.* 79.

Shapes.
†P, Proteus-like . . . all shapes can shew,
Ch. Cr. 43.

Share.
he yet may share the feast: *Bard* 79.
Where our Friends the conflict share, *F. S.* 27.
climb his knees the envied kiss to share. *El.* 24.

Sharp-set.
The hungry Pack their sharp-set Fangs embrued. *Dante* 40.

She, *omitted.*

Shed.
The tear forgot as soon as shed, *Eton* 43.
from the straw-built shed, *El.* 18.
bid it . . . shed The fragrance of its blushing head: *Inst.* 73.
lamps, that shed at Ev'n a cheerful ray *E. G.* 66.

She 'd. *See also* Would.
She 'd issue out her high commission. *L. S.* 51.

Sheep-biting.
Such a sheep-biting look, *C. C.* 6.

Sheet. *See* Winding-sheet.

Shelburne's.
Nor Shelburne's, Rigby's, Calcraft's friendship vain, *View* MS. 18.

Shell.
Sovereign of the willing soul, . . . Enchanting shell! *P. P.* 15.
'T was Milton struck the deep-ton'd shell, *Inst.* 23.
†the rolling Sun Bursts the inactive Shell, *Ode* 44.

Shepherd.
The Shepherd of his flocks, *Prop.*[3] 60.

She-wolf.
She-Wolf of France, . . . That tear'st *Bard* 57.

Shew. *See* Show.

Shews. *See* Shows.

Shield.
spread O'er the youthful King your shield.
F. S. 32.
O'er it hangs the shield of gold; *Odin* 45.
Gwyneth's shield, *Owen* 4.
So glittering shows the Thracian Godhead's shield, *Stat.*[1] 28.

Shine.
There sit . . . The few, whom genius gave to shine *Inst.* 16.
In vain to me the smileing Mornings shine, *West* 1.
Sulphureous veins and liveing silver shine, *Tasso* 59.

Shines.
When blazing 'gainst the sun it shines from far, *Stat.*[1] 30.
From Cynthia all that in my numbers shines; *Prop.*[3] 3.

Shining.
A shining border round the margin roll'd, *Stat.*[2] 26.
Swift shoots the Village-maid . . . adown the shining way, *Tasso* 20.

Shipwrecked.
And mariners, though shipwreck'd, dread to land, *View* 8.

Shiver.
Pikes must shiver, javelins sing, *F. S.* 22.

Shivered.
thunder's fiery stroke, Glancing on the shiver'd oak; *Conan* 8.

Shivering.
To chear the shiv'ring [buried, MS.] Natives dull abode. *P. P.* 57.

Shoe-strings.
His bushy beard, and shoe-strings green, *L. S.* 13.

Shook.
A sudden fit of ague shook him, *L. S.* 119.

Shoot.
Shafts . . . Shoot the trembling cords along.
F. S. 14.
All stones of lustre shoot their vivid ray, *Tasso* 65.

Shoots.
Swift shoots the Village-maid in rustic play *Tasso* 19.
†Or Poppy-thoughts blast all the shoots. *Ode* 12.

Shore.
On dreary Arvon's shore they lie, *Bard* 35.
Talymalfra's rocky shore *Owen* 25.
Nor fear the rocks, nor seek the shore: *Inst.* 92.
oft on Alpheus' shore The pond'rous brass . . . he bore; *Stat.*[1] 36.
Nor yet in prospect rose the distant shore; *Tasso* 5.
scepter'd Alexandria's captive Shore, *Prop.*[3] 45.

Short.
The short and simple annals of the poor. *El.* 32.
Short was his joy. *L. S.* 77.
To start from short slumbers, and wish for the morning — *Am. Lines* 3.
And the short Marble but preserve a Name, *Prop.*[3] 100.

Short-lived.
Obscure his radiance in a short-liv'd night; *Prop.*[2] 34.

Should.
why should they know their fate? *Eton* 95.
Owls should have hooted *View* Nich. 23.
And half disclose those Limbs it should conceal; *Prop.*[3] 10.
No Mountain-Structures in my Verse should rise, *Prop.*[3] 36.
Nor Tale of Thebes, nor Ilium there should be, *Prop.*[3] 37.
Here should Augustus great in Arms appear, *Prop.*[3] 41.
In golden Chains should loaded Monarchs bend, *Prop.*[3] 48.
Thee too the Muse should consecrate to Fame, *Prop.*[3] 53.
Each in his proper Art should waste the Day: *Prop.*[3] 62.
†But why on such *mock* grandeur should we dwell, *Ch. Cr.* 23.

Shout.

Rous'd by the shout of millions: *Agr.* 143.

Show.

Some shew their gayly-gilded trim   *Spring* 29.
shew them where in ambush stand   *Eton* 58.
Her air and all her manners shew it.   *L. S.* 138.
†In Episode, to show my breeding: *Ode* 28.
†P, Proteus-like . . . all shapes can shew,
    Ch. Cr. 43.

Showed.

Shew'd him where empire tower'd,   *Agr.* 46.

Shower.

Iron-sleet of arrowy shower Hurtles   *F. S.* 3.
Sweet is the breath of vernal shower,   *Inst.* 61.

Showers.

scatter'd oft . . . are Show'rs of Violets
    El. Pem. 118 ; *Mas.* 138.
scatter . . . Showers of Plenty o'er the Land.
    E. G. 18.
And batter Cadmus' walls with stony showers,
    Stat.[1] 18.

Shows.

court the times With shows of fair obeisance;
    Agr. 102.
So glittering shows the Thracian Godhead's
shield,   *Stat.*[1] 28.
†and now shews a Pound;   *Ch. Cr.* 38.

Shrieks.

Severn shall re-eccho . . . The shrieks of death,
    Bard 55.
Shrieks of an agonizing King!   *Bard* 56.

Shrill.

The cock's shrill clarion,   *El.* 19.
Or chaunticleer so shrill,   *El. Mas.* 19.
when thou hear'st the organ piping shrill
    Shak. 15.

Shriller.

†In shriller notes Q like a female squeaks;
    Ch. Cr. 48.

Shrine.

heap the shrine of Luxury and Pride   *El.* 71.
Before the Goddess' shrine we . . . bend,
    Prop.[1] 2.

Shrink.

the time To shrink from danger;   *Agr.* 48.

Shun.

†and Thoughts Like Butterflies, their Prison shun
    Ode 45.

Shut.

shut the gates of mercy on mankind,   *El.* 68.

Shuttles.

Shafts for shuttles, dipt in gore,   *F. S.* 13.

Sicily.

And there the ensanguined Wave of Sicily,
    Prop.[3] 44.

Sickening.

Must sick'ning virtue fly the tainted ground?
    E. G. 71.

Sickle.

Oft did the harvest to their sickle yield, *El.* 25.

Sickles.

Oft did the harvest to their sickles yield,
    El. Eg. 25.

Sickly.

Night, and all her sickly dews,   *P. P.* 49.
oft in weak and sickly minds   *Agr.* 72.
sickly Plants betray a niggard Earth,   *E. G.* 1.
The uncertain Crescent gleams a sickly light.
    Tasso 48.

Side.

'T was on a lofty vase's side,   *Cat* 1.
down the steep of Snowdon's shaggy side
    Bard 11.
Side by side as proudly riding,   *Owen* 12.
the Greenwood Side along,   *El. Mas.* 117.
With Freedom by my side,   *Inst.* 34.
Indolence and Pride, Softly rolling, side by side,
    Vic. 62.

Sidelong.

With side-long plough to quell the . . . ground,
    E. G. 91.

Sidney.

The Master of Sidney Is of the same Kidney;
    Satire 9.

Sieges.

†Battles, Sieges, Men, and Arms,   *Ode* 25.

Sigh.

shall [shalt, Lett.[1]] send A sigh,   *Bard* MS. 76.
the passing tribute of a sigh.   *El.* 80.
A sigh of soft reflection.   *Bent.* 28.
A sigh; an unavailing tear;   *Clerke* 14.

Sighing.

"Ah!" said the sighing peer,   *View* 17.

Sighs.

each giant-oak, and desert cave, Sighs *Bard* 24.
languid Pleasure sighs in every Gale. *E. G.* 45.
Sighs sudden and frequent,   *Am.* Lines 5.
For thee fat Nanny sighs,   *Com.* Lines 6.

Sight.

Visions of glory, spare my aching sight, *Bard* 107.
fades the glimmering landscape on the sight.
    El. 5.
Styack has often seen the sight   *L. S.* 103.
not the basilisk More deadly to the sight, *Agr.* 161.
the dazzled sight Of wakeful jealousy. *Agr.* 191.
gems that singly charm the sight,   *Bent.* 22.
lessening from the dazzled sight, Melts into air
    Vic. 15.
Our mother-church, with half-averted sight,
Blush'd   *Toph.* 5.
the champions, trembling at the sight, Prevent
disgrace,   *Stat.*[1] 22.
The diamond there attracts the wondrous sight,
    Tasso 69.
To Chiron Phœnix owed his long-lost Sight,
    Prop.[3] 83.
Speechless my Sight I fix'd, nor wept, *Dante* 53.

Sigismundo.

Lanfranc there And Sigismundo,   *Dante* 33.

Sign.

no sign of grace,   *L. S.* 89.
'T is a sign you have eat just enough *Couplet* 2.

Silence.
Such as in silence of the night Come *L. S.* 101.

Silent:
Melancholy, silent maid,   *Adv.* 27.
Can Honour's voice provoke the silent dust,
                    El. 43.
the silent Tenour of thy Doom. *El. Mas.* 88.
I . . . must be silent,   *Agr.* 85.
In silent gaze the tuneful choir among, *Bent.* 1.
Lo! where the silent marble weeps, . . . a mother
  sleeps: *Clerke* 1.

Silken.
The silken son of dalliance,   *Agr.* 98.

Silks.
But rustling in their silks and tissues. *L. S.* 24.

Silk-worm.
†For one Silk-worm thought that thrives *Ode* 37.

Silly.
No — at our time of life 't would be silly,
                    C. C. 10.

Silver.
Their jewels of silver and jewels of gold?
                    C. C. 26.
Sulphureous veins and lieving silver shine,
                    Tasso 59.
With silver light Relumes her crescent Orb
                  Prop.[2] 21.
†slow down the Silver stream. *Ch. Cr.* 57.

Silver-bright.
Oft woo'd the gleam of Cynthia silver-bright
                  Inst. 32.

Silver-winding.
Wanders the . . . Thames along His silver-
  winding way: *Eton* 10.

Similes.
†Tares of Similes choak the roots, *Ode* 11.

Simper.
With servile simper nod the mitred head. *Toph.* 4.

Simple.
The short and simple annals of the poor. *El.* 32.

Simplest.
The simplest note that swells the gale, *Vic.* 50.

Since.
Since sorrow never comes too late, *Eton* 96.
Vocal no more, since Cambria's fatal day,
                  Bard 27.
Since weeping I forsook thy fond embrace.
                  Ign. 12.
since Of me the Tower of Famine hight *Dante* 23.

Sincere.
his soul sincere,   *El.* 121.
Affection warm, and faith sincere, *Clerke* 5.

Sinew.
every labouring sinew strains, *Eton* 86.
Brac'd all his nerves, and every sinew strung;
                  Stat.[2] 7.

Sinews.
The slacken'd sinews of time-wearied age.
                  Agr. 140.
where unwearied sinews must be found *E. G.* 90.

Sing.
Pikes must shiver, javelins sing, *F. S.* 22.
Songs of joy and triumph sing! *F. S.* 54.
they sing, they laugh, they tattle, *L. S.* 58.
Lubbers, That to eternity would sing, *L. S.* 143.
And I, . . . That live to . . . sing their fall.
                  Hoel 24.
No tree is heard to whisper, bird to sing;
                  View 10.
And sing with what a careless Grace she flings
                  Prop.[3] 15.
†buskin'd Strains, . . . I sing; *Ode* 33.

Singly.
gems that singly charm the sight, *Bent.* 22.

Sings.
Bright Rapture calls, and soaring, as she sings,
                  Bard 123.
through the skies Sings in its rapid way,
                  Stat.[1] 50.

Sink.
They sink, they vanish from my eyes.
             Bard MS. 104.
crush his pride, And sink the traitor *Agr.* 187.
How flames . . . Shall sink this beauteous fabric
                  Prop.[2] 28.

Sinking.
If sinking into Sleep she seem to close *Prop.*[3] 17.

Sinks.
Sinks the fabric of the world. *Odin* 94.
The ponderous mass sinks in the cleaving ground,
                  Stat.[2] 16.

Sinner.
The ghostly Prudes . . . Already had condemn'd the sinner.   *L. S.* 130.

Sir.
far less shall be Our Suffering, Sir, *Dante* 66.

Sire.
thy Sire to send on earth Virtue . . . design'd,
                  Adv. 9.
those of Egypt, Have not forgot your sire:
                  Agr. 116.
the panting Sire Of Strength bereft, *Dante* 37.

Sire's.
No children run to lisp their sire's return, *El.* 23.

Sister.
long rever'd . . . the daughter, sister, wife,
                  Agr. 118.
"Lord! sister," says Physic to Law, *C. C.* 5.
The sun's pale sister, drawn by magic strain,
                  Stat.[1] 54.

Sister-art.
Bentley leads her sister-art along, *Bent.* 3.

Sisters.
Sisters, weave the web of death; *F. S.* 51.
Sisters, cease, the work is done. *F. S.* 52.
Sisters, hence with spurs of speed: *F. S.* 61.
Her sisters denying, and Jemmy proposing:
                  C. C. 20.
where three sisters of old In harmless society
  guttle   *C. C.* 3.

Sisters'.

Whence the seven Sisters' congregated fires, *Prop.*² 35.

Sit.

With me the Muse shall sit, *Spring* 16.

a griesly band, I see them sit, *Bard* 45.

There sit the sainted sage, the bard divine, *Inst.* 15.

benefits . . . sit heavy on the soul, *Agr.* 75.

Let majesty sit on thy awful brow, *Agr.* 145.

Sits.

Her infant image . . . Sits smiling on a father's woe: *Clerke* 10.

Sitting.

Brown sees thee sitting on his nose's tip, *Com. Lines* 4.

Six.

Not I — for a coronet, chariot and six. *C. C.* 18.

Sixth.

e'er the sixth Morn Had dawn'd, *Dante* 74.

Skies.

bright track, that fires the western skies, *Bard* 103.

they speak . . . The liquid language of the skies: *Inst.* 56.

trusts her Blossoms to the churlish Skies. *E. G.* 8.

A brighter Day, and Skies of azure Hue; *E. G.* 55.

opener skies, and suns of fiercer flame *E. G.* 64.

The common sun, the air, the skies, *Vic.* 51.

skies serene Speak not always winter past. *Song* 9.

through the skies Sings in its rapid way, *Stat.*¹ 49.

No Giant Race, no Tumult of the Skies, *Prop.*³ 35.

Then, while the vaulted Skies loud Ios rend, *Prop.*³ 47.

Nor changing Skies can hurt, *Prop.*³ 94.

Skill.

No boding Maid of skill divine Art thou, *Odin* 84.

Skim.

Some lightly o'er the current skim, *Spring* 28.

Skirts.

solemn scenes . . . their glitt'ring skirts unroll? *Bard* 106.

Skulks.

And Shame that sculks behind; *Eton* 64.

Skurry. *See* **Hurry-skurry.**

Sky.

Zephyrs thro' the clear blue sky *Spring* 9.

He gives to range the dreary sky: *P. P.* 51.

the native darkness of the sky; *Ign.* 8.

Sky-lark.

But chief, the sky-lark warbles high *Vic.* 13.

Slackened.

rebrace The slacken'd sinews of . . . age. *Agr.* 140.

Anon, with slacken'd rage comes quiv'ring down, *Stat.*¹ 51.

Thy passing Courser's slacken'd Speed restrain; *Prop.*³ 102.

Slain.

that I was . . . by Treachery slain, *Dante* 17.

Slaughter.

We the reins to slaughter [havock, Pem.] give, *F. S.* 33.

to wade through slaughter to a throne, *El.* 67.

Slaves.

Slaves from the womb, *Agr.* 130.

Sleep. *See also* **Iron-sleep.**

They do not sleep. *Bard* 43.

Where long of yore to sleep was laid *Odin* 19.

Let me, let me sleep again. *Odin* 34.

The rude Forefathers of the hamlet sleep. *El.* 16.

For ever sleep: *El. Mas.* 17.

Now let him sleep in peace *Child* 6.

If sinking into Sleep she seem to close *Prop.*³ 17.

and Sleep Prophetic of my Woes *Dante* 26.

sleep as yet Gave not to know *Dante* 42.

Sad with the Fears of sleep, *Dante* 49.

Sleeping.

The sleeping fragrance from the ground; *Vic.* 6.

Sleeps.

Brave Urien sleeps upon his craggy bed: *Bard* 31.

A friend, a wife, a mother sleeps: *Clerke* 2.

Sleet. *See* **Iron-sleet.**

Sleeve.

safe and laughing in his sleeve, *L. S.* 75.

Slippery.

The slipp'ry verge her feet beguil'd, *Cat* 29.

A slipp'ry weight, *Stat.*¹ 8.

Sloth.

dreaming Sloth of pallid hue, *Inst.* 4.

Slow.

Slow melting strains their Queen's approach declare: *P. P.* 36.

Descending slow their glitt'ring skirts unroll? *Bard* 106.

Slow thro' the church-way path *El.* 114.

pacing forth With solemn steps and slow, *Inst.* 36.

Come on, With sturdy step and slow, Hippomedon; *Stat.*² 2.

Heal the slow Chief, and send again *Prop.*³ 82.

†Slow follow all the quality of State, *Ch. Cr.* 51.

†slow down the Silver stream. *Ch. Cr.* 57.

Slow-consuming.

Poverty . . . And slow-consuming Age. *Eton* 90.

Slowly.

Slowly breath'd a sullen sound. *Odin* 26.

The lowing herd wind slowly o'er the lea, *El.* 2.

Slowly-winding.

rushy Camus' slowly-winding flood *Ign.* 3.

Sluggish.

†And, springing from the sluggish mould, *Ode* 47.

Slumber.

Quench'd in dark clouds of slumber lie *P. P.* 23.

That Slumber brings to aid my Poetry. *Prop.*³ 20.

Slumbering.

The massy sceptre o'er thy slumb'ring line?
    Ign. 16.
She bids each slumb'ring energy awake, *E. G.* 78.
the whilst I slumb'ring lay,   *Dante* 26.

Slumbers.

the slumbers light,   *Eton* 49.
steep in slumbers each benighted sense? *Ign.* 18.
To start from short slumbers, and wish for the
    morning —   *Am. Lines* 3.

Sly.

When sly Jemmy Twitcher had smugg'd up his
    face,   *C. C.* 1.

Small.

In still small Accents whisp'ring   *El.* Mas. 83.
The Muses, . . . Convey'd him . . . To a small
    closet   *L. S.* 72.
The still small voice of gratitude.   *Inst.* 64.
From fumbling baronets and poets small,
     Shak. 6.
and to small distance threw.   *Stat.*[1] 6.
Thro' a small crevice opening,   *Dante* 22.
†And seems small difference the sounds between;
     Ch. Cr. 46.

Smeared.

Smear'd with gore, and ghastly pale: *Bard* 36.

Smile.

A baleful smile upon their baffled Guest. *Bard* 82.
A smile of horror on their baffled guest.
     Bard MS. 82.
Till he on *Hoder's* corse shall smile   *Odin* 69.
Nor Grandeur hear with a disdainful smile *El.* 31.
If equal Justice . . . Smile not indulgent
     E. G. 16.
The social Smile, the sympathetic Tear. *E. G.* 37.
They smile, but reply not —   *Am. Lines* 8.

Smiled.

Malignant Fate . . . smil'd   *Cat* 28.
Stretch'd forth his little arms, and smiled.
     P. P. 88.
She smiled, and bid him come to dinner.
     L. S. 132.

Smileing.   *See* **Smiling.**

Smiles.

The star of Brunswick smiles serene,   *Inst.* 93.
nor to be lured with smiles   *Agr.* 18.
Dispel . . . with smiles, the tim'rous cloud
     Agr. 193.
Morning smiles the busy Race to chear, *West* 9.
Smiles on past Misfortune's brow . . . Reflec-
    tion's hand can trace;   *Vic.* 29.
hag . . . smiles malignant on the labouring
    power.   *Stat.*[1] 59.
Here the soft emerald smiles   *Tasso* 67.

Smiling.

scatter plenty o'er a smiling land,   *El.* 63.
now smiling as in scorn,   *El.* 105.
In vain to me the smileing Mornings shine,
     West 1.
Her infant image . . . Sits smiling on a father's
    woe: *Clerke* 10.

Smoking.

As when from Ætna's smoking summit broke,
     Stat.[2] 18.

Smooth.

Deep, majestic, smooth, and strong.   *P. P.* 8.
Swift shoots the Village-maid . . . Smooth, with-
    out step,   *Tasso* 20.

Smugged.

When sly Jemmy Twitcher had smugg'd up his
    face,   *C. C.* 1.

Smuggle.

resolution To smuggle a few years,   *View* 3.

Snatch.

And snatch a fearful joy.   *Eton* 40.

Snow.

the rose of snow, . . . we spread: *Bard* 91.
The winter's snow, the summer's heat, *Odin* 32.
And all its jetty honours turn to snow; *Prop.*[2] 14.
†My cold soil nips the Buds with Snow. *Ode* 6.

Snowdon's.

down the steep of Snowdon's shaggy side *Bard* 11.
what solemn scenes on Snowdon's height
     Bard 105.

Snows.

the rigour Of bleak Germania's snows. *Agr.* 110.
dauntless goes . . . through Zembla's snows?
     E. G. 77.
A vestment unadorn'd, though white as new-
    fal'n Snows;   *Tasso* 14.

Snowy.

the snowy beard,   *Cat* 8.
snowy veils, that float in air.   *Odin* 78.
Saw the snowy whirlwind fly;   *Vic.* 22.

So.

beech, That wreathes its . . . roots so high,
     El. 102.
Or chaunticleer so shrill,   *El.* Mas. 19.
So Rumor says.   *L. S.* 73.
So cunning was the Apparatus,   *L. S.* 85.
The powerful pothooks did so move him,
     L. S. 86.
And so God save our noble King,   *L. S.* 141.
Where he so soon may —   *Agr.* 165.
no matter What; so 't be strange,   *Agr.* 171.
So Helen look'd,   *Agr.* 194.
So her white neck reclin'd, so was she borne
     Agr. 195.
So draw Mankind in vain the vital Airs, *E. G.* 9.
So fond Instruction on the growing Powers
     E. G. 13.
How rude so e'er th' exterior Form   *E. G.* 26.
so was thought somewhat odd;   *Char.* 3.
So Carădoc bore his lance.   *Caradoc* 4.
— and his eyes are so lewd!   *C. C.* 8.
Then he shambles and straddles so oddly —
     C. C. 9.
He drinks — so did Noah;   *C. C.* 28.
— he swears — so do I: *C. C.* 28.
So York shall taste   *Shak.* 21.
So from our works sublime fumes shall rise;
     Shak. 22.

So the Master of Queen's Is is like as two beans;
     Satire 15.
so grinned the brawling fiend, *Toph.* 1.
So glittering shows the Thracian Godhead's
 shield,   *Stat.*[1] 28.
So from th' astonish'd stars, *Stat.*[1] 53.
So mov'd the Seer,   *Tasso* 23.
Why does yon Orb, so exquisitely bright,
       Prop.[2] 33.
Father, why, why do you gaze so sternly?
       Dante 56.
†I tell her so in Elegy.   *Ode* 30.
†So I to you this Trifle give, *Ode* 53.
†As H the Hebrew found, so I the Jew,
       Ch. Cr. 25.
†So big with Weddings, waddles W, *Ch. Cr.* 58.

Soar.
On expectation's strongest wing to soar *Agr.* 42.

Soaring.
Bright Rapture calls, and soaring, . . . Waves
       Bard 123.

Sober.
To Contemplation's sober eye *Spring* 31.
Their sober wishes never learn'd to stray; *El.* 74.

Social.
buried ashes glow with social fires. *El. Mas.* 108.
The social Smile, the sympathetic Tear. *E. G.* 37.

Society.
In harmless society guttle and scold. *C. C.* 4.

Soft.
Pity, dropping soft the sadly-pleasing tear.
       Adv. 32.
frantic Passions hear thy soft controul. *P. P.* 16.
Vocal no more, . . . To . . . soft Llewellyn's
 lay,   *Bard* 28.
soft the Zephyr blows,   *Bard* 71.
And thus they speak in soft accord *Inst.* 55.
Knows his soft ear the trumpet's . . . voice,
       Agr. 95.
But, soft! why do I waste the . . . hours
       Agr. 154.
the soft springs of pity in my heart, *Agr.* 182.
ignorance! soft salutary power! *Ign.* 9.
The soft Returns of Gratitude *E. G.* 34.
A sigh of soft reflection.   *Bent.* 28.
With . . . whisper soft She woo s the tardy
 spring: *Vic.* 3.
Smiles . . . Soft Reflection's hand can trace;
       Vic. 30.
faith sincere, And soft humanity were there.
       Clerke 6.
Here the soft emerald smiles *Tasso* 67.
These soft inglorious joys my hours engage;
       Prop.[2] 51.
Whence the soft Strain and ever-melting Verse?
       Prop.[3] 2.
That the soft Subject of my Song I make,
       Prop.[3] 14.
Me from myself the soft Enchantress stole;
       Prop.[3] 75.

Soften.
To soften, not to wound my heart. *Adv.* 44.

Softer.
Still may his Bard in softer fights engage;
       Prop.[1] 3.

Soft-eyed.
Freedom by my side, and soft-eyed Melancholy.
       Inst. 34.

Softly.
Indolence and Pride, Softly rolling, side by side,
       Vic. 62.

Soil.
The Soil, . . . will not teem in vain, *E. G.* 6.
manners speak the idiom of their soil. *E. G.* 87.
To seek your Hero in a distant Soil! *Tasso* 28.
†My cold soil nips the Buds with Snow. *Ode* 6.

Solar.
In climes beyond the solar road, *P. P.* 54.

Soldier.
the Soldier of the Fight, *Prop.*[3] 60.

Soldier's.
Weaving many a Soldier's doom, *F. S.* 7.
strengthen it With his plain soldier's oath,
       Agr. 151.

Sole.
Verse, the hero's sole reward. *Conan* 4.

Solemn.
Still on thy solemn steps attend: *Adv.* 29.
Murmur'd deep a solemn sound: *P. P.* 76.
what solemn [. . . , Lett.[1]] scenes on Snowdon's
 height   *Bard* 105.
Virgins . . . That bend to earth their solemn
 brow,   *Odin* 76.
all the air a solemn stillness holds, *El.* 6.
When he the solemn hall had seen; *L. S.* 118.
pacing forth With solemn steps and slow,*Inst.* 36.
mutter'd charms, and solemn invocation, *Agr.* 63.

Solemn-breathing.
Parent of sweet and solemn-breathing airs,
       P. P. 14.

Solid.
and cleaves the solid ground. *Stat.*[1] 52.
What wondrous force the solid earth can move,
       Prop.[2] 30.

Solitary.
A solitary fly!   *Spring* 44.
Molest her ancient solitary reign. *El.* 12.

Solitude.
Amazement in his van, . . . and solitude behind.
       Bard 62.

Solomon.
Why, David lov'd catches, and Solomon whoring:
       C. C. 24.

Some.
Beside some water's rushy brink *Spring* 15.
Some lightly o'er the current skim, *Spring* 28.
Some shew their gayly-gilded trim *Spring* 29.
Some speedy aid to send. *Cat* 33.
While some on earnest business bent *Eton* 31.
Some bold adventurers disdain *Eton* 35.
Some heart once pregnant with celestial fire;
       El. 46.
Some village-Hampden, *El.* 57.
Some mute inglorious Milton *El.* 59.

Some Cromwell guiltless of his country's blood.   *El.* 60.
Some frail memorial . . . erected nigh,   *El.* 78.
On some fond breast the parting soul relies,   *El.* 89.
Some pious drops the closing eye requires; *El.* 90.
If chance that e'er some pensive spirit   *El. Mas.* 95.
Some kindred spirit shall inquire   *El.* 96.
some hoary-headed Swain may say,   *El.* 97.
Such as . . . Come (sweep) along some winding entry   *L. S.* 102.
haply eyed at distance Some edileship,   *Agr.* 40.
To smuggle some years,   *View* MS. 3.
if to some feeling breast   *Bent.* 25.
†Some spin away their little lives   *Ode* 39.
†Some have loved, and loved (they say)   *Rond.* 5.
†Some have lov'd, to pass the time,   *Rond.* 13.

Something.
Yet something he was heard to mutter, *L. S.* 121.

Somewhat.
Teach it . . . as somewhat rare   *Agr.* 135.
so was thought somewhat odd;   *Char.* 3.

Son. *See also* Dragon-son.
Thy son is gone.   *Bard* 68.
he that calls, a Warriour's Son.   *Odin* 38.
Welcome, my noble son,   *Inst.* 67.
the fate Impending o'er your son: *Agr.* 66.
If the son reign, the mother perishes.   *Agr.* 67.
reign the son!   *Agr.* 68.
The silken son of dalliance,   *Agr.* 98.
had her wanton son Lent us his wings, *Agr.* 189.
my Hoel, died, Great Cian's son: *Hoel* 7.
Nor more, for now Nesimachus's son, *Stat.*[1] 13.
And Phœbus' Son recall'd Androgeon *Prop.*[3] 84.

Song.
Learn the tenour of our song.   *F. S.* 58.
The fond complaint, my Song, disprove, *P. P.* 46.
Modred, whose magic song Made huge Plinlimmon bow   *Bard* 33.
OWEN's praise demands my song,   *Owen* 1.
the Woodlark piped her farewell Song,   *El. Mas.* 119.
nature . . . leads the general song: *Vic.* 20.
That the soft Subject of my Song I make,   *Prop.*[3] 14.
†Loath'd the love; and loath'd the song; *Rond.* 15.

Songs.
Songs of joy and triumph sing!   *F. S.* 54.
†gratefully they pay Their little Songs, *Ode* 52.

Song-thrush.
the song-thrush there Scatters his loose notes   *Birds* 1.

Sonnet.
He once or twice had pen'd a sonnet; *L. S.* 125.
†Perhaps Thalia prompts a Sonnet   *Ode* 35.

Sons.
Pain can reach the Sons of Heav'n!   *Odin* 48.
His sable Sons with nearer Course surrounds   *E. G.* 24.
when I beheld My Sons,   *Dante* 62.

Soon.
The tear forgot as soon as shed,   *Eton* 43.
Soon their ample sway shall stretch   *F. S.* 39.
Soon a King shall bite the ground.   *F. S.* 44.
But soon his rhetorick forsook him,   *L. S.* 117.
Where he so soon may —   *Agr.* 165.
Which soon the parent sun's warm powers refine,   *Tasso* 60.
his helpless offspring soon O'erta'en beheld,   *Dante* 38.
too soon they had aroused 'em   *Dante* 48.
†Or, soon as they begin to blow   *Ode* 5.
†but soon pops in again;   *Ch. Cr.* 30.

Sooth. *See* Soothe.

Soothe.
My weary soul they seem to sooth   *Eton* 18.
Can . . . Flatt'ry soothe the . . . ear of death?   *El.* 44.

Soranus.
Soranus there, And Cassius;   *Agr.* 124.

Sorceries.
Sorceries, Assassinations, poisonings — *Agr.* 171.

Sore.
By residence, by marriage, and sore eyes?   *Shak.* 12.

Sorrow.
sorrow never comes too late,   *Eton* 96.
What sorrow was, thou bad'st her know, *Adv.* 15.
Long her strains in sorrow steep: *F. S.* 47.
o'er the cheek of Sorrow throw   *Vic.* 31.
A pang, to secret sorrow dear;   *Clerke* 13.
My struggling sorrow,   *Dante* 69.
what Sorrow could not, Hunger did. *Dante* 81.

Sorrow's.
Sorrow's piercing dart.   *Eton* 70.
and Sorrow's weeping train,   *P. P.* 44.
with Flight combined, And sorrow's faded form,   *Bard* 62.

Sorrows.
Struck the deep sorrows of his lyre. *Bard* 22.
Tell me, whence their sorrows rose: *Odin* 79.

Sought.
They sought, oh Albion! next thy sea-encircled coast.   *P. P.* 82.

Soul.
My weary soul they seem to sooth,   *Eton* 18.
numbs the soul with icy hand,   *Eton* 89.
Sovereign of the willing soul,   *P. P.* 13.
To save thy secret soul from nightly fears,   *Bard* 7.
unborn Ages, crowd not on my soul! *Bard* 108.
They breathe a soul to animate thy clay.   *Bard* 122.
the genial current of the soul.   *El.* 52.
On some fond breast the parting soul relies,   *El.* 89.
Large was his bounty, and his soul [heart, Mas.] sincere,   *El.* 121.
where on their opening soul First . . . ardour stole.   *Inst.* 21.
I . . . Have seen your soul,   *Agr.* 55.

benefits . . . sit heavy on the soul,   *Agr.* 75.

Health and Vigour to the Soul impart,   *E. G.* 11.

What fancied Zone can circumscribe the soul,
E. G. 73.

Rise, my soul! on wings of fire,   *Vic.* 17.

My soul in Bacchus' pleasing fetters bound;
*Prop.*² 8.

†Nature in my Soul implanted: *Ode* 2.

Souls.

rough, stubborn souls That struggle with the
yoke.   *Agr.* 126.

To different Climes seem different Souls assign'd?
E. G. 39.

Sound.

Murmur'd deep a solemn sound: *P. P.* 76.

Slowly breath'd a sullen sound.   *Odin* 26.

But hark! the portals sound,   *Inst.* 35.

Scar'd at the sound,   *Agr.* 32.

say we sound The trump of liberty;   *Agr.* 121.

to sound the Victor's Praise,   *Prop.*³ 32.

Sounding.

the nations . . . Their cymbals toss, and sounding brass explore;   *Stat.*¹ 57.

Her artful hand across the sounding Strings.
*Prop.*³ 16.

Sounds.

Such were the sounds, that . . . scatter'd wild
dismay,   *Bard* 9.

Or roused by sprightly sounds from out the
trance,   *Prop.*² 5.

But yet in low and uncompleated Sounds
Dante 44.

†And seems small difference the sounds between;
Ch. Cr. 46.

Sour.

Sour visages, enough to scare ye,   *L. S.* 106.

Source.

the sacred source of sympathetic Tears. *P. P.* 94.

conscious of the source from whence   *E. G.* 74.

Near the source whence Pleasure flows;   *Vic.* 54.

Of many a flood they view'd the secret source,
Tasso 51.

Back to it's Source divine the Julian Race.
*Prop.*³ 58.

South.

The prostrate South to the Destroyer yields
E. G. 52.

Sovereign.

Sovereign of the willing soul,   *P. P.* 13.

Why then stays my sovereign,   *Agr.* 164.

Spacious.

within the spatious walls,   *L. S.* 9.

This spacious animated Scene survey   *E. G.* 22.

As bright and huge the spacious circle lay,
*Stat.*¹ 26.

And in the midst a spacious arch appears.
Tasso 42.

Spaniard.

Tho' Pope and Spaniard could not trouble it.
L. S. 16.

Spaniel.

Follows them like a spaniel: *Satire* 26.

Spare.

spare the meek Usurper's holy head.   *Bard* 90.

Visions of glory, spare my aching sight,
Bard 107.

Ours to kill, and ours to spare: *F. S.* 34.

Spare the honour of my love.   *Song* 12.

Spares.

†careless spares to weed the Plain;   *Ode* 10.

Spark.

The gen'rous spark extinct revive,   *Adv.* 45.

How shall the spark . . . Blaze   *Agr.* 127.

If any spark of wit's delusive ray   *Ign.* 19.

Sparkling.

Fill high the sparkling bowl,   *Bard* 77.

Sparks.

The Sparks of Truth and Happiness   *E. G.* 29.

Spatious. *See* Spacious.

Speak.

Speak to a Commoner and Poet!   *L. S.* 140.

And thus they speak in soft accord   *Inst.* 55.

The manners speak the idiom of their soil.
E. G. 87.

and skies serene Speak not always winter past.
Song 10.

Speaks.

†K, as a man, with hoarser accent speaks,
Ch. Cr. 47.

Spear.

With dazzling helm, and horrent spear.
Bard MS. 112.

Where he points his purple spear,   *Owen* 33.

Spectres.

Her Spectres wan, and Birds of boding cry,
P. P. 50.

Sped.

Collecting all his force, the circle sped; *Stat.*¹ 48.

Speechless.

Stout Glo'ster stood aghast in speechless trance:
Bard 13.

What Virgins these, in speechless woe, *Odin* 75.

Speechless my Sight I fix'd, nor wept, *Dante* 53.

Speed.

To chase the rolling circle's speed,   *Eton* 29.

Sisters, hence with spurs of speed: *F. S.* 61.

Uprose the King of Men with speed,   *Odin* 1.

beguil'd With more elusive speed the . . . sight
Agr. 191.

Art it requires and more than winged speed.
Tasso 30.

Thy passing Courser's slacken'd Speed restrain;
*Prop.*³ 102.

with fleet and equal Speed   *Dante* 31.

Speedy.

Some speedy aid to send.   *Cat* 33.

Spell.

The Father of the powerful spell.   *Odin* 12.

Prophetess, my spell obey,   *Odin* 59.

But left a spell upon the table.   *L. S.* 80.

Without a spell to raise, . . . it   *Agr.* 16.

Then let me rightly spell of nature's ways;
Prop.[2] 15.

The powerful Mixture and the midnight Spell;
Prop.[3] 86.

Spelt.

their years, spelt by th' unletter'd muse,   *El.* 81.

Sphere.

The sun's pale sister, . . . Deserts precipitant
her darken'd sphere: *Stat.*[1] 55.

Spice.

Better be twisted into caps for spice,   *Shak.* 19.

Spied.

Him the Dog of Darkness spied,   *Odin* 5.
You think, you spied a tear   *Agr.* 10.

Spilt.

By whom shall *Hoder's* blood be spilt? *Odin* 62.

Spin.

†Some spin away their little lives   *Ode* 39.

Spinning.

Your Hist'ry whither are you spinning? *L. S.* 19.

Spires.

Ye distant spires, . . . That crown the . . .
glade,   *Eton* 1.

Spirit. *See also* **Sprite.**

Latium had her lofty spirit lost,   *P. P.* 81.
what daring Spirit Wakes thee   *P. P.* 112.
Some kindred spirit shall inquire   *El.* 96.
If chance that e'er some pensive spirit
     El. Mas. 109.
kind Heaven Had arm'd with spirit,   *L. S.* 30.
the spirit of Britannicus   *Agr.* 14.
They guard with spirit what . . . they gain'd?
     E. G. 95.
†Bids the poetick Spirit flourish;   *Ode* 14.

Spirits.

The spirits pure,   *Eton* 49.
While spirits blest above . . . Join with glad
voice   *Inst.* 87.

Spirit-stirring.

ears to own Her spirit-stirring voice; *Agr.* 124.

Spite.

Spite of danger he shall live.   *F. S.* 35.
Spite of her frail companion dauntless goes
     E. G. 76.
Much have I borne from canker'd critic's spite,
     Shak. 5.

Spoils.

page Rich with the spoils of time   *El.* 50.

Spoke.

He spoke, and headlong . . . plung'd *Bard* 143.

Sport.

With antic Sport[?],   *P. P. MS.* 30.

Sported.

A gentler Lamb ne'er sported on the plain,
     Child 3.

Sportive.

The sportive kind reply: *Spring* 42.

Sports.

With antic Sports, and blue-eyed Pleasures,
     P. P. 30.
oft in Pisa's sports, his native land Admired that
arm,   *Stat.*[1] 35.
And sports and wantons o'er the frozen tide.
     Tasso 22.

Spot.

in this neglected spot is laid   *El.* 45.
On this congenial spot he fix'd his choice; *View* 5.

Spots.

With native spots and artful labour gay, *Stat.*[2] 25.

Spray.

†then perches on the spray,   *Ch. Cr.* 41.

Spread.

Gondula, and *Geira*, spread . . . your shield.
     F. S. 31.
the rose of snow, . . . we spread: *Bard* 92.
For whom yon glitt'ring board is spread, *Odin* 41.
giddy fame Has spread among the crowd;
     Agr. 168.
Spread the young Thought,   *E. G.* 12.
climes, that spread Where Nile redundant
     E. G. 100.

Sprightly.

Full many a sprightly race   *Eton* 22.
Or roused by sprightly sounds from out the trance,
     Prop.[2] 5.

Spring.

The untaught harmony of spring: *Spring* 7.
Eager to taste the honied spring,   *Spring* 26.
thy spring is gone —   *Spring* 49.
To breathe a second spring.   *Eton* 50.
She woo's the tardy spring: *Vic.* 4.
Ere the spring he would return —   *Song* 2.

Springing.

†And, springing from the sluggish mould, *Ode* 47.

Springs.

From Helicon's harmonious springs   *P. P.* 3.
the soft springs of pity in my heart,   *Agr.* 182.
the source from whence she springs,   *E. G.* 74.

Sprite. *See also* **Spirit.**

Who thus afflicts my troubled sprite,   *Odin* 29.

Sprung.

'T was the Lark that upward sprung!   *Song* 5.

Spun.

The thread is spun.   *Bard* 98.

Spurs.

Sisters, hence with spurs of speed: *F. S.* 61.

Sputter.

For thee does Powell squeeze, and Marriot
sputter,   *Com. Lines* 2.

Spy.

Hyperion's march they spy,   *P. P.* 53.
The secrets of th' Abyss to spy.   *P. P.* 97.

Squadrons.

thro' the kindred squadrons mow their way.
     Bard 86.
Squadrons three against him came;   *Owen* 10.
Upon Deïra's squadrons hurl'd   *Hoel* 3.

Square.

Cried the square Hoods in woful fidget *L. S.* 135.

Squeaks.

†In shriller notes Q like a female squeaks;
Ch. Cr. 48.

Squeeze.

For thee does Powell squeeze,   *Com. Lines* 2.

Squib.

Disprov'd the arguments of *Squib*,   *L. S.* 115.

Squire.

But left . . . state to Charles Townshend and
Squire.   *Char.* 6.

St. *See also* **Saint.**

But stint your clack for sweet St. Charitie
Shak. 2.

The Master of St. John's   *Satire* 33.

Owls would have hooted in St. Peter's choir,
View 23.

And foxes stunk and litter'd in St. Paul's.
View 24.

Stain.

Nor Envy . . . Dare the Muse's walk to stain,
Inst. 10.

Stairs.

And up stairs in a whirlwind rattle.   *L. S.* 60.

Stamp.

Stamp we our vengeance deep,   *Bard* 96.

Stand.

shew them where in ambush stand   *Eton* 58.

And from the gallery stand peeping: *L. S.* 100.

Such as . . . at the chappel-door stand sentry;
L. S. 104.

you spied a tear stand in her eye,   *Agr.* 10.

Let him stand forth   *Stat.*[1] 3.

Where flow'd the widest stream he took his stand;
Stat.[1] 38.

Irresolute they stand;   *Tasso* 11.

Stands.

The Dragon-Son of Mona stands;   *Owen* 20.

An ancient pile of buildings stands: *L. S.* 2.

Star. *See also* **Evening-star.**

The star of Brunswick smiles serene,   *Inst.* 93.

the influence of the northern star   *E. G.* 68.

Search to what regions yonder Star retires,
Prop.[2] 19.

Stare.

The Audience stare,   *L. S.* 109.

created but to stare,   *Agr.* 130.

Starry.

Sublime their starry fronts they rear;   *Bard* 112.

Stars.

So from the astonish'd stars,   *Stat.*[1] 53.

Start.

the idle herd . . . yet will start,   *Agr.* 131.

To start from short slumbers, and wish for the
morning —   *Am. Lines* 3.

Starts.

Till April starts, and calls around   *Vic.* 5.

Starves.

flinty Bosom starves her generous Birth,   *E. G.* 2.

State.

At ease reclin'd in rustic state   *Spring* 17.

In gliding state she wins her easy way: *P. P.* 39.

They mock the air with idle state.   *Bard* 4.

Meek Newton's self bends from his state sublime,
Inst. 25.

But left church and state to Charles Townshend
Char. 6.

†Slow follow all the quality of State,   *Ch. Cr.* 51.

Stately.

the stately brow of WINDSOR's heights   *Eton* 5.

Statesmen.

gorgeous Dames, and Statesmen old . . . appear.   *Bard* 113.

Stay.

Stay, oh stay! nor thus forlorn Leave me
Bard 101.

Stayed.

Rap'd at the door, nor stay'd to ask,   *L. S.* 55.

Stays.

Why then stays my sovereign,   *Agr.* 164.

Steadfast.

Who taught this vast machine its steadfast laws,
Prop.[2] 17.

Steady.

Thy steady course of honour keep,   *Inst.* 91.

Steal.

Steal to his closet at the hour of prayer; *Shak.* 14.

Words that steal from my tongue, *Am. Lines* 6.

Steam.

the grateful steam Of flattery's incense, *Agr.* 34.

Steed.

Each bestride her sable steed.   *F. S.* 63.

saddled strait his coal-black steed;   *Odin* 2.

Steel.

steel our hearts to war?   *E. G.* 69.

Steep.

Now rowling down the steep amain,   *P. P.* 10.

Woods, that wave o'er Delphi's steep,   *P. P.* 66.

down the steep of Snowdon's shaggy side *Bard* 11.

Long her strains in sorrow steep: *F. S.* 47.

Down the yawning steep he rode,   *Odin* 3.

To steep in slumbers each benighted sense?
Ign. 18.

And down the steep he led   *Tasso* 43.

Steeps.

Victor he stood on Bellisle's rocky steeps —
Williams 10.

Stem.

OWEN . . . Fairest flower of Roderic's stem,
Owen 3.

wont to stem With stubborn nerves the tide,
Agr. 108.

Step.

One false step is ne'er retriev'd   *Cat* 38.

come on, With sturdy step and slow, Hippomedon;   *Stat.*[2] 2.

Age step 'twixt love and me,   *Prop.*[2] 12.

Swift shoots the Village-maid . . . Smooth, without step,   *Tasso* 20.

Steps.

Still on thy solemn steps attend; *Adv.* 29.
with hasty steps . . . To meet the sun *El.* 99.
pacing forth With solemn steps and slow, *Inst.* 36.
I have pursued your steps, *Agr.* 54.
Behind the steps that Misery treads, *Vic.* 39.
And first to Ascalon their steps they bend,
Tasso 3.

Stern.

Stern rugged Nurse! thy rigid lore *Adv.* 13.

Sternly.

Father, why, why do you gaze so sternly?
Dante 56.

Stiles.

Thro' lanes unknown, o'er stiles they ventur'd,
L. S. 54.

Still.

Still is the . . . hand of Care: *Spring* 21.
Still had she gaz'd; *Cat* 13.
Where grateful Science still adores *Eton* 3.
Still as they run they look behind, *Eton* 38.
Still on thy solemn steps attend; *Adv.* 29.
Onward still his way he takes *Odin* 13.
frail memorial still erected nigh, *El.* 78.
In still small Accents whisp'ring *El. Mas.* 83.
The still small voice of gratitude. *Inst.* 64.
one . . . may still With equal power resume
Agr. 90.
dost thou still oppose Thy leaden ægis *Ign.* 13.
Still stretch, . . . The massy sceptre *Ign.* 15.
For ever gone — yet still to fancy new, *Ign.* 33.
Freedom still withstands Th' encroaching tide,
E. G. 60.
Still, . . . See a kindred Grief pursue; *Vic.* 37.
Art he invokes new horrors still to bring.
View 12.
Still may his Bard in softer fights engage;
Prop.[1] 3.
You ask, why thus my Loves I still rehearse,
Prop.[3] 1.
†Still to ripen 'em is wanted; *Ode* 4.

Stillness.

all the air a solemn stillness holds, *El.* 6.

Stings.

The stings of Falshood those shall try, *Eton* 75.

Stint.

But stint your clack for sweet St. Charitie
Shak. 2.

Stirred.

No Nereid stirr'd: *Cat* 34.

Stirring. *See* **Spirit-stirring.**

Stole.

where . . . First the genuine ardour stole.
Inst. 22.
Me from myself the soft Enchantress stole;
Prop.[3] 75.

Stone.

the lay Grav'd on the stone *El.* 116.
nor wept, for all Within was Stone: *Dante* 54.

Stones.

All stones of lustre shoot their vivid ray, *Tasso* 65.

Stony.

And batter Cadmus' walls with stony showers,
Stat.[1] 18.

Stood.

Stout Glo'ster stood aghast in speechless trance:
Bard 13.
With haggard eyes the Poet stood; *Bard* 18.
He stood as mute as poor *Macleane*. *L. S.* 120.
he stood trembling, Scar'd at the sound, *Agr.* 31.
The Herd stood drooping by: *Vic.* 24.
Victor he stood on Bellisle's rocky steeps —
Williams 10.
Where fix'd in wonder stood the warlike pair,
Tasso 25.

Stop.

Marking . . . Fear to stop, *Owen* 36.

Stopped.

Nor stopp'd till it had cut the further strand.
Stat.[1] 40.

Store.

In one rich mass unite the precious store,
Tasso 61.

Stores.

OWEN . . . nor heaps his brooded stores,
Owen 5.
Instruction . . . idly lavishes her Stores, *E. G.* 14.

Storied.

Can storied urn or animated bust *El.* 41.

Storm.

Now the storm begins to lower *F. S.* 1.

Storms.

sad refuge from the storms of Fate! *P. P.* 45.

Stormy.

tongue, That hush'd the stormy main: *Bard* 30.

Stout.

Stout Glo'ster stood aghast in speechless trance:
Bard 13.
Mov'd the stout heart of England's Queen,
L. S. 15.

Straddles.

Then he shambles and straddles so oddly —
C. C. 9.

Straight.

saddled strait his coal-black steed; *Odin* 2.
straight Ariseing all they cried, *Dante* 64.
†See Folly, Fashion, Foppery, straight appear,
Ch. Cr. 16.

Strain.

the loom, Where the dusky warp we strain,
F. S. 6.
The sun's pale sister, drawn by magic strain,
Stat.[1] 54.
Whence the soft Strain and ever-melting Verse?
Prop.[3] 2.
But nor Callimachus' enervate Strain *Prop.*[3] 55.

Strains.

every labouring sinew strains, *Eton* 86.
Slow melting strains their Queen's approach de-
clare: *P. P.* 36.
What strains of vocal transport round her play.
Bard 120.

a thousand strains Triumphant tell

          Bard MS. 109.

Long her strains in sorrow steep: *F. S.* 47.

Strains of Immortality!   *F. S.* 48.

†Tragick Numbers, buskin'd Strains, *Ode* 31.

Strait. *See* **Straight.**

Strand.

Nor stopp'd till it had cut the further strand.

          Stat.[1] 40.

Strange.

The Poet felt a strange disorder: *L. S.* 82.

so 't be strange, and dreadful.   *Agr.* 171.

Stranger.

A stranger yet to pain!   *Eton* 14.

when yet a stranger To adoration, *Agr.* 33.

Straw-built.

The swallow twitt'ring from the straw-built shed,

          El. 18.

Stray.

Their sober wishes never learn'd to stray; *El.* 74.

Or lawless, o'er their Ivory Margin stray:

          Prop.[3] 8.

Strayed.

Where once my careless childhood stray'd,

          Eton 13.

where lucid Avon stray'd,   *P. P.* 85.

Strays.

while yet he strays Along the . . . vale

          Clerke 11.

Stream. *See also* **Torrent-stream.**

The Genii of the stream: *Cat* 15.

the rich stream of music winds along *P. P.* 7.

Nor wash his visage in the stream, *Odin* 67.

Where flow'd the widest stream he took his stand;

          Stat.[1] 38.

Against the stream the waves secure he trod,

          Tasso 15.

And paint the margin of the costly stream,

          Tasso 64.

Famine at feasts, and thirst amid the stream;

          Prop.[2] 47.

To mourn the Glories of his sevenfold Stream,

          Prop.[3] 50.

†slow down the Silver stream. *Ch. Cr.* 57.

Streamed.

Stream'd, like a meteor, to the troubled air

          Bard 20.

Streams.

Rich streams of regal bounty pour'd, *Inst.* 52.

†Purling streams and cooling breezes *Ode* 20.

Street. *See* **Grub-street.**

Strength.

They guard . . . what by strength they gain'd?

          E. G. 95.

could they catch his strength, *Bent.* 13.

The strength and harmony of Life. *Vic.* 44.

Young Pterelas with strength unequal drew,

          Stat.[1] 5.

Phlegyas . . . Summon'd his strength, *Stat.*[1] 33.

the panting Sire Of Strength bereft, *Dante* 38.

Strengthen.

dress thy plea, and Burrhus strengthen it

          Agr. 150.

Strengthens.

Sings in its rapid way, and strengthens as it flies;

          Stat.[1] 50.

Stretch.

Where'er the oak's thick branches stretch

          Spring 11.

Soon their ample sway shall stretch *F. S.* 39.

His listless length . . . would he stretch, *El.* 103.

Still stretch, . . . The massy sceptre *Ign.* 15.

Stretched. *See also* **Out-stretched.**

She stretch'd in vain   *Cat* 22.

Again she stretch'd,   *Cat* 26.

The dauntless child Stretch'd forth *P. P.* 88.

Earth's monster-brood stretch'd on their iron bed,

          Prop.[2] 41.

Strews.

many a holy text around she strews, *El.* 83.

Strife.

the madding crowd's ignoble strife, *El.* 73.

with Reason and thyself at Strife, *El. Mas.* 85.

And blended form, with artful strife, *Vic.* 43.

Strike.

bade him strike The noble quarry. *Agr.* 46.

Strikes.

Hark! 't is nature strikes the lyre, *Vic.* 19.

Not all that strikes your wand'ring eyes

          Cat MS. 39.

String.

To string our nerves and steel our hearts

          E. G. 69.

Strings. *See also* **Shoe-strings.**

give to rapture all thy trembling strings. *P. P.* 2.

What strings symphonious tremble in the air,

          Bard 119.

Her artful hand across the sounding Strings.

          Prop.[3] 16.

Stripling.

't will profit you And please the stripling. *Agr.* 13.

Strive.

strive to mend A broken character *View* 3.

Stroke.

bow'd the woods beneath their sturdy stroke!

          El. 28.

As the thunder's fiery stroke, *Conan* 7.

Stroked.

She strok'd up her belly,   *C. C.* 22.

And strok'd down her band — *C. C.* 22.

Strokes.

There the thund'ring strokes begin, *Owen* 23.

Strong.

Deep, majestic, smooth, and strong. *P. P.* 8.

Keep the tissue close and strong. *F. S.* 16.

Owen swift, and Owen strong; *Owen* 2.

But none . . . return, Save . . . Conan strong,

          Hoel 21.

Another orb upheaved his strong right hand,

          Stat.[1] 15.

Artful and strong he pois'd the well-known
weight   *Stat.*² 3.
†But their love could not be *strong*.   *Rond.* 16.
†*Strong* to love, — and then to part,   *Rond.* 17.

Strongest.
On expectation's strongest wing to soar *Agr.* 42.

Struck.
Struck the deep sorrows of his lyre.   *Bard* 22.
'T was Milton struck the deep-ton'd shell,
               Inst. 23.

Structures. *See* **Mountain-structures.**

Struggle.
souls That struggle with the yoke.   *Agr.* 127.

Struggleing. *See* **Struggling.**

Struggles.
And struggles to elude my longing Eyes,
               *Prop.*³ 24.

Struggling.
The struggling pangs of conscious truth   *El.* 69.
Nor lofty Carthage struggleing with her Fate.
               *Prop.*³ 40.
I swallow'd down My struggling Sorrow,
               Dante 69.

Strung.
Brac'd all his nerves, and every sinew strung;
               *Stat.*² 7.

Struts.
†Behold K struts,   *Ch. Cr.* 49.

Stubborn.
Their furrow oft the stubborn glebe has broke:
               El. 26.
wont to stem With stubborn nerves the tide,
               Agr. 109.
stubborn souls, That struggle with the yoke.
               Agr. 127.
The stubborn elements confess her sway,
               E. G. 81.

Stung.
Stung by a senseless word,   *Agr.* 133.

Stunk.
And foxes stunk and litter'd in St. Paul's. *View* 24.

Sturdy.
bow'd the woods beneath their sturdy stroke!
               El. 28.
come on, With sturdy step and slow, Hippomedon;   *Stat.*² 2.

Stutter.
And Glyn cut Phizzes, and Tom Neville stutter.
               Com. Lines 3.

Styack.
Styack has often seen the sight   *L. S.* 103.

Subject.
That the soft Subject of my Song I make,
               *Prop.*³ 14.

Sublime.
arms sublime, that float upon the air, *P. P.* 38.
Nor second He, that rode sublime   *P. P.* 95.
Sublime their starry fronts they rear; *Bard* 112.
Meek Newton's self bends from his state sublime,
               Inst. 25.

Sublimer.
So from our works sublimer fumes shall rise;
               Shak. 22.

Submission.
And doff their hats with due submission:
               L. S. 110.

Submit.
Dryden's harmony submit to mine.   *Bent.* 16.

Submits.
Submits the fasces of her sway,   *Inst.* 86.

Substantial.
till substantial Night Has reassum'd   *Odin* 91.

Subterraneous.
Through subterraneous passages they went,
               Tasso 49.

Succeed.
What idle progeny succeed   *Eton* 28.

Succeeding.
All that whole Day, or the succeeding Night
               Dante 58.

Success.
Exalt the brave, and idolize Success;
               El. Mas. 74.

Successful.
successful dost thou still oppose   *Ign.* 13.

Such.
Such is the race of Man: *Spring* 32.
Such forms, as glitter in the Muse's ray, *P. P.* 119.
Such were the sounds, that . . . scatter'd wild
dismay,   *Bard* 9.
such as, wand'ring near her secret bow'r, *El.* 11.
To rid the manour of such vermin.   *L. S.* 52.
'Gainst four such eyes were no protection.
               L. S. 96.
such as . . . Come (sweep) along some winding
entry   *L. S.* 101.
Nero To such a mother owes;   *Agr.* 58.
Who had such liberal power   *Agr.* 89.
Such a sheep-biting look,   *C. C.* 6.
such a pick-pocket air!   *C. C.* 6.
To reject him for such peccadillos, were odd;
               C. C. 29.
With such a gleam affrights Pangæa's field,
               *Stat.*¹ 29.
such as mought entrance find within   *Dante* 60.
†But why on such *mock* grandeur should we dwell,
               Ch. Cr. 23.

Sucked.
And suck'd the eggs, and kill'd the pheasants.
               L. S. 48.

Sudden.
To sudden fate . . . Half of thy heart we con-
secrate.   *Bard* 97.
A sudden fit of ague shook him,   *L. S.* 119.
Sighs sudden and frequent,   *Am. Lines* 5.
And wonder at the sudden Funeral. *Prop.*³ 98.

Suffering.
far less shall be Our Suffering,   *Dante* 66.

Sufferings.
To each his suff'rings: *Eton* 91.

Suffices.
world, you gave him, Suffices not   *Agr.* 59.

Sullen.
the sullen Cares And frantic Passions hear
P. P. 15.
Slowly breath'd a sullen sound.   *Odin* 26.
the sullen year Saw the snowy whirlwind fly;
Vic. 21.
Or the bull, with sullen roar, . . . advance?
Caradoc 2.

Sulphureous.
Sulphureous veins and liveing silver shine,
Tasso 59.

Sultry.
the sultry climes, that spread Where Nile *E. G.* 100.
Nor changing Skies can hurt, nor sultry Air.
*Prop.*³ 94.

Sum.
Gave not to know their Sum of Misery, *Dante* 43.

Summer.
The summer Friend, the flatt'ring Foe; *Adv.* 22.

Summer-bed.
Nile redundant o'er his Summer-bed   *E. G.* 101.

Summer-gale.
Far from the sun and summer-gale,   *P. P.* 83.

Summer's.
The winter's snow, the summer's heat, *Odin* 32.

Summit.
As when from Ætna's smoking summit broke,
*Stat.*² 18.

Summoned.
Phlegyas . . . Summon'd his strength, *Stat.*¹ 33.

Sun.
Quick-glancing to the sun.   *Spring* 30.
Thy sun is set,   *Spring* 49.
Far from the sun and summer-gale,   *P. P.* 83.
With orient hues, unborrow'd of the Sun:
P. P. 120.
Ere the ruddy sun be set,   *F. S.* 21.
Clouds of carnage blot the sun.   *F. S.* 50.
To meet the sun upon the . . . lawn.   *El.* 100.
With whistful eyes pursue the setting sun.
El. Mas. 120.
'T is time to go, the sun is high advanc'd,
Agr. 158.
The common Sun, the air, the skies,   *Vic.* 51.
When blazing 'gainst the sun it shines from far,
*Stat.*¹ 30.
Till a new Sun arose with weakly Gleam,
Dante 59.
†Till again the rolling Sun Bursts   *Ode* 43.

Sung.
'T was the Nightingale that sung!   *Song* 6.

Sunk.
he sunk to endless night.   *Bard* Lett.² 144.

Sun's.
Nor see the sun's departing beam,   *Odin* 68.
The sun's pale sister, drawn by magic strain,
*Stat.*¹ 54.
Which soon the parent sun's warm powers refine,
Tasso 60.

Suns.
opener skies, and suns of fiercer flame   *E. G.* 64.

Sunshine.
The sunshine of the breast: *Eton* 44.
The . . . swarm that wantons in the sunshine
Agr. 147.

Superior.
Heavier toil, superior pain.   *Inst.* 58.

Supple.
bow the supple knee, and court the times
Agr. 101.

Suppliant's.
Oh, gently on thy Suppliant's head,   *Adv.* 33.

Supply.
scarce religion does supply Her muttered requiems,   *Bard* MS. 73.
The place of fame and elegy supply: *El.* 82.

Supreme.
Sailing with supreme dominion   *P. P.* 116.

Sure.
— Sure Delia will tell me!   *Am. Lines* 8.
Sure flew the disc from his unerring hand,
*Stat.*¹ 39.
†For, too sure, they love not *well.*   *Rond.* 24.
†Great D *d*raws near — the *D*utchess sure is come,
Ch. Cr. 1.

Surely.
Surely the Masians too, and those of Egypt,
Agr. 115.

Surge.
How the rude surge its sandy Bounds control;
*Prop.*² 37.

Surges.
And parting surges round the vessel roar;
*Stat.*² 21.

Surrounded.
With beauty, with pleasure surrounded, to languish —   *Am. Lines* 1.

Surrounding.
On surrounding foes advance?   *Caradoc* 3.

Surrounds.
His sable Sons with nearer Course surrounds
E. G. 24.

Survey.
th' expanse below . . . survey,   *Eton* 7.
This spacious animated Scene survey   *E. G.* 22.

Susan.
Nor *Susan* [*Harry*, Wal., Whar., Dods.] heard.
Cat 35.

Suspends.
Suspends th' inferior laws that rule our clay:
E. G. 80.
Suspends the crowd with expectation warm;
*Stat.*¹ 44.

Swain.
some hoary-headed Swain   *El.* 97.

Swains. *See* **Fellow-swains.**

Swallow.
The swallow twitt'ring from the straw-built shed,
El. 18.

Swallowed.

I swallow'd down My struggling Sorrow,
Dante 68.

Swan.

†S, sails the Swan   *Ch. Cr.* 57.

Swarm.

Swarm, that in thy noon-tide beam were born?
Bard 69.

around thee call The gilded swarm   *Agr.* 147.

Sway.

Regardless of the sweeping Whirlwind's sway,
Bard 75.

Soon their ample sway shall stretch   *F. S.* 39.

Submits the fasces of her sway,   *Inst.* 86.

and arbitrary sway: *Agr.* 79.

gloomy Sway have fix'd her Empire there,
E. G. 19.

where the deluge burst, with sweepy sway
E. G. 48.

The stubborn elements confess her sway,
E. G. 81.

Swayed.

the rod of empire might have sway'd,   *El.* 47.

Swearing.

And all the town rings of his swearing and roaring!
C. C. 16.

Swears.

— he swears — so do I: *C. C.* 28.

Sweat.

Have his limbs Sweat under iron harness?
Agr. 97.

Sweep.

Black and huge along they sweep,   *Owen* 17.

Such as . . . Come (sweep) along some winding
entry   *L. S.* 102.

with resistless sweep   *Vic.* 59.

To rush, and sweep them from the world! *Hoel* 4.

How riseing winds the face of Ocean sweep,
Prop.[2] 23.

Sweeping.

Regardless of the sweeping Whirlwind's sway,
Bard 75.

Sweepy.

where the deluge burst, with sweepy sway
E. G. 48.

Sweet.

Parent of sweet and solemn-breathing airs,
P. P. 14.

In loose numbers wildly sweet   *P. P.* 61.

Attemper'd sweet To virgin-grace.   *Bard* 118.

Sweet is the breath of vernal shower,   *Inst.* 61.

The bee's collected treasures sweet,   *Inst.* 62.

Sweet music's melting fall,   *Inst.* 63.

But stint your clack for sweet St. Charitie *Shak.* 2.

Me may Castalia's sweet recess detain, *Prop.*[2] 2.

Sweeten.

hours . . . to sweeten liberty: *Eton* 34.

Sweeter.

sweeter yet The . . . voice of gratitude. *Inst.* 63.

Sweetness.

waste its sweetness on the desert air.   *El.* 56.

Sweets.

No hive hast thou of hoarded sweets, *Spring* 46.

The sweets of kindness lavishly indulg'd *Agr.* 73.

Swell.

as the choral warblings round him swell, *Inst.* 24.

The Soil, . . . Forbids her Gems to swell,
E. G. 7.

Swelling.

†Copious numbers, swelling grain;   *Ode* 8.

Swells.

The pealing anthem swells the note of praise.
El. 40.

The simplest note that swells the Gale,   *Vic.* 50.

Swept.

She swept, she hiss'd, she ripen'd and grew rough,
Par. on Ep. 2.

Swift.

Owen swift, and Owen strong;   *Owen* 2.

Swift at the word, from out the gazing host,
Stat.[1] 4.

Swift shoots the Village-maid in rustic play
Tasso 19.

Swift-descending.

the torrent's swift-descending flood,   *E. G.* 92.

Swifter.

In swifter measures animated run,   *Bent.* 11.

Swiftly.

happiness too swiftly flies,   *Eton* 97.

Swollen.

Swoll'n with new force, and late-descending rains.
Tasso 10.

Sword.

Sword [Blade, Whar.], that once a Monarch
bore,   *F. S.* 15.

Sword with clattering buckler meet,
F. S. Whar. 23.

At Aix, his voluntary sword he drew, *Williams* 5.

Did the sword of Conan mow The crimson harvest   *Conan* 9.

Purg'd by the sword, and purified by fire,
View 21.

Swore.

My Lady . . . Swore by her coronet   *L. S.* 50.

Thyrsis, when we parted, swore   *Song* 1.

Sylla.

Sylla has his friends,   *Agr.* 100.

Syllani.

pitied ghosts Of the Syllani,   *Agr.* 176.

Symmetry.

To local symmetry and life awake!   *Bent.* 8.

Sympathetic.

the sacred source of sympathetic Tears. *P. P.* 94.

By sympathetic musings here delayed,
El. Mas. 110.

The social Smile, the sympathetic Tear. *E. G.* 37.

Sympathy.

a glance . . . They send of tender sympathy
Inst. 20.

my lines a secret sympathy   *Bent.* 26.

Symphonious.
What strings symphonious tremble in the air, *Bard* 119.
Join with glad voice the loud symphonious lay. *Inst.* 88.

Symptoms.
Ah! say, . . . how these symptoms befell me? *Am. Lines* 7.
'T is hard th' elusive Symptoms to explore: *Prop.³* 95.

System.
Has from them his system took; *Satire* 30.

Tabby.
Demurest of the tabby kind, *Cat* 4.

Table.
But left a spell upon the table. *L. S.* 80.
From table she rose, *C. C.* 21.

Tail.
Her conscious tail her joy declar'd; *Cat* 7.

Tainted.
sick'ning virtue fly the tainted ground? *E. G.* 71.

Take.
A thousand rills their mazy progress take: *P. P.* 4.
This pencil take (she said), *P. P.* 89.
take me to thy peaceful shade again. *Ign.* 6.
Another touch, another temper take, *E. G.* 79.
Fix'd by his touch a lasting essence take; *Bent.* 6.
Take back, what once was yours. *Dante* 68.

Taken.
He ne'er was for a conj'rer taken. *L. S.* 128.

Takes.
Onward still his way he takes *Odin* 13.
She curtsies, as she takes her chair, *L. S.* 111.
The Master of Catherine Takes them all *Satire* 20.

Taking.
And Satan's self had thoughts of taking orders. *Toph.* 8.

Tale.
Mortal, thou that hear'st the tale, *F. S.* 57.
Dost . . . their artless tale relate; *El.* 94; *Mas.* 78.
Nor Tale of Thebes, nor Ilium *Prop.³* 37.
And hates the Tale of Troy *Prop.³* 74.
That which yet remains . . . (a horrid tale) *Dante* 19.

Taliessin.
Hear from the grave, great Taliessin [Taliesin, Lett.²] *Bard* 121.

Talk.
dost thou talk to me . . . of danger, *Agr.* 27.

Talks.
— for he talks about God — *C. C.* 30.

Talymalfra's.
Talymalfra's rocky shore *Owen* 25.

Tame.
tame th' unwilling Deep. *E. G.* 43.

Tamer.
Thou Tamer of the human breast, *Adv.* 2.

Tantalus.
May the long Thirst of Tantalus allay, *Prop.³* 89.

Tardy.
The tardy rhymes that us'd to linger on, *Bent.* 9.
She woo's the tardy spring: *Vic.* 4.

Tares.
†Tares of Similes choak the roots, *Ode* 11.

Tarnished.
In peaked hoods and mantles tarnish'd, *L. S.* 105.

Tarts.
Better to bottom tarts *Shak.* 17.

Task.
Hail the task, and hail the hands! *F. S.* 53.
The Heroines undertook the task, *L. S.* 53.

Taste.
Eager to taste the honied spring, *Spring* 26.
The Proud are taught to taste of pain, *Adv.* 6.
So York shall taste what Clouet never knew, *Shak.* 21.
lured . . . To taste of hollow kindness, *Agr.* 19.

Tastes.
And tastes it as it goes. *Vic.* 56.

Tattle.
they sing, they laugh, they tattle, *L. S.* 58.

Taught.
The Proud are taught to taste of pain, *Adv.* 6.
her that . . . taught his novice hand *Agr.* 30.
to Him . . . Who taught this vast machine *Prop.²* 17.

Teach.
Teach me to love and to forgive, *Adv.* 46.
That teach the rustic moralist to die. *El.* 84.
wrinkled beldams Teach it *Agr.* 136.
love could teach a monarch to be wise, *E. G.* 108.

Tea-cup.
Under a tea-cup he might lie, *L. S.* 67.

Team.
How jocund did they drive their team afield! *El.* 27.
a team of harness'd monarchs bend *Ign.* 38.

Tear.
The tear forgot as soon as shed, *Eton* 43.
mocks the tear it forc'd to flow; *Eton* 77.
Pity, dropping soft the sadly-pleasing tear. *Adv.* 32.
afford A tear to grace his obsequies. *Bard* 66.
He gave to Mis'ry all he had, a tear, *El.* 123.
you spied a tear stand in her eye, *Agr.* 10.
The social Smile, the sympathetic Tear. *E. G.* 37.
A sigh; an unavailing tear; *Clerke* 14.
while o'er the Place You drop the Tear, *Prop.³* 106.

Tear, vb.
These shall the fury Passions tear, *Eton* 61.
their flaxen tresses tear, And snowy veils, *Odin* 77.
and all his [he, Lett.⁴] scribbles, tear. *Shak.* 16.
†is to tear the closing wound. *Rond.* 32.

Tearest.
That tear'st the bowels of thy mangled Mate,
Bard 58.

Tears.
in the vale of tears beneath, *Eton* 81.
the sacred source of sympathetic Tears. *P. P.* 94.
From Cambria's curse, from Cambria's tears!
Bard 8.
Their tears, their little triumphs o'er, *Inst.* 48.
At once give loose to Utterance, and to Tears.
Dante 9.
if thou weep not now, Where are thy Tears?
Dante 48.

Tease.
Coarse panegyricks would but teaze her. *L. S.* 34.

Teaze. *See* **Tease.**

Teem.
The Soil, . . . will not teem in vain, *E. G.* 6.

Tell.
Ah, tell them, they are men! *Eton* 60.
a thousand strains Triumphant tell
Bard MS. 110.
Tell me what is done below, *Odin* 40.
Tell me, whence their sorrows rose: *Odin* 79.
Tell your master, His mother shall obey him.
Agr. 2.
tell him too, *Agr.* 88.
tell me! say *Agr.* 92.
Tell them, tho' 't is an awful thing to die,
Stanza 1.
— Sure Delia will tell me! *Am. Lines* 8.
When she died, I can't tell, *C. C.* 14.
nor Callimachus' enervate Strain May tell of
Jove, *Prop.*³ 56.
Sailors to tell of Winds and Seas delight,
*Prop.*³ 59.
†I tell her so in elegy. *Ode* 30.

Telling.
yet if the telling may Beget *Dante* 6.

Tells.
Ah, gallant youth! this marble tells the rest,
Williams 11.

Temper.
Another touch, another temper take, *E. G.* 79.
our master's temper natural Was fashion'd fair
Shak. 9.

Tempered.
Temper'd to thy warbled lay. *P. P.* 26.

Tempest.
raise A tempest that shall shake *Agr.* 91.
Then, with a tempest whirl, and wary eye,
*Stat.*² 8.

Tempestuous.
a River roll'd its flood Tempestuous, *Tasso* 8.

Tempt.
Ambition this shall tempt to rise, *Eton* 71.
To tempt the dangers of the doubtful way;
Tasso 2.

Tempts.
Not all that tempts [strikes, Whar.] *Cat* 40.
Nor tempts he yet the plain, *Stat.*¹ 45.

Tenacious.
tenacious of thy right divine, *Ign.* 15.
The orb on high tenacious of its course, *Stat.*² 10.

Tend.
Antium; there to tend Her household cares, *Agr.* 7.

Tender.
The tender for another's pain; *Eton* 93.
a glance . . . They send of tender sympathy
Inst. 20.
check their tender Hopes with . . . Fear, *E. G.* 20.

Tenderest.
Scatters his freshest, tenderest green. *Vic.* 8.

Tenet.
The Master of Benet Is of the like tenet;
Satire 28.

Tenfold.
Till *Lok* has burst his tenfold chain; *Odin* 90.

Tenor.
Learn the tenour of our song. *F. S.* 58.
the noiseless tenor of their way. *El.* 76.
the silent Tenour of thy Doom. *El.* Mas. 88.

Terrific.
Scared at thy frown terrific, *Adv.* 17.
terrific Maid, *F. S.* 17.

Terror.
The terror of his beak, *P. P.* 24.
Of Terror that, and thrilling Fears, *P. P.* MS. 93.

Terror's.
There Confusion, Terror's child, *Owen* 37.

Terrors.
Not in thy Gorgon terrors clad, *Adv.* 35.
What Terrors round him wait! *Bard* 60.
new terrors still to bring. *View* Nich. 12.
And calm'd the terrors of his claws in gold.
*Stat.*² 27.
The hissing terrors round Alecto's head,
*Prop.*² 42.

Tester.
And o'er the bed and tester clamber, *L. S.* 64.

Text.
many a holy text . . . she strews, *El.* 83.

Texture.
See the griesly texture grow! *F. S.* 9.

Thalia.
†Perhaps Thalia prompts a Sonnet *Ode* 35.

Thames.
Wanders the hoary Thames along *Eton* 9.
Say, father Thames, *Eton* 21.

Than.
More hideous than their Queen: *Eton* 84.
more to Innocence . . . Than Pow'r and Genius
El. Mas. 76.
no other lustre, than the blood Of . . . race,
Agr. 37.
pretensions Drowsier than theirs, *Agr.* 104.
More deadly . . . than is to me The cool inju-
rious *Agr.* 161.
Than thus be patch'd and cobbled in one's grave,
Shak. 20.

Far better scenes than these had blest our view,
View 19.
Tho' wiser than Nestor   *Ext. Keene* 2.
And fairer than Esther,   *Ext. Keene* 3.
Art it requires, and more than winged speed.
Tasso 30.

Thanks.
Thanks to the rosy queen Of amorous thefts:
Agr. 188.

That, omitted.

The, omitted.

Theatre's.
The theatre's green height and woody wall
Stat.² 14.

Theban.
That the Theban Eagle bear   *P. P.* 115.

Thebes.
Nor Tale of Thebes, nor Ilium   *Prop.³* 37.

Thee, omitted.

Thefts.
the rosy queen Of amorous thefts: *Agr.* 189.

Their, omitted.

Theirs.
Gay hope is theirs by fancy fed,   *Eton* 41.
Theirs buxom health   *Eton* 45.
pretensions Drowsier than theirs,   *Agr.* 104.
My struggling Sorrow, nor to heighten theirs:
Dante 69.

Them, omitted. See 'Em.

Then.
and then a claw,   *Cat* 20.
Then whirl the wretch from high,   *Eton* 72.
Then I leave thee to repose.   *Odin* 80.
then was the time To shrink from danger; *Agr.* 47.
fear might then have worn The mask *Agr.* 48.
Why then stays my sovereign,   *Agr.* 164.
Say then, . . . by what Fate confin'd *E. G.* 38.
Then he shambles and straddles so oddly —
C. C. 9.
Then his character, *Phyzzy,*   *C. C.* 13.
If then he wreak on me his wicked will, *Shak.* 13.
Then had we seen proud London's hated walls;
View 22.
Then thus the king: —   *Stat.¹* 1.
Then thus: *Stat.¹* 16.
Then grasp'd its weight,   *Stat.¹* 42.
Then, with a tempest whirl, and wary eye, *Stat.²* 8.
Then let me rightly spell of nature's ways;
Prop.² 15.
Then, while the vaulted Skies loud Ios rend,
Prop.³ 47.
When then my Fates   *Prop.³* 99.
Then to my quiet Urn awhile draw near,
Prop.³ 105.
then on my Children's Eyes . . . my Sight I
fix'd,   *Dante* 52.
for then Hunger had reft my Eye-sight *Dante* 78.
Then with unrelenting Eye   *Dante* 82.
†Then for a Moiety of the Year   *Ode* 41.
†to love, — and then to part,
Rond. 1, 9, 17, 25, 33.

†Then have left, to love anew: *Rond.* 7.
†Then to sever what is bound,   *Rond.* 31.
†Then one faint glimpse of Queen Elizabeth;
Ch. Cr. 10.
†then perches on the spray,   *Ch. Cr.* 41.

There.
Thy philosophic Train be there   *Adv.* 43.
There the Norman sails afar Catch the winds,
Owen 15.
There the thund'ring strokes begin, *Owen* 23.
There the press, and there the din; *Owen* 24.
Hasty, hasty Rout is there,   *Owen* 34.
There Confusion, Terror's child,   *Owen* 37.
There [Oft, Mas.] at the foot of yonder . . .
beech,   *El.* 101.
There scatter'd oft, the earliest of the Year,
El. Pem. 117 ; *Mas.* 137.
loves to build[,] and [&] warble there,
El. Pem. 119 ; *Mas.* 139.
There they alike in trembling hope repose,
El. 127.
His frailties there in trembling hope repose
El. Mas. 151.
The Huntingdons and Hattons there   *L. S.* 3.
A House there is, (and that's enough) *L. S.* 21.
that thereabouts there lurk'd . . . a Poet,
L. S. 43.
The Court was sate, the Culprit there, *L. S.* 97.
There sit the sainted sage, the bard divine,
Inst. 15.
And either Henry there,   *Inst.* 45.
Antium; there to tend Her household cares, *Agr.* 7.
at least there are who know   *Agr.* 15.
there will not want, . . . ears to own *Agr.* 122.
Soranus there, And Cassius;   *Agr.* 124.
a vain tradition, As there were magic in it?
Agr. 135.
there before His high tribunal   *Agr.* 143.
Seneca be there In gorgeous phrase   *Agr.* 148.
gloomy Sway have fix'd her Empire there,
E. G. 19.
There Industry and Gain their Vigils keep,
E. G. 42.
There languid Pleasure sighs in every Gale.
E. G. 45.
faith sincere, And soft humanity were there.
Clerke 6.
There first in blood his infant honour seal'd;
Williams 6.
There pipes the woodlark,   *Birds* 1.
the song-thrush there Scatters his loose notes
Birds 1.
'T was there he aim'd the meditated harm,
Stat.² 22.
The Po was there to see,   *Tasso* 55.
The diamond there attracts the wondrous sight,
Tasso 69.
There bloom the vernal rose's earliest pride;
Prop.² 10.
Nor Tale of Thebes, nor Ilium there should be,
Prop.³ 37.
And there the ensanguined Wave of Sicily,
Prop.³ 44.

Lanfranc there And Sigismundo,   *Dante* 32.
†See Israel, and all Judah thronging there.
           Ch. Cr. 28.

Thereabouts.
that thereabouts there lurk'd . . . a Poet,
           L. S. 43.

These.
These shall the fury Passions tear,   *Eton* 61.
Thine too these golden keys,   *P. P.* 91.
Dear, as the light that visits these sad eyes,
           Bard 40.
Long on these mould'ring bones   *Odin* 31.
What Virgins these, . . . That bend   *Odin* 75.
Nor you, ye Proud, impute to These the fault,
           El. 37.
If Memory to these no Trophies raise.
       El. Dods., Pem., Mas. 38.
these bones from insult to protect   *El.* 77.
in these lines their artless tale relate;
         El. 94 ; *Mas.* 78.
in these consecrated bowers,   *Inst.* 7.
And bad these awful fanes and turrets rise,
           Inst. 53.
much I hope these walls alone   *Agr.* 22.
These were your gift,   *Agr.* 80.
these, by ties confirm'd, Of old respect
           Agr. 113.
These hated walls that seem to mock   *Agr.* 156.
These Ears, alas! for other Notes repine,
           West 5.
A different object do these Eyes require: *West* 6.
Far better scenes than these had blest our view,
           View 19.
Ah! say, . . . how these symptoms befell me?
           Am. Lines 7.
These conscious shame withheld,   *Stat.*[1] 25.
When my changed head these locks no more shall
   know,   *Prop.*[2] 13.
These soft inglorious joys my hours engage;
           Prop.[2] 51.
These miserable Limbs with Flesh you cloath'd;
           Dante 67.
†But, my Dear, these Flies, they say,   *Ode* 49.

They, *omitted.*

Thick.
Where'er the oak's thick branches stretch
           Spring 11.

Thin.
If the thin Coan Web her Shape reveal, *Prop.*[3] 9.

Thine.
and Misery not thine own.   *Adv. MS.* 9.
Thine too these golden keys,   *P. P.* 91.
Be thine Despair, and scept'red Care, *Bard* 141.

Thing.
Tell them, tho' 't is an awful thing to die,
           Stanza 1.

Things.
things that but whisper'd Have arch'd *Agr.* 168.
The Master of King's Copies them in all things;
           Satire 18.
Great things and full of wonder . . . I shall unfold;   *Tasso* 35.

Think.
the Muse shall sit, and think   *Spring* 16.
Nor think to draw them from their dread abode,
           El. Mas. 146.
You think, you spied a tear   *Agr.* 10.
Think too how oft in weak . . . minds *Agr.* 72.
to think, what my poor Heart Foresaw, *Dante* 46.
†in vain you think to find them under E,
           Ch. Cr. 13.

Thinkest.
think'st thou, yon sanguine cloud,   *Bard* 135.

Thinks.
thinks to quench the fire   *Agr.* 84.

Third.
A third arose,   *Stat.*[1] 11.
Third in the labours of the disc come on,
           Stat.[2] 1.

Thirst.
Fell Thirst and Famine scowl   *Bard* 81.
Famine at feasts, and thirst amid the stream;
           Prop.[2] 47.
May the long Thirst of Tantalus allay, *Prop.*[3] 89.

Thirsty.
And drop'd his thirsty lance   *P. P.* 19.

This.
Ambition this shall tempt to rise,   *Eton* 71.
This racks the joints, this fires the veins,
           Eton 85.
This pencil take (she said),   *P. P.* 89.
This can unlock the gates of Joy;   *P. P.* 92.
Who is this, with voice unblest,   *Odin MS.* 35.
This the force of Eirin hiding,   *Owen* 11.
this pleasing anxious being   *El.* 86.
this long deserted shade.   *El. Mas.* 112.
By this time all the Parish know it   *L. S.* 42.
Welcome, . . . To this, thy kindred train, and
   me: *Inst.* 68.
her that arm'd This painted Jove,   *Agr.* 30.
This mighty emperor, this dreaded hero, *Agr.* 93.
to check this dangerous passion,   *Agr.* 106.
not to one in this benighted age   *Bent.* 17.
Ah, gallant youth! this marble tells the rest,
           Williams 11.
On this congenial spot he fix'd his choice;
           View 5.
Why this unavailing haste?   *Song* 8.
That to avoid, and this to emulate.   *Stat.*[2] 5.
Let on this head unfadeing flowers reside,
           Prop.[2] 9.
Who taught this vast machine   *Prop.*[2] 17.
How flames . . . Shall sink this beauteous fabric
           Prop.[2] 28.
And to this bosom give its wonted Peace,
           Prop.[3] 88.
Ruggieri, Pisa's perfidious Prelate this: *Dante* 14.
headed by this The deadliest.   *Dante* 34.
†So I to you this Trifle give,   *Ode* 53.

Tho'. *See* Though.

Thorn.
the stone beneath yon aged thorn.   *El.* 116.
And the buds that deck the thorn!   *Song* 4.

Thorny.

Boar . . . Wallows beneath the thorny shade.

Bard 94.

tost On the thorny bed of Pain,   *Vic.* 46.

Those.

The stings of Falshood those shall try, *Eton* 75.
Those in the deeper vitals rage: *Eton* 87.
Beneath those rugged elms,   *El.* 13.
the Masians too, and those of Egypt, *Agr.* 115.
unfriended, by those kindly Cares,   *E. G.* 10.
If realms beneath those fabled torments know,

*Prop.*² 39.

And half disclose those Limbs it should conceal;

*Prop.*³ 10.

Of those loose Curls, that Ivory front I write;

*Prop.*³ 11.

Thou, *omitted.*

Though.

tho' he inherit Nor the pride, nor ample pinion,

P. P. 113.

Tho' fann'd by Conquest's crimson wing *Bard* 3.
vain tho' kind enquiry   *El. Mas.* 111.
Tho' Pope and Spaniard could not trouble it.

L. S. 16.

though school'd . . . To bow the supple knee,

Agr. 100.

Though by me ye bled, He was the cause.

Agr. 180.

The Soil, tho' fertile, will not teem in vain,

E. G. 6.

And scatter with a free, though frugal, Hand

E. G. 17.

Though now a book, and interleaved you see.

Shak. 4.

And mariners, though shipwreck'd, dread to land.

View 8.

The Bishop of Chester, Tho' wiser than Nestor

Ext. Keene 2.

Tell them, tho' 't is an awful thing to die,

Stanza 1.

A vestment unadorn'd, though white as new-
fal'n Snows;   *Tasso* 14.
†But, tho' Flowers his ardour raise,   *Ode* 15.

Thought.

Thought would destroy their paradise. *Eton* 98.
Immersed in rapt'rous thought profound, *Adv.* 26.
My thought aches at him;   *Agr.* 160.
Spread the young Thought,   *E. G.* 12.
Unmanly Thought!   *E. G.* 72.
See, . . . each transitory thought   *Bent.* 5.
so was thought somewhat odd;   *Char.* 3.
†For one Silk-worm thought that thrives *Ode* 37.

Thoughtless.

The thoughtless day,   *Eton* 48.
Laughter, Noise and thoughtless Joy, *Adv.* 19.
The thoughtless World to Majesty may bow,

El. Mas. 73.

Thoughts. *See also* Poppy-thoughts.

thoughts, that breath, and words, that burn.

P. P. 110.

And Satan's self had thoughts of taking orders.

Toph. 8.

To Providence, to Him my thoughts I'd raise,

*Prop.*² 16.

†and thoughts Like Butterflies, their Prison shun

Ode 44.

Thousand.

A thousand rills their mazy progress take: *P. P.* 4.
From Cambria's thousand hills a thousand strains

Bard MS. 109.

Thousand Banners round him burn: *Owen* 32.
fire A thousand haughty hearts,   *Agr.* 17.
and thousand beauties see   *Prop.*³ 19.

Thracian.

So glittering shows the Thracian Godhead's
shield,   *Stat.*¹ 28.

Thracia's.

On Thracia's hills the Lord of War   *P. P.* 17.

Thrasea.

Vetus, too, and Thrasea,   *Agr.* 125.

Thread.

The thread is spun.   *Bard* 98.

Threat.

Move through the Sacred Way and vainly threat,

*Prop.*³ 52.

Threatening.

With thund'ring voice, and threat'ning mien,

Adv. 38.

Threats.

The threats of pain and ruin   *El.* 62.
waste the fruitless hours In threats unexecuted?

Agr. 155.

Three.

Squadrons three against him came; *Owen* 10.
where three sisters of old   *C. C.* 3.
my other three before my Eyes Died *Dante* 75.
for three days more I grop'd   *Dante* 77.

Threw.

And to small distance threw.   *Stat.*¹ 6.

Thrice.

Thrice he traced the runic rhyme; *Odin* 22.
Thrice pronounc'd, . . . The thrilling verse

Odin 23.

Thrice hath Hyperion roll'd his . . . race,

Ign. 11.

Thrice two hundred warriors go: *Hoel* 12.

Thrilling.

Of Horrour . . . and thrilling Fears, *P. P.* 93.
The thrilling verse that wakes the Dead: *Odin* 24.
the trumpet's thrilling voice,   *Agr.* 95.
warbles high His trembling thrilling ecstasy;

Vic. 14.

Thrives.

†For one Silk-worm thought that thrives *Ode* 37.

Thro'. *See* Through.

Throat.

The Attic warbler pours her throat, *Spring* 5.
His shaggy throat he open'd wide,   *Odin* 6.

Throbbing.

Horrour, Tyrant of the throbbing breast. *Bard* 130.
Horror . . . that chills the throbbing breast.

*Bard Lett.*² 130.

Throne.

The living Throne, the saphire-blaze, *P. P.* 99.
to wade through slaughter to a throne, *El.* 67.
Lethargic nods upon her ebon throne. *Ign.* 24.

Throng.

Bursting through the bloody throng *Hoel* 22.

Thronging.

†See Israel, and all Judah thronging there.
Ch. Cr. 28.

Through.

thro' the clear blue sky *Spring* 9.
how thro' the peopled air *Spring* 24.
flutter thro' life's little day, *Spring* 36.
Thro' richest purple *Cat* 17.
Thro' verdant vales, *P. P.* 9.
Thro' the azure deep of air: *P. P.* 117.
The shrieks of death, thro' Berkley's roofs that
ring, *Bard* 55.
thro' the kindred squadrons mow their way.
Bard 86.
Wading through th' ensanguin'd field, *F. S.* 30.
thro' each winding vale . . . the notes prolong.
F. S. 59.
through the long-drawn isle and fretted vault
El. 39.
to wade through slaughter *El.* 67.
thro' the cool sequester'd Vale of Life
El. Mas. 87.
thro' the church-way path *El.* 114.
Thro' lanes unknown, o'er stiles they ventur'd,
L. S. 54.
to shine Thro' every unborn age, *Inst.* 17.
Thro' the wild waves . . . Thy . . . course of
honour keep, *Inst.* 89.
Through various life I have pursued *Agr.* 54.
dews Lethean through the land dispense *Ign.* 17.
thro' Ages by what Fate confin'd *E. G.* 38.
through Zembla's snows? *E. G.* 77.
Bursting through the bloody throng *Hoel* 22.
Hosannas rung through hell's tremendous borders,
Toph. 7.
through the skies Sings in its rapid way, *Stat.*[1] 49.
Dismiss'd at length, they break through all delay
Tasso 1.
Through subterraneous passages they went,
Tasso 49.
Here gems break through the night *Tasso* 63.
Move through the Sacred Way and vainly threat,
Prop.[3] 52.
Thro' a small crevice opening, *Dante* 22.

Throw.

throw A melancholy grace; *Vic.* 31.
†but fickle throw my trains . . . into the Fire:
Ode 33.

Thrush. *See* **Song-thrush.**

Thunder.

With necks in thunder cloath'd, *P. P.* 106.

Thundering.

With thund'ring voice, and threat'ning mien,
Adv. 38.
Each her thundering faulchion wield; *F. S.* 62.
There the thund'ring strokes begin, *Owen* 23.

Thunder's.

As the thunder's fiery stroke, *Conan* 7.

Thus.

nor thus [here, MS.] forlorn *Bard* 101.
Who thus afflicts my troubled sprite, *Odin* 29.
And thus they speak in soft accord *Inst.* 55.
Thus ever grave and undisturb'd reflection
Agr. 82.
Thus far we 're safe. *Agr.* 188.
Not thus of old, with ensigns . . . unfurl'd,
Ign. 27.
Thus Etough look'd; *Toph.* 1.
Than thus be patch'd and cobbled in one's grave.
Shak. 20.
Then thus the King: — *Stat.*[1] 1.
Then thus: *Stat.*[1] 16.
His course he turn'd, and thus relieved their care:
Tasso 26.
You ask, why thus my Loves I still rehearse,
Prop.[3] 1.
thus Began. Would'st thou revive *Dante* 3.
whom thus I ceaseless gnaw insatiate; *Dante* 7.
†Thus to love, — and then to part — *Rond.* 33.
†Thus great R reigns in town, *Ch. Cr.* 53.

Thwart.

When thwart the road a River roll'd its flood
Tasso 7.

Thy, *omitted.*

Thyrsis.

Thyrsis, when we parted, swore *Song* 1.

Thyself.

with Reason and thyself at Strife, *El.* Mas. 85.

Tide. *See also* **Noon-tide, Torrent-tide.**

'midst the tide Two angel forms were seen
Cat 13.
Deep in the roaring tide he plung'd *Bard* 144.
wont to stem . . . the tide, *Agr.* 109.
Th' encroaching tide, that drowns her . . . lands,
E. G. 61.
rise and glitter o'er the ambient tide *E. G.* 107.
And sports and wantons o'er the frozen tide.
Tasso 22.

Ties.

these, by ties confirm'd, Of old respect *Agr.* 113.

Tiger's.

A tiger's pride the victor bore away, *Stat.*[2] 24.

Till.

Till down the eastern cliffs afar *P. P.* 52.
Till fierce Hyperion from afar *P. P.* MS. 52.
Till o'er the eastern cliffs from far
P. P. MS. 52.
Till the sad Nine in Greece's evil hour, *P. P.* 77.
Till full before his fearless eyes *Odin* 15.
Till from out the hollow ground *Odin* 25.
Till he on *Hoder's* corse shall smile *Odin* 69.
Till *Lok* has burst his tenfold chain; *Odin* 90.
till substantial Night Has reassum'd *Odin* 91.
Till wrapt in flames, in ruin hurl'd, *Odin* 93.
Till April starts, *Vic.* 5.
Till time shall every grief remove, *Clerke* 15.

Nor stopp'd till it had cut the further strand.
Stat.[1] 40.

Till a new Sun arose with weakly Gleam,
Dante 59.

†Till again the rolling Sun Bursts   *Ode* 43.

'Till.

†'Till they loved their love away;   *Rond.* 6.

Time.

What time, where lucid Avon stray'd, *P. P.* 85.
the flaming bounds of Place and Time: *P. P.* 98.
't is time to ride: *F. S.* Pem. 61.
page Rich with the spoils of time   *El.* 50.
By this time all the Parish know it   *L. S.* 42.
then was the time To shrink   *Agr.* 47.
'T is time to go, the sun is high   *Agr.* 158.
Till time shall every grief remove,   *Clerke* 15.
No — at our time of life 't would be silly, *C. C.* 10.
†But the genial Hand of Time   *Ode* 3.
†Some have lov'd, to pass the time,   *Rond.* 13.

Timely.

now the Hour Of timely Food approach'd;
Dante 50.

Times.

Eight times emerging from the flood   *Cat* 31.
The times are alter'd quite and clean! *L. S.* 136.
Oh! times for ever lost!   *Ign.* 31.
court the times With shows   *Agr.* 101.

Time-wearied.

slacken'd sinews of time-wearied age. *Agr.* 139.

Timid.

Carry to him thy timid counsels.   *Agr.* 87.

Timorous.

the tim'rous cloud That hangs on thy clear brow.
Agr. 193.

Tinge.

Howe'er Opinion tinge the . . . Mind, *E. G.* 27.

Tinklings.

drowsy tinklings lull the distant folds: *El.* 8.

Tints.

Chastised by sabler tints of woe;   *Vic.* 42.

Tip.

Brown sees thee sitting on his nose's tip,
Com. Lines 4.

Tip'd. See **Tipped.**

Tipped.

Cobham had . . . tip'd her arrows   *L. S.* 32.

Tires.

And what Bootes' lazy waggon tires; *Prop.*[2] 36.

Tissue.

weave . . . the tissue of thy line.   *Bard* 48.
Keep the tissue close and strong.   *F. S.* 16.

Tissues.

But rustling in their silks and tissues. *L. S.* 24.

Titles.

Her boasted Titles and her golden Fields;
E. G. 53.

Tityus'.

Scarce to nine acres Tityus' bulk confined,
Prop.[2] 43.

To, *omitted.*

To-day.

Nor care beyond to-day: *Eton* 54.
To-day the Lover walks,   *Prop.*[3] 96.

Together.

gems . . . Together dart their intermingled rays,
Bent. 23.

Toil.

Let not Ambition mock their useful toil, *El.* 29.
Heavier toil, superior pain.   *Inst.* 58.
various tracts enforce a various toil,   *E. G.* 86.
Vast, oh my friends, and difficult the toil
Tasso 27.
To paint the Hero's Toil,   *Prop.*[3] 33.

Toiling.

Still is the toiling hand of Care: *Spring* 21.

Toilsome.

He wound with toilsome march his long array.
Bard 12.

Told.

Had told, . . . there lurk'd . . . a Poet,
L. S. 43.
The prophet of Bethel, we read, told a lie:
C. C. 27.
†In pretty Dialogue I told   *Ode* 23.

Tolls.

The Curfew tolls the knell of parting day, *El.* 1.

Tom.

Nor cruel *Tom*, . . . heard.   *Cat* 35.

Tomb.

His Brother sends him to the tomb.   *Odin* 56.
To break the quiet of the tomb?   *Odin* 28.
If Mem'ry o'er their Tomb no Trophies raise,
El. 38.
from the tomb the voice of Nature cries, *El.* 91.
Charity, that glows beyond the tomb. *Inst.* 50.

To-morrow.

To-morrow he repairs the golden flood, *Bard* 137.
to-morrow is no more;   *Prop.*[3] 96.

Toned. See **Deep-toned.**

Tongue.

Cold is Cadwallo's tongue,   *Bard* 29.
with courtly tongue refin'd,   *Inst.* 82.
the frivolous tongue of giddy fame   *Agr.* 167.
Words that steal from my tongue, *Am. Lines* 6.
my Ear, Won by thy Tongue,   *Dante* 12.

Too.

sorrow never comes too late,   *Eton* 96.
happiness too swiftly flies,   *Eton* 97.
Thine Too these golden keys,   *P. P.* 91.
I well remember too (for I was present) *Agr.* 60.
Think too how oft in weak . . . minds *Agr.* 72.
benefits too great To be repaid,   *Agr.* 74.
the Masians too, and those of Egypt, *Agr.* 115.
Cassius; Vetus, too, and Thrasea,   *Agr.* 125.
Too poor for a bribe,   *Char.* 1.
too proud to importune;   *Char.* 1.
Too, too secure in youthful pride,   *Hoel* 5.
Before the Goddess' shrine we too, . . . bend,
Prop.[1] 2.

Thee too the Muse should consecrate to Fame,
                                        *Prop.*³ 53.
too soon they had aroused 'em   *Dante* 48.
†Maggots too will form and nourish;   *Ode* 16.
†For, too sure, they love not *well.*   *Rond.* 24.

Took.
Holland took the pious resolution *View* MS. 2.
And scorn'd repose when Britain took the field.
                                        Williams 8.
The Master of Pembroke Has from them his
   system took;   *Satire* 30.
he took his stand;   *Stat.*¹ 38.

Tooth.
Jealousy with rankling tooth,   *Eton* 66.

Topped. *See* **Cloud-topped.**

Torments.
If realms beneath those fabled torments know,
                                        *Prop.*² 39.

Torn.
lilies . . . From haughty Gallia torn, *Inst.* 40.

Torrent.
With torrent rapture, see it pour; *P. P.* MS. 11.

Torrent's.
Sighs to the torrent's aweful voice beneath!
                                        Bard 24.
the torrent's swift-descending flood,   *E. G.* 93.
Had I but the torrent's might,   *Hoel* 1.

Torrent-stream.
The torrent-stream his ancient bounds disdains,
                                        Tasso 9.

Torrent-tide.
Check'd by the torrent-tide of blood, *Owen* 27.

Torrid.
†Youth, his torrid Beams thay [that?] plays,
                                        Ode 13.

Tortoise.
Her coat, that with the tortoise vies, *Cat* 10.

Torturing.
Whose iron scourge and tort'ring hour *Adv.* 3.

Toss.
yon puny ball Let youngsters toss: *Stat.*¹ 20.
the nations . . . Their cymbals toss,   *Stat.*¹ 57.

Tossed.
tost On the thorny bed of Pain,   *Vic.* 45.

Touch.
Pain can touch the Sons of Heav'n! *Odin* MS. 48.
With damp, cold touch forbid it to aspire, *Ign.* 21.
Another touch, another temper take,   *E. G.* 79.
Fix'd by his touch a lasting essence take; *Bent.* 6.

Toward.
The river boil'd beneath, and rush'd toward the
   Main,   *Tasso* 24.

Towards.
I saw methought Towards Pisa's Mount,
                                        Dante 29.

Tower.
from yonder ivy-mantled tow'r   *El.* 9.
That grim and antique Tower admitted *Dante* 23.
The Tower of Famine hight,   *Dante* 24.

Towered.
Shew'd him where empire tower'd,   *Agr.* 46.

Towering.
By acclamations roused, came tow'ring on.
                                        *Stat.*¹ 14.

Towers.
ye antique towers,   *Eton* 1.
Ye [Grim, MS.] Towers of Julius, London's
   lasting shame,   *Bard* 87.
Ye gothic fanes, and antiquated towers, *Ign.* 2.
your arms shall rase the Tyrian towers, *Stat.*¹ 17.
It towers to cut the clouds;   *Stat.*¹ 49.

Town.
And all the town rings of his swearing and roaring!
                                        C. C. 16.
†Thus great R reigns in town,   *Ch. Cr.* 53.

Townshend.
But left church and state to Charles Townshend
                                        Char. 6.

Trace.
The paths of pleasure trace,   *Eton* 24.
The characters of hell to trace.   *Bard* 52.
in thy lineaments we trace A Tudor's fire,
                                        Inst. 69.
Smiles . . . Soft Reflection's hand can trace;
                                        Vic. 30.
trace Back to it's Source divine   *Prop.*³ 57.

Traced.
Thrice he traced the runic rhyme;   *Odin* 22.

Track.
Her track, . . . Glory pursue,   *P. P.* 63.
In yon bright track [clouds, MS.],   *Bard* 103.

Tracts.
various tracts enforce a various toil, *E. G.* 86.

Tradition.
Stung by a . . . vain tradition,   *Agr.* 134.

Tragic.
†Tragick Numbers, buskin'd Strains,   *Ode* 31.

Train. *See also* **Serpent-train.**
Fair Venus' train appear,   *Spring* 2.
black Misfortune's baleful train!   *Eton* 57.
Thy philosophic Train be there To soften,
                                        Adv. 43.
Disease, and Sorrow's weeping train, *P. P.* 44.
Welcome, . . . To this, thy kindred train,
                                        Inst. 68.
the train of pleasures   *Agr.* 78.
draws his humid train of mud: *Ign.* 4.
So from th' astonish'd stars, her nightly train,
                                        *Stat.*¹ 53.
Whate'er with copious train its channel fills,
                                        Tasso 53.
A train of mourning Friends attend his Pall,
                                        *Prop.*³ 97.
†Q draws her train along the Drawing-room,
                                        Ch. Cr. 50.

Train. *See* **Serpent-train.**   *Inst.* 8.

Trained.
to patient valour train'd They guard   *E. G.* 95.

Trains.

†but fickle throw my trains . . . into the Fire:
Ode 33.

Traitor.

sink the traitor in his mother's ruin.   Agr. 187.

Traitor's.

the telling may Beget the Traitour's Infamy,
Dante 7.

Trance.

Stout Glo'ster stood aghast in speechless trance:
Bard 13.

Forgetful of their wintry trance,   Vic. 11.

Or roused by sprightly sounds from out the trance,
Prop.² 5.

Transient.

Her rapid wings the transient scene pursue,
Ign. 34.

Transitory.

See, . . . each transitory thought   Bent. 5.

Transparent.

Transparent birdlime form'd the middle, L. S. 83.

Transport.

And give to transport   P. P. MS. 2.

What strains of vocal transport round her play.
Bard 120.

Rapt in celestial transport they: Inst. 18.

Traveller.

A Traveller, to thee unknown,   Odin 37.

no Traveller art thou, King of Men,   Odin 81.

Treachery.

that I was . . . by Treachery slain,   Dante 17.

Tread.

As the paths of fate we tread,   F. S. 29.

Nor doubt with me to tread the downward road
Tasso 37.

Treads.

Behind the steps that Misery treads,   Vic. 39.

Treasures.

The bee's collected treasures sweet,   Inst. 62.

Tree. See also Old-tree.

near his fav'rite tree;   El. 110.

No tree is heard to whisper,   View 10.

Tree's. See Yew-tree's.

Treeses.

†reclined beneath the Tree-zes;   Ode 22.

Tree-zes. See Treeses.

Tremble.

Where Angels tremble, while they gaze,
P. P. 100.

What strings symphonious tremble in the air,
Bard 119.

tremble at the phantom I have raised?   Agr. 86.

The theatre's green height and woody wall
Tremble   Stat.² 15.

Trembled.

how she turn'd pale and trembled;   Agr. 9.

Earl Goodwin trembled for his neighbouring sand;
View 6.

Trembling.

give to rapture all thy trembling strings. P. P. 2.

Shafts . . . Shoot the trembling cords along.
F. S. 14.

they alike in trembling hope repose,   El. 127.

The trembling family they daunt,   L. S. 57.

while he stood trembling,   Agr. 31.

o'er the trembling Nations from afar   E. G. 46.

warbles high His trembling thrilling ecstasy;
Vic. 14.

the champions, trembling at the sight, Prevent
disgrace,   Stat.¹ 22.

and in their trembling Flanks   Dante 39.

and rent his trembling Prey.   Dante 84.

Tremendous.

Hosannas rung through hell's tremendous borders,   Toph. 7.

Tresses.

their flaxen tresses tear, And snowy veils, Odin 77.

Tribe.

Shame of the versifying tribe!   L. S. 18.

Tribunal.

before His high tribunal thou and I   Agr. 144.

Tribute.

the passing tribute of a sigh.   El. 80.

The Fields to all their wonted Tribute bear;
West 11.

Sacred tribute of the bard,   Conan 3.

Tricks.

And filching and lying, and Newgate-bird tricks;
C. C. 17.

†P, Proteus-like all tricks, . . . can shew,
Ch. Cr. 43.

Tried.

His vigorous arm he tried before he flung, Stat.² 6.

Tries.

While to retain the envious Lawn she tries,
Prop.³ 23.

Trifle.

†So I to you this Trifle give,   Ode 53.

Trim.

Some shew their gayly-gilded trim   Spring 29.

In gallant trim the gilded Vessel goes; Bard 73.

Trinity.

The Master of Trinity To him bears affinity;
Satire 11.

As to Trinity Hall We say nothing at all. Satire 35.

Triple.

The triple dog that scares the shadowy kind,
Prop.² 44.

Triumph.

To triumph, and to die, are mine.   Bard 142.

Where they triumph, where they die.   F. S. 28.

Songs of joy and triumph sing!   F. S. 54.

Triumph to the younger King.   F. S. 56.

The laurell'd Triumph and the sculptured Carr;
Prop.³ 34.

Triumphant.

a thousand strains Triumphant tell
Bard MS. 110.

triumphant o'er the vanquish'd world;   Ign. 28.

Triumphs.
Their tears, their little triumphs o'er,   *Inst.* 48.

Trod.
I trod your level lawn,   *Inst.* 31.
yet the dread path once trod,   *Stanza* 2.
Against the stream the waves secure he trod,
     Tasso 15.
Nor how the Persian trod the indignant Sea;
     *Prop.*³ 38.

Trojan.
borne By the young Trojan to his . . . bark
     Agr. 196.

Troop.
A griesly troop are seen,   *Eton* 82.

Troops.
Now in circling troops they meet: *P. P.* 33.
On the first marching of the troops   *L. S.* 69.

Trophies.
If Mem'ry . . . no Trophies raise,   *El.* 38.

Trouble.
Tho' Pope and Spaniard could not trouble it.
     L. S. 16.

Troubled.
Stream'd, like a meteor, to the troubled air
     Bard 20.
Who thus afflicts my troubled sprite,   *Odin* 29.

Troy.
And hates the Tale of Troy   *Prop.*³ 74.

True.
'T is true, our master's temper natural Was
   fashion'd fair   *Shak.* 9.
"Ah!" said the sighing peer, "had Bute been true,
     View 17.
True to the mighty arm that gave it force,
     *Stat.*² 11.
†But, I wot, they loved not *true.*   *Rond.* 8.
†*True* to love, — and then to part,   *Rond.* 9.

Trump.
say we sound The trump of liberty;   *Agr.* 122.

Trumpet's.
the trumpet's thrilling voice,   *Agr.* 95.

Trust.
band, Who trust your arms   *Stat.*¹ 17.
That I did trust him, that I was betray'd
     Dante 16.

Trusting.
that I was betray'd By trusting,   *Dante* 17.

Trusts.
trusts her Blossoms to the churlish Skies. *E. G.* 8.

Truth.
To her they vow their truth,   *Adv.* 24.
Mirrors of Saxon truth and loyalty   *Bard* MS. 71.
Truth severe, by fairy Fiction drest.   *Bard* 127.
The struggling pangs of conscious truth   *El.* 69.
The Sparks of Truth and Happiness   *E. G.* 29.

Try.
The stings of Falshood those shall try,   *Eton* 75.
two youths advance, . . . to try the glorious
   chance;   *Stat.*¹ 10.
it be my Fate to try Another Love,   *Prop.*³ 69.

Tudor's.
in thy lineaments we trace A Tudor's fire,
     Inst. 70.

Tully.
Some mute inglorious Tully   *El.* Mas. 59.

Tumbled.
She tumbled headlong in.   *Cat* 30.

Tumult.
No Giant Race, no Tumult of the Skies,
     *Prop.*³ 35.

Tuneful.
How do your tuneful Echo's languish, *P. P.* 71.
Dear lost companions of my tuneful art, *Bard* 39.
In silent gaze the tuneful choir among, *Bent.* 1.

Tunes.
She tunes my easy Rhime,   *Prop.*³ 6.

Turbulent.
Where broad and turbulent it grows   *Vic.* 58.

Turf.
Whose turf, . . . Wanders the hoary Thames
   along   *Eton* 8.
Where heaves the turf in many a . . . heap,
     El. 14.

Turn.
Where his glowing eye-balls turn,   *Owen* 31.
To turn the torrent's . . . flood,   *E. G.* 92.
And all its jetty honours turn to snow; *Prop.*² 14.

Turned.
Decorum 's turn'd to mere civility;   *L. S.* 137.
how she turn'd pale and trembled: *Agr.* 9.
But may not honey's self be turn'd to gall
     Shak. 11.
His course he turn'd, and thus relieved their care:
     Tasso 26.
Askaunce he turn'd him,   *Dante* 83.

Turns.
Where'er she turns the Graces homage pay.
     P. P. 37.

Turrets.
And bad these awful fanes and turrets rise,
     Inst. 53.
Turrets and arches nodding to their fall,
     View 14.

Twenty.
†Twenty more in Embrio dye;   *Ode* 38.

Twice.
He once or twice had pen'd a sonnet; *L. S.* 125.

Twilight-gloom.
The Muse has broke the twilight-gloom
     P. P. 56.

'T will. *See also* **Will.**
't will profit you,   *Agr.* 12.

Twined.
Twined with her blushing foe,   *Bard* 92.

Twinkling. *See* **Many-twinkling.**

Twisted.
Helm, nor Hauberk's twisted mail,   *Bard* 5.
Better be twisted into caps for spice, *Shak.* 19.

Twitcher.
When sly Jemmy Twitcher had smugg'd up his
face, *C. C.* 1.
I 'll be Mrs. *Twitcher* myself. *C. C.* 32.

Twittering.
The swallow twitt'ring from the straw-built shed,
El. 18.

Two.
Two angel forms were seen to glide, *Cat* 14.
Two Coursers of ethereal race, *P. P.* 105.
Thrice two hundred warriors go: *Hoel* 12.
As the Master of Keys Is as like as two pease,
Satire 14.
So the Master of Queen's Is as like as two beans;
Satire 16.
The love of honour bade two youths advance,
Stat.[1] 9.
All but two youths th' enormous orb decline,
Stat.[1] 24.

'Twould. *See also* **Would.**
't would dash his joy *Agr.* 13.
— at our time of life 't would be silly, *C. C.* 10.

Tyrant.
Nor even thy virtues, Tyrant, shall avail
Bard 6.
Horrour, Tyrant of the throbbing breast.
Bard 130.
The little Tyrant of his fields *El.* 58.
Yet would the Tyrant Love permit me raise
Prop.[3] 31.

Tyrant-power.
Alike they scorn the pomp of tyrant-Power,
P. P. 79.

Tyrants.
And purple Tyrants vainly groan *Adv.* 7.

Tyrian.
Their scaly armour's Tyrian hue *Cat* 16.
your arms shall rase the Tyrian towers,
Stat.[1] 17.

Ugolino.
Know, thou seest In me Count Ugolino,
Dante 13.

Ulysses.
And scarce Ulysses scap'd his giant arm.
Stat.[2] 23.

Umbrageous.
Fast by th' umbrageous vale lull'd to repose,
Prop.[2] 3.

Unaccustomed.
Nor I with unaccustom'd Vigour trace *Prop.*[3] 57.

Unadorned.
low as his feet there flows A vestment unadorn'd,
Tasso 14.

Unavailing.
Ye unavailing horrors, fruitless crimes! *Agr.* 177.
A sigh; an unavailing tear; *Clerke* 14.
Why this unavailing haste? *Song* 8.

Unblessed.
Leave me unbless'd, unpitied, here to mourn:
Bard 102.

with voice unblest, That calls me *Odin* 35.

Unborn.
unborn Ages, crowd not on my soul! *Bard* 108.
to shine Thro' every unborn age, *Inst.* 17.

Unborrowed.
With orient hues, unborrow'd of the Sun:
P. P. 120.

Uncertain.
The uncertain Crescent gleams a sickly light.
Tasso 48.

Unclose.
Unwilling I my lips unclose: *Odin* 49.

Unclouded.
equal Justice with unclouded Face *E. G.* 15.

Uncompleated. *See* **Uncompleted.**

Uncompleted.
But yet in low and uncompleated Sounds
Dante 44.

Unconquerable.
Th' unconquerable Mind, *P. P.* 65.

Uncouth.
With uncouth rhimes and shapeless sculpture
El. 79.

Undaunted.
A heart that . . . will mount undaunted, *Agr.* 52.
With eyes of flame, and cool undaunted breast,
Williams 9.

Undeceived.
From hence, ye Beauties, undeceiv'd, *Cat* 37.

Under.
Under a tea-cup he might lie, *L. S.* 67.
Have his limbs Sweat under iron harness?
Agr. 97.
Under the warlike Corbulo, *Agr.* 112.
†In vain you think to find them under E,
Ch. Cr. 13.

Underneath.
The Muses, . . . Convey'd him underneath
their hoops *L. S.* 71.

Undertook.
The Heroines undertook the task, *L. S.* 53.

Undigested.
And embryon metals undigested glow, *Tasso* 58.

Undiscovered.
to shine thro' every . . . undiscover'd clime.
Inst. 17.
who can probe the undiscover'd Wound?
Prop.[3] 92.

Undisturbed.
grave and undisturb'd reflection *Agr.* 82.

Unequal.
Young Pterelas with strength unequal drew,
Stat.[1] 5.

Unerring.
could they catch . . . his unerring line; *Bent.* 14.
Sure flew the disc from his unerring hand,
Stat.[1] 39.

Unexecuted.
waste the . . . hours In threats unexecuted?
Agr. 155.

Unfading.
Let on this head unfadeing flowers reside, *Prop.*[2] 9.

Unfathomed.
The dark unfathom'd caves of ocean   *El.* 54.

Unfeeling.
Th' unfeeling for his own.   *Eton* 94.

Unfelt.
Tyrants vainly groan With pangs unfelt before,
       Adv. 8.

Unfold.
Great things . . . in your ears I shall unfold ;
       Tasso 36.
The Bitterness of Death, I shall unfold.
       Dante 20.

Unformed.
Unform'd, unfriended, by those . . . Cares,
       E. G. 10.

Unfriended.
Unform'd, unfriended, by those . . . Cares,
       E. G. 10.

Unfurled.
with ensigns wide unfurl'd, She rode   *Ign.* 27.

Ungrateful.
power he has to be ungrateful.   *Agr.* 81.
we may meet, ungrateful boy, we may! *Agr.* 140.

Unguarded.
unguarded and without a lictor,   *Agr.* 5.

Unhappy.
they wept, unhappy Boys!   *Dante* 54.

Unheeded.
thy judging eye, The flow'r unheeded shall descry,   *Inst.* 72.
And scornful flung th' unheeded weight *Stat.*[1] 21.

Unhonored.
mindful of th' unhonour'd Dead, *El.* 93; *Mas.* 77.

Unhonoured.   *See* **Unhonored.**

Unite.
In one rich mass unite the precious store,
       Tasso 61.

Universal.
That first, eternal, universal Cause;   *Prop.*[2] 18.

Unkindness'.
hard Unkindness' alter'd eye,   *Eton* 76.

Unknown.
And unknown regions dare descry: *Eton* 37.
What call unknown, what charms presume
       Odin 27.
A Traveller, To thee unknown,   *Odin* 37.
to Fortune and to Fame unknown.   *El.* 118.
Thro' lanes unknown, o'er stiles they ventur'd,
       L. S. 54.
he liv'd unknown To fame, or fortune, *Agr.* 39.
Oceans unknown, inhospitable Sands! *Tasso* 32.
Happy the Youth, and not unknown to Fame,
       Prop.[3] 65.
To thee and all unknown   *Dante* 19.

Unlettered.
their years, spelt by th' unletter'd muse, *El.* 81.

Unlock.
This can unlock the gates of Joy;   *P. P.* 92.

Unmanly.
Unmanly Thought!   *E. G.* 72.

Unpeopled.
Unpeopled monast'ries delude our eyes, *View* 15.

Unpitied.
purple Tyrants . . . unpitied and alone. *Adv.* 8.
Leave me unbless'd, unpitied, here to mourn:
       Bard 102.

Unpledged.
they are aware Of th' unpledg'd bowl, *Agr.* 21.

Unquenchable.
How shall the spark Unquenchable, . . . blaze
       Agr. 129.

Unrelenting.
with unrelenting fangs, That tear'st   *Bard* 57.
Then with unrelenting Eye   *Dante* 82.

Unrequited.
benefits . . As unrequited wrongs.   *Agr.* 76.

Unresisted.
nations own'd her unresisted might,   *Ign.* 29.

Unriddle.
The words too eager to unriddle,   *L. S.* 81.

Unroll.
solemn scenes . . . their glitt'ring skirts unroll?
       Bard 106.
Knowledge . . . her ample page . . . did ne'er
unroll;   *El.* 50.

Unseen.
many a flower is born to blush unseen,   *El.* 55.
There scatter'd oft, . . . By Hands unseen
       El. Pem. 118; *Mas.* 138.
For Ills unseen what Remedy is found? *Prop.*[3] 91.

Untaught.
The untaught harmony of spring: *Spring* 7.

Unthought.
Th' unthought event disclose a whiter meaning.
       Agr. 71.

Untimely.
from an untimely grave.   *Clerke MS.* 12.
Idle notes! untimely green!   *. Song* 7.

Unto, *omitted.*

Unuttered.
The Anguish, that unutter'd nathless wrings
       Dante 5.

Unused.
hearts, unus'd to shake When a boy frowns,
       Agr. 17.

Unveil.
To Him the mighty Mother did unveil *P. P.* 86.

Unwearied.
where unwearied sinews must be found *E. G.* 90.

Unwilling.
Unwilling I my lips unclose: *Odin* 49.
tame th' unwilling Deep.   *E. G.* 43.

Up, *omitted.*

Upheaved.
Another orb upheaved his strong right hand,
Stat.[1] 15.

Upland.
meet the sun upon the upland lawn. *El.* 100.

Upon, *omitted.*

Uprear.
from the dust uprear his reverend head, *Agr.* 142.

Upright.
but hurl'd upright, Emits the mass, *Stat.*[1] 45.

Uprose.
Uprose the King of Men with speed, *Odin* 1.

Upstairs. *See* **Stairs.**

Upward.
'Twas the Lark that upward sprung! *Song* 5.

Urge.
Or urge the flying ball? *Eton* 30.
Years of havock urge their destined course,
Bard 85.
And all that *Groom* could urge against him.
L. S. 116.

Urien.
Brave Urien sleeps upon his craggy bed: *Bard* 31.

Urn.
Scatters from her pictur'd urn *P. P.* 109.
Can storied urn or animated bust *El.* 41.
Then to my quiet Urn awhile draw near,
Prop.[3] 105.

Us, *omitted.*

Used.
rhymes that us'd to linger on, *Bent.* 9.

Useful.
mock their useful [rustic, Mas.] toil, *El.* 29.

Usurper's.
spare the meek Usurper's holy head. *Bard* 90.

Utterance.
At once give loose to Utterance, and to Tears.
Dante 9.

Vain.
How vain the ardour of the Crowd, *Spring* 18.
She stretch'd in vain *Cat* 22.
Ah, fields belov'd in vain, *Eton* 12.
By vain Prosperity received, *Adv.* 23.
has he giv'n in vain the heav'nly Muse? *P. P.* 48.
Mountains, ye mourn in vain *Bard* 32.
with vain tho' kind enquiry *El. Mas.* 110.
Stung by . . . a vain tradition, *Agr.* 134.
penitence, and vain remorse, *Agr.* 179.
In vain the smileing Mornings shine, *West* 1.
The Birds in vain their amorous Descant joyn;
West 3.
I . . . weep the more because I weep in vain.
West 14.
The Soil, . . . will not teem in vain, *E. G.* 6.
draw Mankind in vain the vital Airs, *E. G.* 9.
Nor Mungo's, Rigby's, Bradshaw's friendship
vain, *View* 18.
Nor B—d's promises been vain, *View* Nich. 18.

In vain the nations with officious fear Their
cymbals toss, *Stat.*[1] 56.
Here Arts are vain, *Prop.*[3] 85.
imploreing In vain my Help, *Dante* 74.
†In vain you think to find them under E,
Ch. Cr. 13.

Vainly.
purple Tyrants vainly groan *Adv.* 7.
meaner Beauties . . . vainly ape her art
L. S. 28.
Move through the Sacred Way and vainly threat,
Prop.[3] 52.
†Vainly enamelling the Green. *Ode* 18.

Vale.
in the vale of years beneath *Eton* 81.
thro' each winding vale . . . the notes prolong.
F. S. 59.
the cool sequester'd vale of life *El.* 75.
The meanest flowret of the vale, *Vic.* 49.
Along the lonely vale of days? *Clerke* 12.
To Cattraeth's vale . . . Thrice two hundred
warriors go: *Hoel* 11.
But none from Cattraeth's vale return, *Hoel* 20.
Fast by th' umbrageous vale lull'd to repose,
Prop.[2] 3.

Vales.
Thro' verdant vales, *P. P.* 9.
Insult the plenty of the vales below? *E. G.* 99.
While vales and woods and echoing hills rebound.
Stat.[2] 17.

Valor.
to patient valour train'd They guard *E. G.* 94.

Valour. *See* **Valor.**

Van.
Amazement in his van, . . . and solitude behind.
Bard 61.

Vane.
Here lives Harry Vane *Impr. Vane* 1.

Vanish.
They melt, they vanish from my eyes. *Bard* 104.

Vanquished.
triumphant o'er the vanquish'd world; *Ign.* 28.

Varied.
Opinion tinge the varied Mind, *E. G.* 27.

Variegated.
†And variegated Fancy's seen *Ode* 17.

Various.
Through various life I have pursued *Agr.* 54.
As various tracts enforce a various toil, *E. G.* 86.
What length of sea remains, what various lands,
Tasso 31.
All stones : . . mix attemper'd in a various day;
Tasso 66.

Varying.
In fortune's varying colours drest: *Spring* 37.

Vase's.
'Twas on a lofty vase's side, *Cat* 1.

Vast.
How vast the debt of gratitude *Agr.* 57.
Vast, oh my friends, and difficult the toil *Tasso* 27.
Who taught this vast machine *Prop.*[2] 17.

Vault.

through the long-drawn isle and fretted vault
El. 39.

Vaulted.

Then, while the vaulted Skies loud Ios rend,
*Prop.*³ 47.

Veil.

clouds of carnage veil the sun. *F. S. Whar.* 50.
Oped the dark Veil of Fate. *Dante* 28.

Veiled.

they . . . veil'd their weapons bright and keen
L. S. 39.

Veils.

snowy veils, that float in air. *Odin* 78.

Veins.

this fires the veins, *Eton* 85.
fill their verdant Veins. *E. G.* 4.
Sulphureous veins and liveing silver shine,
Tasso 59.

Velvet.

The velvet of her paws, *Cat* 9.

Velvet-green.

O'er Idalia's velvet-green *P. P.* 27.

Venal.

she . . . no venal incense flings; *Inst.* 79.
Old, and abandon'd by each venal friend,
View 1.

Venerable.

Foremost . . . The venerable Marg'ret see!
Inst. 66.

Vengeance.

Stamp we our vengeance deep, *Bard* 96.
In lieu of penitence, . . . Accept my vengeance.
Agr. 180.

Vengeful.

Not circled with the vengeful Band *Adv.* 36.

Ventured.

Thro' lanes unknown, o'er stiles they ventur'd,
L. S. 54.

Venus'.

Fair Venus' train appear, *Spring* 2.

Verdant.

Thro' verdant vales, *P. P.* 9.
fill their verdant Veins. *E. G.* 4.
Here the soft emerald smiles of verdant hue,
Tasso 67.

Verdure.

From his broad bosom life and verdure flings
E. G. 102.

Verge.

The slipp'ry verge her feet beguil'd, *Cat* 29.
Give ample room, and verge enough *Bard* 51.

Vermeil-cheek.

With vermeil-cheek . . . She woo's the tardy
spring: *Vic.* 3.

Vernal.

Richly paint the vernal year: *P. P.* 90.
Sweet is the breath of vernal shower, *Inst.* 61.
blast the vernal Promise of the Year. *E. G.* 21.
There bloom the vernal rose's earliest pride;
*Prop.*² 10.

Verse.

The verse adorn again Fierce War, *Bard* 125.
The thrilling verse that wakes the Dead; *Odin* 24.
Build to him the lofty verse, *Conan* 2.
Verse, the hero's sole reward. *Conan* 4.
Whence the soft Strain and ever-melting Verse?
*Prop.*³ 2.
No Mountain-Structures in my Verse should rise,
*Prop.*³ 36.
A milder Warfare I in Verse display; *Prop.*³ 61.
A little Verse my All that shall remain;
*Prop.*³ 101.
†If heroïc Verse I 'm reading *Ode* 26.

Versifying.

Shame of the versifying tribe! *L. S.* 18.

Very.

What, in the very first beginning! *L. S.* 17.
The very power he has *Agr.* 81.
No very great wit, *Char.* 4.
Very good claret and fine Champaign.
Impr. Vane 2.

Vessel.

In gallant trim the gilded Vessel goes; *Bard* 73.
And parting surges round the vessel roar;
*Stat.*² 21.

Vestment.

low as his feet there flows A vestment unadorn'd,
Tasso 14.

Vetus.

Vetus too, and Thrasea, *Agr.* 125.

Vice.

Vice, that revels in her chains. *P. P.* 80.

Victim.

the Victim of her Scorn, *Prop.*³ 77.

Victims.

The little victims play! *Eton* 52.
ye manes of ambition's victims, *Agr.* 174.

Victor.

Mighty Victor, mighty Lord! *Bard* 63.
Victor he stood on Bellisle's rocky steeps —
Williams 10.
A tiger's pride the victor bore away, *Stat.*² 24.

Victorious.

Joy to the victorious bands; *F. S.* 55.

Victor's.

to sound the Victor's Praise, *Prop.*³ 32.

Victors.

fair befall the victors. *Agr.* 153.

Victory.

'T is the woof of victory. *F. S.* 20.
The orb . . . joys to see Its ancient lord secure
of victory. *Stat.*² 13.

Vies.

Her coat, that with the tortoise vies, *Cat* 10.

View.

To the view . . . Betray'd a golden gleam, *Cat* 17.
Your helpless, old, expiring master view!
Bard MS. 72.
bring the buried ages back to view. *Ign.* 35.
Approaching Comfort view: *Vic.* 40.

Nor envy dar'd to view him with a frown.
Williams 4.
Far better scenes than these had blest our view,
View 19.
Pisa's Mount, that intercepts the View Of Lucca,
Dante 29.
†See Isaac, Joseph, Jacob, pass in view;
Ch. Cr. 26.
†And brings all Womankind before your view;
Ch. Cr. 59.

Viewed.
Of many a flood they view'd the secret source,
Tasso 51.

Vigils.
Industry and Gain their Vigils keep,   *E. G.* 42.

Vigor.
And lively chear of vigour born;   *Eton* 47.
Cares, That Health and Vigour . . . impart,
E. G. 11.
See the Wretch, . . . At length repair his vigour
lost,   *Vic.* 47.
Nor I with unaccustom'd Vigour trace *Prop.*³ 57.

Vigorous.
His vigorous arm he tried before he flung,
*Stat.*² 6.
vigorous he seem'd in years,   *Tasso* 12.

Vigour. *See* **Vigor.**

Village-Cato.
Some Village-Cato,   *El.* Mas. 57.

Village-Hampden.
Some village-Hampden [-Hambden, Pem.] *El.* 57.

Village-maid.
Swift shoots the Village-maid in rustic play
Tasso 19.

Vindicate.
Redeem, what Crassus lost, and vindicate his
name.   *Prop.*² 54.

Vintage.
quaff the pendent Vintage as it grows.   *E. G.* 57.

Violet.
Ah! what means yon violet flower!   *Song* 3.

Violets.
Scatter'd oft . . . are Show'rs of Violets
El. Pem. 118; Mas. 138.

Virgin-grace.
Attemper'd sweet to virgin-grace.   *Bard* 118.

Virgins.
What Virgins these, . . . That bend to earth
their solemn brow,   *Odin* 75.

Virtue.
thy Sire to send on earth Virtue, . . . design'd,
Adv. 10.
Must sick'ning virtue fly the tainted ground?
E. G. 71.

Virtues.
Nor even thy virtues, Tyrant, shall avail *Bard* 6.
nor circumscrib'd alone Their growing virtues,
El. 66.
within whose sacred cell The peaceful virtues . . .
dwell.   *Clerke* 4.

Visage.
Nor wash his visage in the stream,   *Odin* 67.

Visaged. *See* **Grim-visaged.**

Visages.
Sour visages, enough to scare ye,   *L. S.* 106.

Viscountess.
Why, what can the Viscountess mean? *L. S.* 134.

Visionary.
Before his visionary eyes would run.
P. P. MS. 118.

Visions.
Visions of glory, spare my aching sight, *Bard* 107.

Visits.
Dear, as the light that visits these sad eyes,
Bard 40.

Vital.
draw Mankind in vain the vital Airs,   *E. G.* 9.

Vitals.
Those in the deeper vitals rage: *Eton* 87.

Vivid.
All stones of lustre shoot their vivid ray,
Tasso 65.
What colours paint the vivid arch of Jove;
*Prop.*² 29.

Vocal.
Vocal no more, since Cambria's fatal day,
Bard 27.
What strains of vocal transport round her play.
Bard 120.

Voice.
They hear a voice   *Eton* 39.
With thund'ring voice, and threat'ning mien,
Adv. 38.
Thee the voice, the dance, obey,   *P. P.* 25.
but to the voice of Anguish?   *P. P.* 72.
Sighs to the torrent's aweful voice beneath!
Bard 24.
A Voice, . . . Gales from blooming Eden bear;
Bard 131.
What voice unknown,   *Odin* MS. 27.
Who is he [this, Whar.], with voice unblest,
That calls me   *Odin* 35.
Can Honour's voice provoke the silent dust?
El. 43.
from the tomb the voice of Nature cries, *El.* 91.
sweeter yet The still small voice of gratitude.
Inst. 64.
While spirits . . . Join with glad voice *Inst.* 88.
the trumpet's thrilling voice,   *Agr.* 95.
ears to own Her spirit-stirring voice;   *Agr.* 124.
If . . . my voice ye hear,   *Agr.* 178.
permit me raise My feeble Voice,   *Prop.*³ 32.

Volumes.
Of the dear Web whole Volumes I indite:
*Prop.*³ 12.

Voluntary.
obsequious vows From voluntary realms,
Agr. 36.
At Aix, his voluntary sword he drew,
Williams 5.

Votaries.
we too, love's vot'ries, bend, *Prop.*[1] 2.

Vow.
To her they vow their truth, *Adv.* 24.

Vows.
obsequious vows From voluntary realms, *Agr.* 35.

Vulgar.
Beyond the limits of a vulgar fate, *P. P.* 122.
she No vulgar praise, . . . flings, *Inst.* 79.

Vulture.
Or drive the infernal Vulture *Prop.*[3] 90.

Vultures.
The vulturs of the mind, *Eton* 62.

Vulturs. *See* **Vultures.**

W.
†So big with Weddings, waddles W, *Ch. Cr.* 58.

Waddles.
†So big with Weddings, waddles W, *Ch. Cr.* 58.

Wade.
Forbad to wade through slaughter *El.* 67.

Wading.
Wading through th' ensanguin'd field, *F. S.* 30.

Wage.
Wars . . . with Cynthia let me wage. *Prop.*[1] 4.

Waggon. *See* **Wagon.**

Wagon.
And what Bootes' lazy waggon tires; *Prop.*[2] 36.

Wail.
I heard 'em wail for Bread. *Dante* 45.

Wait.
Yet see how all around 'em wait *Eton* 55.
Confusion on thy banners wait, *Bard* 2.
What Terrors round him wait! *Bard* 60.
pleasures That wait on youth, *Agr.* 79.
†Queer Queensbury only does refuse to wait.
Ch. Cr. 52.

Waits.
Lo! Granta waits to lead her blooming band,
Inst. 77.

Wake.
And wake the purple year! *Spring* 4.
Awake, my lyre: my glory, wake, *P. P.* MS. 1.
No more shall wake them from their lowly Bed.
El. Dods. 20.
might serve belike to wake pretensions *Agr.* 103.

Waked.
Hands, that . . . wak'd to extasy the living lyre.
El. 48.

Wakeful.
the dazzled sight Of wakeful jealousy.
Agr. 192.

Wakes.
what daring Spirit Wakes thee now? *P. P.* 113.
The thrilling verse that wakes the Dead:
Odin 24.
Bright Rapture wakes, *Bard Lett.*[2] 123.

Waking.
DIVINITY heard, between waking and dozing,
C. C. 19.

Walk.
Nor Envy . . . Dare the Muse's walk to stain,
Inst. 10.
And breathe and walk again: *Vic.* 48.

Walks.
linger in the gloomy Walks of Fate: *El. Mas.* 80.
the spirit of Britannicus Yet walks on earth:
Agr. 15.
To-day the Lover walks, *Prop.*[3] 96.

Wall.
The theatre's green height and woody wall
Tremble *Stat.*[2] 14.

Wallows.
Boar . . . Wallows beneath the thorny shade.
Bard 94.

Walls.
from Pomfret's walls shalt send *Bard Lett.*[1] 75.
within the spatious walls, . . . he . . . led the
Brawls; *L. S.* 9.
much I hope these walls alone *Agr.* 22.
hated walls that seem to mock my shame,
Agr. 156.
Then had we seen proud London's hated walls;
View 22.
And batter Cadmus' walls with stony showers,
Stat.[1] 18.
Whose walls along the neighbouring Sea extend,
Tasso 4.
†The walls of old Jerusalem appear, *Ch. Cr.* 27.

Wan. *See also* **Woeful-wan.**
Envy wan, and faded Care, *Eton* 68.
Her Spectres wan, and Birds of boding cry,
P. P. 50.
drooping, woeful wan, like one forlorn,
El. Dods. 107.
with weakly Gleam, And wan, *Dante* 60.

Wandering.
Not all that tempts your wand'ring eyes *Cat* 40.
wand'ring near her secret bow'r, *El.* 11.

Wanders.
Wanders the hoary Thames along *Eton* 9.

Waning.
That monthly waning hides her paly fires,
Prop.[2] 20.

Want.
there will not want, . . . ears to own *Agr.* 122.
The rough abode of want and liberty, *E. G.* 97.

Wanted.
†Still to ripen 'em is wanted; *Ode* 4.

Wanton.
had her wanton son Lent us his wings, *Agr.* 189.

Wantonness.
†With Woe behind, and Wantonness before.
Ch. Cr. 61.

Wantons.
The gilded swarm that wantons *Agr.* 147.
And sports and wantons o'er the frozen tide.
Tasso 22.

Wants.

Their little wants, their low desires refine,
E. G. 82.

War.

on Thracia's hills the Lord of War   *P. P.* 17.
glitt'ring shafts of war.   *P. P.* 53; *MS.* 52.
Fierce War, and faithful Love,   *Bard* 126.
Weave the crimson web of war   *F. S.* 25, 36.
Norman sails afar . . . join the war: *Owen* 16.
He heard the distant din of war.   *L. S.* 76.
the glittering front of war?   *Agr.* 94.
Scythia breath'd the living Cloud of War;
E. G. 47.
steel our hearts to war?   *E. G.* 69.
And, clash'd, rebellious with the din of war.
Stat.[1] 31.
the cloudy Magazines maintain Their wintry war,
Prop.[2] 26.
To paint . . . the Ranks of War,   *Prop.*[3] 33.
and send again to War;   *Prop.*[3] 82.

Warble.

The Red-breast loves to build[,] and [&] warble
there,   *El. Pem.* 119; *Mas.* 139.

Warbled.

Temper'd to thy warbled lay.   *P. P.* 26.

Warbler.

The Attic warbler pours her throat,   *Spring* 5.

Warbles.

But chief, the Sky-lark warbles high   *Vic.* 13.
Where Aganippe warbles as it flows;   *Prop.*[2] 4.

Warblings.

distant warblings lessen on my ear,   *Bard* 133.
as the choral warblings round him swell,   *Inst.* 24.

Warfare.

A milder Warfare I in Verse display;   *Prop.*[3] 61.

Warlike.

Under the warlike Corbulo,   *Agr.* 112.
Where fix'd in wonder stood the warlike pair,
Tasso 25.
Ye Argive flower, ye warlike band,   *Stat.*[1] 16.

Warm.

Warm Charity, the gen'ral Friend,   *Adv.* 30.
O'er her warm cheek, and rising bosom,
P. P. 40.
Dear, as the ruddy drops that warm my heart,
Bard 41.
Left the warm precincts of the . . . day, *El.* 87.
To warm their little Loves the Birds complain:
West 12.
warm the opening Heart.   *E. G.* 12.
Affection warm, and faith sincere, . . . were there.
Clerke 5.
Suspends the crowd with expectation warm;
Stat.[1] 44.
Which soon the parent sun's warm powers refine,
Tasso 60.

Warms.

warms the nations with redoubled ray. *Bard* 138.

Warmth.

Nor genial Warmth, nor genial Juice   *E. G.* 3.

Warned.

By Phlegyas warn'd, and fir'd by Mnestheus' fate,
Stat.[2] 4.

Warp.

Weave the warp, and weave the woof,   *Bard* 49.
the loom, Where the dusky warp we strain, *F. S.* 6.

Warrior.

Is the sable Warrior fled?   *Bard* 67.

Warrior's.

Each a gasping Warriour's head.   *F. S.* 12.
he that calls, a Warriour's Son.   *Odin* 38.
Every warrior's manly neck Chains of regal
honour deck,   *Hoel* 13.

Warriors.

Prostrate warriors gnaw the ground.   *Owen* 30.
issues A brace of Warriors, not in buff,
L. S. 23.
Thrice two hundred warriors go: *Hoel* 12.

Warriors'.

before the warriors' eyes . . . the waves disparted rise;   *Tasso* 39.

Wars.

Wars hand to hand with Cynthia let me wage.
Prop.[1] 4.

Wary.

Then, with a tempest whirl, and wary eye,
Stat.[2] 8.

Was, *omitted.*

Wash. *See also* White-wash.

Nor wash his visage in the stream,   *Odin* 67.

Waste.

pineing Love shall waste their youth,   *Eton* 65.
waste its sweetness on the desert air.   *El.* 56.
why do I waste the fruitless hours   *Agr.* 154.
song-thrush . . . Scatters his loose notes in the
waste of air.   *Birds* 2.
Each in his proper Art should waste the Day:
Prop.[3] 62.

Watches.

While bright-eyed Science watches round: *Inst.* 11.

Watchful.

With watchful eye and dauntless mien, *Inst.* 90.

Water's.

Beside some water's rushy brink   *Spring* 15.

Watery.

She mew'd to ev'ry watry God,   *Cat* 32.
towers, That crown the watry glade,   *Eton* 2.
Lochlin plows the watry way;   *Owen* 14.
broods o'er Egypt with his wat'ry wings,
E. G. 103.
The watery glimmerings of a fainter day
Tasso 45.

Wave.

Who . . . delight to cleave . . . thy glassy
wave?   *Eton* 26.
Woods, that wave o'er Delphi's steep, *P. P.* 66.
their hundred arms they wave,   *Bard* 25.
And there the ensanguined Wave of Sicily,
Prop.[3] 44.

Waves.

Or where Mæander's amber waves   *P. P.* 69.

Rapture . . . Waves in the eye of Heav'n

     Bard 124.

Thro' the wild waves as they roar,   *Inst.* 89.

Morn . . . Waves her dew-bespangled wing,

     Vic. 2.

Scarce the hoarse waves from far were heard to

   roar,   *Tasso* 6.

Against the stream the waves secure he trod,

     Tasso 15.

When mountain-high the waves disparted rise;

     Tasso 40.

Waving.

As waving fresh their gladsome wing,   *Eton* 17.

Way. *See also* Church-way, Sacred Way.

Wanders the . . . Thames along His silver-

   winding way: *Eton* 10.

she wins her easy way: *P. P.* 39.

Yet shall he mount, and keep his distant way

     P. P. 121.

thro' the kindred squadrons mow their way.

     Bard 86.

Onward still his way he takes   *Odin* 13.

Lochlin plows the watry way;   *Owen* 14.

The plowman homeward plods his weary way,

     El. 3.

They kept the noiseless tenor of their way. *El.* 76.

Yet on his way . . . he prefer'd his case,

     L. S. 89.

shades, that . . . blacken round our weary way,

     Vic. 35.

through the skies Sings in its rapid way,

     Stat.[1] 50.

To tempt the dangers of the doubtful way;

     Tasso 2.

Swift shoots the Village-maid . . . adown the

   shining way,   *Tasso* 20.

Discover'd half, and half conceal'd their way;

     Tasso 46.

Ways.

Then let me rightly spell of nature's ways;

     Prop.[2] 15.

Wayward.

Join the wayward work to aid: *F. S.* 19.

Mutt'ring his wayward fancies   *El.* 106.

We, *omitted*.

Weak.

how oft in weak and sickly minds   *Agr.* 72.

Weakly.

Till a new Sun arose with weakly Gleam,

     Dante 59.

Wealth.

all that wealth e'er gave,   *El.* 34.

Alone in nature's wealth array'd,   *Hoel* 9.

Weapons.

they . . . veil'd their weapons bright and keen

     L. S. 39.

Wear.

Thy form benign, oh Goddess, wear,   *Adv.* 41.

Wearied. *See* Time-wearied.

Weary.

My weary soul they seem to sooth,   *Eton* 18.

Who thus afflicts a weary sprite,   *Odin* MS. 29.

Now my weary lips I close; [:]   *Òdin* 57, 71.

The plowman homeward plods his weary way,

     El. 3.

shades, that . . . blacken round our weary way,

     Vic. 35.

Weave.

And weave with bloody hands   *Bard* 48.

Weave the warp, and weave the woof, *Bard* 49.

Weave we the woof.   *Bard* 98.

Weave the crimson web of war[.]   *F. S.* 25, 36.

Sisters, weave the web of death;   *F. S.* 51.

And with her Garlands weave   *Prop.*[3] 54.

Weaving.

Weaving many a Soldier's doom,   *F. S.* 7.

Web.

The web is wove.   *Bard* 100.

Weave the crimson web of war   *F. S.* 25, 36.

Sisters, weave the web of death: *F. S.* 51.

If the thin Coan Web her Shape reveal, *Prop.*[3] 9.

Of the dear Web whole Volumes I indite:

     Prop.[3] 12.

Weddell.

Weddell attends your call,   *Com. Lines* 1.

Weddings.

†So big with Weddings, waddles W,   *Ch. Cr.* 58.

Weed.

†careless spares to weed the Plain: *Ode* 10.

Weep.

No more I weep.   *Bard* 43.

Long his loss shall Eirin weep,   *F. S.* 45.

I . . . weep the more because I weep in vain.

     West 14.

And I, . . . That live to weep . . . their fall.

     Hoel 24.

To weep without knowing the cause of my an-

   guish: *Am. Lines* 2.

oh! if thou weep not now,   *Dante* 47.

Weeping.

Disease, and Sorrow's weeping train, *P. P.* 44.

weeping I forsook thy fond embrace. *Ign.* 12.

Weeps.

where the silent marble weeps, . . . a mother

   sleeps: *Clerke* 1.

Where melancholy friendship bends, and weeps.

     Williams 12.

Weight.

And furthest send its weight   *Stat.*[1] 2.

A slipp'ry weight, and form'd of polish'd brass.

     Stat.[1] 8.

and scornful flung th' unheeded weight *Stat.*[1] 21.

Then grasp'd its weight,   *Stat.*[1] 42.

Artful and strong he pois'd the well-known

   weight   *Stat.*[2] 3.

Weights.

and the weights, that play below,   *F. S.* 11.

To judge of weights and measures;   *Agr.* 41.

Welcome.

Welcome, my noble son,   *Inst.* 67.

Well.

'T is well, begone!   *Agr.* 1.
Go! you can paint it well   *Agr.* 12.
I well remember too   *Agr.* 60.
She eyes the clear chrystalline well,   *Vic.* 55.
†For, too sure, they love not *well*.   *Rond.* 24.
†*Well* to love, — and then to part,   *Rond.* 25.

Well-known.

Artful and strong he pois'd the well-known weight   *Stat.*[2] 3.

Wench.

†A Wench, a Wife, a Widow, and a Whore,   *Ch. Cr.* 60.

Wenching.

What a pother is here about wenching and roaring!   *C. C.* 23.

Went.

He went, as if the Devil drove him.   *L. S.* 88.
A wooing he went,   *C. C.* 3.
Through subterraneous passages they went,   *Tasso* 49.

Wept.

Chatillon . . . That wept her bleeding Love,   *Inst.* 42.
Speechless my Sight I fix'd, nor wept, *Dante* 53.
they wept, unhappy Boys!   *Dante* 54.
They wept, and first my little dear Anselmo Cried,   *Dante* 55.
yet wept I not, or answer'd   *Dante* 57.

Were, *omitted.*

West.

In the caverns of the west,   *Odin* 63.

Western.

bright track, that fires the western skies,   *Bard* 103.
Western gales . . . Speak not always winter past.   *Song* 9.

What.

What female heart can gold despise?   *Cat* 23.
What Cat's averse to fish?   *Cat* 24.
What sorrow was, thou bad'st her know, *Adv.* 15.
What others are, to feel,   *Adv.* 48.
What idle progeny succeed   *Eton* 28.
Man's feeble race what Ills await,   *P. P.* 42.
What time, where lucid Avon stray'd, *P. P.* 85.
what daring Spirit Wakes thee   *P. P.* 112.
What Terrors round him wait!   *Bard* 60.
What pitying eye, what heart, afford A tear   *Bard MS.* 65.
what solemn scenes on Snowdon's height   *Bard* 105.
What strings symphonious tremble in the air,   *Bard* 119.
What strains of vocal transport round her play.   *Bard* 120.
What call unknown, what charms *Odin* 27.
Tell me what is done below,   *Odin* 40.
What dangers *Odin's* Child await,   *Odin* 53.
What Virgins these, . . . That bend to earth their solemn brow,   *Odin* 75.
What, in the very first beginning!   *L. S.* 17.

Why, what can the Viscountess mean? *L. S.* 134.
What is grandeur, what is power?   *Inst.* 57.
What the bright reward we gain?   *Inst.* 59.
What if you add, how she turn'd pale   *Agr.* 9.
no matter What; so 't be strange,   *Agr.* 171.
thro' Ages by what Fate confin'd   *E. G.* 38.
what seasons can control, . . . the soul, *E. G.* 72.
What fancied Zone can circumscribe *E. G.* 73.
What wonder, if to patient valour train'd   *E. G.* 94.
They guard with spirit what . . . they gain'd?   *E. G.* 95.
What wonder in the sultry climes,   *E. G.* 100.
Whom what awaits,   *Clerke* 11.
What a pother is here   *C. C.* 23.
But what awaits me now is worst of all. *Shak.* 8.
So York shall taste what Clouet never knew,   *Shak.* 21.
Ah! what means yon violet flower! *Song* 3.
What length of sea remains, what various lands,   *Tasso* 31.
Search to what regions yonder Star retires,   *Prop.*[2] 19.
What colours paint the vivid arch of Jove;   *Prop.*[2] 29.
What wondrous force the solid earth can move,   *Prop.*[2] 30.
And what Bootes' lazy waggon tires; *Prop.*[2] 36.
Redeem, what Crassus lost,   *Prop.*[2] 54.
And sing with what a careless Grace she flings   *Prop.*[3] 15.
For Ills unseen what Remedy is found?   *Prop.*[3] 91.
nor on what Errand Sent hither: *Dante* 10.
what scant Light That . . . Tower admitted   *Dante* 22.
to think, what my poor Heart Foresaw, *Dante* 46.
What would you have? yet wept I not, *Dante* 57.
Take back, what once was yours.   *Dante* 68.
The fourth, what Sorrow could not, Hunger did.   *Dante* 81.
†Then to sever what is bound,   *Rond.* 31.
†What Ease and Elegance her person grace,   *Ch. Cr.* 7.

Whate'er.

Whate'er the frivolous tongue . . . Has spread   *Agr.* 167.
In brief whate'er she do, or say, or look,   *Prop.*[3] 27.
Whate'er with copious train its channel fills,   *Tasso* 53.

Wheel.

The pendent rock, Ixion's whirling wheel,   *Prop.*[2] 46.

Wheels.

Save where the beetle wheels his droning flight,   *El.* 7.

When.

Less pleasing when possest;   *Eton* 42.
When first thy Sire to send on earth Virtue, . . . design'd,   *Adv.* 9.
When Latium had her lofty spirit lost, *P. P.* 81.
Yet when they first were open'd *P. P. MS.* 118.
the night, When Severn shall re-eccho *Bard* 54.

When he had fifty winters o'er him,   *L. S.* 10.
When he the solemn hall had seen;   *L. S.* 118.
When a boy frowns,   *Agr.* 18.
when yet a stranger To adoration,   *Agr.* 33.
when I Oped his young eye   *Agr.* 44.
When in a secret and dead hour   *Agr.* 61.
Ev'n when its will seem'd wrote   *Agr.* 70.
when the idle herd . . . yet will start, *Agr.* 130.
but when, extends Beyond their chronicle —
     Agr. 137.
When love could teach a monarch to be wise,
     E. G. 108.
when conspiring in the diamond's blaze, *Bent.* 21.
And scorn'd repose when Britain took the field.
     Williams 8.
When sly Jemmy Twitcher had smugg'd up his
   face,   *C. C.* 1.
When she died, I can't tell,   *C. C.* 14.
When thou hear'st the organ piping shrill
     Shak. 15.
To close my dull eyes when I see it returning;
     Am. Lines 4.
Thyrsis, when we parted, swore   *Song* 1.
When you rise from your Dinner as light as be-
   fore,   *Couplet* 1.
When blazing 'gainst the sun it shines from far,
     Stat.[1] 30.
As when from Ætna's smoking summit broke,
     Stat.[2] 18.
When thwart the road a River roll'd its flood
     Tasso 7.
when lo! appears The wondrous Sage: *Tasso* 11.
As on the Rhine, when Boreas' fury reigns,
     Tasso 17.
When mountain-high the waves disparted rise;
     Tasso 40.
As when athwart the dusky woods by night
     Tasso 47.
And when, . . . Age step 'twixt love and me,
     Prop.[2] 11.
When my changed head these locks no more shall
   know,   *Prop.*[2] 13.
When Pindus' self approaching ruin dreads,
     Prop.[2] 31.
When, less averse, and yielding to Desires,
     Prop.[3] 21.
When then my Fates   *Prop.*[3] 99.
and when she frown'd, he died.   *Prop.*[3] 108.
The Morn had scarce commenc'd, when I awoke:
     Dante 41.
when at the Gate Below I heard   *Dante* 50.
when I beheld My Sons,   *Dante* 61.
When Gaddo, at my Feet out-stretch'd,
     Dante 73.
†First when Pastorals I read,   *Ode* 19.
†But when once the potent dart   *Rond.* 29.

Whence.

Tell me, whence their sorrows rose: *Odin* 79.
Say from whence their sorrows rose: *Odin* MS. 79.
House . . . From whence one fatal morning is-
   sues   *L. S.* 22.
the source from whence she springs,   *E. G.* 74.
Near the source whence Pleasure flows; *Vic.* 54.

And whence, . . . Relumes her crescent Orb
     Prop.[2] 21.
And whence the cloudy Magazines maintain Their
   wintry war,   *Prop.*[2] 25.
Whence the seven Sisters' congregated fires,
     Prop.[2] 35.
Whence the soft Strain and ever-melting Verse?
     Prop.[3] 2.

Where.

Lo! where the rosy-bosom'd Hours,   *Spring* 1.
Where China's . . . art had dy'd   *Cat* 2.
Where grateful Science still adores   *Eton* 3.
Where once my careless childhood stray'd,
     Eton 13.
shew them where in ambush stand   *Eton* 58.
where ignorance is bliss,   *Eton* 99.
Where shaggy forms . . . roam,   *P. P.* 55.
Or where Mæander's amber waves   *P. P.* 69.
Where each old poetic Mountain   *P. P.* 73.
where lucid Avon stray'd,   *P. P.* 85.
Where Angels tremble, while they gaze,
     P. P. 100.
where Dryden's less presumptuous car, *P. P.* 103.
the loom, Where the dusky warp we strain,
     F. S. 6.
Where our Friends the conflict share, *F. S.* 27.
Where they triumph, where they die. *F. S.* 28.
Where long of yore to sleep was laid   *Odin* 19.
Where his glowing eye-balls turn,   *Owen* 31.
Where he points his purple spear,   *Owen* 33.
Save where the beetle wheels his droning flight,
     El. 7.
Where heaves the turf in many a mould'ring heap,
     El. 14.
Where through the long-drawn isle   *El.* 39.
In Britain's Isle, no matter where,   *L. S.* 1.
Where, . . . He heard the distant din of war.
     L. S. 75.
where on their opening soul First . . . ardour
   stole.   *Inst.* 21.
Where willowy Camus lingers with delight!
     Inst. 29.
Shew'd him where empire tower'd,   *Agr.* 46.
Where he so soon may —   *Agr.* 165.
Where rushy Camus' slowly-winding flood
     Ign. 3.
Climes, where Winter holds his Reign, *E. G.* 5.
where the rolling Orb, that gives the Day,
     E. G. 23.
where the deluge burst, with sweepy sway
     E. G. 48.
where the face of nature laughs around, *E. G.* 70.
where unwearied sinews must be found *E. G.* 90.
Where Nile redundant o'er his Summer-bed
     E. G. 101.
where rosy Pleasure leads,   *Vic.* 37.
Where broad and turbulent it grows   *Vic.* 58.
Mark where Indolence and Pride,   *Vic.* 61.
Lo! where the silent marble weeps, . . . a mother
   sleeps: *Clerke* 1.
Where melancholy friendship bends, and weeps.
     Williams 12.
where three sisters of old In harmless society
   guttle   *C. C.* 3.

Where flow'd the widest stream he took his stand;
Stat.[1] 38.

Where Ocean frets beneath the dashing oar,
Stat.[2] 20.

Where fix'd in wonder stood the warlike pair,
Tasso 25.

Further they pass, where ripening minerals flow,
Tasso 57.

Where Aganippe warbles as it flows; *Prop.*[3] 4.

Where lie th' eternal fountains of the deep,
Prop.[2] 24.

if thou weep not now, Where are thy Tears?
Dante 48.

Where'er.

Where'er the oak's thick branches stretch
Spring 11.

Where'er the . . . beech O'er-canopies the glade;
Spring 13.

Where'er she turns the Graces homage pay.
P. P. 37.

where'er the Goddess roves, *P. P.* 63.

Whether.

Whether she fear'd, or wish'd to be pursued.
Agr. 199.

Which.

The captive linnet which enthral? *Eton* 27.

gratitude which Nero . . . owes; *Agr.* 57.

And realis'd the beauties which we feign:
View 20.

a bad face which did sadly molest her.
Mrs. Keene 2.

silver . . . Which soon the parent sun's warm
powers refine, *Tasso* 60.

Lips, which on the clotter'd Locks . . . he wiped,
Dante 2.

That which yet remains . . . I shall unfold.
Dante 18.

For Anguish, which they construed Hunger;
Dante 64.

While. *See also* **Awhile.**

While whisp'ring pleasure as they fly, *Spring* 8.

We frolick, while 't is May. *Spring* 50.

While some on earnest business bent *Eton* 31.

Where Angels tremble, while they gaze,
P. P. 100.

While proudly riding o'er the azure realm
Bard 72.

While . . . Foam and human gore distill'd:
Odin 7.

While, . . . Prostrate warriors gnaw the ground.
Owen 29.

While o'er the Heath we hied, *El. Mas.* 118.

While bright-eyed Science watches round!
Inst. 11.

While spirits blest . . . Join with glad voice
Inst. 87.

while he stood trembling, *Agr.* 31.

While mutual Wishes, mutual Woes endear
E. G. 36.

While European Freedom still withstands
E. G. 60.

while their rocky ramparts round they see,
E. G. 96.

While Bentley leads her sister-art along, *Bent.* 3.

While Hope prolongs our happier hour, *Vic.* 33.

while yet he strays Along the . . . vale
Clerke 11.

While Nancy earns the praise to Shakespeare due,
Shak. 23.

While frighted prelates bow'd *Toph.* 2.

and while they wished him dead, *Toph.* 3.

While vales and woods and echoing hills rebound.
Stat.[2] 17.

While to retain the envious Lawn she tries,
Prop.[3] 23.

Then, while the vaulted Skies loud Ios rend,
Prop.[3] 47.

While Prows, that late in fierce Encounter mett,
Prop.[3] 51.

while o'er the Place You drop the Tear,
Prop.[3] 106.

He lived, while she was kind; *Prop.*[3] 108.

†while different far, Rests in Retirement,
Ch. Cr. 53.

Whilst.

the whilst I slumb'ring lay, *Dante* 26.

Whirl.

Then whirl the wretch from high, *Eton* 72.

Then, with a tempest whirl, and wary eye,
Stat.[2] 8.

Whirling.

The pendent rock, Ixion's whirling wheel,
Prop.[2] 46.

Whirlwind.

And up stairs in a whirlwind rattle. *L. S.* 60.

Saw the snowy whirlwind fly; *Vic.* 22.

As the whirlwind in its course; *Conan* 6.

Whirlwind's.

Regardless of the sweeping Whirlwind's sway,
Bard 75.

Whisk.

Out of the window, whisk, they flew, *L. S.* 79.

Whisker.

A whisker first and then a claw, *Cat* 20.

Whisper.

With . . . whisper soft She woo's the tardy
spring: *Vic.* 3.

No tree is heard to whisper, *View* 10.

Whispered.

things, that but whisper'd Have arch'd *Agr.* 168.

Whispering.

whisp'ring pleasure as they fly, *Spring* 8.

In still small Accents whisp'ring *El. Mas.* 83.

Whistful. *See* **Wistful.**

White.

So her white neck reclin'd, *Agr.* 195.

A vestment unadorn'd, though white as new-
fal'n Snows; *Tasso* 14.

Whiter.

Th' unthought event disclose a whiter meaning.
Agr. 71.

White-wash.

With a lick of court white-wash, and pious
grimace, *C. C.* 2.

Whither.

Your Hist'ry whither are you spinning? *L. S.* 19.

Who.

Who foremost now delight to cleave *Eton* 25.
who o'er thy country hangs The scourge of
Heav'n. *Bard* 59.
Who thus afflicts my troubled sprite, *Odin* 29.
Who is he, . . . That calls me *Odin* 35.
say, . . . Who the Author of his fate. *Odin* 54.
say, Who th' Avenger of his guilt, *Odin* 61.
Who ne'er shall comb his raven-hair, *Odin* 66.
Who their flaxen tresses tear *Odin* MS. 77.
who to dumb Forgetfulness a prey, *El.* 85.
thee, who mindful *El.* 93; *Mas.* 77.
Alas, who would not wish to please her! *L. S.* 36.
Imp . . . Who prowl'd the country *L. S.* 45.
Who will, believe. *L. S.* 73.
at least there are who know *Agr.* 15.
your servant's fears, who sees the danger *Agr.* 24.
the rest is heav'n's; who oft has bade, *Agr.* 69.
one Who had such liberal power *Agr.* 89.
theirs, who boast the genuine blood *Agr.* 104.
the soul, Who conscious of the source *E. G.* 74.
who could not save His all *Clerke* MS. 11.
band, Who trust your arms *Stat.*[1] 17.
to Him . . . Who taught this vast machine
Prop.[2] 17.
Who measured out the year, *Prop.*[2] 38.
who can probe the undiscover'd Wound?
Prop.[3] 92.
I know not, who thou art; *Dante* 10.
†They who just have felt the flame *Rond.* 21.

Whoe'er.

Whoe'er the quoit can wield, *Stat.*[1] 1.

Whole.

Of the dear Web whole Volumes I indite:
Prop.[3] 12.
All that whole Day, or the succeeding Night
Dante 58.

Whom.

They, whom once the desart-beach Pent *F. S.* 37.
For whom yon glitt'ring board is spread, *Odin* 41.
Drest for whom yon golden bed. *Odin* 42.
By whom shall *Hoder's* blood be spilt? *Odin* 62.
Whom meaner Beauties eye askance, *L. S.* 27.
The few, whom genius gave to shine *Inst.* 16.
Whom what awaits, *Clerke* 11.
the Traitour's Infamy, whom thus I ceaseless
gnaw *Dante* 7.

Whore.

†A Wench, a Wife, a Widow, and a Whore,
Ch. Cr. 60.

Whoring.

They say he 's no Christian, loves drinking and
whoring, *C. C.* 15.
Why, David lov'd catches, and Solomon whoring:
C. C. 24.

Whose.

Whose turf . . . among Wanders the hoary
Thames along *Eton* 8.
whose shade . . . among Wanders the hoary
Thames along *Eton* 8.

whose flowers among Wanders the hoary Thames
along *Eton* 8.
Whose iron scourge and tort'ring hour *Adv.* 3.
This pencil . . . whose colours clear *P. P.* 89.
a rock, whose haughty brow Frowns *Bard* 15.
Modred, whose magic song Made huge Plinlim-
mon bow *Bard* 33.
thee, whose influence breathed from high *Ign.* 7.
Whose flinty Bosom starves her generous Birth,
E. G. 2.
A heart, within whose sacred cell *Clerke* 3.
Whose walls along the neighbouring Sea extend,
Tasso 4.
You whose young bosoms feel a nobler flame
Prop.[2] 53.
Whose heart has never felt a second flame.
Prop.[3] 66.
†Whose influence first bid it live. *Ode* 54.

Why.

why should they know their fate? *Eton* 95.
Why, what can the Viscountess mean? *L. S.* 134.
why do I waste the fruitless hours *Agr.* 154.
Why then stays my sovereign, *Agr.* 164.
Why yet does Asia dread a Monarch's nod,
E. G. 59.
Why, David lov'd catches, *C. C.* 24.
Why this unavailing haste? *Song* 8.
Why does yon Orb, . . . Obscure his radiance
Prop.[2] 33.
You ask, why thus my Loves I still rehearse,
Prop.[3] 1.
Father, why, why do you gaze so sternly?
Dante 56.
†But why on such *mock* grandeur should we dwell,
Ch. Cr. 23.

Wicked.

lurk'd A wicked Imp they call a Poet, *L. S.* 44.
If then he wreak on me his wicked will,
Shak. 13.

Wide.

Wide o'er the fields of Glory *P. P.* 104.
Far and wide the notes prolong. *F. S.* 60.
His shaggy throat he open'd wide, *Odin* 6.
with ensigns wide unfurl'd, She rode *Ign.* 27.

Widest.

Where flow'd the widest stream he took his stand,
Stat.[1] 38.

Widow.

The Widow feels thee in her aching hip;
Com. Lines 6.
†A Wench, a Wife, a Widow, and a Whore,
Ch. Cr. 60.

Wield.

Each her thundering faulchion wield; *F. S.* 62.
Whoe'er the quoit can wield, *Stat.*[1] 1.

Wife.

long rever'd . . . the daughter, sister, wife,
Agr. 118.
A friend, a wife, a mother sleeps: *Clerke* 2.
— but he once had a wife; *C. C.* 14.
†A Wench, a Wife, a Widow, and a Whore,
Ch. Cr. 60.

Wild.

Theirs . . . wild wit,   *Eton* 46.

moody Madness laughing wild   *Eton* 79.

Wild Laughter, Noise, and thoughtless Joy,
                                               Adv. 19.

the sounds, that . . . scatter'd wild dismay,
                                               Bard 10.

With Horror wild,   *Bard* Lett.[2] 130.

There . . . Conflict fierce, and Ruin wild,
                                               Owen 38.

Thro' the wild waves   *Inst.* 89.

With headlong rage and wild affright   *Hoel* 2.

Wildly.

In loose numbers wildly sweet   *P. P.* 61.

Their raptures now that wildly flow, No . . .
   morrow know;   *Vic.* 25.

Will.

its will seem'd wrote in lines of blood, *Agr.* 70.

If then he wreak on me his wicked will,
                                               Shak. 13.

Will, *vb. See also* **I 'll, Nill, 'T will, You 'll.**

Who will, believe.   *L. S.* 73.

That will he, nill he, . . . He went,   *L. S.* 87.

A heart that . . . will mount undaunted, *Agr.* 52.

there will not want, . . . ears to own   *Agr.* 122.

the idle herd . . . yet will start,   *Agr.* 132.

ere mid-day, Nero will come to Baiæ.   *Agr.* 159.

I will not meet its poison.   *Agr.* 163.

Yes, I will be gone,   *Agr.* 165.

The Soil, . . . will not teem in vain,   *E. G.* 6.

As lawless force from confidence will grow
                                               E. G. 98.

A fairer flower will never bloom again: *Child* 4.

Sure Delia will tell me!   *Am. Lines* 8.

The Bishop of Chester, . . . If you scratch him
   will fester.   *Ext. Keene* 4.

†Maggots too will form and nourish;   *Ode* 16.

Willey. *See* **Willy.**

Williams.

Young Williams fought for England's fair renown;
                                               Williams 2.

Willing.

Sovereign of the willing soul,   *P. P.* 13.

The willing homage Of prostrate Rome, *Agr.* 76.

Willowy.

Where willowy Camus lingers with delight!
                                               Inst. 29.

Willy.

'T is Willy [Willey, Lett,[4]] begs,   *Shak.* 3.

Wind.

a voice in every wind,   *Eton* 39.

Wind, *vb.*

The lowing herd wind slowly o'er the lea, *El.* 2.

Winded. *See* **Long-winded.**

Winding. *See* **Silver-winding, Slowly-winding.**

thro' each winding [echoing, Whar.] vale . . . the
   notes prolong.   *F. S.* 59.

Such as . . . Come (sweep) along some winding
   entry   *L. S.* 102.

Winding-sheet.

The winding-sheet of Edward's race.   *Bard* 50.

Window.

Out of the window, whisk, they flew,   *L. S.* 79.

Windows.

Rich windows that exclude the light,   *L. S.* 7.

Winds.

Norman sails afar Catch the winds,   *Owen* 16.

Command the Winds, and tame th' unwilling
   Deep.   *E. G.* 43.

How riseing winds the face of Ocean sweep,
                                               Prop.[2] 23.

Sailors to tell of Winds and Seas delight,
                                               Prop.[3] 59.

Winds, *vb.*

The lowing Herd winds slowly o'er the Lea,
                                               El. Dods. 2.

the rich stream of music winds along *P. P.* 7.

Windsor's.

the stately brow Of WINDSOR's heights   *Eton* 6.

Wing.

The insect youth are on the wing,   *Spring* 25.

As waving fresh their gladsome wing,   *Eton* 17.

With ruffled plumes, and flagging wing: *P. P.* 22.

Tho' fann'd by Conquest's crimson wing *Bard* 3.

On expectation's strongest wing to soar *Agr.* 42.

Morn . . . Waves her dew-bespangled wing,
                                               Vic. 2.

Winged.

Art it requires, and more than winged speed.
                                               Tasso 30.

Wings. *See also* **Seraph-wings.**

On hasty wings thy youth is flown;   *Spring* 48.

Waves . . . her many-colour'd wings. *Bard* 124.

had her wanton son Lent us his wings,   *Agr.* 190.

Her rapid wings the transient scene pursue,
                                               Ign. 34.

By reason's light on resolution's wings, *E. G.* 75.

broods o'er Egypt with his wat'ry wings,
                                               E. G. 103.

Rise, my soul! on wings of fire,   *Vic.* 17.

†Expand their wings of flimzey Gold.   *Ode* 48.

Wins.

she wins her easy way: *P. P.* 39.

Winter.

Climes, where Winter holds his Reign,   *E. G.* 5.

the Brood of Winter view A brighter Day,
                                               E. G. 54.

and skies serene Speak not always winter past.
                                               Song 10.

And winter binds the floods in icy chains,
                                               Tasso 18.

Winter's.

The winter's snow, the summer's heat, *Odin* 32.

Winters.

When he had fifty winters o'er him,   *L. S.* 10.

Wintry.

Forgetful of their wintry trance, The Birds . . .
   greet: *Vic.* 11.

the cloudy Magazines maintain Their wintry war,
                                               Prop.[2] 26.

Wiped.

Of th' half devoured Head he wiped,   *Dante* 3.

Wisdom.

Wisdom in sable garb array'd   *Adv.* 25.

Wise.

'T is folly to be wise.   *Eton* 100.

love could teach a monarch to be wise, *E. G.* 108.

Wiser.

Tho' wiser than Nestor   *Ext. Keene* 2.

Wish.

With many an ardent wish,   *Cat* 21.

Alas, who would not wish to please her ! *L. S.* 36.

Did I not wish to check this . . . passion, *Agr.* 106.

To start from short slumbers, and wish for the
morning —   *Am. Lines* 3.

Wished.

He gain'd . . . ('t was all he wish'd) a friend.
   El. 124.

she fear'd, or wish'd to be pursued.   *Agr.* 199.

And while they wished him dead,   *Toph.* 3.

Wishes.

Their sober wishes never learn'd to stray; *El.* 74.

anxious Cares and endless Wishes   *El.* Mas. 86.

mutual Wishes, mutual Woes endear   *E. G.* 36.

To Cynthia all my Wishes I confine;   *Prop.*³ 68.

Wistful.

With whistful eyes pursue the setting sun.
   El. Mas. 120.

Wit.

Theirs . . . wild wit,   *Eton* 46.

Heaven Had arm'd with spirit, wit, and satire:
   L. S. 30.

No very great wit,   *Char.* 4.

With, *omitted.*

Withdrawing-room.

†Open the doors of the withdrawing-room; *Ch.Cr.* 2.

Withheld.

These conscious shame withheld,   *Stat.*¹ 25.

Within.

desart-beach Pent within its bleak domain,
   F. S. 38.

within the spatious walls,   *L. S.* 9.

the spark . . . that glows within their breasts,
   Agr. 128.

A heart, within whose sacred cell   *Clerke* 3.

nor wept, for all Within was Stone: *Dante* 54.

within That House of Woe.   *Dante* 60.

Without.

Without design to hurt the butter,   *L. S.* 123.

unguarded and without a lictor,   *Agr.* 5.

Without a spell to raise,   *Agr.* 16.

To weep without knowing the cause of my anguish: *Am. Lines* 2.

Swift shoots the Village-maid . . . Smooth, without step,   *Tasso* 20.

Pangs without respite, fires that ever glow,
   *Prop.*² 40.

Withstands.

Freedom still withstands Th' encroaching tide,
   E. G. 60.

Withstood.

The little Tyrant of his fields withstood,   *El.* 58.

a River . . . all further course withstood; *Tasso* 8.

Wit's.

If any spark of wit's delusive ray   *Ign.* 19.

Woe.

laughing . . . Amid severest woe.   *Eton* 80.

she learn'd to melt at others' woe.   *Adv.* 16.

Robed in the sable garb of woe,   *Bard* 17.

With fury pale, and pale with woe, *Bard* Lett.¹ 17.

Orkney's woe, and *Randver's* bane.   *F. S.* 8.

What Virgins these, in speechless woe, *Odin* 75.

Her infant image . . . Sits smiling on a father's
woe: *Clerke* 10.

Chastised by sabler tints of woe;   *Vic.* 42.

within That House of Woe.   *Dante* 61.

†With Woe behind, and Wantonness before.
   Ch. Cr. 61.

Woeful.

woeful wan, like one forlorn,   *El.* Dods. 107.

Cried the square Hoods in woful fidget *L. S.* 135.

Woeful-wan.

drooping, woeful-wan, like one forlorn,   *El.* 107.

Woes.

The rival of her crown and of her woes, *Inst.* 44.

mutual Wishes, mutual Woes endear   *E. G.* 36.

But pictured horrour and poëtic woes. *Prop.*² 50.

and Sleep Prophetic of my Woes   *Dante* 27.

Woful. *See* **Woeful.**

Wolf. *See also* **She-wolf.**

A Wolf full-grown;   *Dante* 31.

Womankind.

†And brings all Womankind before your view;
   Ch. Cr. 59.

Woman's.

Her household cares, a woman's best employment.   *Agr.* 8.

Womb.

Slaves from the womb,   *Agr.* 130.

Won.

my Ear, Won by thy Tongue,   *Dante* 12.

Wonder.

The hapless Nymph with wonder saw: *Cat* 19.

What wonder, if to patient valour train'd *E. G.* 94.

What wonder in the sultry climes,   *E. G.* 100.

Great things and full of wonder . . . I shall unfold;   *Tasso* 35.

Where fix'd in wonder stood the warlike pair,
   Tasso 25.

And wonder at the sudden Funeral. *Prop.*³ 98.

Wondered.

Have seen your soul, and wonder'd at its daring :
   Agr. 55.

Wondrous.

when lo! appears The wondrous Sage: *Tasso* 12.

attracts the wondrous sight,   *Tasso* 69.

What wondrous force the solid earth can move,
   *Prop.*² 30.

A wond'rous [giant, MS.] boy shall *Rinda* bear,
   Odin 65.

Wont.
legions wont to stem With stubborn nerves
                                                            Agr. 108.

Wonted.
in our Ashes live their wonted Fires.   *El.* 92.
The Fields to all their wonted Tribute bear;
                                                            West 11.
And to this bosom give its wonted Peace,
                                                            *Prop.*³ 88.

Wood.
Hard by yon wood,   *El.* 105.
Nor up the lawn, nor at the wood   *El.* 112.
brave the savage rushing from the wood,
                                                            E. G. 93.

Woodlark.
the Woodlark piped her farewell Song,
                                                        El. Mas. 119.
There pipes the woodlark,   *Birds* 1.

Woods.
Woods, that wave o'er Delphi's steep, *P. P.* 66.
How bow'd the woods beneath their . . . stroke!
                                                            El. 28.
While vales and woods and echoing hills rebound.
                                                            *Stat.*² 17.
As when athwart the dusky woods by night
                                                            Tasso 47.

Woody.
The theatre's green height and woody wall
Tremble   *Stat.*² 14.

Wooed.
I . . . Oft woo'd the gleam of Cynthia *Inst.* 32.

Woof.
Weave the warp, and weave the woof, *Bard* 49.
Weave we the woof.   *Bard* 98.
'T is the woof of victory.   *F. S.* 20.

Wooing.
A wooing he went,   *C. C.* 3.

Woos.
She woo's the tardy spring: *Vic.* 4.

Word.
Stung by a senseless word,   *Agr.* 133.
Swift at the word, from out the gazing host,
                                                            *Stat.*¹ 4.

Words.
Thoughts, that breath, and words, that burn.
                                                            P. P. 110.
The words too eager to unriddle,   *L. S.* 81.
Words that steal from my tongue, *Am. Lines* 6.

Wore.
The laureate wreath, that Cecil wore *Inst.* 84.

Work.
The work is done.   *Bard* 100.
Join the wayward work to aid: *F. S.* 19.
Sisters, cease, the work is done.   *F. S.* 52.

Works.
So from our works sublime fumes shall rise;
                                                            Shak. 22.

World.
Sinks the fabric of the world.   *Odin* 94.
leaves the world to darkness and to me. *El.* 4.

The thoughtless World to Majesty may bow,
                                                        El. Mas. 73.
the world, you gave him, Suffices not *Agr.* 58.
The world, the prize;   *Agr.* 153.
triumphant o'er the vanquish'd world; *Ign.* 28.
To rush, and sweep them from the world!
                                                            Hoel 4.
Beyond the confines of our narrow world:
                                                            Tasso 34.
Shall sink this beauteous fabric of the world;
                                                            *Prop.*² 28.

Worm. *See* **Silk-worm.**

Worn.
fear might then have worn The mask *Agr.* 48.

Worst.
But what awaits me now is worst of all. *Shak.* 8.

Worthier.
Receive a worthier load;   *Stat.*¹ 19.

Wot.
†But, I wot, they loved not *true*.   *Rond.* 8.

Would. *See also* **I'd, She'd, 'T would.**
Thought would destroy their paradise. *Eton* 98.
Yet oft before his infant eyes would run
                                                            P. P. 118.
His listless length . . . would he stretch, *El.* 103.
Mutt'ring his . . . fancies he would rove,
                                                            El. 106.
Coarse panegyricks would but teaze her. *L. S.* 34.
Alas, who would not wish to please her!
                                                            L. S. 36.
The Godhead would have back'd his quarrel,
                                                            L. S. 93.
Numbers would give their oaths upon it,
                                                            L. S. 127.
Lubbers, That to eternity would sing, *L. S.* 143.
would have dropp'd, but that her pride restrain'd
it?   *Agr.* 11.
Owls would [might, MS.; should, Nich.] have
hooted in St. Peter's choir,   *View* 23.
Ere the spring he would return —   *Song* 2.
Yet would the Tyrant Love permit me raise
                                                            *Prop.*³ 31.
Not Marius' Cimbrian Wreaths would I relate,
                                                            *Prop.*³ 39.
What would you have? yet wept I not, *Dante* 57.

Wouldest.
Would'st thou revive the deep Despair, *Dante* 4.

Wound.
To soften, not to wound my heart.   *Adv.* 44.
He wound with toilsome march his long array.
                                                            Bard 12.
Gor'd with many a gaping wound: *F. S.* 42.
She felt the wound she left behind, *Clerke* 8.
who can probe the undiscover'd Wound?
                                                            *Prop.*³ 92.
†is to tear the closing wound.   *Rond.* 32.

Wove.
The web is wove.   *Bard* 100.

Wrapped.
wrapt in flames, . . . Sinks the fabric of the
world.   *Odin* 93.

Wrapt. *See* **Wrapped.**

Wreak.

If then he wreak on me his wicked will,
Shak. 13.

Wreath.

The laureate wreath, that Cecil wore   *Inst.* 84.

Wreathed.

Chains . . . Wreath'd in many a golden link:
Hoel 15.

Wreathes.

Beech, That wreathes its old . . . roots so high,
El. 102.

Wreaths.

Not Marius' Cimbrian Wreaths would I relate,
*Prop.*³ 39.

Wretch.

Then whirl the wretch from high,   *Eton* 72.
See the Wretch, that long has tost   *Vic.* 45.
and known To many a Wretch   *Dante* 25.

Wrings.

that unutter'd nathless wrings My inmost Heart?
Dante 5.

Wrinkled.

Wrinkled beldams Teach it   *Agr.* 135.

Write.

Of those loose Curls, that Ivory front I write;
*Prop.*³ 11.
†I burn to write;   *Ode* 27.

Wrongs.

benefits . . . As unrequited wrongs.   *Agr.* 76.
now hear My Wrongs,   *Dante* 15.

Wrote.

Wrote on the stone beneath yon aged thorn.
El. Mas. 136.
its will seem'd wrote in lines of blood, *Agr.* 70.
†cooling breezes I only wrote of;   *Ode* 21.

Wrought.

in fancy's airy colouring wrought   *Bent.* 7.

Yawning.

Down the yawning steep he rode,   *Odin* 3.

Ye, *omitted.*

Year.

And wake the purple year!   *Spring* 4.
thy rigid lore . . . many a year she bore: *Adv.* 14.
Richly paint the vernal year: *P. P.* 90.
Mark the year, and mark the night, *Bard* 53.
There scatter'd oft, the earliest of the Year,
El. Pem. 117; *Mas.* 137.
blast the vernal Promise of the Year. *E. G.* 21.
Yesterday the sullen year Saw . . . whirlwind
fly;   *Vic.* 21.
Who measured out the year,   *Prop.*² 38.
†Then for a Moiety of the Year   *Ode* 41.

Years.

Years of havock urge their destined course,
Bard 85.
their years, spelt by th' unletter'd muse, *El.* 81.

resolution To smuggle a few years, *View* 3.
vigorous he seem'd in years,   *Tasso* 12.
†Not like yon Dowager deprest with years;
Ch. Cr. 6.

Yell.

long pursues, with fruitless yell, The Father
Odin 11.

Yes.

Yes, we may meet, ungrateful boy, *Agr.* 140.
Yes, I will be gone,   *Agr.* 165.

Yesterday.

Yesterday the sullen year Saw . . . whirlwind
fly;   *Vic.* 21.
Their raptures . . . No yesterday, nor morrow
know;   *Vic.* 26.

Yet.

Yet hark, how thro' the peopled air *Spring* 23.
A stranger yet to pain!   *Eton* 14.
Yet see how all around 'em wait *Eton* 55.
Yet, ah! why should they know their fate? *Eton* 95.
Yet oft before his infant eyes   *P. P.* 118.
Yet when they first were open'd *P. P. MS.* 118.
Yet shall he mount,   *P. P.* 121.
Yet never can he fear   *P. P. MS.* 122.
they linger yet, Avengers of their native land:
Bard 45.
Yet thou, proud boy,   *Bard MS.* 75.
he yet may share the feast: *Bard* 79.
Yet awhile my call obey;   *Odin* 73.
Yet . . . these bones from insult to protect
El. 77.
nor yet beside the rill,   *El.* 111.
Yet on his way . . . he prefer'd his case,
L. S. 89.
Yet something he was heard to mutter, *L. S.* 121.
Yet hop'd, that he might save his bacon: *L. S.* 126.
Yet hither oft a glance . . . They send *Inst.* 19.
sweeter yet The . . . voice of gratitude. *Inst.* 63.
Yet 't would dash his joy To hear *Agr.* 13.
the spirit of Britannicus Yet walks on earth:
Agr. 15.
when yet a stranger To adoration, *Agr.* 33.
Nor am I yet to learn how vast the debt *Agr.* 56.
the idle herd . . . yet will start, *Agr.* 131.
Yet if your injur'd shades demand my fate,
Agr. 184.
Yet Morning smiles the busy Race to chear,
West 9.
yet still to fancy new,   *Ign.* 33.
Why yet does Asia dread a Monarch's nod,
E. G. 59.
while yet he strays Along the . . . vale *Clerke* 11.
Yet Nature could not furnish out the feast,
View 11.
yet the dread path once trod,   *Stanza* 2.
Nor tempts he yet the plain,   *Stat.*¹ 45.
Nor yet in prospect rose the distant shore;
Tasso 5.
Yet would the Tyrant Love permit me raise
*Prop.*³ 31.
yet if the telling may Beget   *Dante* 6.
That which yet remains . . . I shall unfold,
Dante 18.

to grace thy youthful brow, The laureate wreath,
Inst. 83.

Too, too secure in youthful pride, *Hoel* 5.

Youth's.
Be love my youth's pursuit, *Prop.*[2] 52.

Youths.
The love of honour bade two youths advance,
Stat.[1] 9.

All but two youths th' enormous orb decline,
Stat.[1] 24.

Zembla's.
dauntless goes . . . through Zembla's snows?
E. G. 77.

Zephyr.
soft the Zephyr blows, *Bard* 71.

Zephyrs.
Cool Zephyrs thro' the clear blue sky *Spring* 9.

Zone.
What fancied Zone can circumscribe the soul,
E. G. 73.